BUSINESS AND POLITICS IN INDIA

IIMA Monograph in Business History-III

Business and Politics in India

A Historical Perspective

Edited by
DWIJENDRA TRIPATHI

MANOHAR
2020

The publication of this book has been financially supported by the Indian Council of Historical Research and the responsibility for the facts stated or opinions expressed is entirely of the authors and not of the Council.

First published 1991
Reprinted 2020

ISBN 978-81-85425-59-7

Published by
Ajay Kumar Jain *for*
Manohar Publishers & Distributors
4753/23 Ansari Road, Daryaganj
New Delhi 110 002

Printed at
Replika Press Pvt. Ltd.

For I.G. Patel

Contents

Acknowledgements

This volume emerged from a seminar, held from 29 to 31 March 1989, in the IIMA Seminar Series in Business History. In addition to those whose contributions are included here, a number of other scholars participated in the deliberations and thus contributed to the quality of these essays. They include Dharma Kumar (University of Delhi), K. Mamkootam (Indian Institute of Public Administration, New Delhi), M. J. Mehta and Shirin Mehta (both of Gujarat University), Gyanendra Pandey (University of Delhi), Raojibhai Patel (Baroda), P.C. Randeria (Ahmedabad), Sunanda Sen (Jawaharlal Nehru University, New Delhi), Ghanshyam Shah (Centre for Social Studies, Surat), N.R. Sheth (Indian Institute of Management, Ahmedabad), and B.R. Tomlinson (University of Birmingham). Dharma Kumar and S. Bhattacharya (Jawaharlal Nehru University, New Delhi) provided critical help in the academic planning of the seminar.

Financial support came from the Indian Council of Historical Research, New Delhi (which has also subsidised the publication of this volume) and the Kasturbhai Lalbhai Fellowship Fund instituted by the Lalbhai Group of Companies at the Indian Institute of Management, Ahmedabad.

Priti Ramchandran, Gita Ranchan and Sanjay Thakur assisted in organizing the seminar. Ashok Jhambekar (Vikram Sarabhai Library, Indian Institute of Management, Ahmedabad) and A. Tikekar and his associates (Bombay University Library) and the staff of the Nehru Memorial Museum and Library, New Delhi provided missing details in some of the footnotes. Sonal Shah compiled the bibliography, P.S. Seshadri prepared the index and G. John produced the press copy.

To all these persons and organizations I owe a deep sense of gratitude. None except myself, however, should be held responsible for shortcomings that might have remained.

D.T.

Introduction

The second volume in the IIMA Monograph Series in Business History, *State and Business in India : A Historical Perspective* (Manohar, 1987), concentrated primarily on the impact of the policies and actions of various ruling systems that governed the country from the Mughals up to the end of the Nehru era. It did not dwell on how the Indian business reacted to political twists and turns, how it related to various political formations, and what influence it had on the processes and events in the transition from a colonial to an independent polity. These are the foci of the present volume. In view of the fact that these aspects have received scant attention from historical scholarship, the volume addresses itself to a neglected but vital facet of business behaviour in the country. And it has covered a fairly long period, unlike the few scattered studies that have dealt with the subject, with a view to providing a broader perspective.

The volume opens up with a generalized account of the place of business in Indian society. S. Ambirajan has argued that the businessman occupied a position of honour well up to the end of the 16th century. With the emergence of the Mughals as the supreme power, however, things began to change because except the banking community, which had close nexus with the nobility, other classes of businessmen had little relevance for Mughal scheme of things. This had inevitable consequence for the social image of business. The general attitude to business in the subsequent age, however, was more favourable because the colonial legal system accorded due recognition to individual pursuit of profit and sanctity of private property, and the nationalist movement was not anti-capitalist.

Ambirajan's account is primarily based on literary sources. Using more tangible data, Lakshmi Subramanian and Rajat K. Ray have arrived at almost similar conclusions. According to them, the Mughal empire, with its surplus revenue and organized treasury, did not at its zenith need businessmen, but the successor regimes with no such advantages did. Consequently while the relationship between various business groups and the ruling power in the age of the Great Mughals depended primarily on the whims of the officer on the spot, the merchant emerged as a major force in the innumerable principalities that arose in the wake of the disintegration of the Mughal power. He propped up native regimes as long as they served his purpose, but later became the lynchpin in the political convulsions which paved the ground for the rise of the English East India Company as the paramount political power. Strangely enough, the merchant communities, out of which the future business class would be fashioned, never exhibited the desire or will to mould a regime in which they would be at the centrestage. Instead, the period between the fall of the Mughal Empire and the end of the East India Company regime witnessed a spectacle of shifting allegience on their part to whosoever in their judgement was better placed to safeguard their interest.

That this was as much true for the later periods as well has been demonstrated by the next three papers. Surveying the entire span of the Crown government in India, Dwijendra Tripathi finds the emerging industrial class full of goodwill for the imperial regime during the pre-Gandhi phase. But as the national movement gained in strength and prestige under Gandhi's leadership, the industrialists had to take note of its potential as a possible ally in wresting concessions and privileges vital for them from the ruling power. This called for a judicious blend of making common cause with the Congress during peaceful times and distancing from it when it set off on paths of confrontation. Under these conditions there was no question of the capitalist class influencing the nature and course of national movement in any direct manner. This in fact is the thrust of Bhagwan Josh's paper which argues that the simplistic characterization of the Indian National Congress as a bourgeois formation must be discarded. Instead, it should be viewed as a broad anti-imperialist movement and the Indian capitalists, who had by 1930s developed a distinct political vision vis-a-vis imperialism, contributed to it without hurting their class interests. This is the reason that while favouring constitutional forms of the freedom struggle, they kept aloof from non-constitutional mass upsurge such as non-cooperation and civil disobedience movements. These conclusions, arrived at on the basis of a macro view of the situation, have been reinforced by Gita Piramal's close look at the changing attitude of the burgeoning entrepreneurial community of Bombay - the cradle of Indian capitalism.

B.R. Nanda and Bhikhu Parekh have also argued that the Indian bourgoisie never had great influence on the counsels of the Congress, even though their respective frameworks of analysis are somewhat different. Using hitherto unused data, Nanda has debunked the oft-repeated leftist view that the capitalists kept the Congress flush with funds and thus established a claim on its gratitude. The fact is that the Congress most of the time had to manage its affairs with pitifully small amount of money raised from members or small donors; the large capitalists as a rule shied away from contributing to the Congress coffers. Nanda also rejects the view that with their access to Gandhi, some captains of Indian industry influenced his thinking and action to suit their purpose; Gandhi was too astute for such machinations. Parekh supports this line of reasoning by pointing out that Gandhi cannot be properly comprehended with reference to capitalism or socialism and that it is patently wrong to describe him as a supporter or sympathiser of either system. Basing his judgement on a content analysis of Gandhi's thoughts and actions rather than factual details, Parekh concludes that Gandhi developed a distinctive language of discourse aimed at developing the Congress into a forum of national consensus where different segments of Indian society could sensitise one another with their needs and aspirations. Such a leader, according to Parekh, cannot be accused of being the spokesman or agent of capitalism as the leftist critics of Gandhi have attempted to do.

The rest of the papers in the volume relate to the attitude of the Indian business to specific events, groups, or issues. The partition of India by any yardstick was one of the most important events in Indian history. Did the Indian business play a role in it and if so what? This is the focus of Claude Markovits's enquiry. As we are still too close to the event and the crucial sources of data are still unavailable, he understandably suspends a final judgement. He, however, suggests that the Indian big business, irrespective of community affiliation, did not oppose partition and from 1942 onwards seems to have been increasingly favourable to it. The Muslims were naturally lured to the idea. For others the alternative to Pakistan in the mid-1940s seemed to be a loose federal structure with a weak centre and this they did not like. Markovits, however, concedes that even if the big business had opposed partition, it would not have been able to prevent it. He, thus, indirectly supports the view that the Indian business at best had only a marginal impact on the course of events.

The attitude of big business towards peasantry is the subject-matter of Kapil Kumar's paper in which he has argued that the while the Indian capitalists were willing to tolerate the presence of the peasantry in the freedom struggle, they sought to keep it within manageable limits. For, a politically conscious peasant class might ultimately threaten their own existence as many capitalists owned large landed estates. This is the reason that they used their money power to thwart the Kisan Sabha movement. And if the Kisan Sabhas were banned by the Congress ministries in the late 1930s, it was partly because many Congress leaders were beholden to the capitalists for various kinds of material benefits.

Two papers in this category deal with how political developments affected the internal dynamics of different business groups. One of these by Raman Mahadevan is concerned with the development of business associations in colonial Madras. He is of the view that the politics of businessmen in the southern region was moulded considerably by their immediate economic interests. To support his contention he points out that well until the rise of militant nationalism, the native businessmen in the south played rather insignificant role in trade associations all of which were dominated by Europeans. However, as the national movement gained momentum, and the native business developed a sense of identity, a number of such bodies controlled by the Indians came to the fore. These associations were not merely interest groups; they represented the articulation of business class identity through a process of realignment between various sub-groups.

Maria Misra dwells on how the expatriate British businessmen responded to the threat posed by the rising tide of Indian nationalism. Basing her analysis on the private papers of some expatriate firms, she finds no support for the view that the colonial government unduly favoured British firms operating in India or that the expatriate houses exercised great influence over the government. These firms or individuals controlling them, in fact, exhibited little interest in political developments almost up to the onset of 1920s when it seemed to them, rightly or wrongly, that the political reforms introduced by the government would jeopardise their competitive position vis-a-vis the rising Indian business class. This realization led to a moderate politicization of this class which responded to the danger by a series of measures - all of them half-hearted and largely ineffective.

The last paper is a comprehensive account of the process through which the Indian business class got converted to the idea of economic planning. Raghabendra Chattopadhayay tracing the evolution of the concept of planning suggests that the Indian business elite played a crucial role in the process both before and after Independence. This by no means was parodoxical because planning in India was always visualized as a mere instrument of rapid industrialization, in which the industrial class had a crucial stake, instead of a process of total transformation of society as conceived in the Soviet model, which was an anathema to them.

A common thread, thus, runs through these papers, although the authors did not coordinate their efforts in any direct way and they have followed their own frameworks of analysis. Understandably, therefore, one finds some overlappings, some repetitions, here and there. This only adds to, and does not detract from, the richness of this work. While the volume does not claim to have exhausted the subject - exhausting a subject is a myth anyway - it surely presents an integrated view of a theme which has a great deal of relevance for comprehending our present. And this ultimately is the purpose of all historical enquiries.

Ahmedabad
10 June 1991 **Dwijendra Tripathi**

1

Changing Attitudes towards Business in India*

S. Ambirajan

'What is business?' is a difficult question to answer. Is the farmer cultivating his land with or without hired help and selling his surplus engaged in business? Is a physician or a lawyer doing business? Was the nobleman of ancient Carthage, who had land, capital and slave labour and was able to have a large household economy (*oikos* in Greek), a businessman or an aristocrat? It is difficult to determine who is doing business or merely performing his professional duties or just following a traditional occupation. For the present discussion, we shall regard as business an activity that involves commercial, trading, financial and industrial transactions to provide goods and services.

The rise of business, the part it has played in the economy, attitudes towards it by the society at large are all of great relevance to understand the economic and social changes in that society over long periods. Different societies, or the same society at different stages, experience the impact of business in different ways. How did the social appreciation of business in India change during its long history? Our sources of information for the pre-Mughal period are too scanty and scattered to enable us to come to a definitive conclusion. To go by literary and epigraphic sources, albeit limited, it would appear that much before the end of the sixteenth century, business had come to occupy a significant place in the Indian society, and businessmen were treated with respect and civility. Very often the leading merchants were close to the king and acted as his advisers and were regarded, because of their philanthropy, as an instrument of social good. Indeed, an archaic Tamil term for merchant *(ilamkokkan)* also signifies the son or younger brother of a king. And the small merchant and the artisan in the vast countryside had symbiotic relationship with the agriculturist who was regarded as the linchpin of society.[1]

We are, however, concerned with the later periods about which our sources are more authentic. For analytical convenience, we would divide these periods into two – one covering about three centuries from 1500 to 1800, the heyday of the Mughal supremacy, and the other the age of British paramountcy. As we shall see later, there was a distinct difference in the ways Indian society viewed business in these two periods.

I

Many questions have been raised about the economic evolution of India during the period between the sixteenth and eighteenth centuries, when the foundations of the Industrial Revolution, that was to bring so much economic development to Britain, Germany and western Europe, were laid. How was the economic experience of India different from that of Europe? Were the necessary preconditions for the development of capitalism present in India? Was there developing in India an incipient middle class of the type that ushered in the Industrial Revolution? If not, what prevented its emergence? What happened to the structure of the business community that the sixteenth century inherited from the past?

Looking at the structure of business, the sixteenth-century India seems to have had many similarities with the sixteenth-century Europe such as (a) existence of powerful merchant princes, (b) a substantial body of merchants in urban centres with access to capital, (c) a self-confident artisan class organized in influential corporate organizations, and (d) close links with rulers who sought to keep the trade/artisan class contented through royal patronage. Yet, India did not take the path that west European countries took. One reason was the way attitudes towards business altered drastically in the next four centuries with far reaching consequences. In the preceding centuries there had been a gradual rise in the status and privileges of the merchant communities, reflecting their steadily growing role in the economy. Business communities as also individual businessmen had received support from and given help to the kings. In general, the rulers had a pro-trader/artisan orientation in the pre-Mughal period when, in the absence of a dependable public financial system, the mercantile community tended to be a steady source of needed resources. As K.N. Chaudhuri has pointed out:

> Pre-modern rulers, forced to depend on the economic surplus of agriculture, always suffered from the twin scourges of a shortage of ready cash and unending military expenditure. They knew only too well that ill-paid, mutinous soldiers were as much a threat to their power and authority as any known enemy outside. If the great merchants could be persuaded to become, partially at least, indirect paymasters of the army, so much the better. Persuasion could take the form of granting special privileges to the mercantile class....[2]

Businessmen, conscious of their power and importance, also had a very positive attitude about their own class. This self-confidence is an extremely important aspect of the role of business in the economic history of India. Society in general, too, had a positive regard for businessmen and believed that honest business was possible notwithstanding some stray evidence to the contrary.

The three hundred years roughly between 1500 and 1800 witnessed many changes that altered the social attitudes towards business almost radically. This was the period of the glory and decline of the great Mughal empire followed by the time when India became the happy hunting ground of various European mercantile adventurers.

More than any previous rulers, the Mughal administration was able to keep its control on the country. A significant characteristic of the Mughal empire was its centralised bureaucracy. While the earlier rulers presided over a relatively decentralized political structure, the Mughal emperors retained a lot of power with themselves. Not only was the Mughal system bureaucratic, but it was also based on a form of feudal aristocracy that derived its power from military might. The feudal aristocracy, which was the 'steel frame' of the Mughal empire, was able to extract the surplus of the peasantry for its sustenance and luxurious living, and hence was hardly interested in other types of economic activity such as trading and manufacturing. M. Athar Ali has shown that out of 1,061 members of the Mughal nobility under Aurangzeb, who had *mansabdaris* vested in them, only two – Mir Jumla and Nurulla Khan – were merchants before becoming members of the Mughal aristocracy. The Mughal nobles by virtue of their *jagirs* were able to accumulate vast fortunes but very few of them used them to good mercantile purposes. Some of them like Mir Jumla and Shaista Khan were exceptions in that they indulged in trading activities. Mir Jumla, according to Athar Ali, 'was in a real sense a merchant prince'.[3] A few other nobles seem to have invested in manufacturing establishments known as *karkhanas* to produce luxury items.

Even those nobles who involved themselves in trading and manufacturing were more interested in extracting the most out of traders by hook or by crook. According to Streynsham Master (a servant of the East India Company), Shaista Khan's 'officers oppress the people, monopolize most commodities, even as low as grass for beasts, calves, firewood, thatch, etc.' And according to Job Charnock his 'darogha hath so abused the merchants that they are almost all run away'. Athar Ali has also cited the case of Prince Azimushshan who had engaged in very many unfair practices.[4]

Distance from the capital did not give much protection to the business communities from the rapaciousness of the nobility. During the early Mughal period, i.e. mid-sixteenth century onwards, there was much maritime activity especially on the western coast. During this period a large body of merchants, mostly Muslims, began to operate from these ports. They held, according to W. H. Moreland, a 'privileged position, maintaining cordial relations with the local authorities, and enjoying . . . . more freedom than was granted to the ordinary inhabitants'.[5] But this was not to last long. Ashin Das Gupta informs us that mercantile property in the most important western Indian port of Surat came to be more and more threatened by local political potentates who had cut loose from the Mughal tether in the first half of the eighteenth century.[6] Oppression of inland trade and commerce became so bad during the Mughal rule that Aurangzeb had to issue a *firman* (notification) to prevent this kind of behaviour from the nobility.

The troubles of the traders and merchants were nothing as compared with the fate of the artisan at the hands of the nobility and the bureaucracy. Francisco Pelsart, chief of the Dutch factory at Agra, wrote in 1626: 'The second scourge is the oppression of Governor, nobles, Diwan, Kotwal, Bakhshi, and other Imperial officers. If one of these wants a workman, the man is not asked if he is willing to come, but is seized in his house or in the street, well beaten if he should dare to raise any objection.'[7] Another traveller, Francois Bernier reported similarly:

> When an Omrah or Mansabdar requires the services of an artisan, he sends to the Bazar for him, employing force, if necessary, to make the poor man work; and after the task is finished the unfeeling lord pays, not according to the value of labour but agreeably to his own standard of fair remuneration; the artisan having reason to

> congratulate himself if the *Korah* [whip] has not been given in part payment . . . .[8]

Conditions could not be any worse for business activity. As Athar Ali says of the Mughal rule:

> In trade and commerce corruption prevailed everywhere and no assistance was rendered by the authorities unless they were paid for it . . . . It should be remembered that the interference of the state in economic affairs was taken for granted in medieval times, as also the seeking of special favours, including the creation of monopolies by suitable bribes, presents, etc.[9]

In this sort of situation only those who could give costly bribes could prosper. No wonder that between the artisan and the trader, the latter suffered less, and the rich merchant was better off.[10] The uncertaintly was still ever present because if the rich merchant's benefactor lost out in the political game, he dragged the merchant as well to economic ruin. These circumstances led the merchants to escape from the plunder and oppression by the Mughal bureaucracy to the protection of the welcoming European East India companies, if possible. Similarly, the artisans tried to escape repression by resorting to various means including conversion to Islam, which explains the high level of conversion among them in the medieval period.

To this steady decline of the prestige and power of the business class during the Mughal period, there is one significant exception, i.e. the rise of the banking and moneylending community. Recent researches of Tapan Raychaudhuri, Irfan Habib and others have shown that the Mughal centralized bureaucracy based on the *mansabdari* system managed to extract virtually all the available surplus from the peasantry, that the Mughal economy was highly monetized, and that the attitude at any rate of the early Mughals towards foreign commerce was favourable.[11]

All this required a kind of expertise to organize, calculate and speculate in the finance sector and very soon it was forthcoming. The general expansion of trade in the Indian Ocean in the late sixteenth to the early eighteenth centuries also needed this kind of financial infrastructure. The rise of the Marwari bania businessmen of Rajasthan from the sixteenth century onwards has to be explained in terms of this demand for financial services. Thomas Timberg has pointed out that this community had experience in long-range trade and high finance even before the Mughal arrival in India, but the Marwaris spread outside Rajasthan only during the Mughal period. The initial migration was as 'commissary officers' of the units of Mughal armies commanded by Rajasthan princes.[12] Soon they settled in the big cities such as Murshidabad, Banaras, Surat, Hyderabad, Baroda, under the protection of the Mughal empire, and established an invisible all-India network of banking services. The bankers had, to quote Moreland, 'developed a conventional morality of their own. . . . Its merit lay in the fact that it provided a system under which commerce could be effectively carried on, and. . . . it was substantially fair to everyone who knew the rules of the game'. He thought the merchants should be placed 'in the highest class' and quoted Tavernier in support : 'The Jews engaged in money matters in the Turkish empire are usually considered to be exceptionally able, but they are scarcely fit to be apprenticed to the money-changers of India.[13]

The Mughal emperors had a love-hate relationship with these banking/moneylending traders. In general the ruling class perception of the trader was not very flattering. Abul Fazal in his *Ain-i-Akbari* was forthright: 'Honesty and conscientiousness are rare, especially among traders.[14] This may have been due to the Islamic injunction against usurious practices of any kind. And yet the Mughal government often utilized the services of the merchants to transmit funds from one corner to the other. They slowly became very useful instruments of exploitation by the Mughal nobility, helping in the transfer of money from the *jagirs* to the capital. The more impecunious of the nobility and princes found in the bania a good source of ready cash for borrowing. Even after the decline of the Mughal emperors, powerful regional satraps found the big merchants a useful financial arm. For example, in Bengal, merchant princes like Jagat Seth, Omi Chand and Khwaja Wazid controlled the finances of the country for the nawab.[15]

The general anti-trader bias of the Mughal polity, however, restricted the development of business communities. It did not take long for the latter to foresee the impending decline of the Mughal empire and the increasing ascendancy of the European companies in India. The companies had realized long ago their need for the middleman-comprador. Thus emerged the Indian business - European companies nexus at the beginning of the eighteenth century – the 'Anglo-Bania alliance, as Lakshami Subramanian terms it – which was mainly responsible for the swift expansion of the British interests in India. Though details may vary in regions, this switch in loyalty from the earlier rulers to the English East India Company cannot be seriously questioned. It was a beneficial arrangement for both. The British got their empire and the bania a 'new range of opportunities'.[16]

The attitude of the state towards business during this period cannot be neatly summarized. It may not even be correct to assume that either the Mughal state was an unchanging entity or that the economic environment remained stable from the fifteenth to the eighteenth century. Certainly, in the period of the Great Mughals considerable investment in commerce took place through powerful merchants in ports as far away as Surat in western India, Hughli in eastern India and Masuliapatnam in south India. Again, kingdoms on the periphery of the powerful Mughal empire were not always unfriendly to the business communities. As Arasaratnam has shown, the sultans of Golconda and Bijapur followed policies to encourage commerce in their territories.[17] But after the Great Mughals and especially since the end of the seventeenth century, this involvement in commerce as well as even the mild tolerance shown towards the business class disappeared. The steady decline of Mughal patronage of and the increasing hostile attitude towards business drove the business communities into the arms of the European trader-colonist who had developed a 'policy of protection of the Fair Trader'. But the pro-business attitude of the companies was as much politically motivated as it was economically induced.

In the three centuries with which we are concerned, one cannot help feeling that the business class lost the esteem of society as well as its own. This was due in part to merchants in general concealing their wealth to avoid the greedy eye of the bureaucrat or nobility. According to Pelsart, 'the shopkeeper is distinctly better off than the workman, and some of them are even well-to-do; but they must not let the fact be seen, or they will be victims of a trumped-up charge, and their property will be legally confiscated'.[18] This was also due to the merchants taking unfair advantage of the fallen state of artisans, as Bernier testified: 'If money be gained, it does not in any measure go into his [artisan's] pocket, but only serves to increase the wealth of the merchant'.[19]

The declining self-confidence among the business class was reflected in the decline of the corporate entities that had existed in the earlier centuries. Vijaya Ramaswami has drawn our attention to the fact that in the seventeenth century, whenever merchants are mentioned in the records, it is only in their individual capacity and not as part of a mercantile corporation or guild.[20] Ashin Das Gupta says that the merchants of Surat 'never evolved a comprehensive impersonal body to take care of all their common interests'.[21] Not only did the class feeling decline, but caste feeling increased to such an extent that business transactions often took place within the same subcaste. For example, in Bengal in the eighteenth century, as Sushil Chaudhury has pointed out recently, 'the commercial organization of Calcutta merchants was caste based'.[22] He cites the example of how the Jagat Seths refused to work with members of other castes when in 1748 the East India Company asked them to contract for investment. Fluidity in the caste structure, witnessed during the earlier period especially among the artisan class, disappeared and a particular profession got locked up into a particular caste. Artisans became very much economically dependent either on the European companies or the merchants and lost their respected position in society long before the end of the eighteenth century.

II

Once the British were firmly entrenched in India by the first decade of the nineteenth century, attitudes towards business also began to change. The relationship of the English East India Company and Indian business was no longer based on equality. As the company became the government, its objectives became very different from what they were in the previous century and the altered perception of its interests was bound to affect its attitudes towards business. In this context, two contradictory aspects of the British rule have to be noticed.

First, the British brought with them a belief in the market mechanism. Their ideal was capitalism which had served them well in Britain, and no doubt would do in India. Central to this belief was their faith in the sanctity of the institution of private property. The legal system which the British lawgivers gave India emphasizes this again and again. While the imperial policy would not grant political equality resulting in self-government, the new legal system recognized freedom for the individual to pursue his self-interest without any state interference. Secondly, the new colonial government, fashioned out of a British trading outfit, could not be completely neutral between the British business community and the Indian business community.

To these two, we must add another circumstance, namely the Industrial Revolution, that was to alter the British view of the utility of India as well as the attitudes of the colonial state towards the Indian business class. Unlike the East India Company in the eighteenth century, which was concerned more with exporting finished goods from India to Europe, the interests of the colonial rulers were very different. They needed raw materials for British industries and markets for finished goods. Consequently, it was clearly perceived that private business should be encouraged to achieve these twin objectives. As for the banking and credit aspects of Indian business, these were no longer of concern to the British rulers as they began overseeing the formation of a new type of financial infrastructure that could help achieve colonial economic objectives.

In short, business as such was not a favoured element as it was in the pre-Mughal economy, nor was it despised as it was when the Mughal state was strong, but something in between. The attitude of the colonial state towards business depended on the circumstances and the people they were dealing with. Before 1813, there was not much love lost between the so-called free European merchants and the East India Company merchants. When the company had not achieved the total political domination that it achieved in the nineteenth century, it was almost a free-for-all in the market place, the participants being the company merchant, the company servant as a private trader, the company soldier, the free European merchant and the Indian merchant. But when, with the passage of time, the free merchants, known as interlopers, became respectable gentlemen, formed clubs and chambers of commerce, and cultivated the company of the officials, the government became solicitous of their interests. Hence, business during the nineteenth century cannot be treated as a homogeneous entity even for academic convenience. We have to differentiate between the resident European business interests engaged in manufacturing, mercantile pursuits and railway transport on the one hand and Indian manufacturing and mercantile interests as well as those in the unorganized sector such as moneylenders and small traders on the other.

Each category, however, was not a separate watertight compartment. The various categories competed in certain areas and collaborated in others in a free legal atmosphere. Nevertheless, because by and large the colonial government was favourably disposed towards the European business interests, Indian business felt – and rightly so – discriminated against. Though there was undoubtedly a racial element in the formation of British attitudes, it seems that the desire to keep the empire intact was a more powerful motive. One cannot also dismiss completely the suggestion that some members of the Indian administration genuinely believed in encouraging Indian business. But they faced far too many obstacles as, for example, Alfred Chatterton in Madras did.[23]

Again, the British rulers were not averse to going against their own principles of administration if it was to help prevent the weakening of the empire. We can cite various acts against moneylenders. It was the legal system introduced by the British that unleashed many economic forces that resulted in large-scale rural indebtedness and wholesale transfer of land from agriculturists to moneylenders. Despite the belief in free trade and in the sanctity of private property, legislation militating against these principles was passed to help the moneylender so as to prevent serious political problems for the empire. Similarly, during the period before the First World War, the British policy was one of strict formal (as against effective) neutrality between Indian and British manufacturing interests. After the war, however, this attitude changed so that a small measure of protection was provided to the Indian industries. This was not done to favour business in India as such, but to achieve a measure of economic development in order to have a militarily stronger India.

How did the Indian society view business activity and businessmen during the British rule? At one level, the public perception of the businessmen – traders and moneylenders – was not flattering. This no doubt was due to the increasing (and very well-utilized) legal opportunities made available to them to exploit the poor. Ravinder Kumar points out that in western India in the second half of the nineteenth century 'the relationship of trust and confidence between the *ryots* and the *vanis*' that had existed during the pre-colonial times 'had been transformed through the institution of the courts of law, and the promulgation of the regulations, into a relationship of acute antagonism'.[24] The petty shopkeeper too did not have a good image. A character in a novel written by the great pioneer Tamil novelist and an outstanding judicial officer of the nineteenth century, Munsif Vedanayagam Pillay, in 1876 articulates what was apparently a commonly held view of small traders – in this case a textile merchant:

> The frauds perpetrated by the cloth merchants are universally known. You may be able to count the lines of the cloth but not their tricks. They will convert old clothes into new, turn white into black, black into red. . . . They pay one rupee to the weaver but sell it for ten rupees. No wonder cattle, sheep, and birds prefer to remain nude. The merchants' fraudulent character alone can explain why the Jains prefer to be *Digambaras* and Lord Shiva to take recourse to tiger or elephant skins.[25]

The petty shopkeeper and the small moneylender came to be looked upon by the poor villagers as parasites because the class to which they belonged was seen as the destroyer of the society based on *dharma*, i.e. the moral order.

Despite the contempt exhibited by the public for petty trading and moneylending, for some under-privileged groups it was still an attractive career to enter. A clear case is that of the Nadars of what is now Chidambaranar, Tirunelveli and Ramnad districts. They were originally eking their livelihood as toddy tappers, but thanks to altered circumstances during the British rule and a remarkable sense of community feeling, they developed themselves into a highly visible business community in south India.

At the same time, at another level society's attitude towards business was very favourable. The rich merchant in the nineteenth century was no different from his predecessors in so far as acts of piety and charity were concerned. He built temples, donated liberally to good causes, erected *choultries,* and fed the poor and needy during periods of famine or drought. This invariably earned him a good name.

There was yet another level of attitudes towards business. The rising new intelligentsia since the 1860s – educated in English and with high hopes for the country's future – pinned its faith in the Indian business communities to develop the Indian economy. As Mahadeva Govinda Ranade, for example, wrote in 1893:

> About twenty-two years ago, I had occasion to notice this collapse of domestic industries, and the gradual rustication of our chief occupations. . . . Things were as bad as could be about 1870-1875; since then the tide has turned, and India has shown signs of revival which marks its first step in the transition from a purely agricultural into a purely manufacturing and trading country . . . . I have placed before you what appears to me to be good grounds for the hope I entertain that India has now fairly entered upon the path which, if pursued in the same spirit which has animated its capitalists hitherto, cannot fail to work out its industrial salvation.[26]

As the movement for political freedom gained momentum, Indian (as opposed to British) business, by its cooperation with the nationalist elements and as the instrument through which the swadeshi policy would be implemented, came to be placed high in the public esteem. Not only Jamsetji Tata but also many other leading industrialists became folk heroes for championing the Indian cause against the British. It is no doubt true that the middle class ambition was to enter the professions or government service, but that did not prevent Indian business from being given importance in the Indian society.

This gave the business class a high degree of self-confidence. From the second half of the nineteenth century onwards one can notice the formation of a distinct business class that was in many respects different from that of the earlier periods. Indian merchants and traders with initiative found new opportunities in the competitive world of capital cities. After the initial period of collaboration with European capital, the Indian businessmen began to feel oppressed. This was no doubt due to the aggressive self-confidence of European business communities in India which was reflected, among many other things, in the foundation of chambers of commerce dominated by them. The Bengal Chamber of Commerce was formed in 1834, and those in Bombay and Madras in 1836. Within a few years many more such associations of European businessmen to cater to particular areas and businesses were formed.

In the wake of the nationalist movement at the turn of the century, Indian businessmen also began to acquire some self-confidence and assert their importance. A series of industrial conferences were organized along with the annual meetings of the Indian National Congress to discuss the problems of India's manufacturing sector and, if possible, to put pressure on the colonial government to do something to encourage Indian economic development. Another expression of the new-found self-confidence of the Indian business class was the formation of many purely Indian chambers of commerce starting with the one in what is now Kakinada in Andhra Pradesh. Quite a few early leaders of the Indian National Congress like Dadabhai Naoroji, Dinshaw Wacha, Ibrahim Rahimtoola, Vithaldas Thackersay and Purushotamdas Thakurdas were highly respected businessmen. At a later stage, many of India's leading businessmen – G.D. Birla, Lala Shri Ram, Jamnalal Bajaj, and many Ahmedabad millowners – came under the spell of Mahatma Gandhi. FICCI (the Federation of Indian Chambers of Commerce and Industry), which began in 1927 as the apex body of all the Indian chambers of commerce, gave its full backing to Gandhi's passive resistance movement in the 1930s. When the second Round Table Conference failed and Gandhiji was arrested, FICCI passed a unanimous resolution condemning the arrest and the subsequent police measures.

Lala Shri Ram as the president of FICCI wanted the Congress to consult with the organization before taking decisions on economic matters and requested the Mahatma to take the necessary steps to develop 'a sort of convention for the future that in all matters pertaining to the realm of economics, the Congress before making up its mind will allow us to offer it our suggestion and if necessary have discussion with our members'. Echoing sympathy for the suggestion Gandhi advised the businessmen to 'regard yourselves as trustees and servants of the poor . . . and you must be satisfied with earning an honest penny. I do not for a moment believe that commercial prosperity is incompatible with strict honesty'.[27]

Another measure of the rising self-confidence of the Indian business class was the aggressive invasion by it of what was traditionally the preserve of the European businessman. For example, the shipping industry which was dominated by the giant British India Navigation Company had to contend with Walchand Hirachand who daringly entered this field and achieved a measure of success despite the unhelpful attitude of the government. Again the Marwari businessmen quietly created a revolution by getting control of large chunks of European-owned companies – especially in Bengal – expanding their operations during the 1930s and 1940s.[28]

When India became free, the Indian business class was at its most popular phase. The new independent state expected the Indian business class to propel the country into a prosperous future. The captains of industry and their business were looked upon almost as national institutions by the government and the society at large, and at long last the business class was very confident of itself. It was no longer a despised poor relation as it had been under the Raj but capable of calling the shots. Indeed in the next forty years, while there would be times when it seemed that the private business class would once again lose its importance, it would retain and augment its autonomy and position in society.

III

If we compare the changing attitude to business in India with that in Europe, we would find a great deal of intrinsic differences, similarities if any being superficial. For instance, in Europe before the fifteenth century the merchants, traders or artisans did not enjoy a high position in society. Anyone wanting to rise on the social ladder chose soldiering or religion; commerce and industry were not the routes to social eminence. It was most certainly a period which was dominated by an anti-business ideology. The next two hundred years, however, witnessed a high degree of social and occupational mobility, the rise of powerful merchant princes, and the growth of an influential middle class. These developments were aided by a sort of intellectual revolution characterized by reason and science.[29]

All this brought about a sea change in the attitudes towards business and businessmen by the seventeenth century. It was a period when politically influential mercantile families came into their own. Jacques Coeur of Bourges, the Fugger family of Augsburgh, Dick Whittington of London, Roberto Strozzi and the Medici of Florence and many others throughout Europe became important in the social and political life.

These merchant princes represented only the icing on the cake because there had simultaneously grown a large trading community. As Charles Wilson points out: 'Everywhere along the seaboards of western Europe and the Mediterranean, the sixteenth and seventeenth centuries saw trade grow, and with it, important merchant communities'.[30] And by intermarrying with nobility, they increased their social standing. Even more important, the views of merchants were significant inputs in the making of national economic policies. Mercantilist economic policy was very much the result of the ascendancy of commercial interests on the European economic scene.

Along with the creation and expansion of the national and international business system in the sixteenth and seventeenth centuries, two powerful and inter-related intellectual movements captured the European mind. They were the Scientific Revolution and the idea of progress. By stressing Reason as the appropriate style of discourse and showing a definite goal for man to strive for, these two intellectual movements provided to the European nations both the desire and the wherewithal to achieve economic development. And once the Industrial Revolution occurred in the eighteenth and nineteenth centuries, it enabled the business class to take off and eventually capture an exalted and respected place in European society even above that of the military and clergy.

In contrast, in India there was never an anti-business ideology until the Mughal arrival. The pre-sixteenth century ethos was supportive of business activity but business had no specific place in the Mughal order of things. It was not an essential element of the Mughal system. It was only in the nineteenth century that conditions became somewhat conducive for Indian business to attempt to regain its old position in society in spite of the country being under an alien rule. Some like Dipesh Chakrabarty would even argue that the altered attitudes towards business and businessmen were all parts of the phenomenon of colonialism in the larger context.

The nineteenth century marks a divide in the way Indians looked at the World, Nature, Society and Man. This had an indirect but powerful link with the reorientation given in the educational policies of the colonial rulers. The consequences for the attitudes towards economic development in general and business activities in particular were considerable. Until the onset of the nineteenth century the concern of Indian thinkers and scholars were fundamental questions of life, existence, death and soul. Specific questions about physical phenomena were not asked, much less answered. Science as it developed in the west since the seventeenth century did not develop in India, and a high level of craftsmanship developed without any connection to scientific results. Overarching all this was a philosophy of self-denial that precluded accumulation of wealth for the sake of one's pleasure. Though accumulation of wealth did take place, it was always considered something for one to be defensive about. And the Indian view of history saw the future as dismal.[31]

All these attitudes began to be attacked incessantly by the intellectual forces unleashed from Europe in India in the nineteenth century. The Bengal renaissance is a supreme example of how rationalism and westernism were introduced into India with far-reaching results. Westernism implied, to quote Susobhan Chandra Sarkar, 'the rights of man as man in the secular sense, its rationalism undermines change resisting religious and social orthodoxy, its social reform holds out the prospect of emancipation for the oppressed'.[32] Westernism also implied bringing to India the very same elements that brought industrial development to Britain, such as business enterprise, investment, sales, rates of return, and so on. Dipesh Chakrabarty has pointed out how the important figures of the Bengal renaissance despite their divergent opinions, were all united in their belief in benefits that would accrue to India with the introduction of railways.[33]

Above everything else, India also absorbed the idea of progress which is to say that in terms of happiness derived from material consumption, the present is better than the past, and the future better than the present. That the nineteenth-century Indian intelligentsia was sure of a bright future for India need not be disputed. There was, for example, Raja Rammohan Roy who had what Sarkar calls 'an unaltering vision of their [Indian people's] bright modern destiny'.

Bankim Chandra Chattopadhyaya, another influential figure of the century, was clear as to what would happen in the future:

> Of the two necessary conditions for the growth of civilization – desire for knowledge and desire for wealth – the latter is more pervasive and hence ultimately beneficial for mankind . . . . A steady growth in human happiness and welfare has been the end result of such material aspiration.[34]

Ranade is another example of how leading Indian thinkers had absorbed the idea of progress. Having noticed that industrial regeneration had taken place after a temporary setback, he too projected a future thus: 'Whether we wish it or not, the transformation of Industries . . . is inevitable, and we must make the best of it'.[35]

It is not as though only the western educated intelligentsia internalized the idea of progress. We have the example of a Tamil Pandit, Veeraswami Chettiar, writing in the 1860s in the form of a discussion between one *Supatchan* and another *Vipatchan* – protagonists of the present and of the past respectively. For every objection that *Vipatchan* makes to the current developments, *Supatchan* argues against and invariably gets the better of the argument. No matter what the subject – education, manufacture, agriculture, commerce, life of the common man, administration – *Supatchan* argues that things have improved and will improve further. Although the discussion goes on to praise the colonial rule, the underlying attitude is clear: India has to progress and progress inevitably would bring much happiness to the ordinary people through the means of the capitalist path.[36]

Although more than a century has passed since this was written, this attitude towards progress and business has sustained itself.

Notes

*My discussion with Prof. S. Arasaratnam helped me in clarifying my ideas for which I am grateful.

1. The literary sources are too varied to be documented. Among the secondary works which throw some light on the subject are : N.Subranmanyam, *Sangam Polity* (Bombay 1966); E.H. Washington, *The Commerce between the Roman Empire and India* (Cambridge 1928); T.W. Rhys Davids, *Buddhist India* (London 1911); Pushpa Niyogi, *Contributions to the Economic History of Northern India from the Tenth to the Twelfth Century A.D.*(Calcutta 1962); R.N.Saletore, *Early Indian Economic History*(Bombay 1973); A.Appadorai, *Economic Conditions in Southern India, 1100-1500 A.D.* (Madras 1936); Meera Abraham, *Two Medieval Merchant Guilds of South India* (Delhi 1988); G.L. Adhya, *Early Indian Economics; Studies in the Economic Life of Northern and Western*

India, c.1200 B.C. to 300 A.D. (Bombay 1966).

2. K.N. Chaudhuri, *Trade and Civilization in the Indian Ocean: An Economic History from the Rise of Islam to 1750* (Cambridge 1985), p.11.

3. M. Athar Ali, *The Mughal Nobility under Aurangazeb, (Bombay 1970)*, p. 155.

4. Ibid., pp. 156-57.

5. W.H. Moreland, *India at the Death of Akbar* (Delhi 1962), pp. 229-30.

6. Ashin Das Gupta, 'The Merchants of Surat, c. 1700-50' in E. Leach & S. N. Mukherji. (eds.), *Elites in South Asia* (Cambridge 1970), p. 221.

7. Quoted in W.H. Moreland, *From Akbar to Aurangzeb: A Study in Indian Economic History* (London 1923), p.199.

8. Quoted in Athar Ali, *The Mughal Nobility*(n.3), p.157.

9. Ibid., pp. 158-60.

10. Merchants also did well by supplying goods to the expanding foreign trade under the early Mughal kings. See Om Prakash, *The Dutch East India Company and the Economy of Bengal 1630-1720*. (Delhi 1988), p.259.

11. Tapan Raychaudhuri, 'The Mughal Empire' in T. Roychudhuri and Irfan Habif(eds.) *The Cambridge Economic History of India,* vol. I. c 1200-c 1750 (Cambridge 1982) pp. 172ff.

12. Thomas Timberg, *The Marwaris: From Traders to Industrialists* (New Delhi 1978), pp. 41-42.

13. Moreland, *India at the Death of Akbar*(n.5), p.233.

14. Abul Fazal, *Ain-i-Akbari*, tr. by H.Blochmann (Delhi 1965, reprint), p. 232.

15. Om Prakash, *The Dutch East India Company*(n.10), p.32.

16. Lakshmi Subrahmaniam, 'Banias and the British: The Role of Indigenous Credit in the Process of Imperial Expansion in Western India in the Second Half of the 18th Century', *Modern Asian Studies*, XVII (1987), pp. 473-510.

17. See S. Arasaratnam, 'India and Indian Ocean: The Seventeenth Century' in Ashin Das Gupta and M.N. Pearson (eds.), *India and the Indian Ocean 1500-1800* (Calcutta 1987), pp. 104-24. S. Arasaratnam, 'The Coromandel-South East Asia Trade, 1650-1740', *Journal of Asian HIstory*, XVIII (1984), pp. 114-16. See also Ashin Das Gupta, 'Indian Merchants and the Western Indian Ocean: The Early Seventeenth Century', *Modern Asian Studies,* XIX (1985), pp. 481-99, where the complexity of the changing relationships between the state and business is emphasized.

18. Cited in Moreland, *From Akbar to Aurangzeb,* (n.7), p. 200.

19. Ibid., p.203.

20. Vijaya Ramaswami, *Textiles and Weavers in Medieval South India* (Delhi 1985), p.145.

21. Ashin Das Gupta, 'The Merchants of Surat' (n.6), p. 220. See also his 'India and the Indian Ocean in 18th century' in Das Gupta and Pearson(eds), *India and the Indian Ocean* (n.17).

22. Sushil Chaudhary, 'Merchants, Companies and Rulers: Bengal in the 18th Century', *Journal of the Economic and Social History of the Orient,* XXXI (1988), p. 82. Christopher Bayly however believes that while caste was important in commercial organization, it was not the 'prime parameter of mercantile organisation in complex cities' such as Benaras. 'Indian Merchants in a Traditional Setting: Beneras, 1780-1830' in Clive Dewey and A.G.

Hopkins (eds.), *The Imperial Impact: Studies in the Economic History of Africa and India (London 1978)*,p.192.

23. See Padmini Swaminathan, 'State Intervention in Industrial Development: A Case Study of Madras Presidency', paper presented at a Seminar on *South Indian Economy* held at Trivandrum, 25-27 April 1988.

24. Ravinder Kumar, *Western India in the Nineteenth Century* (London 1968), p. 154.

25. Vednayagam Pillay, *Pratapa Mudaliar Charittiram* (Madras 1957), p. 147.

26. M.G. Ranade, *Essays on Indian Economics: A Collection of Essays and Speeches* (Madras 1906), p. 126.

27. Cited in Khushwant Singh and Arun Joshi, *Shri Ram: A Biography* (Bombay 1968), pp. 201-02.

28. See Omkar Goswami, 'Then Came the Marwaris: Some Aspects of the Changes in the Pattern of Industrial Control in Eastern India', *Indian Economic and Social History Review*, XII (1985), pp. 225ff.

29. George Unwin, *Industrial Organisation in the Sixteenth and Seventeenth Centuries* (London 1963), passim.

30. Charles Wilson, *England's Apprenticeship, 1603-1763* (London 1965), p. 10; also, Sydney Checkland, *The Rise of Industrial Society in England, 1815-1885*. (London 1964), p. 74.

31. See for an elaboration of this point: S.Ambirajan and R.Rajagopalan, 'Science: Teacher, Servant or Master? in *Bulletin of the Madras Institute of Development Studies*, XVI (1986), pp. S117-S205.

32. Susobhan Sarkar, *On the Bengal Renaissance* (Calcutta 1985), p. 75.

33. See Dipesh Chakrabarty, 'The Colonial Context of the Bengal Renaissance; A Note on Early Railway Thinking in Bengal' *Indian Economic and Social History Review*, XI (1974) pp. 92-111.

34. See Tapan Raychaudhuri, *Europe Reconsidered: Perceptions of the West in Nineteenth Century Bengal* (Delhi 1988), pp. 161-62.

35. Ranade, *Essays on Indian Economics* (n.26), p.126.

36. Veeraswami Chettiar, *Vinodarasamanjari* (Madras 1931), 74-109.

2

Merchants and Politics: From the Great Mughals to the East India Company*

Lakshmi Subramanian and Rajat K. Ray

I

A typical quartet figuring in Bengal's folk-tales consists of the wandering prince (*rajaputra*), the minister's son (*mantriputra*), the commandant's son (*kotalputra*)[1] and the merchant's son (*saudagarputra*). The combination of these four important figures reflects the popular notions of political and social precedence in the older Indian society. The wealthy merchant who acts as the prince's banker is seen in sixteenth-century sources to occupy a place of honour and importance in the court, be he the minister of a Rajput raja (such as Bhamashah, the minister of Rana Pratap Singh of Mewar) or the *diwan* of a Pathan sultan (such as Rai Dhana, the chief *potedar* of Sulaiman Sultan, independent Pathan king of Bengal).[2] The incorporation of these smaller dominions into the growing empire of Akbar relegated the merchants and bankers to obscurity in the long imperial century that followed. Despite the increased commercial prosperity induced by the administrative integration of the maritime regions of Gujarat and Bengal with the land mass of Hindustan, the *shahs* and *seths* had no place in the affairs of state under the rule of the Mughal *umara*. In the centralized imperial system of the seventeenth century, power and wealth were concentrated to an enormous degree in the hands of the ranking commanders of Mughal horse (*mansabdars*). Even in areas of unusual concentration of wealthy merchants and bankers, such as Surat (the Bandar Mubarak of the Great Mughals) and Bengal, the imperial officer posted on the spot, whether it was the *mutasaddi* of Surat or the *nazim* of Bengal, represented an Olympian imperial power before which the wealthiest of subjects was levelled. But the merchants and bankers were destined to occupy an important place in the smaller successor regimes of the eighteenth century. One of these local successor regimes, the English East India Company (*diwan* of Bengal from 1765), gradually triumphed over the rest. The *sahukars* (bankers) and *saudagars* (merchants), having occupied the limelight for a brief period during the interregnum, helped the company prevail over its greatest rival, the Maratha Confederacy, by providing the former with crucial financial services.

The revenues claimed by the Great Mughals and their *mansabdars* amounted virtually to a half of the crops produced in the empire. Of the amounts realized in taxes, as much as 82 per cent went to the *mansabdars* – an imperial ruling corps of officers, commanders and noblemen (*umara*) numbering just 1,671 persons in the latter part of Akbar's reign.[3] As the Mughal *umara* needed the entire amount in cash, there was a higher degree of commercialization and monetization of the products of the empire at the beginning of the seventeenth century, a process reflected in the transition from the copper coin to the silver rupee (which made possible bigger units of revenue and trade transactions) and the development of the great *hundi* exchanges between Surat and Agra, and between Agra and Dacca.[4] The *mansabdars* and their regiments, subject to frequent transfers from one end of the empire to the other, found it useful to avail of the private commercial facilities for the transfer of moneys offered by the *hundi* bankers. It must be emphasized, however, that the imperial regime constructed by Akbar was not in any critical sense dependent on the *shahs*, *seths*, *sahukars* and *saudagars*. Despite the fairly frequent resort to the *hundi* as a useful auxiliary facility, the empire basically relied for its enormous transfers of moneys on despatch of treasure by secure imperial highways. In addition, it regularly remitted money through the far-flung imperial system of closely interlinked provincial treasuries drawing *barats* (bills) one upon the other.[5] There was no pressing need to farm out the taxes and the mints to wealthy traders and moneyed men in the seventeenth century, for the salaried revenue establishments in every *sarkar* and every *pargana* collected the revenues regularly and there were accumulated balances of treasure in the central treasury for countering emergencies, amounting at the death of Akbar at around fifteen crore rupees.[6] Far from traders and bankers financing the imperial military-bureaucratic class, the Mughal officers had enough accumulated savings to finance and fit out overseas fleets for the purpose of trade to Achin at one end and Mokha at the other through the better part of the seventeenth century.[7]

Private bankers and merchants were an entirely subordinate class in the Mughal empire and their attitude to the imperial officers, as reflected in the contemporary Hindi literature, was an indication of their fear and deference. The great and unbridgeable distance between the Mughal officers and the generality of Hindu merchants, the merchants' abject subservience to the officers and their dependence on the latter's caprice for their lives and property come out in one of the incidents of Banarsidas's trading career. He describes in a passage how two Mughal officers calmly debate between themselves in Persian whether a party of merchants they have just arrested are thugs or genuine merchants. The soldiers are entirely casual in bringing up nineteen iron spikes for despatching Banarsidas and his eighteen companions. Most striking of all is the gratitude with which the author, on his unexpected release by the *hakim's diwan*, begs the latter not to blame himself for the mistake: 'Sir, you are our noble master, and it is all the consequence of our past deeds.'[8]

The set of relationships prevailing within the social formation described above makes it evident that there was no question of the merchants taking a hand in the fall of the Mughal empire, or of the bankers diverting their financial support from the Mughals to their opponents.[9] On the contrary, the *mahajans* and Khatris of the Punjab exhibited a definite preference for the local Mughal rulers as against the Sikh rebels pillaging the towns. In the same manner, the mercantile community of Surat was behind the local Mughal administration as against the bands of roving Maratha horse levying blackmail.[10] It may be imagined, however, that the breakdown of the unified rule of the imperial military-bureaucratic class, and the emergence of a series of autonomous local nawabs from Surat at one end to Murshidabad at the other, all left by Delhi to their own devices in coping with the light Maratha horse, would open up new possibilities for the merchants and bankers of the Mughal empire. One of these possibilities was for the bankers and merchants to seize power in areas where they were strong, on the pattern of the Venetian, Florentine and Dutch republics. The nearest they ever came to this was their rebellion in Surat in 1730, a stillborn revolution which ended up by replacing one nawab with another. The other possibility, the one that was actually realized, was for the bankers and merchants to become essential elements in the new regimes that were being shaped out of the fragments of the Mughal empire.

As civil wars, rebellions and succession disputes broke out all over the empire, money became urgent for campaigns that would not wait.

With the accumulated balances in the treasury exhausted in endless military operations,[11] it was not possible to wait for the inflow of the next instalment of revenue. Rulers and generals began to borrow money from bankers and merchants on the security of the next *kist* (instalment) and to farm out taxes and mints to whoever was willing to supply ready money. Thus Farrukhsiyar, proclaiming himself emperor in Bengal, undertook his successful expedition to Delhi with the money raised form the bankers of Patna and Banaras;[12] and when, upon his triumph, the disorganization of the entire revenue system of the empire pressed the necessity of fresh financial expedients upon the central government, Ratanchand, the *diwan* of the all-powerful and hated Sayyid brothers, hit upon the device of farming out the revenues and the very mint of the empire to the lowly *baqqals* (shopkeepers, banias).[13] Ratanchand, who hailed from a trading caste, was accused by the *umara* of having turned statecraft into shopkeeping (*baqqaliat*). But the noblemen, beggars themselves, were in no position to be choosers; and in the beleagured Punjab *subah*, they began around 1716 to farm out their own *jagirs* to the *mahajans*.[14]

Juridically, the Mughal empire was still intact, the court of Delhi still the sovereign legitimizer of appointments in the now virtually autonomous *subahs*. Many of the noblemen serving in these new *subahdari* (nawabi) administrations, still had their homes and families in Delhi.[15] The *jagirs* as well as the lands of the *khalisa*, continued to be spread around in many parts of the empire. But as the separate nawabi administrations set up by the *nazim* of Bengal, the *wazir* of Awadh, the *nizam* of Hyderabad and even the petty *mutasaddi* of Surat became better articulated, *de facto* borders carved out the theoretically integral territory. In these circumstances, the gigantic imperial money transfers system operating through the mutual *barats* of the far-flung treasuries of the empire ceased to function. With the roads increasingly insecure, and even the imperial highway from Murshidabad to Delhi being infested by Rohilla and Rajput rebels near Etawah,[16] the physical despatch of treasure had become more difficult than ever. There was, however, one way still of remitting money safely. The private commercial credit transfer links fostered in the heyday of the Mughal empire had survived. The *hundi* links between Delhi, Agra, Kora, Allahabad and Banaras, for instance, were in active use right through the reign of Shah Alam II.[17] In an age when so many freshly drawn frontiers had to be crossed, the bankers' credit constituted, as the French adventurer Jean Law commented, a chain that extended everywhere.[18]

It was these private financial facilities that noblemen, commanders and officers of the empire now relied upon almost exclusively to remit the fortunes accruing out of their official salaries and *jagirs*.[19] The same practice was resorted to in the *khalisa* lands of the empire. The revenue collectors sent *hundis* for the amount realized, and the bankers of Delhi encashed the *hundis* and sent the sum to the office of the *wazir*. The growing dependence of the *wizarat* on the goodwill and cooperation of the bankers was underscored by the fact that the latter would often suppress the news of the receipt of the *hundis* from their agents, for fear that the collection might not have been actually made in the *mahals*.[20] As the revenues of the empire dried up and in consequence, the court at Delhi was forced to rely on the annual tribute from Bengal, the method of remittance through *hundi* transactions between Jagat Seth's *kothis* in Murshidabad and Delhi assumed critical importance, the whole tribute, amounting to a crore rupees, being negotiated in this manner between 1720 and 1740. Following the later Mughal precedents, the Marathas also resorted to bankers' *hundis* for remitting the *chauth* imposed on the princely states of Rajputana to their headquarters in Malwa.[21] In the same fashion, but on a bigger scale, the English East India Company remitted huge portions of the Bengal revenue to Bombay through the house of Manohardas Dwarkadas in the late eighteenth century, a device which, as we shall see, played a critical part in the mobilization of financial resources for the English military operations against the Maratha Confederacy.

The Mughal state on more than one occasion professed its intentions of augmenting the prosperity of the realm by extending protection and fair deal to the trader and banker. Emperor Jehangir, almost immediately after his accession, proclaimed through one of his twelve regulations that merchants travelling through the country were not to have their bales or packages of any kind opened without their consent. When they were perfectly willing to dispose of any article of merchandise, purchasers were to deal with them without 'offering any species of molestation'.[22] The emperor was equally solicitous about respecting the inviolability and sanctity of private property, individual commercial fortunes inclusive, and stated:

> When a person shall die and leave children, the individual not being in the employment of the State, no man whatever was to interfere a pin's point in his territory nor to offer the slightest molestation to the children, but when there were neither children nor direct or

> unquestionable heirs, the inheritance was to be applied to defray the expenses incurred for mosques and talaub or water tanks, so as to secure perpetual blessings on the soul of the departed.[23]

So much for the Mughal maxims of statecraft regarding the merchants. Did these in any sense reflect the real condition that prevailed in the seventeenth-century Hindustan? And, equally important, how did the merchants perceive their own lot under the dispensation of the Great Mughals? A careful reading of the available sources reveals that the actual situation was complex, and that the treatment of the merchants varied greatly from time to time and place to place. Merchants were especially concerned about the imperial postings to their own area, for much depended on the immediate officer in command and the gap between principle and practice might be specially pronounced under a venal or arbitrary officer. Merchants were never quite sure of what was in store for them, and there was no guarantee of an enlightened imperial administration actuated by the highest notions of benevolence and predictability of efficient bureaucratic mechanisms. A lot depended on personal whim.

It is, however, especially difficult to get at what merchants felt and how they coped with the situation. There was no tradition of writing memoirs, autobiographies or histories among merchant communities in India. Fortunately, there is an exception – a source that enables us to see things from their own point of view. The *Ardha Kathanaka*[24] ('Half a Tale') of Banarsidas, a Jain merchant of the seventeenth century, graphically mirrors the reality of the social and political milieu in which the Indian merchant operated. Banarsidas, like his father Kharagsen, was a resident of Jaunpur which was part of the Mughal empire from 1560. Under Akbar, Jaunpur remained the chief town of a large territory until 1575 when the provincial capital was shifted to Allahabad, and Jaunpur itself reduced to the status of a *sarkar* in the *subah* of Allahabad. These variations in administrative status do not appear to have made an appreciable dent on the commercial fortunes of Jaunpur which together with Allahabad and Agra constituted a major arterial point in the internal trade of northern India. Enterprising business communities - Jains, Khatris and banias – were active in trade and moneylending and maintained extensive contacts with their correspondents in far-off towns. The business of provisioning imperial troops was also important; Banarsidas's grandfather Muldas Biholiya was a case in point.[25]

The advantages of Mughal employment, however, came to an abrupt end with Muldas's demise in 1555 (v.s. 1613) when his possessions were confiscated by the Mughal *amir*, notwithstanding the legitimacy of his son Kharagsen's claims. The latter left Nurwar for Jaunpur where his assaying skills commanded immediate notice. By 1575, he had become a merchant of repute and had set up a commercial firm in partnership with Ramdas Agarwal. The firm seems to have handled a lucrative business in money and precious stones (diamonds, rubies and corals), Kharagsen at the same time taking pains to extend his business contacts by arranging for his son Banarsidas's marriage with a well-to-do merchant's family in Khairabad. Happy days soon came to an end when a year later (1592), Nawab Qilij Khan, the governor of the city, vented his wrath on the city's jewellers and moneyed men. Failing to persuade the merchants to meet a large cash contribution well beyond their capacity, the governor stood them in a row and whipped them with a spiked lash. The merchants who had nearly turned corpses, to echo Banarsidas's eloquence, as a result of the beating they had taken, fled the town to protect their person and property.[26] Overnight, Kharagsen with his family crossed the Ganga and left for Shahzadpur where he was unexpectedly befriended by Karamchand Mahur, a helpful bania who knew him before. The association sustained Kharagsen and his family, enabling him to establish and extend his business contacts further to Allahabad, and encouraging young Banarsidas to dabble in the cowrie trade. Allahabad was then under the fostering care of Akbar's son Danyal – 'a benefactor of the entire world'.[27] Kharagsen's trade prospects considerably improved in Allahabad where he engaged in moneylending as well.

The departure of Governor Qilij Khan in 1598 encouraged the emigres to return and, in Banarsidas's words, 'to surface like people long lost in the bowels of the earth'.[28] The new governor, the younger Qilij, popularly known as Nuram Sultan, was, as his nickname indicated, well disposed towards the merchants. The 'personal factor' did not, however, immunize the merchants against the larger crisis of the empire. Thus, when Prince Salim threatened to march to Jaunpur defying imperial orders, the merchant population once more contemplated going away until the danger passed, but the crisis soon blew over. In due course, Kharagsen consolidated his position extending his contacts to Patna and making unexpectedly high profits. In 1603, he accepted an invitation from Hiranand, an Oswal Jain and a *mukim* of Prince Salim, to accompany a pilgrimage party from Prayag to Samet.

The following year did not augur well. Uncertainty prevailed – the news of Emperor Akbar's demise triggering off a chain reaction of panic among Jaunpur's citizens. This panic, nation wide in impact, became in Banarsidas's perception a great leveller: 'the rich to ward off any possible extortion donned the garbs of the poor and secreted their wealth underground. Shops had their shutters pulled down, while the more resourceful took to flight abroad'.[29] The description reveals as nothing else does the inherent insecurity that the Indian merchant had to cope with. Imperial politics mattered fundamentally; it had its manifestation at the local level and this invariably involved the possibility of extortion and plunder.

The dismal prospects of civil war soon faded and the situation quickly returned to normalcy. The news of Salim's succession as Emperor Jehangir was celebrated with much festivity and fanfare. Kharagsen's firm had by now, i.e. 1609, become one of repute. Exploiting the growing demand for cloth and jewellery from the ruling elite in Agra, the firm did brisk business. Banarsidas was given the responsibility of setting up a trading mission in Agra where his contact was his brother-in-law Bansidas, a well-to-do resident of Moti Katra. His ventures did not take off as well as anticipated, and his misfortunes were conveyed to his father through his elder brother-in-law Uttamchand, a well-to-do merchant and dealer in precious stones in Agra. Kharagsen's disappointments forced Banarsidas to stay back in Agra and recoup his losses. Entering into partnership with Dharamdas, an Oswal Jain merchant, he worked up a modest trade in precious stones only to wind it up in 1612. Largely due to his extravagance, Banarsidas was left with no personal savings. Throwing himself on his wife's support, he ventured into business again. This time, making use of his father-in-law's establishment in the well-known market of Katra Parvez in Agra, he met with a degree of success. Associations were forged with Narrottamdas, Thanmal Badaliya, and Tarachand Mothiya – the latter persuading Banarsidas to venture out to Patna as well.

The nucleus of the business, however, lay at Banaras, where the firm's trade in precious stones flourished. Branches were established at Patna and Jaunpur, where Banarsidas handled the business. His position and prospects improved with the coming of Cini Qilij Khan as governor who favoured him and invested him with a *sirpao*. Indeed, it is possible that this connection with Qilij Khan was a decisive factor in Banarsidas's business success, although the merchant himself refused to disclose the secret behind it.[30]

In marked contrast to Cini Qilij Khan, his successor Agha Noor was a terror to the trading community. The conditions in Jaunpur changed dramatically. Coercion and extortion became the order of the day and, as Banarsidas put it, 'all the *kothiwals* [bankers], *hundiwals* [billbrokers], *sarrafs* [money changers], *jauharis* [jewellers] and *dalas* [brokers] were seized without distinction between right and wrong'.[31] Banarsidas remained outside Jaunpur until Agha Noor was abruptly recalled to Agra. The return of sanity meant that Banarsidas could resume his business and undertake a journey to Agra. Accompanied by several influential Maheswari merchants, Banarsidas went on a trip dogged by trouble and ill luck. A Brahman in the travelling team was cheated by a silversmith who later had the audacity to accuse the former of having given him counterfeit coins in the first place. The whole body of traders and travellers were accused by the capricious *kotwal* of being thugs and were nearly put on iron spikes. Fortunately for Banarsidas and his companions, the *faujdar's* deputy was a man of milder character, and suitable contacts were found which convinced him of their innocence. The next few years were spent mostly in pilgrimage and remarriage. (Banarsidas had lost his second wife and son in 1621.)

What emerges most clearly from Banarsidas's autobiographical tale is the fact that merchants were never quite sure of the caprice of the local administration. The latter was not guided by clearly defined rules and self-aggrandizement was often a powerful motive behind administrative action. In the absence of dependable patronage by the administration, substitutes were found in the form of long established familial, caste and business connections. Note with what facility Banarsidas and his father were able, in times of stress in Jaunpur, to find a niche for themselves in the business world of Agra on one occasion and Allahabad on the other. Merchants were equally adept at building unofficial contacts with the administration, whenever possible. For the most part, the administration was more feared than admired, and the mercantile community had learnt to reckon with the necessity of keeping their immediate rulers placated by timely bribes and presents. The question of merchants having an honoured role in the affairs of state or even of their exerting any sustained pressure on administration did not arise.

II

The complexion of things was somewhat different in Surat, the premier port of Mughal India, where there was a dramatic expansion of trade in the seventeenth century. Surat's growing trade with the Red Sea and Persian Gulf was undoubtedly due to the larger benefits of

Mughal rule in terms of improved communications, a larger and more integrated market network and somewhat greater security of person and property.[32] The monetization of the land revenue, moreover, added significantly to the value of trade and made possible the consolidation of the credit lines fanning out from Surat to different parts of the empire. The merchants of the Bandar Mubarak could not but respond to the new opportunities arising from the consolidation of the Ottoman, Safavid and Mughal empires and the increased volume of exchange between these huge trading blocks. Several merchants rose to become men of wealth and eminence. They had sufficient weight to carry the administration with them on several important matters. What was especially striking was the manner in which the Great Mughals were willing to back them against the European East India companies. The Muslim shipowners of Surat looked up to the Mughal administration for support against the intruding English. The latter naturally did not have a favourable view of the policy of the Great Mughals. The contemporary English perception was that 'the King hath no content . . . . expects great presents and jewels and regards no trade but what feeds his insatiable appetite after stones, riches and rare pieces of art'.[33]

The bone of contention between the Great Mughals and the English East India Company was permission for the latter to participate in the Red Sea trade – a line that was zealously guarded by the Muslim merchants of Gujarat. In defending their preserve the Surat shipowners found a ready ally in the administration whose shipping and commercial interests, intermittent but important, were closely interwoven with theirs. Ishaq Beg, the *mutasaddi* of Surat in 1619, went so far as to issue a general prohibition of trade by the English and impose 'a penalty on all the brokers as well as of Brodera [Baroda] and Baruch as of this place and Nunserry [Navsari] that sell the English any cloth and [write] also the Governors of the said places to that effect'.[34] Ishaq Beg was in this case acting at the instance of Prince Khurram, the viceroy of Gujarat. The Muslim merchants had petitioned to Prince Khurram that the Red Sea was the only trade preserve left open to them, and that if this were thrown open to the English, Surat would be beggared.[35] The English decision to blockade and attack Surat's shipping from the Gulfs eventually gave them the opening they desired. Neither the Mughal administration nor the Muslim merchants were prepared to push matters to the point of facing an expensive and prolonged naval blockade.

The triumph of the English was ephemeral. It did not enable them to compete effectively with the Muslim merchant shipowners who dominated the scene with their medium-size ships.[36] The families of Mulla Abdul Ghafur (Bohra) and Ahmed Chellabi (of Turkish descent), alongside others of Persian extraction, dominated the high seas at the beginning of the eighteenth century, and were held in esteem by the Mughal administration whose patronage they naturally enjoyed. Influence and wealth did not, however, breed interest in active politics except negotiations involving the Europeans and their convoy arrangements.[37]

Official patronage did not extend to other trading groups in the city – the banias and the Parsis – in the same manner. But unlike Banarsidas and his colleagues in the north, they did not have to take recourse to frequent change in residence, which is indicative of their ability to cope with the situation. Nor do we have any contemporary records of an indigenous merchant describing his travails. We have to depend for the most part on English factory records which bring to light occasional instances of government excesses and the merchants' responses thereto.

Administrative interference usually assumed the form of engrossing goods, extorting a percentage of brokers' commissions and of hoarding bullion imports instead of releasing them into the market. In 1622, the Cambay factors wrote to the Surat factory about the governor's misdoings – that he insisted on the city brokers to present daily statements and accounts of their sales and purchases and to make over to him a percentage of their proceeds. The governor also ordered the brokers to confine their negotiations to the bazaar. Merchants, however, refused to comply with these demands; trade suffered and in due course the orders were withdrawn.[38]

Noncooperation did not always work. In 1628, we hear of the gates of Ahmedabad city being locked for two days so as to enable Prince Khurram to extort nearly two crore rupees from the city's banias.[39] The citizens of Surat seem to have enjoyed a relative degree of immunity, although there were occasional instances of interference. In 1662 the governor of Surat chose to engross the bullion imports of merchants into his own hands. 'That hath frightened most of the merchants from this place, that to this day there is not a ship gone out of this port to Persia'.[40] Such acts were, however, sporadic, and the merchants had learnt to deal with them. The administration, while by no means benevolent in its disposition, was not totally arbitrary in Surat.[41] There was, thus, no question of abandoning one's home to escape the caprices of a particularly venal governor. It was only when matters of religion and religious sentiment were involved that such an extreme step could be contemplated.

Whether the disturbances of 1669 in Surat were the culminating point of a growing proselytizing tendency on the part of the Mughal government is difficult to say. What is clear from the available English records on the issue is that considerable pressure was being exerted on the city's banias and Parsis so much so that Tulsidas Parakh, a *shroff* working for the English company, was compelled to convert to Islam and committed suicide. There were other instances too – 'a Persian [Parsi] scrivan . . . was forcibly circumcized for no other reason but that five years past he had eaten part of a water melon which the Cozzy [Kazi] had eaten of'.[42] Under the circumstances, five leading bania citizens including Bhimji Parakh, the English broker, approached Gerald Aungier, the president of Bombay, on 22 November asking for his protection. Although fully aware of the advantages that bania migration held for the rising settlement of Bombay, Aungier was unwilling to enter into any confrontation with the Mughals. Instead, he advised the banias to proceed to Broach, and approach the governor of Ahmedabad for redress and protection. On 23/24 November 1669, about 8,000 banias, leaving their wives and children in Surat, left for Broach where they were given a favourable reception. A petition was drawn up to be presented at the *durbar*.[43]

Meanwhile, the bania *mahajan* (association of banias) went into action and all commercial operations were suspended. The mint and custom house were closed, and trade came to a standstill. As the English president observed in his despatch to the English company:

> Ever since the flight of the Bannians the trade of Surat hath suffered great obstruction and it is the opinion of many wise men that it will prove of fatal consequence to the utter ruin of it, in case the King doth not take some effectual healing order for the making up this breach for most of the Sheroffs and moneyed men doe think of calling their stocks and according to the custom of this countrey, burying the greatest part under ground, so the bulke of trade which is maintained and carried chiefly on credit must necessarily fall.[44]

Only when the administration relented did the *mahajan* lift its boycott and normalcy was restored. Interestingly, this weapon was not used in resisting the occasional 'monetary demands' of the administration. That the bania merchants encountered such problems is without doubt. For instance in 1672, we hear of the administration calling all eminent merchants, Moors and banias alike, and proposing to them collection of Rs. 45,000 to raise 500 horses and 3,000 foot to defend the city against the anticipated attack of Shivaji. In reality, it was the banias who were expected to make good the contribution; as the English factors observed:

> The Moors readily subscribed to it, knowing that the burthen of the tax would fall on the Banias. They stood off a little to pause on the business but have all subscribed. We hear of no soldiers raising, but there are officers employed in taking an account of every Banias house in towne, of which the Governor will no doubt make good improvement to his particular benefit.[45]

The Hindu merchants had little choice but to accept the situation and the question of entertaining political preferences just did not arise. For one thing, the Mughal political structure as it stood in the seventeenth century was not dependent in any manner either for its revenues or for its monetary transactions on the mercantile groups, as its successor regimes indeed were in the later part of the eighteenth century. Admittedly, imperial arrangements for disbursal of salaries and *jagir* accounts to the military commanders and the militia, which were generally in the form of *barats*, were integrated into the existing credit system of the country.[46] At a later date Manucci spoke at length of the manner in which generals and officers paid off their soldiers, and how the latter were obliged to borrow from the *shroffs* or money changers at excessive interest rates '. . . these men lend to them at the command of the general or officer, and these latter have an understanding with them about the profit from interest, which they share between them. Sometimes soldiers sell their papers to these money changers who for a note of hand of Rs. 100 will give them 20 or 25.'[47] Interestingly, the Bikaner Banking Enquiry Committee of 1930 recorded the fact that the forefathers of most of the 1930 bankers had during the time of the Mughals attached themselves to regiments and transacted the business of arranging salaries for the militia. Definitive evidence of how the Mughal forces on the move were actually paid is lacking and we have no means to ascertain whether state *barats* were, like the *hundis*, negotiable instruments and whether these could be used interchangeably. The *barats*, however, undoubtedly represented an extensive system of official drafts for payment of soldiers' salaries, on which the paymaster *(bakshi)* might rely if necessary without resorting to private commercial paper.

To sum up, the relationship between the Mughal state and the Hindu/Jain merchants was characterized by a certain degree of flexibility and give and take. The state did not in any sense actively foster trade and commerce by protectionist devices, except in so far as guaranteeing the basic infrastructural requirements of tradesmen. In so far as it traded on its own account, it was alive to the dangers of English competition but did not have the naval expertise nor inclination for that matter to withstand the European presence on the seas. As if this was not enough, there was always the unpredictable personal factor – the whim and caprice of an individual governor who had sufficient power to harass the merchants. The latter for the most part had learnt to deal with the vagaries of the situation, and notwithstanding moments of stress and strain, a working relationship between them and the administration had been evolved. The Muslim merchants operated with an added advantage – official patronage – which they utilized to their fullest benefit, particularly when dealing with European trading companies and the elaborate convoy arrangements they were pursuaded to provide.[48]

The existing equations rapidly changed in course of the first half of the eighteenth century when a series of developments dislocated the delicate balance of forces between the state, the merchants and the companies, and set the stage for the latter to play politics. The implications of Mughal decline were serious for the west coast of India where two developments operated in conjunction. Maratha forays into Gujarat which the Mughal forces were unable to contain exerted pressure on the local administration, the situation becoming particularly serious after the occupation of Surat Athavisi in 1723 from where the city drew its principal revenues. From this as their base, the Maratha *sardars* repeatedly held the Surat administration to ransom, forcing it to pay tribute. Hemmed in, the administration turned to 'taxing' its traders – a decision which was ill-timed coming as it did in the wake of a slump in the city's overseas trade. The expansion of English private trade in the western Indian Ocean was the other developments that put additional pressure on the Muslim merchants. The stage was, thus, set for the first concrete expression of an organized merchant resistance to the Mughal administration. Leadership came from the Muslims, with Mulla Abdul Ali, a descendant of Mulla Abdul Ghafur, playing the lead role.

Signs of protest appeared among the Muslim merchants of Surat between 1723 and 1726.[49] The immediate cause for the agitation lay in the government's policy of extortion which no longer spared the Muslim shipowners. The resistance assumed the form of a general cessation of business activity, forcing the government to negotiate. Three out of five confrontations were organized personally by Mulla Muhammed Ali during Mutasaddi Sohrab Khan's tenure (1725-33). Calling the governor's bluff, the merchants staged an impressive walkout. The Chellabis, who were rivals of the mulla, also joined forces. Ahmed Chellabi's participation was the direct result of an abusive slander campaign against him by Gadai Beg Khan, the *waqianavis* of Surat. A public apology was demanded and on 29 June 1726 a *mazhar* was drawn up wherein Ahmed Chellabi was declared an honest and well-behaved man. This was followed up by a petition drawn up and sent on 6 July to the court where, among other things, the two nephews of Qiladar Beglar Khan – Gadai Beg and Teg Beg – were accused of forcibly extracting from the merchants four lakh rupees each. They were also accused of illegally collecting ten to twelve lakh rupees under the guise of fee for permission (*rukhasatnama*) to build new houses.[50]

The bania and Hindu traders of the city did not at this stage entertain any design of a general boycott or even of presenting their own specific charter of demands. Predictably, they supported the agitation of the Muslim merchants while at the same time exploring new solutions and strategies. Those working for the English as brokers were beginning to realize their growing influence in the trade to the Gulfs and their role in local politics, however marginal. There was a Dutch faction too and it remained to be seen how the Europeans would react to the changing political scenario.

It was in 1730-32 that the resistance movement organized by Mulla Muhammed Ali assumed significant proportions. Using his base at Athwa, about five kilometres south of Surat where Mulla Abdul Ghafur had built one of his warehouses, he succeeded in mobilizing several strands of merchant opinion, and raising the banner of revolt against the local authorities. Laldas Vithaldas, the bania broker attached to the English East India Company, prevailed on the English to lend their support to the resistance. Perhaps a section of the bania community was keen to win the assistance of the English in meeting the crisis they faced. The rebellion climaxed in 1732 when the merchants recruited troops, fought pitched battles in the streets of Surat, and won a resounding victory by driving out Sohrab Khan. This was an event without parallel in the history of Indian business. But so limited were their political conceptions that in the moment of victory they could only think of replacing the ousted governor with his rival Teg Bakht Khan, a Mughal nobleman who eventually turned out to be as incompetent and oppressive as his predecessor. The fleeting moment when a merchants' republic might have been set up in Surat was soon past.

The revolt came to naught; the administration asserted itself and the movement, largely due to its inherent contradictions, collapsed. Mulla Muhammed languished in prison and died. It was not clear at this stage whether the Muslim shippers would once again take the offensive. By 1733, one important political change had already occurred in Surat – this was the declaration of independent rule by the Surat governor. Teg Bakht Khan assumed the title of nawab in 1733, with the offices of *qiladar* and *naib* being held by his brothers Beglar Khan and Safdar Khan respectively. The 'new administration' found itself coping with yet another pressure group: the English company authorities had covetous eyes over the imperial fleet which was under the control of the *sidi*, the Mughal admiral. They solicited the assistance of Damaji Gaekwad against the nawab, and in 1735 blockaded the city in an attempt to settle the issue by force. The nawab did not relent on the issue of the fleet, but promised to guarantee security for English trade. The city's merchants were once more allowed to transact business with the English[51] – a concession that must have created a favourable impression on the merchants about the strength of the company. They could not but have been aware that the company was entertaining clear political ambitions like control of the admiralty, and that a timely connection with the English might well immunize them against the exactions by the administration. Needless to say, not all shades of merchant opinions were inclined to this view. There were Muslim shipowning merchants who could not but react adversely to the English. Furthermore, those banias and Parsis who were engaged in business with the Dutch could hardly be expected to favour the English company. There is no doubt, however, that by the late 1730s merchant groups were groping for new solutions, new allies and new political connections.

The process was hastened during the 1740s and 1750s when a series of developments upstaged the English, as it were, and improved their political prospects. The political situation deteriorated rapidly because of rival political claims to the nawabship of Surat. For the Muslim merchants in particular, succession disputes became a matter of central concern. Chellabi took the initiative and in 1748 espoused the claims of Meah Achan as nawab against Safdar Khan (who had been nominated nawab by Teg Bakht Khan in 1747) and Qiladar Wakhar Khan. The English threw in their lot with the Achan clique which won the day.[52] For a short while Chellabi's political influence increased and moulded government policy in several cases. In 1749 for instance, when Meah Achan threatened to seize the effects of the Persian ambassador Mahomet Beg and of the captain of a Persian vessel, then anchored at Surat, as an act of reprisal against Nadir Shah's recent invasion, Chellabi warned him against such a course which might result in Persian retaliation.[53] Meah Achan seems to have been persuaded by these arguments and desisted from the contemplated action.

Chellabi's pro-Achan stand was not, however, representative of the Muslim merchants at large and it would be wrong to conclude that all Muslim shipowning merchants preferred to align themselves with the administration. As a block they undoubtedly preferred the Mughal rule, but this is not to suggest that none ever contemplated alliance with the European trading companies, although admittedly the commercial interests of the Muslim shippers and the European companies were irreconcilable. Among the instances of collaboration was that of Mulla Fakhruddin, great-grandson of Ghafur who, handling Governor William Wake's private trade, was more responsive to the company connection. A marked man in Surat, he sought English protection which on more than one occasion enabled him to secure exemption from the government's demands. The alliance was not, however, without tension and did not stand the test of time. The situation took a new turn in 1751 when Meah Achan was overthrown by Safdar Khan, who became governor with the support of the Dutch East India Company and its partisans.

The Hindu or bania merchant community of Surat did not overtly show the same initiative. To them, any long-term alliance with the administration was no longer attractive. For an increasing number, the issue boiled down to the question of accepting either English or Dutch protection and jurisdiction with all its implications. Migration to the island city of Bombay which was being developed as an alternative entrepot was a variant of the first; indeed the English authorities at Bombay repeatedly expressed their willingness to offer security and safety for the fair trader. Company pronouncements did not take immediate effect and migrations in the 1740s remained only of marginal consequence,[54] merchants preferring on the whole to retain their principal establishments at Surat. It was in the 1750s that a sequence of events strengthened their resolve to back the company's tentative political claims and to rely on their increasing political influence to gain redress for the grievances suffered at the hands of the Mughal officials.

The company authorities, in their attempt to secure greater political leverage, projected the image of a benevolent patron of the 'fair trader' – the latter becoming a convenient cover for the company's self-aggrandizement. This endeared them to the bania merchant population which in time found English protection to be a better immunity against the excesses of incumbent administration. The first concrete illustration of this came in 1752 when the English authorities conducted negotiations with the *durbar* to let off 'merchants under English protection' from the general tax Sidi Masud had proposed to pay off the Marathas. The task was by no means easy. The negotiations were marked by discord but eventually the English demands were conceded. In the final arrangement it was stipulated that an assessment of ten lakh rupees would be levied on all substantial merchants of the city, but that merchants under English protection need not pay.[55]

The administration, thwarted by the Surat factors, was determined to strike back. The blow came sooner than expected when in 1754 Ali Navas Khan, a leading government official, seized and detained Jayaram Navaram, an English-protected merchant employed in the textile contract business of the company. The administration justified its action on the ground that Jayaram had conducted subversive activities against the state and was, therefore, not entitled to English protection. On a later occasion, the administration reiterated its stand and argued that Jayaram was in fact a registered 'Mughal' merchant who had been systematically cheating the government of its revenues by evading payment of customs.[56] The Surat factor paid no heed to these statements and successfully pressed for his release. A year later, when Baboojee became prey to the demands of the government, the English once again found it to their interest to advocate his 'cause' before the adminiistration. These events must have impressed on the merchants the usefulness of the English connection, while at the same time discrediting them with the ruling establishment. The latter never let go any apportunity to harass them and, as the Surat factors reported to their superiors at Bombay on 12 November 1757, the merchants under company protection were generally fearful of government designs against their person and property.[57] For a few months thereafter, there were fewer interruptions to trade but the situation changed by April 1758 when the Surat factors informed Bombay that 'the interruptions and insults they had been exempt from ever since Safdar Khan's death .... had since their return from the Bar begun again.'[58]

The Surat *shroffs*, meanwhile, had decided to take the initiative and approached Ellis, the English chief of Surat, with a proposal to take over control of the castle which they believed would ensure 'security to their own persons or fortunes'. Further, they agreed to hold themselves responsible for 'whatever deficiency shall happen during the term of five years ensuing if the revenues accruing thence to the Honourable Company in that time do not amount to the tune of Rs. 2 lakhs per annum'.[59] The merchants in fact executed a bond that they would pay up to two lakh rupees in taxes to recompense the shortfall in revenues. This in effect guaranteed the expenses of the English campaign.

This bond constituted the financial basis of the so called Castle Revolution of 1759. The English, emboldened by the proposal of the banias, conducted the campaign in which they captured the castle and the admiralty. The Chellabis, who kept aloof from the other merchants, watched sullenly as the English consolidated their hold over a part of the government in the city. The English chiefs at Surat used their new-found political power to declare a monopoly over shipping to the Gulfs, delivering thereby a body-blow to the Muslim shipowning merchants of Surat. The banias, on the other hand, had the satisfaction of having the custom rates payable by them brought virtually at par with those applicable to the Muslims and the Armenians. Diarchy had begun at Surat. The Muslim administration and Muslim merchants were hemmed in more and more until they were entirely squeezed out by the turn of the century.

III

At the opposite end of the Mughal empire from Surat, in 'Subah Jinnat-ul-Bilad Bangala' (a name long in use after the death of Emperor Aurangzeb who gave that name, implying 'Paradise of Nations'), the breakdown of centralized Mughal control did not disrupt trade and finance, as it did in the Bandar Mubarak of the Great Mughals. Not only did the bankers and merchants of the Bengal *subah* make unprecedented fortunes under the autonomous nawabs from Murshid Quli Khan to Sirajuddaulah,[60] they also acquired an influence at the new nawabi court at Murshidabad, altogether unknown under the Great Mughals. While the Mughal power had been at its centralized height, the viceroys and their officers had been in the habit of engrossing the most lucrative branches of the trade,[61] and no need had been felt to accord private bankers and merchants places of honour at the then provincial court at Dacca. During the viceroyalty of Azim-ush-shan around 1700, Emperor Aurangzeb severely condemned the practice of *sauda-i-khas* (monopoly trade by officers) at the cost of *sauda-i-am* (free trade by private merchants).[62] As the practice of monopoly by the Mughal officers diminished during the next viceroyalty of Murshid Quli Khan, trade became free, freer at any rate than it had been under the Great Mughals or was ever to be under the East India Company. For the younger generation at Murshidabad who lived to see the ruthless monopolies imposed by the English, the pre-Plassey years stood out as a memory of a happier time when the Mughal, Armenian, Gujarati, Hindustani and Kashmiri merchants had been rich and influential.[63]

The political ascendancy of the bankers and merchants in the Murshidabad court was a consequence of the transition from the imperial Mughal system, in which the ranking commanders of Mughal horse posted from Delhi monopolized power, to the autonomous nawabi system in which the Mughal *umara*, now no longer centrally appointed, had to accommodate the zamindars, bankers and merchants in the financial arrangements made by Murshid Quli Khan and maintained by his successors. In explaining the working of these arrangements to the English after they became the ruling power, a Murshidabad nobleman made the revealing observation: 'The Departments of Trade and Revenue are chiefly connected'.[64] He had in mind the intimate connection of the mint, the treasury and the revenue realizing machinery with the private system of commercial credit and money transfers, on which the nawabs of Bengal had successfully based the local Mughal state power, but of which the centralized Mughal regime in the days of its imperial grandeur had been quite independent.

The shift in the position of the classes accommodated in the *durbar* was seen in the drastic reduction made by Murshid Quli Khan both in the number of horses under the ranking commanders and the amount of revenues assigned to them as *jagir* – the two essential features that had underpinned the dominance of the *mansabdars*. The petty estates of the *subah* were agglomerated in fifteen large *ihtamams* (charges) from which the *diwani* department withdrew its direct presence. These were made over to as many rajas and zamindars who were held responsible for the revenues from their respective *ihtamams* which they had to deposit directly at headquarters. For this purpose, an annual ceremony called the *punyaha* was instituted where they paid court to the nawab and received dresses of honour. They would then assemble at the house of the Jagat Seth to negotiate a fresh supply of funds for the coming year.[65] From the time Jagat Seth Fateh Chand was appointed 'Treasurer General of Bengal' on Murshid Quli Khan's recommendation to the emperor,[66] his house held the keys to the treasury by virtue of this office, received the revenues, encashed the drafts drawn upon their house by the government and charged 10 per cent commission from the zamindars for standing security to their commitment made at *punyaha*. No less than two-thirds of the revenues of Bengal were realized by means of the seths giving *paats* or receipts to the government for the amount deposited by the zamindars; the seths in return realized *patwan* from the zamindars amounting to ten lakhs.[67] This was a system that ensured punctual payment of revenue at a low cost and made Bengal the source of the largest revenue surplus in the eighteenth-century India. Murshid Quli Khan also allowed the Jagat Seths' office of treasurer-general a permanent farm of the Murshidabad mint, enabling them to recoin annually fifty lakhs at a profit of three and a half lakhs, which added to their power to control the flow of credit as well as the rates of exchange in Bengal.[68]

Developments following Murshid Quli Khan's death reinforced the Jagat Seth's position as a key figure in the political affairs of Bengal. Shujauddin Khan, Murshid Quli's son-in-law, secured the viceroyalty by raising one and a half crores as *nazar* (present) for his patrons in Delhi and by remitting the entire sum through the banking agency of the Jagat Seth. Fateh Chand, the head of the house, along with Haji Ahmed (elder brother of Alivardi Khan) and Alamchand (the Rai Rain), formed a council which managed all affairs of state while Shujauddin Khan indulged himself in wine and women. The triumvirate, when on the point of being dismissed by the next nawab (Sarfaraz Khan), entered into a conspiracy with Alivardi Khan, the deputy governor of Bihar, who seized the *masnad* at Murshidabad by a violent coup in 1740 with the help of Jagat Seth Fateh Chand. During the time of troubles that followed – with the Marathas laying Bengal waste right up to the west bank of the Ganga and swooping down upon Murshidabad itself – Fateh Chand was one of the closest financial and political advisers of Nawab Alivardi Khan Muzaffar Jang.[69] Controlling of the credit system by which the war against the Marathas was being financed, he could adopt a high tone in his dealings with the nawab: 'How can I be in safety when there is no kind of government in the city?' His presence at Murshidabad amidst Maratha raids was 'as necessary to the Government as to the merchants',[70] and the nawab had to plead with him to return to the capital when he withdrew to Dacca. Together with Chain Rai, the *diwan*, he was in charge of mobilizing the large sums of money that the army required from the merchants and the European companies, an onerous duty that he performed with skill and diplomacy amidst great difficulties.[71] His heirs, Jagat Seth Mahtab Rai and Maharaj Swarupchand, continued to support the nawab through exceptional difficulties, contributing 'mighty sums' for the suppression of an Afghan uprising in Patna at the time of the Maratha invasion in 1749.[72]

Alivardi Khan, who took notice of the English and the French fortifying themselves during the Maratha raids and setting up rival puppets in the Carnatic, was sufficiently disquieted by these developments to give strong support to the merchants of the Mughal empire in their disputes with the European companies. The merchants, despite competition and mutual rivalries, were tied together by the long established mercantile customs of the country. It was this invisible bond that induced Khoja Wajid, the informal leader of the merchant community, to come to his rival Amirchand's defence when the English dragged the latter's brother Deepchand to the mayor's court of Calcutta in 1744, ignoring Amirchand's protest that the dispute (one involving saltpetre accounts) be settled by the arbitration of 'indifferent persons of the Indostan people' in accordance with the custom of the country. When a security bond of seventy-eight thousand rupees was slapped down for Deepchand's release, Khoja Wajid administered the following rebuke to the English: 'You have overset the custom of the merchants'.[73] The aggrieved brothers, Amirchand and Deepchand, appealed subsequently to the nawab who intervened in their favour in 1745, and appointed Deepchand as the *faujdar* of the rich saltpetre district of Sarkar Saran.[74] The same intangible bond among the merchants and the Murshidabad *durbar* won for them the support of the latter against the English in 1749 – even though they had shown extreme reluctance to make financial contributions for the common defence against the Marathas – when a complaint by 'the Syeds, Moguls, Armenians, & c., merchants of Hooghly',[75] moved the nawab to put a stop to the trade of the English at Kasimbazar and Dacca, charging that the English had seized some Armenian ships returning from Mokha. The English were compelled on this occasion to pay twelve lakhs to the nawab through the house of the Jagat Seth.[76]

With the European companies emerging as powers to reckon with in the Bengal *subah*, the influence of the *sahukars* (bankers) and *saudagars* (merchants) as the natural intermediaries and ambassadors between the court and the companies increased correspondingly. Even independently of this, the process by which the official monopolies in opium, saltpetre, salt, etc. had been increasingly farmed out in the eighteenth century had identified the merchants as influential figures at the court. At one time traded in by the imperial officers themselves, these commodities were now farmed out to the highest bidders. It was a system that gradually resulted in the trade of these commodities being concentrated in the hands of great auction monopolists well entrenched in the court, especially Khoja Wajid of Hughli and Amirchand of Calcutta – the two great commercial rivals of mid-eighteenth-century Bengal. These two merchant princes were apparently able to hold more than their own both against the members of the Mughal nobility still participating in these trades, and also against the European companies.

Thus we see Amirchand in the English records cornering saltpetre and opium on several occasions to the great inconvenience of the Dutch and English companies, and even outwitting the nawab's daughter Amina Begum;[77] he presented 'a large Persia cat' to Muzaffar Jang which enabled him to send down his boatload to Hughli before that of the Begum herself.[78] His portfolio of opium, saltpetre, banking,[79] copper and grain was so diverse that he suffered no reverse when the jealous English factors of Calcutta turned him out of his other occupation as *dadni* merchant and supplier of cloth to the company.[80] The only man capable of worsting him was Khoja Wajid– 'the principal merchant of the province',[81] an owner of five ships trading to Surat, the Persian Gulf and the Red Sea, and a monopolist of the salt contract of Bengal who also succeeded in snatching the saltpetre monopoly of Bihar from the Amirchand-Deepchand brothers in 1749-53.[82] The Dutch, who attached themselves to him believed that the secret of his influence with the court lay in the rich presents he gave to the nawab, willingly rather than under coercion; according to a popular rumour, on one occasion alone this great Armenian merchant, who held the honoured title of Fakhr-ut-Tujjar (Prince of the merchants) in the *durbar* of Muzaffr Jang, gave to the nawab fifteen lakhs as his new-year gift.[83] This figure seems, however, highly exaggerated, for according to a well-informed source Amirchand did not spend more than fifteen or at most twenty thousand a year on presents to the ruler and the same source – an English doctor who treated the nawab on his death-bed – also testified: 'Presents to the Nabob of trifles was the principal method he [Amirchand] used, and a little money distributed among the officers'. Yet the influence that Amirchand exercised in the court by this method was by no means trifling: witness, as did Dr. Forth, the 'respect paid his gomastah, Baulkissen, by the principal men at the Durbar, always made much of whilst our *vakeels* were never looked on or had liberty to go to the Durbar but when sent for . . . '.[84]

A well-established ritual at the court cemented the close personal relationships between the ruler and his great mercantile subjects: the latter would make presents (*nazars*) to the nawab, and would in turn be invested with titles and robes of honour (*khilats*). These were not empty gestures for Roger Drake, the English chief at Calcutta towards the end of Alivardi Khan's life, greeted with consternation the rumour that his antagonist Omichand (Amirchand) had been given honours and privileges comparable to those of Jagat Seth.[85] Nor was the significance of the title Fakhur-ut-Tajjar conferred on Khoja Wajid around 1755 lost on the Dutch factors at Kasimbazar who recommended that friendship with the great Armenian merchant and shipowner would be useful to the Dutch company as he was truly the maintainer of the riches of the court of Alivardi Khan.[86]

The very nature of the bankers' and merchants' business made if necessary for them to get closely involved with the politics of the *durbar*; they could not stay on in that sort of business – farming the mints, guaranteeing the revenues and engrossing the reserved commodities – if they were to lose their influence at the court. Towards the end of Muzaffr Jang's viceroyalty, Jagat Seth Mahtab Rai and Maharaja Swarupchand, the heirs of Fateh Chand, Khoja Muhammad Wajid, the Armenian merchant prince of Hughli, and Amirchand, the Calcutta merchant and banker, were among the most influential figures at the court. Together with a lesser Armenian merchant of Calcutta named Khoja Petross Arratoon , they were almost automatically marked out as intermediaries between the court and the companies when upon the death of Alivardi Khan in 1756 a dispute broke out between Sirajuddaulah and the English. In their bid to maintain their position and influence at the court, they mediated secretly between the Muzaffarjangi *umara* and the English next year and thus assisted in the conspiracy by which the senior Muzaffarjangi *amir*, Mir Muhammad Jafar Khan, replaced Sirajuddaulah in the *nizamat*, or viceroyalty, of Subah Jinnat-ul-Bilad Bangala, Bihar and Orissa. It was no part of their interest as a class to abolish the existing system they had done so well out of,[87] nor did they see at the outset that the English, with whom their interests clashed at many points,[88] would emerge as the real masters of the land.[89] Their entanglement in the conspiracy grew individually out of their close involvement in the politics of the *durbar*. Throughtout the conspiracy they acted in rivalry with one another, prompted by individual and divergent motivations, and by no means as a group united by any common desire to promote the rising English power.

The hot-headed young Sirajuddaulah, who offered at one time to circumcise the Jagat Seth brothers,[90] and his upstart minister Mohan Lal, who was 'a sworn enemy of the Seths',[91] created powerful enemies among the Muzaffarjangi *umara* by their insolent behaviour towards the bankers, officers and noblemen of Alivardi Khan. But initially at any rate Khoja Muhammad Wajid ('my friend, Choja Mhameth Wajed',[92] as the nawab referred to him) and Amirchand ('not a friend in Calcutta but Omichand'[93]) were in high favour with Sirajuddaulah, who used Khoja Wajid as his trusted agent to reduce the English at Calcutta to the level of the Armenians and other merchants of the Mughal empire in matters of trade. This meant that the English had to demolish their new fortifications, pay duties at the Armenian rate, provide no shelter to fleeing Mughal subjects, wind up their mayor's court and accept the jurisdiction of the Mughal *faujdar*.[94] And when the English defied and the nawab marched on Calcutta, Wajid's agent Siva Babu took advantage of the situation to settle an old score with a rival by informing Drake that Amirchand was behind the attack.[95] Amirchand, who was released form the English prison by the nawab's force after Calcutta was occupied, decided to bear no grudge against the English, and responded favourably to Khoja Petross Arratoon's (he had been despoiled in the sack of Calcutta) intervention on behalf of the English at Falta to ensure that they were not starved of supplies in the island and were not altogether driven out of Bengal.[96] When, however, the English approached Khoja Wajid for being allowed once more to trade from Calcutta, he told them that there was no question of returning Fort William to them, and that they must not expect re-settlement on better terms unless they were prepared to come back from Madras in force.[97]

The Seths and the old Muzaffarjangi *umara*, who at this stage had no notion of the English as possible allies in their conspiracy against Siraj, looked hopefully to Shaukat Jang of Purnea – 'a Subahdar to the taste of the house of Jagat Seth and the chief Moors and Rajas'.[98] He had obtained a patent from Delhi appointing him the legitimate governor of the province on promise of resuming the tribute stopped since the Maratha raids. The nawab reproaching Jagat Seth for not getting the *farman* for himself, ordered him to raise three crores from the merchants for the campaign against Purnea and put him behind bars when he pleaded his inability. Mir Jafar and other officers who had set out for Purnea with a scheme to remain inactive in battle, returned immediately to the capital, insisting that Jagat Seth be set at liberty.[99] Due to Shaukat Jang's faults of character, the plot in which Jagat Seth was involved[100] miscarried, and the nawab's cousin and rival was killed in battle. A solution to their practical problems within the framework of Mughal legitimacy having escaped them, the Seths and the discontented *mansabdars* were eventually forced to try other means.

Even so the Seths did not immediately welcome the English when the latter, having refused to carry on business on terms applicable to the Armenians, took Khoja Wajid at his word and brought forces from Madras to reoccupy Calcutta. Resort to arms by the English climaxing with the burning and plunder of the 'Moor town' of Hughli filled Jagat Seth and Khoja Wajid with outrage.[101] As there were growing prospects of war with the French, the English were anxious to reach an accommodation with the court through the mediation of Jagat Seth and Khoja Wajid, but were insistent that the French be kept out of the settlement. Khoja Wajid, the principal patron of the French at the *durbar*, refused to mediate, except through the council of Chandernagore,[102] but the Seths were eventually won over and they deputed their ablest agent Ranjit Rai to accompany the nawab on his second march upon Calcutta. This man, assisted by Amirchand and Khoja Petross, who also acted on behalf of the court, succeeded in working out the peace of Alinagar between the nawab and the English.[103] But when Clive pressed Ranjit Rai to secure permission from the durbar to attack the French, he refused as his master had invested heavily in the French company.[104]

According to Amirchand, who now accompanied Watts to the *durbar*, the Jagat Seth had thirteen lakhs outstanding to the French, and was therefore reluctant to engage himself in the interest of the English. Khoja Wajid, whose dealings were principally with the French and the Dutch, was reported to be even actively engaged in helping the French. Amirchand told Watts that taking advantage of his (Amirchand's) absence from the court, the Khoja had persuaded the nawab to send a lakh to the French and orders to the *faujdar* of Hughli to defend Chandernagore against any English attack.[105]

Amirchand, having no stake in the French company, could wholeheartedly work for the English in this respect. He helped Watts bribe Nanda Kumar, the acting *faujdar* of Hughli, not to carry out the nawab's orders. The Seths, although no friends of the English as aginst the French, were also keen to prevent a conjunction between the nawab and the French. What they would have liked, as the French chief at Kasimbazar surmised, was a conjunction between the English and the French to overthrow a nawab who had levied exactions from both. If there had to be a fight between the English and the French, the Seths insisted on keeping the court out of it. Khoja Wajid, who, as the French chief at Kasimbazar put it, was 'one of the most timid of men' and was desirous of being 'on good terms with everybody', possibly 'did not love the Seths but he feared them, which was sufficient to make him useless to us'.[106] Chandernagore was eventually taken by the English and at their insistence the nawab ordered Jean Law, the French chief at Kasimbazar, to leave for Patna. The way was now clear for the Seths to act more decisively. As Law wrote in retrospect: 'They are, I can confirm the *originators* of the revolution; without them the English would never have carried out what they have'.[107] Two principal courtiers on whom Law had counted for support, Rai Durlabh and Khoja Wajid, fell in with their plans after his departure.[108]

The conspiracy now developed in two distinct conclaves, Watts being the common factor in both. The earlier of these was formed by the energetic Amirchand who was constantly to be found at the mansion of the Jagat Seth in the evenings, conferring with them, their agent Ranjit Rai[109] and also possibly some discontented Hindu rajas and zamindars who were in the habit of assembling at the Seth's residence to discuss the business of the country.[110] Amirchand's pet proposal was to promote to the *masnad* a middle-ranking *mansabdar* named Khuda Yar Khan Latif, who approached Watts through him on 23 April with the promise to join the English on condition of their making him nawab.[111] As the man drew a private stipend from the Seths to defend their house, Amirchand imagined that he would be 'supported by Jaggutseat'.[112] But distrustful of Amirchand, the Seths were in touch with a conclave developing separately from that of Watts-Amirchand-Khuda Yar Khan. The night after Khuda Yar Khan established contact with Watts through Amirchand, Mir Jafar, the paymaster of the army (*bakshi*) and a commander of far higher rank, made a secret overture to Watts through Khoja Petross, who was also in Watts' entourage in Murshidabad. The Jafar-Khoja Petross plan had the backing of the entire Muzaffarjangi *umara* and it was this scheme that Watts recommended to Clive.[113]

Mir Jafar was not known to Amirchand except through Watts[114] and the very fact that he chose Khoja Petross as his agent showed his distrust of him – a distrust possibly communicated to him by the Seths with whom he had long been on friendly terms. Chagrined at being deprived of the exclusive management of the conspiracy from which he had expected financial and political advantages, Amirchand now entered into a complicated game of at once hobnobbing with the conspirators and winning the confidence of the nawab by discrediting his fellow conspirators. At the time of his second march upon Calcutta, the nawab had promised 20,000 gold *mohurs* to Ranjit Rai and Amirchand for the purpose of bribing the English chiefs of Calcutta into peace. Ranjit Rai and Amirchand, the peacemakers of Alinagar, had plotted then to divide the sum between themselves. As the Seths' man of affairs was now pressing the nawab to pay the gold *mohurs,* Amirchand instigated him to turn the man out of court. The nawab was so pleased with saving the money that he ordered the treasury to pay Amirchand his losses suffered in the sack of Calcutta. The Seths would have been embroiled too, had they not disowned their agent and disclaimed all knowledge of the gold *mohur*.[115] They were furious with Amirchand, and it was probably at their instance that Mir Jafar insisted through Khoja Petross that Amirchand be kept out of the conspiracy as he was 'an intriguing gentoo without fortitude and honesty'.[116] Khoja Wajid, who had in the meanwhile secretly defected from the nawab to the English out of fear of isolation in the court, also supplied Watts with damaging evidence against his old rival,[117] as also the more vital fact that the nawab had ordered Law to remain in readiness to come back to Murshidabad.[118]

With no inkling of this conspiracy, Clive had no plan for engineering a revolution in Murshidabad and was thinking of going back with his troops for operations against the French in the Carnatic.[119] The first hint he got of it was when Siva Babu, Khoja Wajid's *diwan*, approached him in Chandernagore through a broker named Lakhai Kundu,[120] from whom, it seems, he first learnt of Mir Jafar's discontent. This set him thinking in a new direction and he wrote to Madras: 'There is a conspiracy carrying on against him [the nawab] by several of the great men, at the head of whom is Juggut Seth himself, as also Khoja Wajid'.[121] Subsequently, he sanctioned Watts's proposal to set Mir Jafar up as nawab on a heavy payment of two and a half crores. The English were to get a zamindari near Calcutta, a mint in the town and confirmation of duty-free trade. As none of these privileges went beyond those already conferred by Farrukshiyar's *farman* of 1717 and the Alinagar treaty of 1757, and since no demand was made for any change in the structure of the *nizamat* to accommodate the English, Mir Jafar happily agreed to these proposals through his agent Khoja Petross.[122]

All seemed set when Amirchand suddenly turned round, appearing to his English patrons as the proverbial snake in the grass. Sensing his exclusion from the secret negotiations, he demanded five per cent of the nawab's treasure for himself, and an undertaking from Mir Jafar that he would not tax the zamindars more than what Murshid Quli Khan had levied from them.[123] The latter was symptomatic of the close financial relations that had evolved under the nawabi system between the bankers and the zamindars. A further demonstration of this close financial connection came soon when the nawab issued an order on the Raja of Burdwan to pay back his debts to the banker. This was a favour granted by the nawab in return for concocted 'top secret' information from Amirchand that Monsieur Bussy was coming from the Deccan to join the English. The wily merchant, riding two horses at the same time, had informed Watts beforehand what he intended to tell the nawab. Watts and Khoja Petross had tried strenuously to dissuade him, but in vain; Amirchand was determined to extract what he could from the nawab in view of the uncertainty of what he might obtain from the coup.[124] Clive at this stage entered into a formal agreement with Mir Jafar. Amirchand, however, was not, shown the genuine document, written on white paper, but a false counterpart on red sheets, containing the five per cent he had insisted upon. Amirchand's suspicions were not allayed and he told Rai Durlabh, as Watts found out form the much maligned Ranjit Rai who did not miss a chance to inform upon his enemy, 'that if we were once permitted to march this way, we should not quit Muxadabad for three years'.[125]

Warned by Amirchand, Rai Durlabh raised objections to the hard financial terms Mir Jafar had so thoughtlessly conceded to the English. Watts was in despair and convinced that all was lost[126] when the Seths intervened. At their instance, Ranjit Rai became active again[127] and Rai Durlabh was brought around with a promise of five per cent of the take.[128] In a covered palanquin meant for the ladies of the zenana, which Khoja Petross had procured, Watts went and saw Mir Jafar and had him swear on the Quran that he would abide faithfully by the treaty.[129] Next day Ranjit Rai informed the Englishman that his master had secured the support of Khuda Yar Khan Latif who would 'act in conjunction' with Mir Jafar.[130] Thus the conspiring groups at the court were merged into a solid bloc against the nawab at the instance of the Seths, and in the battle of Plassey Sirajuddaulah was abandoned by Mir

Jafar, Rai Durlabh and Khuda Yar Khan to his fate.

The bankers and merchants undoubtedly played a critical role in the mid-century revolution in Bengal but it is equally certain that they did not play the dominant role in it. The limits to their political influence were defined by the things the European companies were prepared to do, and the merchants were not. They could not think of running their own town, maintaining their own court of law and mounting their own guns on their own fort, but the English had already done so in Calcutta and the French and the Dutch wanted to do likewise in Chandernagore and Chinsura. Nawab Sirajuddaulah wanted to eliminate the distinction between the north European companies and other merchants under Mughal protection. The English were not prepared 'to submit to inhabit in these dominions as Armenians',[131] and were prepared to fight for the right to conduct duty-free trade from a fortified settlement. That was why Khoja Wajid could suggest quite naturally to the English at Falta that 'the only method to reestablish Calcutta upon creditable terms would be to proceed to Madras and there concert measures with the Governor and Council, and to return with strength sufficient to enforce any petitions we had to make'.[132] He must have been convinced enough that the merchants under the Mughal protection would never think of following the advice he had given to the English and try to create their own political order. Past masters though they were in court manoeuvres, the *sahukars* and *saudagars* were nonetheless incapable of wielding state power themselves. They would therefore not aspire to be anything more than influential pawns in the revolution that was being wrought in Bengal, and were destined to be pulled down once the principals had consolidated their power.

Not only did the bankers and merchants involved in the coup not derive any benefit from it, each of them suffered a cruel fate within the six years that followed Plassey. Amirchand and Khoja Petross, the two agents whose rivalries Watts had exploited so effectively, earned no returns on the considerable investments they had made in the revolution. As the real treaty between Mir Jafar and the English came to be read out at the house of Jagat Seth after the battle, Amirchand, who had invited himself, cried out: 'This cannot be the treaty, it was a red treaty that I saw'. To stage as melodramatic a scene as possible Clive replied: 'Yes Omichand, but this is a white treaty'.[133] Amirchand died next year, leaving a large estate, but with the loans to the Raja of Burdwan still unrealized and destined to be pared down by Clive in a settlement he imposed in favour of the raja in 1765. Khoja Petross, who was treated a little more gently, complained one year after his associate's death: '. . . though I have gone through such great travil, pain, anxiety and dangers . . . . Your Honours have not taken the least notice or mention of me . . . . Even the expenses we disbursed have not been repaid us.'[134] Ironically it was Watts, along with whom he had risked his life at Murshidabad in 1757, who recommended during the war with Mir Qasim that he be turned out of Calcutta as 'Petruse is well known to be an intriguing person'.[135]

Clive's behaviour towards his temporary ally, Khoja Wajid, was even more ruthless. He identified him as a 'villain' soon after the coup on the suspicion that he was a secret supporter of the French. Hardly had four months elapsed after Plassey when the English captured one of his trading vessels on the pretext that it was flying under French colours, but the real reason was that a shipowner and merchant magnate of his standing and independence could not be tolerated in the new commercial system the English were imposing on Bengal. Clive resolved to destroy him and the opportunity came in 1759 when the Khoja plotted unsuccessfully with the Dutch to have the English thrown out. He was captured and put in jail where he 'poisoned' himself.[136] The Seths, who remained important for a few more years on account of their crucial position within the revenue system, met their fate at the hands of the next nawab, Mir Qasim, who executed Jagat Seth Mahtab Rai and Maharaja Swarupchand during the war with the English on account of their close association with the latter. That association did not, however, ensure any consideration for the house afterwards, for Johnstone, Middleton and Leister extorted a lakh and a quarter from Jagat Seth Khushal Chand, when Mir Jafar's son ascended the throne. Clive, after securing the *diwani* in 1765, rebuked him for 'that tendency you seem to have to avarice' exhibited in his clinging to the keys to the treasury.[137] With their control broken over both the mint and the treasury, the Jagat Seths were reduced to poverty, replaced in due course by the Banaras house of Gopaldas Manohardas as the leading bankers in eastern India.

Behind the precipitate fall of the bankers and merchants lay the collapse of the political system and the withdrawal of the court patronage on the basis of which they had built their prosperity since the days of Murshid Quli Khan.[138] On the eve of the battle of Plassey, Khoja Wajid held the monopolies of salt of Bengal and saltpetre of Bihar; Amirchand was the leading trader in opium and had even cornered it for some time; the Seths had apparently established mastery over the Murshidabad mint and treasury. These flexible monopolies which had been recycled into the indigenous economy of the *subah* to assist in capital formation and strengthening of the credit system, were taken over one by one. Immediately after Plassey, the company servants broke into the salt trade in a large way, despatching large quantities from lower Bengal to Patna which forced the *faujdar* of Hughli to remind Clive, though in vain, that the English had previously never traded in salt.[139] One year later, Khoja Wajid was pushed out of saltpetre which became a monopoly of the English through a grant of Mir Jafar. All that the Khoja could do was to complain bitterly that the English had destroyed his business and had driven him to the brink of ruin.[140] Plassey also gave control of the production and trade of opium in Patna to the company servants stationed there: the *naib nazim* of Bihar had to issue an order in 1761 that nobody should purchase opium until the chief of the Patna factory had completed his investment which engrossed virtually the whole of the crop.[141]

There was now no place in Bengal for merchants of the standing of Amirchand and Khoja Wajid. The Society of Trade that Clive set up in 1765 formalized the English monopolies over trade in salt, betelnut and tobacco, leaving to the Indian merchants only the retail trade of the Society's goods.[142] Jagat Seth's control over the monetary and revenue system was also broken with the passing of the *diwani* to the English. This drastically contracted the place of the Seths in the Bengal economy, and when the treasury was shifted to Calcutta in 1772, the last links of the family to the revenue system were snapped off and they ceased to be bankers to the government. The top levels of the most lucrative branches of trade since the days of Murshid Quli Khan – state banking, revenue insurance, minting, saltpetre, salt and opium – were now barred to Indians

The fall of the great banking and commercial magnates produced a general crisis by destroying the extensive trading connections, credit links and political ramifications that had bonded the old society together. What these links meant for the economy, was explained in a remarkable exposition by the last *naib nazim* of Bengal Muhammed Reza Khan on the eve of the famine of 1770.[143] Deploring the coercive system of monopoly the English had imposed on the trade of the *subah*, he pointed out its adverse impact on the revenues of the land. The close connection he had observed between the freedom of trade and the large volume of revenue during the viceroyalty of Alivardi Khan boiled down, in his view, to the question of money supply and the smooth functioning of the traditional banking system. The considerable supplies of silver that Indian merchants, both Hindu and Muslim, had at one time brought from Hindustan, Gujarat and the Deccan to purchase Bengal's cloths and silks, had been reduced to a trickle – from seventy lakhs to seven lakhs according to his estimates – because of the growth of the coercive private trade of the English company servants and their *gumashtahs* (agents). 'Men of credit and large capital' were forcibly retired and the consequence was a 'sudden failure of the usual supplies of specie' by which the merchants had carried on their trade and the peasants had paid their taxes. The result was that business had come 'almost to a total stand' and the rrevenues were 'extorted rather than collected.' Declaring that 'the true spirit of trade' was 'the mutual satisfaction of buyer and seller', Khan pleaded that if 'the illegal and oppressive grade' of the *gumashtahs* was stopped and the freedom of trade restored as in the time of Alivardi Khan, the merchants would be able to renew commerce and import specie as formerly, and the revenues would then be 'collected with ease and without recourse to rigourous methods'.

Another important link in the system now snapped, which according Reza Khan had aggravated the scarcity of money, was the close association of the bankers with the treasury. This had previously provided the backing of revenues for the commercial system of paper credit by means of which the *sahukars and shroffs* financed the trade of the country. The English, upon acquisition of the *diwani*, stopped the ancient practice under which the *amils* and zamindars negotiated the gross revenues with the merchants and bankers who paid the amount in sikka rupees into the treasury on behalf of the former for a discount. 'This', Reza Khan pointed out, 'established the credit of the bankers and their business flourshed'. They had formerly imported large quantitits of specie from Agra, Delhi and Banaras. The mode of remitting the gross revenues into the treasury adopted by the English damaged the system of credit and 'the business of the bankers and merchants suffers thereby a total stagnation'. If they were permitted once again to handle the conversion of the gross revenues (paid in various coins) into the legal tender of the realm, then the 'business of the bankers and merchant would be restored to credit, the scarcity of specie less severly felt and the revenues collected with ease'. Reza Khan saw no reason why this should not be done as the government derived no considerable advantage from the new mode of revenue collection.

But he pleaded in vain. The English were determined to build a financial and monetary system independent of any native influence. It took them time, of course, to build the system that made the Government of India so powerful a regime in the reign of Queen Victoria. In the meantime they still needed the support and services of the bankers – no longer in running the financial system of Bengal, but in extending their conquests to other parts of India. That was the logic behind the distress of Jagat Seth Khushal Chand of Murshidabad, and the prosperity of his younger contemporaries, Gopaldas Sahu and his son, of Banaras.

IV

A careful survey of the political system of Awadh under the independent nawabs and of Banaras, initially part of the *subah* of Awadh but eventually becoming independent under Mansa Ram and Balwant Singh (1739-70), reveals the extent of mercantile penetration into the working of the administration and of the agricultural economy of Hindustan at large. Indeed, even as the state of Awadh was in the process of emerging as an autonomous political unit, the commercial and moneyed elements occupied a special position, playing the role of financial and diplomatic guarantees to the different gradations of local chiefs and zamindars. Sleeman in his journey through Awadh[144] noted a popular legend about the Kulhuns family of Rajputs which is worth recalling here:

> Achul Sing .... about a century and a quarter ago [i.e. around 1729] reigned over the district intervening between Gonda and Wazeergunge, and resided at the capital of Koorassa. The Raja had a dispute with one of his landholders, whom he could not get into his power. He requested Rutun Pandee, the banker, to mediate a reconciliation, and invite the landholder to an amicable adjustment of accounts, on a pledge of personal security. The banker consented, but made the Rajah swear by the river Sarjoo which flowed near the town, that he should be received with courtesy and escorted back safely. The landholder relied on the banker's pledge and came, but the Rajah no sooner got him into his power, than caused him to be put to death. The banker could not consent to live under the dishonour of a violated pledge, and abstaining from food died in twenty-one days invoking the vengeance of the river Sarjoo on the head of the perfidious prince. In his last hour, the banker was visited by one of the Rajah's wives who was then pregnant and implored him to desist from his purpose in mercy to the child in her womb; but she was told by the dying man that he could not consent to survive the dishonour brought upon him by her perjured husband; and that she had better quit the place and save herself and child, since the incensed river Sarjoo would

not spare anyone who remained with the Rajah. She did so. The banker died, and his death was followed by a sudden rise of the river and tempest.[145]

Whatever its credibility, the legend emphasizes in unequivocal terms the centrality of the banker's position in the loose and fluid political and financial arrangements that charcterized the political situation in Awadh in the first decades of the eighteenth century. The consolidation of power and independence by Saadat Khan (1720-39) and Safdar Jang (1739-54) gave no setback to the influence of the bankers.[146] Although we do not have direct evidence for the earlier period (as we do in the case of Bararas) of the bankers' participation in administration and revenue collection, it would not be far-fetched to surmise that the extent of mercantile penetration in the system was substantial, and that the involvement of the Banaras bankers and that of the house of Lala Kashmiri Mal in the 1780s[147] had its beginnings even earlier. In Banaras on the other hand, the bankers right from the start were a conspicious group, involved in politics by virtue of the fact that all revenue of the region passed through their hands on its way to the raja's (i.e. the central) treasury.[148] Revenue farmers or *mustajirs* and *amils* or collectors were systematically backed by individual bankers or firms who made it a practice to issue *dakhillas* or credit notes on future revenues to the state. Banaras was thus truly, as Lauriston commented in 1758, '*la ville des Saokers ou Banquiers*'.[149]

The growing influence of the mercantile community was closely linked to the emergence and consolidation of the Banaras Raj in the late 1750s and 1760s. The bankers represented a new generation; their older counterparts had suffered bankruptcy and insolvency in the troubled 1740s and early 1750s when Rohilla incursions had resulted in considerable contraction of the *hundi* business.[150] Two among the new bankers – Gowaldas and Gopaldas – demonstrated great enterprise and emerged as small-time 'king makers', the former backing Mir Rustam Ali Khan, the chief *mustajir* of Jaunpur, Banaras, Chunar and Ghazipur, and the latter supporting Mansa Ram, a revenue official in Rustam Ali's employ, who eventually founded the independent principality of Banaras.[151] In 1739, Balwant Singh, Mansa Ram's successor, secured the title of raja from the emperor after which he seems to have stopped paying regular tribute to Awadh. Financial backing for the new raj was provided by the rising banking house of Gopaldas Manohardas, soon to emerge as the most powerful banking group commanding virtually the entire corpus of remittance transactions that crisscrossed the subcontinent – principally involving Awadh, Banaras and Bengal. Acting as the principal bankers of the raja, the nawab of Awadh, the Marathas[152] and eventually the English East India Company, they were immediately recognizable as a critical component in the complex welter of tribute transfers that the English authorities initiated, and it was not a matter of surprise that their assistance was continually solicited by the company in times both of peace and war.

The consolidation of the Banaras raj on the one hand and the growing thrust of the Bengal-based English power on the other generated a wide specturm of opportunities for the banking groups already well ensconced in the political system. Awadh in the late 1750s and 1760s came into direct contact with the English company – this being the logical outcome of Nawab Wazir Shujauddaulah's intervention in Bengal affairs on the side of Mir Qasim, the deposed nawab of Bengal. The allied forces were defeated at Buxar in 1764 and Shujauddaulah fled to Jajman where the Awadh army was once agin worsted in 1765. In the peace arrangements that followed, Awadh was preserved as a buffer state against potential Maratha incursions. The company took the first step in this direction in 1773 when a resident was appointed at the court of nawab Wazir and subsidized British forces were stationed in his territories – the unkeep of which came from the country's land revenue.[153]

These preliminary arrangements did not as yet threaten the independence of the Banaras raj where Balwant Singh and his successor Chait Singh maintained their autonomous status. Political security yielded dividends and this was reflected in the growing numbers and influence of the resident banking community. By 1770, the *kothis* of Bhyaram Gopaldas and Kashmiri Mal had been firmly established with a host of others – Sukhlal Sahu, Bhikharidas, Ramchand Gopalchand, Laljimal Sahu and Vrichandas Vishandas – following suit. In 1775, with the death of Shujauddaulah, a new treaty was concluded at Faizabad which increased the subsidy from Awadh for the use of the British troops, diverted the tribute paid by the zamindar of Ghazipur to the company, and most important, provided for the Banaras region to be ceded to the company. Chait Singh was, however, allowed by the company to continue managing his zamindari. Until 1781, he maintained his autonomy, collecting the revenues and overseeing the administration of the mint and criminal justice. In return, he was obliged to pay Rs. 2,340,249 as the annual revenue of Banaras to the company.

The arrangements for the transmission of revenue and subsidy payments involving Banaras, Awadh and the company essentially hinged on the *hundi* network operated by the bankers of Banaras and other cities in north India. The house of Gopaldas Manohardas followed by that of Kashmiri Mal, the official bankers of the nawab of Awadh, dominated the business of remitting the stipulated payments to Calcutta. Their *hundi* operations were subsequently integrated into the Bengal-Bombay *hundi* line as well, the company authorities making increasing use of their bills to bolster the deficit-ridden Bombay presidency.[154] The accelerated pace of *hundi* transactions in the 1780s and 1790s was sustained by the revival of trade and commercial activity generated by the growing influence of the Calcutta and Bombay trading poles. The expansion of Bombay's trade with Poona and the Deccan, and of Calcutta's with the Maratha domains in central India (the entrepot town being Mirzapore), the acceleration of the pilgrim traffic under the protection and patronage of the Marathas and the annual flow of tribute payments from northern and central India to Poona resulted in the emergence of new cross-country trade and credit routes that worked to the decided advantage of the bankers.[155]

The pro-company stance of the Banaras banking house of Gopaldas did not endear the banker to Chait Singh, the raja's relations with Gopaldas Sahu deteriorating some time in the 1780s.[156] On a flimsy pretext, the elderly banker was detained in Vijaygarh Fort in 1781 when Manohardas requested the company authorities at Fort William to intervene on behalf of his father. Even as the English were contemplating suitable action, the banker was released.[157]

The expulsion of Chait Singh in 1781 and the appointment of Mahip Singh as raja with considerably reduced powers subjected Banaras to direct British interference. The annual revenue payable by the raja was increased and fixed in perpetuity at four crore rupees.[158] The growing volume of tribute was as ever funnelled through the *kothis* of the Banaras bankers either to the company's treasury at Calcutta, or alternatively despatched, again by *hundis*, to Bombay to tide over the company's requirements. Large sums to the tune of nearly one and a half crore rupees per annum were remitted to the Bombay government in the 1780s and 1790s – these proving particularly crucial in 1781 to finance General Goddard's fighting forces in Gujarat.[159] By 1789, the arrangements were further systematized by the introduction and adoption of the so-called contract system. The Bombay government entered into an annual agreement with the Surat agent of the house of Manohardas Dwarkadas who undertook to supply the government with four crore rupees within a period of twelve months in exchange for company bills on Bengal at the rate of Bombay Rs. 93 to Banaras sicca Rs. 100.[160] The contract system worked well up to the last years of the eighteenth century when the Fort William authorities under pressure from the Court of Directors replaced it with a system of public loans and subscriptions.[161]

Successive failures on the part of the nawab of Awadh to defray expenses of the British subsidy provided the company authorities the convenient occasion for reprisals in the form of further exactions of territory: the fort at Allahabad in 1797 and the crescent comprising Rohilkahnd, the lower Ganga-Jamuna doab and Gorakhpur in 1801.[162] The loss of these territories was accompanied by the nawab's excessive and growing dependence on the Banaras bankers as well as the house of Lala Kashmiri Mal and Bachhraj for loans. The debts so incurred became a staggering burden by the time of Asafuddaulah's reign (1775-97) when Cherry, the English resident at Lucknow, was instructed by Lord Cornwallis and later by Sir John Shore to look into the matter and assist the nawab 'in ascertaining his true and just debts with a view to their being put into a train of payment'.[163] In 1794,the Banaras bankers had advanced to Nawab Asafuddaulah himself a sum of Rs. 1,158,700 for the use of his government on the security of bonds bearing interest at 36 per cent.[164] This loan had been necessitated partly by the difficult financial situation the nawab faced and partly because he had to pay off the large subsidy to the English East India Company.[165]

In accordance with the governor-general's instructions, the resident entered into a laborious investigation of the debts and transmitted a list of those which he considered admissible. Whether the statement was the product of his own enquiries or merely a duplicate copy of the list given by Raja Tickait Rai of the outstanding debts of the Awadh government, as the company authorities claimed at a later date,[166] is difficult to say. In any event, only in 1797 did the nawab under the relentless pressure of his creditors come up with a compromise solution. Instead of paying compound interest at 36 per cent per annum, he proposed that the claims should be adjusted at 18 per cent per annum up to a certain period, and that the European creditors were to be paid off by instalments stretching over a period of five years while the claims of the indigenous bankers would be settled over a period of six years.[167] This differential treatment was accepted by some of the bankers but peremptorily rejected by Mansaram, the agent of the house of Manohardas, who expressed 'his readiness to agree to receive the principal in the same manner as settled with Europeans'.[168] The nawab paid no heed to his appeals while Lumsden, Cherry's successor, confessed to his inability to persuade the nawab to settle the claims on a more equitable basis.[169]

The issue could not, however, be entirely ignored by the company authorities given the vital nature of their own arrangements with indigenous bankers. In 1798, Sir John Shore concluded with Saadat Ali (1798-1814, successor of Asafuddaulah) a preliminary engagement which contained an article obliging the new nawab to liquidate the just debts of his late brother in course of three years. The article did not find place in the definitive treaty of Allahabad, for the British, characteristically enough, were unwilling to make the company appear a guarantor for the liquidation of the debts. As it happened, Saadat Ali was not inclined to pay any attention to the claims of the creditors and went so far as to state in 1801: 'The payment of the debts of my predecessor Asoph-ul-Dowlah is not stipulated in the existing treaty. I am moreover unable to liquidate the debts contracted in the late reign, but this is an affair for which the Company are in no shape responsible'.[170] Lord Wellesley, refused to acknowledge British liability in the matter. Explaining his predicament after retirement, in a letter addressed to Lord Hastings dated 3 May 1814, he argued: 'My discussions with the Nabob Vizier on other points of the most arduous nature, precluded the possibility of preferring matters, however weighty in the scale of justice, of inferior consideration in a political and national view'. But, he added, 'I repeat to your Excellency my earlier conviction of the strength of this claim, and the propriety of urging it upon the consideration of the Nabob Vizier, who I trust will be induced to discharge so clear a debt of honour'.[171]

Investigations instituted by Lord Hastings revealed interesting particulars. In the first place, the bankers though not Europeans were recognized as British subjects and entitled to the good offices of the company government. Secondly, the money borrowed from the bankers had been for the purposes of discharging the subsidy arrears due to the company. Thus Lord Hastings admitted the validity of the case of the indigenous creditors but confessed to his inability to put pressure on the nawab to discharge his debts.[172]

Ironically enough, it was under the governor-generalship of Lord Wellesley that the cooperation of the indigenous bankers in making available large funds for the British troops, fighting against the Marathas in western and central India, assumed significant dimensions. Whether it was Lord Lake leading the advance in Bundelkhand or Colonel Murray in Ujjain, it was the banking fraternity that came forward with credit in the form of bills of exchange that could be discounted when and where the generals wanted. In January 1804, Lord Lake was informed that Mannu Lal and Beniparshad, both bankers of Banaras, had agreed not merely to finance British war operations; they also wanted an assurance that the British 'would honour them with a preference on being permitted to furnish supplies of cash that may be required for the use of the army'.[173] Similar arrangements with other eminent bankers followed – particularly noteworthy was the contract entered into with Trawady Arjunjee Nathjee of Surat on 9 November 1804 which provided for monthly supplies of six lakh rupees towards payment of the Bombay troops.[174] Ready and regular supplies sustained the British war operations enabling them to crush the Maratha Confederacy in the second Anglo-Maratha War (1802-5) and subsequently emerge as the paramount power in 1818. Just how extensive the involvement of the house of Manohardas Dwarkadas was in the war is difficult to estimate, but there is no doubt that the house virtually monopolized remittance operations for the English during the war and enabled the deficit Bombay government to hold its own against the Marathas.[175]

These considerations seem to have been studiously ignored by the company authorities once they had achieved their aim. Indeed, they found it imperative to implement immediate reforms in the field of currency which would reduce their dependence on the indigenous creditors and 'clip the wings of the bankers'.[176] By the third decade of the nineteenth century, the *hundi* was no longer the exclusive remitting agency for tribute, revenue or military supplies, replaced as it had been by a network of district treasuries where company bills could be regularly encashed. Not surprisingly therefore, the company adopted a disdainful stance towards old claims of indigenous bankers, the house of Gopaldas Manohardas in particular. In a letter dated 1 March 1833 to the secretary of the India Board, the Court of Directors disclaimed any responsibility for repayment of dues owed to the Calcutta bankers, namely the house of Manohardas, pointing out that the bankers had themselves to blame for not having accepted the compromise proposal of Nawab Asafuddaulah. 'Whatever loss they sustained by this refusal', the letter stressed 'is chargeable only on themselves. But men must be left to bear the consequences of their own acts. It would be a monstrous rule that Government should employ extraordinary and dangerous expedients for repairing these consequences'.[177]

The ability of the company authorities to nobilize successfully the resources and cooperation of the indigenous banking community for their political enterprise may be explained partly by their solvency and partly by the belief that they would provide security and good government. To the *shroffs*, company rule implied greater political security – a fact that was pointed out by Trawady Shankar, himself a victim of the Surat riots of 1795. Presenting himself before an enquiry committee instituted by the company in 1795, he asserted: 'I have seen Banaras, the people are all happy there under the English Government. Nowhere have I seen such a thing happen where you English are'.[178] This sentiment, further backed by the conviction that bills issued would be duly honoured by the company and that they would not suffer monetary losses, enhanced the relative prospects of the company in its negotiations with the bankers for loans and bills.

The close association of the bankers with the company administration was characteristic of their dealings with other regimes as well – Hyderabad and the Maratha Confederacy being cases in point. The difference lay in the fact that unlike the company which had its foothold firmly in the fertile province of Bengal with its impressive revenue surplus, the Marathas did not enjoy the same degree of solvency and operated from areas where cash reserves had dwindled, if not dried up. As for Hyderabad, its association with the British moulded the bankers' participation in the state's political system to an important extent, enabling both the British and the bankers to derive advantages at the expense of the court. One difference here lay in the fact that the bankers were not abruptly dislodged from the political system as the British consolidated their hold.

The centrality of the bankers' position in the workings of the Nizam's administration predated its subordination to the British. They occupied a pivotal position in Hyderabad's political system which itself was a complex mesh of patron-client relationship.[179] As in Awadh, they advanced loans to the administration in anticipation of future revenues and to the soldiery. The burden of debt thus incurred increased alarmingly with the stationing of the British subsidiary force in Hyderabad. Further, Hyderabad's participation in the second Maratha War also strained the resources of the Nizam's government which found itself saddled with an enormous debt to the *sahukars*.[180] A critical situation was reached in 1816-17 during the third Anglo-Maratha War, when the *sahukars* refused to advance any loans to the Nizam for the maintenance of the English force except through the English agency house of Palmer & Co.[181] Indeed in a letter addressed to the proprietors of East India Stock dated 1825 and signed 'By an Enemy to oppression', it was mentioned that the Nizam's credit had fallen so low (by 1814) that he could not aspire to raise money on any terms from the native bankers and was obliged to

> resort to Gosains and Patans (a powerful set of villainous money-lenders that no one will have anything to do with that which can help it) who lent their money on such terms as the following – If the Minister wanted to borrow a lac of Rupees, one half probably paid in money, the rest in goods which he could not sell for more than 20,000 Rupees. He actually received only 70,000 Rs. but had to repay a lac and to repay interest on the whole lac at 3 pc per month so that on 70,000 Rs. raised in this way, he had a premium to pay of 43 pc besides 50 pc per annum interest.[182]

This state of affairs resulted in two separate but interrelated developments. On the one hand, the company through its resident at Hyderabad, named Russell, entered into an informal arrangement with Palmer & Co. for its pecuniary requirements, while on the other, indigenous *sahukars* formed a combine to work with the English agency house. Whether the decision was spontaneous and actuated by considerations of security or whether it was forced upon Palmer & Co. became later a matter of debate when in the 1820s a member of parliament, John Smith, accused Lord Hastings and the English resident at Hyderabad of having extended special and unlawful favour to the agency house in their pecuniary dealings. The controversy need not detain us here, the facts of the case being that in 1814 Palmer & Co. was granted permission by the company authorities to conduct banking and agency transactions and to supply timber from forests on the banks of river Godavari for purposes of shipbuilding.[183] Within a short period of two years the house emerged as a principal factor in the credit system of the state by virtue of the special protection it enjoyed in extensive monetary dealings with the Nizam government. According to a contemporary source, through 'pecuniary speculations, borrowing money from the native sahukars at a very inferior rate of interest to that which they themselves charged to the Government and by the large personal allowances to the partners and all the dependents granted by the Minister [i.e. Chandoo Lal] Mr. William Palmer and his associates appear to have acquired a complete command of the money market of Hyderabad.'[184]

Under the circumstances, it was natural that the company authorities as well as their ally Chandu Lal, the Nizam's minister, would negotiate with Palmer & Co. for their financial requirements. In 1816, a formal licence was granted to the house to enter into pecuniary dealings with the Nizam. This was considered imperative in view of the third Maratha War in which the company relied on the Nizam's cooperation. On 31 December 1816, Resident Russell reported: 'For the pay of 2000 Sirkar horse in Berar, an arrangement has been made with Raja Govind Buksh who has engaged that they shall not be more than one month in arrear, and for payment of the Sirkar horse that have gone from Hyderabad, the house of Messrs Palmer & Co. have agreed with Chundoo Lal to provide the monthly sum of 52,000 Rs. at Aurangabad.'[185] The agreement yielded successful results and the resident in his report on 14 June 1817 observed that the Russell brigade had distinguished itself equal to the native corps of the company's own army.[186]

With the successful termination of hostilities in 1818, the company turned its attention to 'reform' of the Nizam's administration in Hyderabad. The crushing burden of debt, the decay in cultivation and the arrears of pay to the armed forces required immediate attention. Once more, the onus to provide funds fell on Palmer & Co. The Aurangabad Contract of 1818 and the loan of 1820 followed.[187] Under the contract, the house agreed to supply two lakh rupees monthly for the punctual payment of the regular and reformed troops at Aurangabad, the security being the revenues of certain districts in Berar. Lord Hastings reviewed the arrangement with approval. In his view, it was justifiably founded on the 'experienced inability or fear of the shroffs to render the necessary aid to administration'.[188] The governor general's reading was probably not entirely accurate. As Stuart, his opponent, pointed out in his minute dated 10 November 1819, the house was 'in collusion with certain Soucars who had preoccupied the traffic at Berar'.[189] What seems likely is that the indigenous bankers were not prepared to advance money directly to the Nizam's government, exposing themselves to the risk of loss, and therefore decided to participant in the 1820 loan through the agency house.

In 1820, Chandu Lal represented to the English resident the immediate and urgent need of a sizeable loan which would enable the administration to discharge arrears due to various establishments, advance *taqavi* to the cultivating ryots, and repay debts incurred to *sahukars* and others on account of war which bore very high rate of interest. The minister proposed applying for a loan from Palmer & Co. which enjoyed the 'confidence of the monied men'[190] who would make the necessary contributions to the proposed loan. The agency house advised the minister to state the exact amount of money needed and the method of repayment because that alone would reassure its local business partners whose cooperation was imperative. To quote: 'You must state to us the exact amount you need, because we should not be able to raise the necessary sum without the cooperation of the bankers and monied men, and we must apprise them of the purpose for which we require their aid'.[191] Eventually, it was agree that Palmer & Co. would advance a loan of sixty lakhs and that the whole capital with the interest would be paid off in six years for which purpose an assignment of territorial revenue furnishing sixteen lakhs annually would be granted to the house.[192] The assignment was calculated to yield ninety-six lakh rupees in six years or six lakhs per year as interest income – a rate of 10 per cent provided that no part of the debt was liquidated in the meantime.[193]

The validity of authorizing a British agency house to advance a sizeable loan to the Nizam's government became a major issue of debate in the 1820s when the Court of Directors questioned the arrangement and accused Lord Hastings of executing an injudicious agreement. The legality of the Court's position or the defence of the Marquis of Hastings need not concern us but the affair highlights the nexus between the English and indigenous bankers. The raising of the loan was in fact a collective affair with the indigenous *shroffs* advancing a sizeable sum to Palmer & Co. for this purpose. The very *shroffs,* who on earlier occasions had been reluctant to loan money to the Nizam, now came forward to help. They were apprehensive of any financial dealing with the Hyderabad government except through the house of Palmer which enjoyed English protection. 'Their willingness', as was pointed out in a letter dated 28 November 1821 to the Bengal council,' proceeded not so much from confidence in the house as in that of the British government'.[194] The loan was thus made possible by a general combination of the Hyderabad *shroffs* and arranged through the clout Palmer & Co. enjoyed with the company authorities.[195]

Clearly, then, political considerations of security and guarantees of repayment were important factors in determining the attitudes of the indigenous banking groups towards the English company. The latter, securely based in Bengal with its revenue surplus, was in a position to pay its creditors, unlike its Indian counterparts. In marked contrast, the Marathas who made repeated bids for mastery over Hindustan both before and after Panipat floundered in mobilizing the funds of the *sahukars*. Based on the arid land of the Deccan, the Confederacy under the Peshwas could not attract loans large enough to pay off the huge arrears due to the soldiery. The regions where they extended their sway – Delhi-Agra and Rajasthan-central India – were moreover starved of cash on account of foreign invasions (Nadir Shah's sack of Delhi in 1740 followed by that of Ahmad Shah Abdali in 1760-61) and political turmoil (Rajput, Rohilla and Jat activities).

The inadequate financial basis of Maratha imperial expansion to the north was revealed from its very outset in the pecuniary embarrassments of the Poona government. Even while the Maratha generals were sweeping everything before them in Malwa and Gujarat, we find Peshwa Baji Rao in 1736 enmeshed inextricably in unredeemed debts incurred on account of the vast army he had to keep constantly on the field. With his troops heavily in arrears, he found the *sahukars*, to whom he owed a personal debt of many lakhs of rupees, bold enough to refuse any further advances. Complaining bitterly of the mutinies and clamours in his camp, he wrote in a letter to his religious preceptor: 'I have fallen into that hell of being beset by creditors, and to pacify soucars and sillidars [self-equipped mercenary troops], I am falling at their feet, till I have rubbed the skin from my forehead.[196]

In these circumstances, the Maratha Confederacy could hardly expect the solid support from large banking houses of the scale of Gopaldas Manohardas and Trawady Arjunjee Nathjee. That is not to say that the Peshwa and his subordinate chiefs did not make extensive use of the bankers and their credit instruments in their military and tribute transfer operations. Poona bankers were from the beginning closely associated with the operations of the Maratha horse outside the Desh, and the extension of Maratha arms to Gujarat, Malwa and Rajasthan saw some of them, such as the Hari Bhakti, set up new and important establishments at places like Baroda, Indore and Gwalior.

A recent monograph on the Maratha system under the Peshwas has emphasized the centrality of the *sahukars*' position in the revenue structure of the Maratha regimes both at the centre and in the confederate areas.[197] The formal subordination of the Maratha Confederacy to the centre expressed itself through transmissions of tribute which subsequently enlarged the scope of the bankers' activities. A chain of *hundi* dealers operated the transmission of tribute from Baroda, Ahmedabad, Mhow and Nagpur to Poona.[198] The family firm of Hari Bhakti provided the financial basis of the Gaekwad's regime in Baroda and assumed the responsibility of remitting tributes to Poona on the one hand, and of maintaining the Bahendari force on the other.

The close association of the bankers in Maratha military operations was vividly recounted by Broughton who served in the Sindhia's army in 1809. He observed that the usual method of raising money even in a military encampment was by making out *paats* (statements of sums required for public expenditure) which were negotiated with bankers of the camp and fetched a price regulated by the value set by these bankers upon securities offered by government for repayment. The securities took the form of revenue assignments of a province under the Sindhia's authority or bills upon different states from whom tribute claims were enforced. *Paats* were saleable at a considerable discount and once the bargain was concluded, the purchasers accepted bills, drawn upon them generally at a long date, called *barats* which were assigned to the troops as pay. Those who received them were generally 'so much in want of ready cash that they are obliged to sell drafts often at a discount of 20-30 pc to procure a present supply of necessities and the bankers on whom they are drawn eagerly purchase them at this rate. You will no longer be at a loss to conceive the distress of government supported by such a system of finance as this or that the bankers by whose means it is entirely conducted should be the richest and most powerful set of people attached to it'.[199] Broughton's observations were echoed by Webbe (he participated in the third Maratha War) who noted Daulat Rao Sindhia's dependence on the *shroffs* which in his opinion was 'so great that no order contrary to their interests could be passed'.[200]

Indeed the emergence of the bankers as diplomatic and financial guarantors bolstering the eighteenth-century regimes had become an all India phenomenon. Not surprisingly, therefore, in the negotiations that followed in the 1770s between Sindhia and Emperor Shah Alam, bankers' bills assumed critical importance in determining monetary negotiations.[201] The revival of Maratha power in northern India under the Sindhia in the 1770s resulted in Delhi emerging as the latter's base and as a converging point for the complex welter of claims and counter-claims registered by the opposing power groups like the Rohillas, Rajputs and the Sikhs.

The fact that Delhi had become a battlefield for the Rohillas, Rajputs and the Marathas to test their strength and assume the role lof 'protector' of the Mughal emperor had several implications. The most serious of these was that the Delhi region was steadily denuded of adequate cash reserves. This in turn meant that huge arrears accumulated and that the soldiery whether of the Rohillas or of the Sindhia was in a perpetual state of semi revolt. More often than not, the contestants were bankrupt. Thus we have the emperor pleading with the Maratha *sardars* in a letter dated 8 February 1772: 'For six months, not a dam has been paid to my soldiers as their salary. In my stables *filkanah* and all the *karkhanas* they get their food once after three or four days of fasting. Whence can I pay the money?'[202] The situation deteriorated further in the 1780s when Zain-ul-Abidin on behalf of the imperial forces summoned the bankers and jewellers and demanded money on the security of the jewels of the emperor. The jewellers pleaded poverty and asked for exemption, but in vain. After considerable persuasion, they advanced a paltry loan of twelve thousand rupees, hardly adequate to defray the expenses of the reprisal measures against the Sikhs.[203]

The situation in the Sindhia camp was no better. Arrears of pay, threat of defection and mutiny in the army continually plagued him. His repeated approaches to the bankers for assistance were rarely productive, as the following message of the Sindhia to Ramanand Bhau on 25 July 1787 indicates: 'The soldiers' pay for two months is Rs. 25 lakhs. Give them bills for five lakhs'.[204] Contrast this with the smoothness of the financial transactions of the English East India Company with the big banking firms of western India and Banaras whose cooperation had been sustained and uninterrupted in the crucial decades of empire building. A guaranteed revenue surplus, generating confidence among the indigenous moneyed groups and thus resulting in their timely cooperation, worked in conjunction with a professionally organized army and a commissariat department. The paramountcy that the British eventually achieved was due to this configuration.

V

The establishment of British paramountcy in 1818 and the subsequent organization of a modern colonial state had a profound impact on the mercantile social formation in India. The immense profits accruing to the bankers and the merchants from revenue handling, coinage, money changing and military-political fund transfers ceased slowly as the paramount power proceeded to organize a new system of finance and administration. In a bid to end the 'imposition of the shroffs', the new colonial regime closed the Farrukhabad mint (1824) and the Banaras mint (1821), bringing about 'a lack of money'[205] that assumed more critical proportions with the imposition all over India of the uniform silver rupee in 1835, a measure necessarily accompanied by huge demonetizations of other currencies that aggravated the depression prevailing in the bazaar in many parts of India. The *shroffs* continued, indeed, to push the Farrukhabad rupees in some parts of Hindustan,[206] but the money-changing component of their business was atrophying.[207] Their profits from handling the revenues also fell off as an independent system of treasuries and coin chests was set up in every British district. The widespread network of British district treasuries, reinforced by money-orders encashable at every post office, took away much of the remittance business of the *hundi* bankers.[208] As the *hundi* ceased to be deployed for remittance, exchange and insurance, it assumed more and more the form of a trade bill operating as an instrument for financing inland trade.

Shorn of the charges[209] of remittance, coin-changing and insurance, the *hundi* emerged as a purely financial instrument for raising credit in the bazaar and for financing the movements of country produce and imports of manufactured goods.[210] C.N. Cooke, an official of the Bank of Bengal who welcomed the integration of the *hundi* business into the colonial system of trade and finance, gave his opinion that the indigenous banking occupation, far from being gone, had 'merely shaken off the trammels with which tradition and conventional forms formerly bound it'. He saw this 'extensive system of banking' of 'a less peculiar character than before'[211] consolidate itself as a subordinate part of the world-wide imperial economy centred on London. The process of transformation was reflected in the decline of the old Patna and Banaras *shroffs* and their replacement by new Marwari trading and banking firms which rose in the nineteenth century.[212] The biggest among the bankers who had assisted the rise of the English power, namely the house of Gopaldas Manohardas, was pauper by the mid-nineteenth century, their claims for the recovery of the loans taken from them by the nawab of Awadh for paying the subsidy to the British having been ungratefully set aside by the latter.[213]

The bankers and merchants were, thus, deprived of many traditional sources of income by the consolidation of British rule in India. All the same, most of them were linked to the company raj by solid ties of attachment and loyalty. It is true that the reassertion of a single imperial authority on the Indian subcontinent relegated them once more to the subservience they had been used to under the Great Mughals, and no longer did they form the strong current they had represented in the tide of political fortunes in the eighteenth century. But they were appreciative of the new imperial power for the security it guaranteed to person and property. In one other respect, too, the colonial regime was more attractive to them than the Mughals and their successors. There was now better facility for the recovery of private loans – an advantage guaranteed by the legislation that made land a collateral for debt. This attached the banker and merchant to the colonial regime, but alienated him from the landlord as well as the peasant. The consequences of these new social realignments were revealed in sharp outline during the rebellion of 1857.

Among the moneyed groups that were most solidly identified with the new colonial order in a subordinate capacity were the Bengalis and the Parsis. The Bengali was the Englishmen's *banian* in Calcutta, the Parsi his guarantee broker in Bombay. Further south, the Tamil *dubash* discharged the same functions in Madras. These roles, similar to that of the comprador in nineteenth-century China, identified a section of the Indian mercantile community with the corporate European supremacy that the first generation of the Victorians were asserting in Indian trade and finance. The connection reflected itself politically in an overt ideology of loyalty that made the Bengali and the Parsi, along with the native Christian, the natural targets in those stations where rebellion broke out in 1857.[214] 'Patriotism' in the context of the colonial port city was the very opposite of that of the mutineers of Hindustan. It meant 'fidelity to the British Crown', as the significant exchange between Jamsetji Jeejeebhoy and his British patrons made amply clear on the occasion of his being made the first Parsi knight. The coin that he received from Queen Victoria bore the inscription – 'Sir Jamshedji Jijibhai, Knight, from the British Government in honour of his munificence and his patriotism'. And his acknowledgement of the same conveyed the promise: 'I shall hand down this medal to my children's children with pride and reverence! They shall be taught that fidelity to the British Crown is their first duty, – loyalty the first virtue'.[215] The 'munificence' for which he received the medal was catalogued by the Governor of Bombay in the presentation ceremony in a manner that left no doubt as to its general direction:

> When the bones of thousands of heroic men, Europeans and sepoys, were whitening in the snows of Kabul, when famine decimated the highlands of Scotland, when a mysterious dispensation of Providence deprived the poor Irishmen of their daily food, when the widows and orphans of the brave men who died for the right at Alma and Inkermann stretched forth their hands for aid, none

> evinced a more general sympathy, none showed more alacrity in giving bread to the hungry and binding up the wounds of the broken hearted than the benevolent Parsi knight.[216]

The catalogue had no place in it for the terrible famines that laid waste Hindustan twice in close succession in 1833 and 1837.

When news of the mutiny reached Bombay and Calcutta, the Parsis and the Bengalis rushed forth with assurances of loyalty and support.[217] More surprising was the measure of support the British received from the banias in the towns of Hindustan. The pattern of their behaviour demonstrated how far the generality of traders had been incorporated into the new colonial economic and political order even in those areas where discontent against it was most pronounced.

Travelling through Awadh in the last years of its autonomy, Colonel Sleeman recorded in his diary of 1850 a typical example of the manner in which the Hindustani merchants' identification with British power had insensibly taken place:

> Morowa is a large town, well situated and surrounded with groves of the finest trees, and in great variety and to the surprise of the officers with me, they saw a respectable house, of burnt brick. It belongs to the most substantial banker and agricultural capitalist in these parts, *Chundun Lal*. These capitalists and their families are, generally, more safe than the others as their aid is necessary to the government and its officers, and no less so to the landholders, cultivators and people of all classes. Their wealth consists in their credit in different parts of India; and he who has most of it, may have little at his house, while the government officers stand generally too much in daily need of his services and mediation to molest him. A pledge made by these officers to landholders and cultivators, or to these officers, by such persons, is seldom considered safe or binding, till the respectable banker or capitalist has ratified it by his mediation, to which all refer with confidence.[218]

Awadh, it may be borne in mind, was a storm centre of the rebellion, where the *taluqdar* and the sepoy alike identified the merchant as belonging to the enemy camp. The contrast between the behaviour of the merchants and that of the rest of the population struck the beleaguered district officers of the upper Ganga valley quite early. The magistrate of Allahabad, who believed 'the zamindars and the agricultural population' to be enemies wrote to his superior, '... I have ... no doubt but that excepting the mercantile classes the people of the country are one and all against us'.[219] The commissioner of Rohilkhand, too, was inclined to the same belief: 'I would except from the imputation of the desire to change the Govt. those classes among the Hindoos who owe all they possess to the existence of the avowedly strongest and most just government; I mean the trading and banking class'.[220] The magistrate of Hamirpur (Bundelkhand) saw in the confrontation between the rebels and the merchants in his district a general phenomenon: 'This, however, must have been equally the case all over the country, but it is strange that in no instance do the class so favoured by our rule, the bankers and other traders, appear to have been able to keep their own in the struggle'.[221]

That is not to say that the merchant communities of upper India instinctively preferred the foreign to the native government. After all, the name first to appear on the lips of any Lucknow bania as he took his seat in his shop in the morning was that of the liberal and munificent Asafuddaulah of Awadh, in whose memory he would intone *'Jis ko na de Maula, tis ko de Asif-ud-daula'*.[222] The long inbred tradition of loyalty among the banias to the princely ruler revealed itself in the manner in which the *sahukars* of Jhalra Patan came forth with the money to get rid of the hungry regiments of Nana Sahib and Tantia Tope when the hard pressed and captive raja of Jhalawar fled the town, leaving behind his women and childran.[223] Some of the bankers of Delhi had connections with the court of Bahadur Shah, and the Gurwala family in particular acted as bankers to the mutineers.[224]

There were other instances of such cooperation from the traders, shopkeepers and bankers in towns occupied by the mutineers. This attitude was , however, strictly temporary and was dictated more by prudence than by sympathy. On the whole, the *sahukars* and banias as a class were inclined to the British because of hard calculations of their economic interests and expectation of the latter's eventual victory. As the English army came back to lay siege to Delhi, the underlying preference of the bankers for British rule came out openly. 'All the Mahajans and Sahukars of the town ...', complained Ghulam Murtaza to Emperor Bahadur Shah, 'conspired with the *Kafirs*. They created bad blood among the chiefs of the army and made matters all the more [sic] worse. The army grew despondent and it marched towards Lucknow'.[225] In marked contrast with the way the court at Delhi was deserted *en masse* by the bankers, the native rulers who remained loyal to the British could count on solid support of the merchant communities. Thus the news from Rampur read:

> Nawab Yusuf Ali Khan, the ruler of Rampur, has taken over the district of Moradabad which was once included in his hereditary dominions. He has appointed a Nazim for that district. Its Govt. has become intact within such a short period. All the Hindus, Musalmans, merchants and bankers of that place feel safe and secure. They are happy and offer prayers. To Chandausi, the paragana of Moradabad some of whose residents had for some time been in great trouble and straits at the hands of the infidel plunderers, he had also deputed an Amil with an army in order to extinguish the fire of tumult and disturbance. Within a period of two days, such excellent arrangements have been made that maladministration has been totally wiped out.[226]

This was the type of administration the bankes and merchants preferred instinctively – not white administration as such, but the sort of protected native administration that offered adequate security. It is not a coincidence that the one leader of the war of 1857 who got the unstinted support of the banias and merchants was Rani Lakshmi Bai of Jhansi who took care to nurture and cherish the bonds of sympathy between herself and her moneyed subjects. She borrowed moderate sums 'from the Mahajans to whom a written undertaking of return was given'.[227] Convinced that the levelling of 'the richest Hindoo city'[228] would act as a warning to the whole of central India, General Rose took terrible revenge on Jhansi by turning it into 'a fiendish burial ground'[229] sparing neither rich[230] nor poor. Upon her expulsion from Jhansi, the rani accompanied Nana Sahib and Tantia Tope in their expedition to Gwalior, and upon entering the city, she ensured that the bankers were spared and that no shops were plundered.[231] Nana Sahib and Tantia Tope shared her view of the importance of the merchant communities, but Tantia Tope's bitter complaints regarding lack of financial support from them show that his success in this direction was limited.[232]

The Muslim princes were considered to be less sensitive to the fears and requirements of the banias. But they, too, finally realized the value of conciliating so important a community. Emperor Bahadur Shah of Delhi and Prince Birjis Qadr of Lucknow issued proclamations against the plunder of the citizens by the rebels.[233] Unfortunately, the proclamations did not guarantee the sort of security the bankers and merchants had become accustomed to under the British administration. Yusuf Khan, the commander-in-chief at Lucknow, laid the town to plunder on account of chronic shortage of funds,[234] and sepoys made a habit of shooting tradesmen in their shops for resisting their arbitrary demands.[235] In Delhi the mutineers asked the emperor to give them two months' pay or their daily rations. The following is a contemporary account of what happened then:

> [Bahadur Shah] summoned all the shroffs and *mahajuns* telling them that if they did not meet the demands of the mutineers they would all be murdered; on which the shroffs agreed to give them *dal rotee* for 20 days, adding they could not afford more. The mutineers replied, 'We have determined to die. How can we eat *dal rotee* for the few days we have to live in this world?' Whereupon the King ordered (four) 4 annas a day. . . . The great banker Luchmee Chund Seit, from feeding the mutineers daily, has saved his firm from sharing the fate of the others and is the only shroff who has not been plundered.[236]

As the above narrative suggests, the moral notions of the mutineers about the right economic order were in conflict with the interests and aspirations of the banias. The reversion to the older notions of the right economic and social order was reflected in the summons that went to the *chaudhuris* and grain merchants of Delhi ordering them to keep their stores open for sale and to sell grain at a fixed and reasonable price.[237] The merchants, having tasted the fruits of free buying and selling under the British administration in Delhi, could not but react unfavourably to the restoration of the Mughal-style grain control. Bahadur Shah issued a proclamation stating plainly that the infidel British government had monopolized the trade of all the fine and valuable merchandise, leaving only 'the trade of trifles to the people' and '. . . the people have merely a trade in name'. He added further: 'When the Badshahi Government is established, all these aforesaid fraudulent practices shall be dispensed with, and the trade of every article, without exception, shall be open to the native merchants of India. . .'. He enjoined that it was the duty of every merchant to take part in the war and aid the Badshahi government with men and money, either secretly or openly.[238]

There was substance in the complaints against the monopolistic activities of the British. But while the soldiers were going round the town with naked swords, terrorizing the shopkeepers and plundering the shops of the sweetmeat sellers, vegetable vendors and cloth merchants, the merchants were unlikely to give credence to all the fine promises in Bahadur Shah's proclamation.[239] Ghulam Ali Khan, the man the mutineers appointed *kotwal* in Farrukhabad, was 'decidedly popular with the mahajans and Buniahs' because he clandensitely tried to protect them from the plundering expeditions of the sepoys. The soldiers discovered this and he was promptly put into prison. The manner in which the banias had aggrandized themselves under the alien British laws had deeply offended the moral notions and material instincts of the classes involved in the rebellion, and had alienated the prince and the peasant alike. Therefore, no social and political alliance based on real community of sentiment and interest was possible between the merchants and the mutineers. The rebel government set up in Awadh did not contain a single bania,[240] while the influential Sobha Ram, a part of the rebel administration in Rohilkhand, was used as an instrument for taxing the bankers and merchants of Bareilly coercively.[241] In the perception of the rebels themselves, the categories of people who would suffer most if the British came back did not include the merchant class.[242] On the contrary, their view of the political economy manifested in their action betrayed an instinctive antipathy to the bania. As the magistrate of Hamirpur wrote in his mutiny narrative: 'I need scarcely say that the great feature in the rebellion here has been the universal ousting of all bankers, *Buniyas*, Marwarees etc, from landed property in the district, by whatever means they acquired it'.[243]

Thus the Khatris, Sarogis, Kayasths and Bhats of Sikandarabad were plundered by the armed Gujars who attacked the town from the surrounding region of rural Bulandshahr. The Sayyid zamindars of Muzaffarnagar invited the 'malefactors of the rural area' and they along with the weavers, butchers and *chamars* of the town plundered the cloth merchants and shopkeepers. The zamindars and villagers of Sahranpur took full advantage of the spreading chaos 'to obtain from the *Mahajans* and *Buneahs* their books of business and bond debts etc.' The Thakurs of the surrounding Badaun country collected five or six thousand people and plundered the town of Bilsi for seven days running, while the *sahukars* watched helplessly; the Chohans of the Aligarh country called in the Jats to plunder and destroy the houses of 'the Bunyahs and Mahajuns' of Khair; and in Mathura the disturbances took the form of 'chiefly attacks on Bunniahs and ejectment of new *zamindars* by the old'.[244] Everywhere the older village proprietary bodies and the rural population aimed at murdering or expelling the auction purchasers in a bid to reassert their rights to hereditary holdings held 'dearer than life'.[245]

The reasons for the systematic character of the support the banias and *sahukars* extended to the British conquest of Hindustan, thus, stand out very clearly indeed. Strategically, the support was important because it enabled the British to control some of the key points in the communication network of the upper Ganga valley, even while the rebels seemed to be carrying everything before them. The fact that the pro-British social front of the raja of Banaras and the great bankers of the town remained intact was crucial because, as the joint magistrate of Jaunpur reflected in hindsight, 'the loss of Banaras would have left us the whole country to reconquer almost from the gates of Calcutta'.[246] Even further up the valley, the market town of Hathras, which successfully defended itself against the mutineers, provided a base for Major Montgomery's operations against the forces under Muhammad Ghaus Khan and Maulvi Abdul Jalil. As the magistrate of the district recalled:

> At this time Hattras was the only town and *tehseel* post in which British Authority could be said to exist. This town lies on the direct road from Agrà to Aligarh 20 miles distant from the former. Its inhabitants, for the most part wealthy Hindoo traders had with the assistance of the neighbouring Jat Rajah of Moorsan, Tekum Singh, and also Thakur Gobind Singh, (now Rajah), been able to preserve order in the town, and ward off every threatened attack from the plunderers.[247]

Here, therefore, the outnumbered force of Major Montgomery could find a safe haven from which to carry out raids on Aligarh town and to prevent the siege of Agra by the rebels who had gathered in Aligarh. In Agra itself, where the British were besieged for a time and had to retire into the fort, the garrison was able to hang on to its position by borrowing from the city at high rates of interest and by encashment of supply bills.[248] Lala Joti Prasad of Agra, the great commissariat contractor in the Afghan and Sikh wars, supplied the garrison besieged in the fort with provisions for several months. 'Without Joteeprasad', recalled a grateful Englishman, 'we could not have held Agra'.[249] The story was much the same in Mathura: 'The great protection of the city consisted in the Seths Radha Kishen and Gobind Dass, who raised a large body of men at their own expense and by their influence kept the other inhabitants quiet. They also lent Captain Nixon two brass guns'.[250]

It is not surprising, then, that the British came to stereotype the faithful bania for his 'passive fidelity'.[251] Yet they would have done well not to take the bania's support for granted. When the Englishmen besieged in the Agra fort returned in triumph to the city, making themselves obnoxious to every native townsman, they resolved in their racial arrogance to put down 'the insolence of the natives who do not make *Salaams* to passing Europeans'.[252] According to a correspondent of the *Hindoo Patriot*, a systematic persecution of the native inhabitants commenced at once: 'Salamming continues to be rigidly exacted in the thoroughfares especially by what our correspondent calls the gentlemen of the Farrukhabad breed. A poor shopkeeper in the Chowk had his head battered by one of the worthies for omission to pay respect to the white skin'.[253] Passive the bania might have been, but he still had his typical weapon, the *hartal*, waiting to be transformed by the greatest man of that community into the wider militant device of non-cooperation and civil disobedience. The social realignments brought about by the British legislation regarding land, debts and property had made the banias the opponents of the rebellion of 1857. But merely six or seven decades would elapse before another series of social realignments would turn them into supporters and sympathizers of the national movement after Gandhi's emergence. The support the British had obtained earlier would then be turned round against them with the same solidity, and everywhere the district magistrates would comment on the same systematic character of the bania's alignment.[254] Only this time he would be on the opposite side of the fence.

VI

Before the Indian capitalist class acquired a voice in the shaping of the political and social order of the country during the period between the two world wars, the merchant communities out of which that class was fashioned exhibited neither the desire nor the capacity to mould a regime in which they would be the ruling element. In the long political tradition of the country from the Great Mughals to Queen Victoria, the bankers and merchants were a subservient element, dependent on whatever warrior group held power or showed promise of capturing it. As a rule they had no place of distinction in the great affairs of state, nor were they as a group with any consistent political vision. The agrarian bureaucratic empire of the Great Mughals and the colonial regime of the Victorians had well-organized financial systems that brooked no dependence on the services of private bankers and merchants. Chiefs, rajas and zamindars might aspire to honours and prerogatives in such imperial regimes, but the *saudagars* and *sahukars* could hardly hope to be leading figures at those imperial courts.

The one exception to this was the interregnum between the passing of the Great Mughals and the attainment of the British paramountcy – a period when there was no centralized bureaucratic regime with an integrated and well-ordered financial system. It was then that the private commercial system of credit emerged as the one agency capable of transferring funds for the purposes of war and tribute and mobilizing cash supplies in anticipation of forthcoming revenues. The importance acquired by the bankers and merchants in the successor regimes of the eighteenth century falls into perspective when we remember the financial needs of the contending commanders and the absence of any regular financial machinery to meet these urgent requirements. The English East India Company, an international capitalist corporation with a developed sense of the importance of regular repayment of debt and with the biggest revenue surplus available in the eighteenth-century India to offer as collateral for large contract loans, was the best placed to tap the resources of the indigenous system of commercial credit. The *seths* and *saudagars* of Bengal and the banias of Surat played a key role in the mid-century coups (Plassey 1757 and Surat Castle 1759) that made the English company a political power to reckon with. Curiously, the merchants and bankers never once contemplated, whether at Surat or at Murshidabad, seizing power for themselves. The limits of their political influence did not stretch beyond supplanting one set of rulers with another, and they remained as dependent on the one as on the other. The bankers and merchants upon whom the company relied for the sinews of war were later subordinated to an international system of finance and trade centred on London. But their strength, sophistication and resilience enabled them to find a space in the new imperial economy.

The security guaranteed for private property in the colonial system rallied the merchants to the company in 1857, but it was a conditional commitment capable of being transferred to another party that might guarantee the same sort of security. The leaders of the 1857 rebellion, tied to a vanishing social order, were not capable of offering that: but the Congress under Gandhi was. The bankers and merchants coalescing gradually into a class impatient of its subordination, consequently, put its increasing social and financial weight behind the nascent order of Indian nationalism.

Notes

*The authors are grateful to the Ganitra Sadana, Viswa Bharti, for crucial help. Special thanks to Shri D.K. Kar and Dr. S.N. Ojha.

1. Kotal is derived from the Persian word Kotwal, the commandant of the town.

2. Banarsidas, *Half a Tale* (the *Ardhakathanaka* of Banarsidas) ed. by Mukund Lath (Japiur 1981) verses 49-50.

3. Shireen Moosvi, *The Economy of the Mughal Empire, c1595* (Delhi, 1987), pp. 118,121.

4. Jean Baptiste Tavernier, *Travels in India*, tr. by V. Ball, ed. by W. Crooke (London 1925), vol. I pp. 36-38.

5. Ibid, pp. 33-34. In addition to soldiers and officers, traders and travellers also availed of the *barat* or treasury bill of exchange.

6. Moosvi, *Economy* (n.3), p. 200.

7. It was only in the 1690's that the Mughal voyages from Hughli to south-east Asia ceased. On the Surat-Mokha run, however, the Mughals were replaced by private Muslim ship-owners sometime after the middle of the seventeenth century.

8. Banarsidas, *Ardhakathanaka*, (n.2) verses 521-538.

9. This is the argument of Karen Leonard, "The Great Firm Theory of the Decline of the Mughal Empire", *Comparative Studies in Society and History*, hereafter *CSSH*, XXI (1979). pp. 151-167. For a contrary argument, see J.F.Richards, "Mughal State Finance and the Pre-Modern World Economy", *CSSH*, XXIII (1981), pp. 285-308.

10. Muzaffar Alam, *The Crisis of Empire in Mughal North India: Awadh and the Punjab, 1707-1748*, (Delhi, 1986) pp. 151-152, 174-175, 177, 183-84, 203. Also see Ashin Das Gupta, *Indian Merchants and the Decline of Surat, 1700-1740* (Wiesbaden, 1979), passim.

11. At the death of Emperor Aurangazeb, the imperial treasury at Agra contained nine crores of rupees. By 1720, the cash at Agra fort amounted to no more than one crore 80 thousand. Alam, *Crisis*, (n.10), p.38.

12. Ghulam Hussain Khan, *The Riyaz-us-Salatin*, tr. by Abdus Salam (Calcutta, 1902), p. 269.

13. Alam, *Crisis* (n.10), p.42.

14. Ibid, p.199.

15. This was so as late as 1757 when many noblemen refused to accompany Sirajuddaulah on his expedition against Shaukat Jang, who had obtained the imperial appointment to the nizamat of Bengal, for fear of threat to their families in Delhi.

16. Alam, *Crisis*, (n.10), pp.33, 261.

17. Ibid.

18. C.S. Bayly, *Rulers, Townsmen and Bazaars: North Indian Society in the Age of British Expansion, 1770-1870* (Cambridge, 1983), p. 172.

19. Fakhruddin Hussain Khan, a dismissed faujdar of Purnea, inherited an immense fortune in ready money and jewels from his father. Banished from Bengal by the viceroy for his contumacy, he remitted this entire fortune to Delhi through "the channel of some bankers of Purnea and Maldah". Seid Ghulam Hossein Khan, *The Seir Mutaqherin*, tr. by Nota Manus, (Delhi 1986, reprint), vol. II, p.90.

20. Alam, *Crisis* (n.10), p. 37.

21. National Archives of India, *National Register of Private Records, Part I: Descriptive List of Documents in the Kapad Dwara Collection, Jaipur*. (New Delhi 1971), nos. 1069, 1070 and 1072.

22. *Memoirs of the Emperor Jehangir* written by himself and translated from a Persian manuscript by Major David Price. (Calcutta 1904), p.9.

23. Ibid, p.9.

24. Banarsidas, *Ardhakathanaka* (n.2).

25. "Muladasa Biholiya, Banik Vritti ke Bhesa. Modi Hai Kai Mugal Kau, yau Malvdesa" (Muladasa Biholiya, of the profession Banik by name, a Modi of some Mughal, to the land of Malwa he came.) Ibid., verse 14. Translation ours.

26. Ibid, verse 113.

27. Ibid, verse 133.

28. Ibid, verse 148.

29. Ibid, verse 253.

30. Ibid, verse 459.

31. Ibid, verse 468.

32. Das Gupta, *Indian Merchants* (n.10) passim.

33. Sir Thomas Roe at Ahmedabad to Sir Thomas Smythe, in William Foster (ed.), *English Factories in India*, (hereinafter E.F.I.) *1618-1621* (Oxford 1906), pp. 23-24.

34. Thomas Kerridge, Thomas Rastell and Giles James at Surat to William Biddulph & c at Burhanpur 6-7 April 1619, ibid, pp. 88-89.

35. William Biddulph and James Willoughby at the Mughal camp to the Company, 25 December 1619, ibid, p. 172.

36. Ashin Das Gupta, "The Early Seventeenth Century", *Modern Asian Studies*, IXX (1985), pp 488-499. Also see his "India and the Indian Ocean in the Eighteenth Century", in A. Das Gupta & M.N. Pearson (eds.), *India and the Indian Ocean 1500-1800*, (Delhi 1987), pp. 104-24.

37. Das Gupta, *Indian Merchants* (n.10) passim.

38. Joseph Salbank and Nicholas Crisp at Cambay to the Surat factory, 8 December 1622, *E.F.I*, 1622-23, pp. 169-170.

39. Ibid, 1624-29, pp. 190-191. Also see M.J. Mehta, "Some Aspects of Surat as a Trading Centre", *The Indian Historical Review*, I (1974), pp. 247-248ff. Mehta sets out two instances of extortion by the local administration.

40. Surat to the Company, 27 February 1662, Shiva Charitra Karyalaya, *English Records on Shivaji, 1659-82*, hereinafter *E.R.S.*, (Poona 1934) p.36.

41. Das Gupta, *Indian Merchants* (n.10), passim.

42. President at Surat to the Company, 26 November 1669, *E.R.S.*, p. 136.

43. Ibid, pp 136-137ff.

44. Ibid, p. 138.

45. Surat to Bombay, 21 June 1672, ibid., p. 220.

46. Abul Fazl, *Ain-i-Akbari*, ed. by Blochmann (Calcutta 1927), vol. I p. 272ff.

47. N. Manucci, *Storia da Mogor* tr. by Sir William Irvine (London 1097) vol. II pt III, pp. 378-79ff.

48. Note for instance Hasan Amadani's relations with the English in 1701. See *Selections from letters, Despatches and Other State Papers Preserved by the Bombay Secretariat. Home Series*. ed. by G.W. Forrest (Bombay 1887) vol. I, pp. 230-231, 260, 264-265.

49. M.P.Singh, "Mulla Muhammed Ali: the Merchant Prince of Surat", Indian History Congress, *Proceedings*, (Bhubaneswar 1977), pp. 291-297.

50. Ibid.

51. Govt. of Bombay *Gazetteer of the Bombay Presidency*, vol. II: Surat and Broach. (Bombay 1877), p. 134-5.

52. Lakshmi Subramanian, "Bombay and the West Coast in the 1740's", *Indian Economic and Social History Review* XXVIII (1981), pp. 208-09.

53. Letter from Surat, 15 July 1749 and the President's letter to Meah Achan 18 July 1749, Public Department Diary of Bombay Government, hereinafter P.D.D., no. 22 (II) of 1749, Maharashtra State Archives, Bombay.

54. L. Subramanian, "Bombay and the West Coast" (n.52).

55. L. Subramanian, "The Castle Revolution of 1759 and the Bania Community of Surat. Changing British-Indian Relationships in Western India" in D. Tripaths (ed.), *State and Business in India. A Historical Perspective* (New Delhi, 1987) pp. 107-108.

56. Ibid.

57. P.D.D. no. 30B of 1757.

58. Letter from Surat, 6 April 1758, P.D.D. of 1758.

59. Letter from Surat, 22 January 1758 and received by Bombay on 27 January 1758, Secret and Political Department Diary of the Bombay government, no. 4 of 1758, Maharashtra State Archives, Bombay.

60. This enabled them to make substantial contributions to Alivardi's successful operations against the Marathas in the 1740's without feeling the pinch too much. G.H. Khan, *The Seir Mutaqherin*, (n.19), vol. I, p. 393. Extract from Richard Becher's letters, *The Letter Copy Books of the Resident at Murshidabad 1769-70*, ed. by W.K. Firmingher (Calcutta 1919), pp.XI-XIV.

61. The overseas trade of Hughli was dominated by the Mughal officers till the 1690's. Om Prakash. *The Dutch East India Company and the Economy of Bengal, 1660-1760* (Cambridge 1978) pp. 67. 84.

62. G. H. Khan, *Riyaz* (n.12), pp. 246-247.

63. Ibid., p. 70.

64. Abdul Majed Khan, *The Transition in Bengal, 1756-75* (Cambridge 1969), p. 172.

65. G. H. Khan, *Riyaz* (n.12) pp. 249, 257; James Grant, "Analysis of the Finance of Bengal", *The Fifth Report from the Select Committee on the Affairs of the English East India Company* (London 1812), pp. 236-237, 252, 259-72; Yusuf Ali, *Ahwal-i Mahabatjang*, tr. by J.N. Sarkar in *Bengal Nawabs* (Calcutta 1952), p. 154; J.H. Little, *The House of Jagatseth* (Calcutta 1967), p. 29.

66. G.H. Khan, *Riyaz* (n.12) p. 174.

67. Luke Scrafton noted in 1757: " Juggetseat is in a manner the government's banker: about two thirds of the revenues are paid into his house and the government gave their draught on him in the same manner as a merchant on the Bank". See Sushil Chaudhuri, "Merchants, Companies and Rulers: Bengal in the Eighteenth Century", *Journal of the Economic and Social History of the Orient* Vol. XXXVI (1988), pp. 91,96.

68. Ibid., p.93.

69. Bengal Public Consultations, 16 November 1744, qouted in Little, *House of Jagatseth* (n. 65) p. 134.

70. Little, *House of Jagatseth* (n.65) pp. 120-121.

71. The English engaged to pay three and a half lakhs, a sum Jagat Seth paid against an English interest note. ibid, pp. 130-133.

72. G.H. Khan, *Seir* (n.19), vol. II, p. 47.

73. Undated letter from Coja Momed Avazed to Thomas Braddyl, Bengal Public Consultations, 24 December 1744, qouted in Kumkum Bandhopadhyaya, "Indigenous Trade, Finance and Politics: A Study of Patna and It's Hinterland, 1757 to 1813", Ph.D. thesis (Calcutta University 1987), pp.11, 113.

74. Ibid, p. 133.

75. Bengal Public Consultations, 9 December 1749, translation of the Nabob's perwannah, in J.Long, *Selections from the Unpublished Records of Government* (Calcutta, 1973), no.41.

76. Ibid, nos. 42 and 46.

77. Amina Begum, Nawab Alivardi Khan Muzaffar Jang's younger daughter was the mother of Siraj.

78. Forth to Drake, 16 December 1756, in *Indian Records Series. Bengal in 1756-57*, ed. by S.C. Hill (London 1905), vol.II, pp. 63-64.

79. He farmed the Patna mint in 1741 and had large loans outstanding to the zamindars. The Raja of Burdwan owed him four lakhs. See note below and ibid., p. 386.

80. Bandhopadhyaya, "Indigenous Trade" (n.73) pp. 104-105; Chaudhuri, "Merchants, Companies and Rulers" (n.67), pp. 97-99.

81. Robert Orme, *A History of the Military Transactions of the British Nation in Indostan* (London 1768), vol.II, p. 58.

82. G.H. Khan, *Seir* (n.19), vol. II, p. 400; *Bengal in 1756-57* (n.78), vol. II, no. 144, Bandhopadhyaya, "Indigenous Trade" (n.73), passim, and Sushil Chaudhuri, "Sirajuddaulah, the English Company and the British Conquest of Bengal. A Reappraisal" *Indian Historical Review*, Vol.XIII (1986-87) pp. 109-134.

83. Chaudhuri, "Merchants, Companies and Rulers", (n.67), p. 102; G.H.Khan, *Seir* (n.19), vol. II, p. 400.

84. Forth to Drake, 16 December 1756, *Bengal in 1756-57* (n.78), vol. II, p.63.

85. "Narrative of the Succession of Souraqud Dowlet, and the Siege of Calcutta by Governor Drake, 19 July 1756", ibid, vol. I, p. 141.

86. Chaudhuri, "Merchants, Companies and Rulers" (n.67), p.102.

87. Forth to Drake, 16 December 1756, *Bengal in 1756-57* (n.78), vol. II, pp. 63-64.

88. Jagat Seth had a monopoly of silver and coinage at Murshidabad that the English had tried repeatedly but so far in vain to break through. Khoja Wajid was recognised by the

English themselves as a strong patron of their rivals, the French and the Dutch. Amirchand, who had been dismissed from the post of *dadni* merchant by the English, was imprisoned by Drake on suspicion of combilicity with the nawab and his men actually showed the way to the nawab's forces into Calcutta.

89. Watts to Clive, 6 June 1757, *Bengal in 1756-57* (n.78), vol. II, p.400.

90. G.H. Khan, *Seir* (n.19), vol. II, p.225.

91. "Memoir of Jean Law"; *Bengal in 1756-57* (n.78), vol. III, p.190.

92. Perwannah of Sirajuddaulah to the Dutch, 22 June 1756, ibid, vol. I, p. 26.

93. Forth to Drake, 16 December 1756, ibid, vol. II, p.64.

94. Nawab to Coja Wajid, 28,May 1756, ibid, p.3: "Drake's Narrative", ibid, vol. I, p.54 and passim. J.Z. Holwell to Court of Directors, 17 July 1756, ibid I, pp. 117-19. Luke Scrafton, *Reflections on the Government of Indostan* (London 1763, reprint Calcutta 1975), p. 58.

95. "Drake's Narrative" in *Bengal in 1756-57* (n.78), vol. I p.135.

96. Khoja Petross Arrattoon to Court of Directors, 25 January 1759, ibid, vol. III, pp. 364-365.

97. Implicit in this was the requirement that the English must live like the Armenians under Imperial Mughal jurisdiction, i.e. under the jurisdiction of Manikchand, appointed governor of Alinagar by Siraj. Watts and Collet to Court of Directors, 17 July 1756, ibid, vol. I, pp. 117-118.

98. "Law's Mamoir", ibid, vol. II, p.173.

99. Ibid, p. 174; Consultations on Board the Phoenix Steamer, Falta, 5 September 1756, Long, *Selections* (n.75) no. 198.

100. G.H. Khan, *Seir* (n.19), vol. II, p.193.

101. Jagat Seth to Clive, 14 January 1757, *Bengal in 1756-57* (n.78), p. 104; Clive to Coja Wajid, 21 January 1757, ibid, p.125.

102. Translation of Coja Wajid's reply to the Gentlemen of the Council, Chandernagore, ibid, p. 127.

103. Orme, *Indostan* (n.81), II, p. 128; Clive to Piggot, 25 January 1757, *Bengal in 1756-57* (n.78) vol. II, p. 133; Ranjit Rai to Colonel Clive, 6 February 1757, ibid, p. 214; Watts to Clive, 14 May 1757, ibid, p. 381.

104. Clive to Secret Committee, 22 February 1757, ibid, p. 240.

105. Watts to Clive, 18 February 1757, ibid, pp. 228-229.

106. "Law's Memoirs", ibid, pp. 193-194.

107. Ibid, p. 185.

108. Ibid, pp. 189-191; Clive to Piggot, 30 April 1757, ibid, p.368.

109. "Law's Memoirs", ibid, pp. 193-194.

110. Raja Krishnachandra of Nadia is known definitely to have entered into the conspiracy with the English. Rajivlochan Mukhopadhyay, *Maharaja Krishnachandra Rayasya Charitram* (Calcutta, V.S. 1343) pp. 26-38; *Bengal in 1756-57* (n.78), vol. II, p. 375, p. 392.

111. Watts to Clive, 23 April 1757, *Bengal in 1756-57*, vol. II, pp. 353-354.

112. Scrafton to Walsh, 18 April 1757, ibid, pp. 342-343.

113. Watts to Clive, 26 April 1757 ibid, pp. 342-343, 363.

114. Ibid, vol. III, p. 316.

115. Watts to Clive, 14 May 1757, ibid, vol. II, p. 381; "Law's Memoir", ibid, vol. III, p.208.

116. Orme, *Indostan* (n.81), vol. II, p. 150.

117. Watts to Clive, 17 May 1757, *Bengal in 1756-57* (n.78), vol. II, p. 381.

118. Watts to Clive, 17 May and 23 May 1757, ibid, pp.386-387., 392.

119. Clive to Select Committee, 16 April 1757, ibid, p. 359.

120. Clive to Watson, 26 April 1757, ibid, p. 362; Watts to Clive, 3 May 1757, ibid, p. 374.

121. Clive to Pigot, 30 April 1757, ibid, p. 368.

122. Orme, *Indostan* (n.81), vol. II, p.150.

123. Watts to Clive, 14 May 1757, *Bengal in 1756-57* (n.78), vol. II p. 381.

124. Watts to Clive, 17 May 1757, ibid, p. 386.

125. Watts to Clive, 6 June 1757, 6 p.m., ibid, p.400.

126. Watts to Clive, 3 June 1757, ibid, p. 396-97.

127. Watts to Clive, 6 June 1757, 6 p.m., ibid, p. 400.

128. Watts to Clive, 4 June 1757, ibid, p.398; Orme, *Indostan* (n.81), vol. II, p. 160.

129. Petross Arratoon to Court of Directors, 25 January 1759, *Bengal in 1756-57* (n.78), vol. III, p.366.

130. Watts to Clive, 6 June 1757, 6 p.m., ibid, p.400.

131. "Drake's Narrative", ibid, vol. I, p. 154.

132. Messrs. Watts and Collet to Court of Directors, 17 July 1756, ibid, pp. 117-119.

133. Clive's evidence to Parliament, 1772, ibid, vol. III, p.325.

134. Petross Arratoon to Court of Directors, 25 January 1759, ibid, 367.

135. Long, *Selections* (n.75) nos. 647, 687. Petross' father, Gurgin Khan, was a general of Mir Qasim; hence the suspicion directed against him.

136. Sushil Chaudhuri, "Armenians in Bengal Trade and Politics: A Study of Khwaja Wajid in Mid-eighteenth Century Bengal" forthcoming article in *Indian Historical Review*. We are indebted to Professor Chaudhuri for supplying us a draft of his unfinished article.

137. Little, *House of Jagatseth* (n.65), p.226; Long, *Selections* (n.75), nos. 819, 830.

138. Bandhopadhyaya, "Indigenous Trade" (n.73), passim.

139. P.J. Marshall, *East Indian fortunes: The British in Bengal in the Eighteenth Century* (Oxford 1976), p. 120.

140. Chaudhuri, "Armenians in Bengal" (n.136).

141. Marshall, *East Indian Fortunes* (n.139), p. 118.

142. Ibid, p. 131.

143. Reza Khan's "propositions", Bengal Public Consultations, 28 March 1769, extracts given in A.M. Khan, *The Transition in Bengal* (n.64), p. 171ff.

144. *Sleeman in Oudh in 1849-50*, edited with an introduction and notes by P.D. Reeves. (Cambridge 1971)

145. Ibid, p. 80.

146. It was under Safdar Jang that Awadh assumed truly independent status, Safdar even appropriating the imperial prerogative of conferring titles and mansabs. See Alam, *Crisis* (n.10) pp. 281-282.

147. Besides handling of the tribute transfer business, the Benaras banking house of Gopaldas Manohardas was extensively involved in advancing loans to the Awadh administration to defray its other civil and military expenses. Sums amounting to nearly Rs. 700,000 were advanced in the 1880s as a debt towards the cattle department. See letter addressed by the Company to the secretary of the India Board, 11 March 1833. *Blue book: East India Papers*, vol. XLIV of 1834. "Claims on the King of Oude".

148. B.S. Cohn, "The Initial British Impact on India: A Case Study of the Benaras Region", *Journal of Asian Studies*, XIX (1960), pp. 312-320.

149. Jean Law de Lauriston, *Memoires sur quelques affaires de l' empire Mogol 1756-61* (Paris 1913) p. 291.

150. Moti Chandra, *Kashi ka Itihas*. (Banaras 1985) pp. 314-315.

151. Alam, *Crisis* (n.10), p.251.

152. Chandra, *Kashi* (n.150), p. 314ff.

153. For a brief survey of Awadh's political history see Reeves' introduction in *Sleeman in Oudh* (n.144).

154. Lakshmi Subramanian, "The West Coast of India: The Eighteenth Century". Ph.D. thesis (Viswa Bharati University, Santiniketan, 1984), passim.

155. Bayly, *Rulers, Townsmen and Bazaars* (n.18), passim.

156. Chandra, *Kashi* (n.150), p. 316.

157. Ibid, pp. 316-317.

158. K.P. Mishra, *Banaras in Transition, 1738-1795: A Socio-Economic Study* (New Delhi 1975), passim.

159. Lakshmi Subramanian, "Banias and the British: The Role of Indigenous Credit in the Process of Imperial Expansion in Western India in the Second Half of the Eighteenth Century", *Modern Asian Studies*, XXI (1987), pp.493-497.

160. Lakshmi Subramanian, "The West Coast of India" (n.154) passim.

161. Ibid.

162. *Sleeman in oudh* (n.144), Introduction.

163. Letter from the Commissioners for the affairs of India, 15 December 1832, House of Commons, *Parliamentary Papers*. vol. XLIV of 1834, p. 119.

164. Letter from John Forbes Esq recorded on the Proceedings of the Court of Directors of 26 February 1834, ibid., p. 160.

165. Ibid.

166. Letter from the secretary of the East India Company to the secretary of the India Board, ibid., p.127.

167. Ibid, p. 160ff.

168. Ibid, p. 119.

169. "I am", wrote Lumsden to Sir John Shore "concerned that it is impossible to persuade the Wazir and his ministers that his own credit and true policy required him to offer the same terms to his ;native creditors which he had granted to the Europeans". ibid, p. 119ff.

170. Ibid., p.120.

171. Ibid., p.121.

172. Ibid., p. 122ff.

173. Letters issued by Agent to Governor General. Extracts from Volumes (Registers) 1-21 Commissioner Benaras pre-Mutiny Agency Records. We are grateful to C.A. Bayly for enabling us access to these records. Also see letter to Lord Lake, 21 January 1804. C.A. Bayly's collection.

174. Copy of Trawady's contract, 9 November 1804.Board's Collections, India Office Library and Records f/4/265, 1809-1810. India Office Library, London.

175. L. Subramanian, "The West Coast of India" (n.154), passim.

176. Qouted in L. Subramanian, "Banias and the British" (n.159), p. 509.

177. *Parliamentary Papers*, (n.163), p. 128.

178. Quoted in L. Subramanian, "Banias and the British" (n.159), p. 510.

179. Karan Leonard, "The Hyderabad Political System and Its Participants", *Journal of Asian Studies*, XXX (1971), pp.569-574.

180. *Hyderabad Papers: Printed for the use of the East India Proprietors by the Hon. Douglas Kinnard* (London 1823), p. 100ff. These and sources cited in notes 181 and 182 below are available in Cambridge University Library, Official Documents Collection.

181. *Hyderabad Papers 1815-23: Papers relative to certain pecuniary transactions of Messrs. William Palmer & Co. with the Govt. of His Highness the Nizam* (London, 1824), pp. 35-37.

182. Anonymous, *A Short Examination of the Hyderabad Papers as far as they relate to the house of William Palmer & Co. in a letter addressed to the Proprietors of East India Stock.* By an enemy to oppression. (London 1825), pp. 21-22.

183. *Hyderabad Papers*, (n.181), p. 1ff.

184. Ibid., Bengal Political Letter, 26 July 1823.

185. *Hyderabad Papers*, (London 1825), p.45.

186. Ibid., p.47.

187. Ibid., pp. 48-51.

188. Lord Hasting's Minute, ibid, pp. 79-84.

189. Ibid, pp. 70-79.

190. Translation of a note from Chundoo lal who states his reasons for wanting money: enclosure 1, ibid., p. 100ff.

191. Translation of a note from Palmer & Co. to Chundoo Lal in reply to his request for aid: enclosure 2, ibid., p.101-102ff.

192. Ibid, pp. 103-104, 112-115.

193. Calculation of the interest rate at 10 p.c. by Hastings was challenged and it was estimated that the rate was actually 16 p.c., Minutes of Stuart and Fendall, ibid., p. 115-122.

195. Letter from the Marquis of Hastings, 20 October 1822, ibid., p. 122.

196. James Grant Duff, *A History of the Mahrattas* (Calcutta 1912) vol. I, p. 431.

197. Andre Wink, *Land and Sovereignty in India: Agrarian Society and Politics under the Eighteenth Swarajya. (Cambridge 1986), passim.*

198. Ibid.

199. Thomas Duer Broughton, *Letters from a Mahratta Camp during the year 1809* (reprint Calcutta 1977), p. 123.

200. Quoted in L. Subramanian, "The west Coast of India" (n.154), p. 249.

201. Delhi news letters of 24 January 1770 and 24 July 1771 in *Persian Records of Maratha History* I: *Delhi Affairs (1761-88), News Letters from the Parasnis Collection*, translated by J. N. Sarkar. (Bombay 1953) nos. A-7 and A-18B.

202. Sevak ram to Madhav Rao, 2 January 1772, ibid, no. A-23. Delhi news letter, 8 February 1772, ibid., no. A-26A.

203. Letter to the Peshwa, 1 May 1783, ibid., no. B-9a.

204. J.N. Sarkar, *Fall of the Mughal Empire*. (Bombay 1954), vol. II, P.8ff.

205. Bayly, *Rulers, Townsmen and Bazaars* (n.18) p.274.

206. Amiya Kumar Bagchi, *The Evolution of the State Bank of India. The Roots, 1806-1876*. (Bombay 1987) part II, pp. 174-175.

207. In the North West Provinces, Company rupees substantially replaced Farukhabad rupees in 12 years from 1835 to 1846. After the conquest of Punjab, steps were taken in 1849 to replace Nankshahi rupees. Thomason's despatches from Calcutta 1858 in *Selections from the Records of the Government of the North Western Provinces*. vol. II, PP.77-78.

208. Government of India. *Rules for Bills of Exchange with Additional Rules for transfer, receipts, letters of credit and cheques prescribed by the Board of Audit*. (Calcutta 1861). pp.5,10.

209. Tavernier's account implies that the hundis of Mughal times bore these charges, a fact confirmed by B.K. Bhargava, *Indigenous Banking in Ancient and Medieval India*. (Bombay 1934), pp. 179-180.

210. This becomes evident when we compare the functions of hundis, as described by Irfan Habib, "Banking in Mughal India", in Tapan Ray Chaudhuri (ed.), *Contributions to Indian Economic Hisstory* . (Calcutta 1960), pp. 1-20 with the functions of the hundi as described in various provincial banking enquiry committee reports of 1929-30.

211. C.N. Cooke, *The Rise, Progress and Present Condition of Banking in India*. (Calcutta 1863), p.13.

212. *Report of the Bihar and Orissa Provincial Banking Enquiry Committee, 1929-30*. (Patna 1930), vol. I, pp.85-86.

213. "Papers relative to certain claims against the late native government of Oudh", House of Commons, *Parliamentary papers*, vol. XLV of 1863, p.7.

214. "The best and most convincing proof of the loyalty of the Parsis will be found in the fact that, if there was an individual of this sect at any station where the revolt occurred, he suffered equally with the Europeans at the hands of the rebels, the sympathy of his race with the government so well known". D.F.Karaka, *History of the Parsis* (London 1884), vol. II, p.282.

215. Ibid, pp. 96-99.

216. Ibid, p. 100.

217. Ibid, p. 282.

218. *Sleeman in Oudh* (n.144), pp. 154-155, 162-163.

219. Magistrate, Allahabad, to Commissioner, 21, July 1857. Govt. of U.P., *Freedom Struggle in Uttar Pradesh*. (Lucknow, 1957-1960), vol.I, p.477.

220. Commissioner, Rohilkhand to Secy, N.W.P., 30 November 1858, ibid., vol. V, p.165.

221. Mutiny Narrative, Hamirpur, ibid, vol. III, p.121.

222. "To whom the Lord Himself will not give Asif-uddaulah will". *Gazetteer of the Province of Oudh.* (Lucknow 1877), vol.II, pp.365-374.

223. Trial Proceedings of Government vs. Rao Saheb in *Freedom struggle* (n.219), vol. III, p.557.

224. News letter of the Durbar at Shahjehanabad, 11 May 1857, ibid., vol.V, pp. 984-985.

225. Ghulam Murtaza's letter addressed to the king, ibid., vol. II, p.136.

226. Rampur News, ibid vol. V, p.330.

227. Deposition of Labu Bakshi, ibid., vol., III p.56.

228. Major general Hugh Rose (Commanding Central Indian Force) to the chief of staff, 30 April 1858, ibid., p. 338.

230. "In Halwaipura mansions of rich people were engulfed in the flames". ibid, p.339.

231. Ibid., pp.414, 419,458.

232. Tantia Tope was heard complaining: "This is the country of my grandfather and great grandfather, and yet no one gives me supplies", ibid, p.530.

233. Translation of pamphlet "Futteh Islam", ibid, p.56.

234. Ibid, vol. II, p. 600.

235. Ibid, p.141.

236. Letter from the Indian Munshi, ibid, vol., III, pp. 965-966.

237. News letter from the Durbar, 11 May 1857, ibid vol., V, p.981.

238. Proclamation of Bahadur Shah, 25 August 1857, ibid., vol., I, p.456.

239. News letter of Durbar, 11 May 1857, ibid., vol. V, pp.979-984.

240. Statement of Syed Eusuf, ibid., vol., II, p. 113.

241. Petition to Governor General by Khan Bahdur Khan, 14 February 1860, ibid., vol. V, pp. 197-98.

242. Pamphlet entitled "Futteh Islam", ibid., vol. III, p.151.

243. Mutiny Narrative, Hamirpur, ibid., vol. IV, p.121.

244. Ibid., vol. V, passim.

245. Ibid, p.214.

246. Narrative of events by Jt. Magistrate, Jaunpur, ibid., vol. IV, P.25.

247. Mutiny Narrative, Aligarh, ibid., vol. V, p.669.

248. Narrative of events by Col. J.R.H. Birch, 9 September 1857, Ibid., p.895.

250. Mutiny Narrative, Mathura, ibid., vol. V, p.686.

251. Mutiny Narrative, Agra, ibid., p. 634.

252. *Hindoo Patriot*, 18 February 1858.

253. Ibid., 15 March 1858.

254. For contrast between 1857 and 1930 see D.A. Low, "The Forgotten Bania: Merchant Communities and the Indian National Congress" in D.A. Low (ed.), *Indian National Congress: Centenery Highlights* (Delhi, 1988), pp. 129-154.

3

Congress and the Industrialists* (1885-1947)

Dwijendra Tripathi

Writings, all of recent origin, on the attitude of the captains of Indian industry towards the Indian National Congress can be divided into two broad categories. While one group of scholars sees a 'grand design' shaping their response to the political scenario in the country, particularly after the emergence of Gandhi, another view would have us believe that they reacted to the situations in an ad-hoc rather than a coherent manner.[1] Interpretations of the motive force behind their attitude also differ. According to one school of thought, the industrialists were guided essentially by their class interests, while some other scholars, without necessarily rejecting this view, have stressed on a long tradition of philanthropy in Indian business as an additional but important source of their inspiration.[2] How different are these interpretations? To answer this question, it is necessary to start off with a synoptic view of the forces that contributed to the evolution of an industrial bourgeoisie in India.

I

The rise of this class was one of the byproducts of the British rule, though wholly unintended by the rulers. With the growth of secular education and spread of western ideas, the religious dogmas and superstitious beliefs beat a defensive retreat, and infrastructural changes of far-reaching consequences expanded the size of the Indian market. The activities of British entrepreneurs in India at the same time pointed to new business opportunities, and India's link with the British empire, then the paramount industrial power in the world, brought it face to face with a superior technology with the guarantee that trained manpower to handle the new machines would be available in plenty. The cumulative effect of all these factors was the beginning of factory industry around the middle of the nineteenth century. In spite of the unhelpful attitude of an imperial regime, wedded to *laissez-faire* principles very popular among British economists and policy-makers in the nineteenth century, the number of Indian industrial establishments registered a successive rise up to the end of the First World War.[3]

It is one of the ironies of history that the burgeoning Indian entrepreneurial spirit manifested itself most tellingly in the realm of textile manufacturing. Throughout the latter half of the nineteenth century, during which period the Indian cotton textile industry gained maturity, English manufacturers looked upon this field as their exclusive preserve and frowned on any encroachment on their near-monopolistic position. It is an interesting question to examine how a backward colony, unaccustomed to modern manufacturing processes, succeeded in establishing its own industry largely under Indian management and with Indian capital, and eventually wrested a major part of the domestic market from the hands of the 'mother country' in the face of subtle and very often open hostility of the English producers, who enjoyed powerful political leverage. The phenomenon cannot be explained with reference simply to the easy availability of essential inputs, such as raw material and labour, or the existence of a vast domestic market alone, as has been done by some scholars. But this is not the occasion to go into this question. What is important is that by 1919 the share of Manchester in India's domestic consumption had declined to less than 40 per cent and the Indian mills had already demonstrated their capacity to capture external markets.

The early founders of cotton mills in India were invariably those who had been influenced by the demonstration effect of British entrepreneurs or had imbibed western ideas, in whatsoever limited measure, through their direct or indirect interaction with the ruling class. But once the viability of new industrial ventures was firmly established, traditional mercantile communities, engaged primarily in trading and moneylending till then, moved into the new fields with great vigour and established their domination on the industrial scene. Most of the later entrants too had imbibed, in varying degrees, the spirit of reform and liberalism that was injecting a new ethos into the Indian society. Appreciation rather than hostility was the distinguishing feature of the attitude of these Indian industrialists towards the British rule and British business methods. This appreciation was so deeply entrenched that not even the imposition of excise duty upon the indigenous production of cotton goods in 1894 – a measure intended to placate the powerful Manchester lobby – generated any vigorous protest from the Indian mill magnates.[4]

The success of Indian entrepreneurship in other areas of industrial activities was not equally spectacular. It is somewhat strange that jute manufacturing, started around the same time as cotton textiles, did not attract Indian investors even though raw materials and cheap labour were available in plenty, and the cost of setting up a jute mill was by no means prohibitive. Perhaps the Bengali entrepreneurs, who had burnt their fingers in a series of unsuccessful modern ventures between 1830 and 1850[5] were too shy to grasp the opportunity when the outbreak of the Crimean War (1854-56) sounded the death-knell of the Scottish jute industry and created a favourable climate for jute manufacturing in India. Marwari capital, concentrated in eastern India, was still steeped in moneylending, thanks to highly favourable rates of interest, and the entrepreneurs in other parts of the country were either too busy exploiting opportunities nearer home or were put off by the sheer distance between the source of raw material and their own regions at a time when the transport facilities in the country were still quite primitive. Whatever the reasons, jute textiles became almost an exclusive preserve of foreign interests whose monopolistic ring was further fortified by the establishment of the Indian Jute Mills Association (IJMA), a cartel-type organization which barred the entry of Indians with remarkable success. This served to eliminate the Indians from some other fields as well, such as coal-mining, steam-shipping and inland navigation, as the European managing agencies controlling the jute mills also controlled most of the companies in these sectors and exercised considerable influence on the railway companies which were the main users of coal.

Free imports on the one hand, and limited demand on the other for other consumer items, such as glass, paper, sugar, and matches, inhibited Indian initiative in these fields. Tea and coffee plantations were developed by and remained in the hands of foreign interests because of their easy access to international markets which were the main consumers of these articles; and input industries such as basic chemicals had no chance to develop as long as the industrial base was as narrow as it was in the nineteenth century. Besides cotton textiles, therefore, the only other major area which attracted Indian entrepreneurship was steel. But here too, J.N. Tata's initiative took a long time to fructify and remained an isolated, almost solitary, example of Indian investment in a basic capital-intensive industry, involving a great deal of risk and a long gestation period.

This industrial scenario which prevailed in India up to the end of the nineteenth century offered little possibility of conflict between the Indian and non-Indian interests. Their respective areas of operation were, by and large, separate and the room for direct competition between them was limited indeed. Reinforcing this economic reality was the hangover of the attitude that the Indian mercantile classes had towards British businessmen in India during the early phase of the Indo-British economic interaction. The Indians, by and large, had acted as collaborators and compradors to the alien interests well up to the middle of the nineteenth century. The Parsis were the most active in providing critical support to British merchants in India,[6] but the role of other Indian communities – such as Gujarati banias, Jains, Bhatias, Khatris and Marwaris – was no less significant. Nothing happened in the latter half of the nineteenth century to disturb the general harmony that had marked the relationship between the two groups in the earlier period. The Indian industrialists, thus, acquiesced in, if not appreciated, the British ruling presence, and accepted their British counterparts operating in India as partners rather than competitors in industrial activities. Admittedly, there were occasional whispers advocating the use of indigenous products[7] but they generally related to goods produced by artisans rather than factories. And in the absence of any meaningful support from the objective conditions then prevailing, these pleas proved too feeble to cause major ripples in the placid waters of Indo-British cordiality in the realm of business.

The attitude of the Indian industrialists towards the British entrepreneurs in India, it must be stressed, was more or less in tune with the attitude of the informed sections of the Indian population towards the British rule and British institutions in the post-1857 period. The bitterness and disappointment caused by the suppression of the revolt soon yielded place to a general appreciation of the imperial regime on the part of the emerging middle class either because of a feeling of helplessness or the policy of reconciliation adopted by the Crown government, as symbolized in the Queen's proclamation of 1858. It is significant that the prominent pioneers of the nationalist school in Hindi poetry, writing in the decades which followed the uprising, sang the praise of the new regime[8] – and the Hindi heartland had been the principal scene of the revolt. It is also worth recalling that publicists like Dadabhai Naoroji, Mahadev Govind Ranade, and Romesh Chandra

Dutt, who voiced Indian economic grievances so eloquently, were not opponents of the British rule as such,[9] and the Indian National Congress which comprised the educated elite functioned more as a pressure group, or at best Her Majesty's loyal opposition, rather than an anti-imperialist platform.[10] Sporadic and occasional uprisings there were but they were provoked by local grievances; to regard them as the manifestation of general antipathy towards the Crown government would be a misreading of history. Racial biases in various administrative measures affecting the Indian economy undeniably existed[11] but they were yet to cause a serious disillusionment among the political or economic elite in the country.

Lord Curzon's ill-conceived measure to divide Bengal in 1905 was perhaps the first significant act of the imperial regime which created serious doubts about the bonafides of the British intentions. Unfortunately for the empire, it came at a time when a small but powerful section of the Indian National Congress led by Lala Lajpat Rai in Punjab, Bipin Chandra Pal in Bengal, and Bal Gangadhar Tilak in Bombay, was trying to recast the organization into a more militant mould. The moderates in the Congress, who controlled the organization, had to react to Curzon's folly more stridently in the face of the rising extremist challenge than they might have done otherwise. The result was that the call to boycott foreign goods and patronize *swadeshi* (indigenous) products became a general battle-cry against the government move. But India was not in a position to supply most of the industrial products needed in the country, since cotton textiles was the only industry which was in a position to meet the excess demand created by the boycott. As the Indian market for Manchester cloth remained depressed, the production capacity of the older establishments was expanded and a number of new mills were floated. In doing so, however, the millowners were swayed by the pulls of demand rather than of the nationalist appeal. In fact, the Bombay mill industry seems to have taken undue advantage of the scarcity to raise the price of certain varieties of goods during the crisis – much to the chagrin of the nationalist leadership.[12]

The swadeshi wave, however, proved too transitory to expand the popular base of the Congress, or to radicalize it. It also made little dent on the traditional attitude of the Indian industrialists towards British rule. Neither those who were active in the Congress organization – and their number was legion – nor those who maintained a discrete distance from it, diluted in any appreciable measure their goodwill and support for India's imperial connection. There is no gainsaying the fact, however, that the swadeshi movement created a closer bond between the Congress and the cotton manufacturers, who benefitted considerably from it, and the promoters of other industries such as the Tatas whose steel venture would have otherwise been starved of funds. To cement this bond, as it were, the Congress continued to reiterate its support for swadeshi even after the movement had lost its *elan* following the annulment of the partition in 1911, and to oppose measures such as the cotton excise duties which militated against the interest of the Indian industrialist. The attitudes of the Congress and emergent industrial bourgeoisie towards the alien rule, thus, seemed to converge.[13]

Below the surface, however, the gulf between the Indian industrial elite and the empire was widening. This can be attributed to three major factors. As the racial discrimination against the Indians continued, overtly or covertly, even after the 1857 holocaust, the hopes that the new imperial order would accord a more equitable treatment to the Indians receded into the background. Secondly, as the opportunities for industrial ventures increased thanks to salutary infrastructural changes, the social base of the Indian industrial class continued to expand, with the result that the people who had only faint memory of the comprador role of their forefathers or no direct experience of it emerged on the Indian industrial front. Some of them, like Laxmanrao Kirloskar, had been the victim of racial biases, and some others, like Walchand Hirachand, had been influenced by nationalist writings during the impressionable phase of their careers.[14] And thirdly, with the gradual accretion in indigenous technical competence to handle modern manufacturing processes, the Indian industrialists were no more overly dependent on English technicians to help them carry on their operations. It is significant that the English engineers, who had occupied critical positions in every establishment during the initial phases of industrialization, had been outnumbered, by the close of the nineteenth century, by Indians 'in almost every category of the higher posts of departmental heads' in the cotton mills of India.[15] That the Indian industrial class was becoming increasingly conscious of its identity and interests is reflected in the growing number of trade organizations during this period. Up to the close of the 1880s, all the chambers of commerce in India were primarily British. Beginning with 1885, however, when the first such organization was promoted by the Indians, the growing number of Indian chambers of commerce indicated a new sense of independence on the part of Indian industrialists. The most important of such bodies were the Bengal National Chamber of Commerce (1887) and the Indian Merchants Chamber of Bombay (1907).[16]

The First World War strengthened these trends still further. As the English engineers were no longer available, Indians rose on the organizational ladder, and the disruption in imports, augmenting demand for indigenous products, brought an increasingly larger number of Indian entrepreneurs to the fore. Some of the merchant communities, such as the Marwaris, which had so far remained confined to trading and money-lending, moved into the industrial field.[17] All new entrepreneurs did not, however, come from the merchant castes. For some of them, business was an entirely new experience. As a result of the enterprising success of Indians, the English monopoly in fields such as coal became a thing of the past, and even the steel produced by the Tatas, though much inferior to the products of British factories, achieved a measure of respectability.

Larger in number, stronger in professional expertise, and varied in social composition, the new entrepreneurial class displayed a remarkably mature attitude to the ruling masters. Like the industrialists of the preceding generation, it continued to profess loyalty to the empire. At the same time it was not willing to give up the advantages it had gained for itself. It was ready to accept, even support, India's imperial connection, but it was no longer prepared to play second fiddle to British business interests. Exactly as the Indian National Congress, in which several Indian industrialists were active[18], was clamouring for a position of equality for Indians with the British subjects of the empire, the emerging industrial elite considered itself entitled to the same kind of treatment as the British entrepreneurs received from the government.

II

This was the scenario when Gandhi appeared on the political firmament of India. Even before returning to the country in 1915, he had attracted the attention of Indian political circles for his 'heroic endeavours'[19] against racial discrimination in South Africa. His method of countering injustice evoked as much praise as his success against the South African government. Here perhaps was a leader whom the Indians were waiting for – a leader who could adopt a most militant posture and yet preach the gospel of peace and non-violence; who was second to none in professing loyalty to the Crown and yet was not willing to settle for anything less than what he considered to be the rightful place of India in the British imperial order; who used the most civil and polite language while advocating the national cause or pressing for the rights of his people and yet left no one, friend or foe, in any doubt about the seriousness of his purpose. Never did the Indians have a leader who was at once so complex and so simple, a bewildering enigma and yet as transparent as glass, a shrewd and calculating politician and yet a deeply religious man. His was a voice the like of which had never been heard before – a voice that rose above all other voices, as Jawaharlal Nehru put it.[20]

The Indian industrialists found Gandhi's charm irresistible, as did other sections of the Indian population. His stress on truth, non-violence, peace, and self-reliance appealed to them immensely as these virtues seemed to conform to their own cultural orientation. His saintly demeanour created the kind of aura around him which has always made a deep impression on the Indian people in general and business in particular. He symbolized the general urge among Indians for self-rule, but his determination not to deviate from peaceful means under any circumstances fitted in admirably with the businessman's abhorrence of conflict. Gandhi's doctrine of trusteeship was particularly appealing to them, for it held no immediate threat to the capitalist system which was experiencing increasingly severe strains after the success of the Bolshevik Revolution.[21] There was much in the Gandhian scheme of things with which the industrialists could have little sympathy – his emphasis on *gram swarajya* or village self-sufficiency, his advocacy of cottage and small-scale industries, and his stress on the abrogation of wealth[22] – but as long as coercion was ruled out as a means, these planks in Gandhi's programme were of no immediate relevance. Never in the history of the Congress organization did any of its leaders succeed in establishing such an intimate bond with the Indian industrialists as Gandhi did. While their relationship with the organization during the first thirty years of its history was purely institutional, it became intimately personal after 1915, thanks to the spell that Gandhi cast on them.

The Ahmedabad millowners, most of whom were Jains and Vaishnava banias, were the first to come under his influence, partly because of their physical proximity – he had settled down in the textile town after returning from South Africa – and partly because he seemed to personify and articulate the Vaishnava-Jain ethos. They met him frequently, attended his prayer meetings, and treated him and his advice with utmost deference. Not only persons with a traditional outlook, such as Mangaldas Girdhardas and Kasturbhai Lalbhai, but also more westernized individuals, like Ambalal Sarabhai, were irresistibly drawn towards him. As the saint of Sabarmati grew in stature and influence, industrialists belonging to other parts of the country joined the growing herd of his disciples. Among the most important and useful discoveries were Ghanshyam Das Birla, a Calcutta-based industrialist who was fast emerging as the principal spokesman of Indian business interests, and his fellow Marwari in Bombay, Jamnalal Bajaj.[23] A large number of traders and merchants of lesser standing were attracted to him in the Bombay presidency – the 'keep of Gandhism',[24] in the words of a British official. This is not to suggest that all business leaders flocked to Gandhi's banner. Many, including some of the most influential ones such as Purshotamadas Thakurdas of Bombay, remained sceptical of his aims and methods. But there is no doubt that Gandhi's leadership won for the Congress a much wider base of support and sympathy among the Indian businessmen than ever before. More than anything else, his charisma, his precepts, and his personal life-style served to politicize the Indian business class beyond measure.

It must be stressed, however, that the industrialist admirers of Gandhi did not always see eye to eye with him or submit to his judgement. Far from it. Ambalal Sarabhai, for example, whose anonymous donation is reported to have saved the Sabarmati Ashram from premature closure, gave, in his capacity as the President of the Ahmedabad Millowners Association, a determined fight to the politician-saint when the latter led a protracted labour strike in Ahmedabad in 1918.[25] Kasturbhai Lalbhai's 'great respect for Mahatmaji' did not prevent him from castigating the 'outsider' for meddling in an industrial dispute; the fast undertaken by Gandhi to force the millowners into an amicable settlement was, in the eyes of this Ahmedabad millowner, a coercive measure.[26] Even Birla who looked upon himself as one of Gandhi's 'pet children' acted against his advice on several occasions.[27] Gandhi was, however, too clever or too catholic a leader to permit minor frictions to interfere with enduring relationships. After all, his industrialist followers were not the only ones who disagreed with him; some of his closest political disciples and coworkers, including Jawaharlal Nehru, had even more violent differences with him.[28] But there was something in the nature of the man which helped him discriminate between the community of intrinsic interests and the grounds of extrinsic divergence and, shape his strategies accordingly. He needed the support of the industrialists to build a national consensus against the alien rule, and their money to finance his numerous constructive programmes. And the industrialists, in their turn, had no doubt whatsoever that if there was one man who could restrain the Congress from adopting a rabid anti-capitalist posture, it was Gandhi, and that their economic demands could not be secured without the help of the Congress.[29]

Even the most ardent supporters of Gandhi and most vocal sympathizers of the Congress among the Indian industrialists, however, were not prepared to alienate the government of the day. This can be explained in the context of the growing clash of interest between the Indian and British business classes. As the former became increasingly more conscious of their distinct identity and destiny, the European interests began to experience a mounting threat to their position of superiority which they had no intention of giving up. The process of estrangement was somewhat subtle in the beginning, but the gulf between the two groups became unbridgeably wide because of post-war developments. The prospect of an increasing role for Indians in the governance of the country, as promised in the Montagu Declaration of 1917, made the Europeans exceedingly uneasy and the Indians could not view with equanimity the determined efforts of manufacturers in England to regain their position in Indian markets which they had nearly lost during the war. The growing rift between the two groups was reflected in the formation, first, of the Associated Chambers of Commerce(ASSOCHAM) in 1921, and later, and as a reaction to it, of the Federation of Indian Chambers of Commerce and Industry (FICCI) in 1927. The former was a coalition of all European trade organizations in the country and the latter was an apex body of the Indian chambers.[30] The 1920s thus witnessed for the first time a clear polarization between the two groups of businessmen – now much more suspicious of each other than ever before – and a hostile administration could tilt the delicate balance unduly against the Indians.

Fortunately, the government was as keen to retain the goodwill of Indian big business. In an era of mounting mass political activity, which Gandhi's leadership had ushered in, the landed gentry and industrial-mercantile interests were perhaps the only groups whom the alien rulers could hope to prevent from gravitating towards the Congress. The basis of representation as provided in the Reform Act of 1919 was a clear pointer to the government strategy. The legislatures created under the act were to comprise, among others, the representatives of various interest groups including labour and capital, and capital was further subdivided into various categories such as millowners, merchants, Indian business, European business, etc. The system of interest representation was expected to preclude the domination of nationalist elements over the legislatures and prevent them from developing into a united forum against the government. Another indicator of the government anxiety not to alienate Indian business interests was its flat refusal to lower the import duty on Manchester goods in 1920 in spite of severe pressure. The duty had been raised as a revenue measure during the war, when English producers, unable to export goods to India, could not have been overly exercised over the decision.[31] Admittedly, 'the mystic bond of racial affinity'[32] with the rulers of the land, to use Bagchi's picturesque pharse, was a factor in favour of the British business interest in India. The government, nevertheless, was keen to project an unbiased image of itself and, thus, its support for European interest could not be taken for granted. Any move on the part of the Indian big business to align itself unequivocally with the Indian National Congress under these conditions would have been counter-productive.

Consequently, the visible affiliation of Indian industrialists with the Congress, a characteristic feature of national politics before the First World War, declined as the organization set off on an agitational course under Gandhi. Not a single important leader of Indian business was actively associated with the Congress after 1919. A policy of equidistance from the government and the Congress was considered to be more appropriate. Even a man like Birla, whose personal loyalty to the Mahatma was beyond question, assumed the role of 'having to defend Bapu before Englishmen and Englishmen before Bapu.[33] With free access to the Congress leaders and the ruling authorities alike, he could act as unofficial mediator between the two parties and, thus, enjoy considerable leverage with both. Behind this facade of equidistance, however, we can detect a four-pronged strategy: (a) keep aloof from the confrontational-agitational aspects of the freedom struggle, (b) support with funds such constructive activities which were indirectly linked with the Congress organization, (c) influence policy formulation by the Congress to ensure that its thinking on major issues affecting business interests was in tune with their own, and, (d) act in unison with the nationalist-minded elements in the legislatures to press the demands of Indian industry.

The strategy unfolded itself only gradually; various elements of it emerged in response to the exigencies of the situation rather than as part of a pre-planned grand design. Also the Indian business class as a whole did not support this strategy. For, there was a very strong section of Bombay-based industrialists, including Dorabji Tata, Ibrahim Rahimtoola and Cowasji Jehangir, who differed from this approach which seemed to be heavily weighted in favour of the Congress.[34] Socially closer to the ruling race, these elements remained suspicious of the Congress leadership and leaned more towards the government. Further, there were groups within groups. For instance, those who sympathized with the Congress were divided between the moderate and militant nationalists. There were divisions within the loyalist group as well. Some were more vocal in their support for the government, others were more subdued, and a few found it difficult to take an unequivocal position.

None perhaps personified the loyalist dilemma more than Purshotamdas Thakurdas who was intimately connected with the house of Tatas. Sometimes he sided with the Tatas, and on other occasions with the Birlas. In 1920, when the loyalists decided under Dorabji Tata's inspiration to form an anti-noncooperation society in Bombay to counter the agitational plan of the Congress, Purshotamdas cooperated with them. But later in 1929, when Tata and some other pro-government industrialists attempted to form a capitalist association in the legislative assembly in cooperation with European interests, the cotton king of Bombay reacted sharply against the move. Pointing to the inherent clash of interests between indigenous and foreign business, he added that 'Indian commerce and industry are only an integral phase of Indian nationalism and that deprived of its inspiration in Indian nationalism, Indian commerce and Indian history stand reduced to mere exploitation'.[35] These words could as well have been spoken by G.D. Birla whose nationalist bias was more pronounced. Again, while the Tatas remained aloof from the FICCI, Purshotamdas was one of its founder members.[36]

The Bombay cotton merchant was not the only one to alternate between the two positions; innumerable groups and individuals shifted their sympathy from one side to the other depending on the issues, or adopted postures entirely independent of the two. To view the Indian business class as a cohesive entity or divide it neatly into various groups with reference to its attitude to the Congress would be misleading indeed. And yet it can be safely maintained that those who generally sympathized with the nationalist cause and subscribed, consciously or unconsciously, to the four-pronged strategy outlined above represented the more dominant coalition.

III

A brief discussion on the reaction of the Indian business class to specific issues and developments would support the conclusion reached at the end of the preceding section. The first major event that unfolded the Gandhian technique of political action and marked a break from the earlier period was the non - cooperation movement of 1921. Whatever their private sympathies, the public posture of big industrialists and merchants, by and large, was one of utter indifference, and some like Purshotamdas Thakurdas, were downright hostile. While deprecating the 'listlessness' of the government in attending to 'genuine and apparent grievances' he chastised the Congress for having given to 'the masses the very dreary and dangerous satisfaction of resting content with destructive work'.[37] Birla, Ambalal Sarabhai, Kasturbhai Lalbhai or other industrialist disciples of Gandhi remained silent; we at least have no record of their views. In fact the major part of the financial support for the agitation came from traders and speculators in Bombay rather than big industrialists, even though the boycott of foreign goods benefited the millowners. After the withdrawal of the movement, however, when Gandhi decided to devote his time and energy to constructive programmes, industrialists of all hues favoured the legislative route to reform even though the Mahatma was unequivocally opposed to entry into the assembly. Instead of accepting the ticket of the Swaraj Party which had captured the leadership of the Congress, those representing Indian business interests came to the assembly either as independents or as nominees of the less militant Nationalist Party, led by Lajpat Rai and Madan Mohan Malaviya, with whom Gandhi had a 'fundamental difference of opinion'.[38]

Within the assembly, however, the industrialist members worked closely with the Swarajists. Kasturbhai, elected at the initiative and with the support of Vallabhbhai Patel to represent the Ahmedabad Millowners Association, had a close liaison with Motilal Nehru and Vithalbhai Patel whose candidacy for the speakership he actively supported. Though he avoided joining any faction, he attended most of the private meetings of the Swarajists and invariably voted with them. Motilal Nehru, in fact, regarded him as a better Swarajist than any of the regualr members of his party.[39] Purshotamdas Thakurdas, who represented the Indian Merchants Chamber, had no particular sympathy for the Swarajists and yet his positions on major issues were often similar to those of Kasturbhai, one of his closest friends. So was the case with G.D. Birla who had a brief stint as a legislator in 1926-27 on the ticket of the Nationalist Party. Not the party label or the lack of it but the community of interests bound these somewhat disparate elements together.

This can be supported by their utterances and voting behaviour in the assembly. Both Kasturbhai and Purshotamdas championed the cause of Indian shipping and pleaded for setting up nautical colleges and schools for the training of Indian seamen; the revenue realized from the merchant marine could be used to finance such activities. Both impressed on the government the need to purchase its requirements for the armed forces in India itself, and demanded safeguards against fraudulent practices adopted by foreign suppliers because of which the indigenous match industry was suffering. The issue which forged the greatest measure of unity between the industrialists and non-industrialists members of the assembly was that of the countervailing excise duty on Indian textile production. Moving the resolution to repeal the measure – 'so imperative that it cannot be effected a day too soon' – Kasturbhai spoke like a firebrand nationalist: 'In the age we are living, Sir', he thundered, 'political domination is sought to be utilized for economic domination of the subject race and the levy of the cotton excise is an instance . . . . This duty is a standing emblem of India's political subservience'. Quoting scholars like Romesh Chandra Dutt, Mahadev Govind Ranade, and Gopal Krishna Gokhale, he asserted bluntly that the levy had been imposed to please Lancashire and concluded with a fervent plea to eliminate this source of 'insult to our national sense of self-respect'. Those who supported Kasturbhai's move included Motilal Nehru, Purshotamdas Thakurdas, and Mohammad Ali Jinnah. The repeal of the contemptible impost pleased not only those who fought for it in the legislature, but also those nationalists who had opted to remain out of it.[40]

Protection for Indian industry was another issue which united the industrialists and nationalists of all hues. What was only a feeble whisper before the First World War became a battle-cry after 1919. The imposition of revenue duty at a level sufficiently high to provide some kind of protection to the match industry in 1922 and the creation of the Tariff Board in the following year were grudging concessions to the critics of the hands-off policy of the government. Instead of pacifying nationalist opinion, however, these gestures only encouraged them to be more aggressive. It is significant that all sections of Indian opinion, both in and out of the central legislature and irrespective of their political sympathies, supported the proposal to grant protection to Indian steel which was then synonymous with the house of Tatas.[41] In fact, one of the most powerful speeches ever delivered on the issue was that of G.D. Birla, his differences with Dorabji on matters of political strategy notwithstanding.[42]

The strong sentiments of the Indian members of the assembly, regardless of their political connection, are reflected in the fight for raising the duties on imported piece-goods. As a result of the growing competition from Japan after the First World War, the Indian textile industry was experiencing severe pressure. All members of the Tariff Board, consisting of a British president and two Indian members, which conducted an inquiry into the matter in 1927 agreed that the Japanese threat was too real to be ignored, but they differed on remedial measures. The president recommended a 4 per cent duty on all imported piece-goods, with an additional impost on Japanese yarn. As this would have done little to check the inflow of Manchester goods, the majority pleaded for a bounty on yarns above 30 counts along with a duty of 4 per cent on all imported cloth, irrespective of their place of origin. Under pressure from the British interests, however, the government rejected both the recommendations and took some half-way measures to pacify Indian public opinion. As the competition from Japan became more severe, the Government of India asked G.S. Hardy of the commerce department in 1929 to study the whole question afresh and submit his recommendation. Hardy found that the Japanese competition was the severest in medium-quality goods, and that Lancashire had a preponderant share in the Indian market for the finer varieties of coloured and grey piece-goods and bleached products. He, therefore, recommended an increase of tariff on the imports of medium varieties.[43]

Instead of acting on this recommendation, however, the government introduced a bill based on the principle of imperial preference which sought to differentiate between the imports from British and non-British sources. This aroused the ire of virtually all the elected members of the legislature. G.D. Birla, who had resigned from the assembly in 1927 but returned to it in 1928, made one of his most impassioned and forceful speeches against the measure which, while providing 'a small protection to the Indian industry' would enable Lancashire to 'wrest her lost territory' from Japan.[44] Except Purshotamdas Thakurdas and the nominated members, all Indian representatives took the same position and, when the government stuck to its guns, the members belonging to the Nationalist Party, to which Birla belonged, and the New Swaraj Party walked out of the house and later resigned their seats in protest. Gandhi 'was filled with joy' when he heard of the resignation by Birla and others.[45]

During all these years, there was yet another question which was raising serious doubts in the mind of the Indian business leaders about the bonafides of the government. This related to the rupee-sterling ratio. The problem had defied a satisfactory solution for a long time – ever since it arose in the last quarter of the nineteenth century. The First World War aggravated it still further. The rising price of silver threw the old ratio, fixed around the turn of the century, out of gear and by the time the war ended the value of the rupee, a silver coin, had increased to 2s. The recommendation of the Babington Smith Committee in 1919 to fix the value of the rupee at 2s gold shot up the exchange rate to 2s 10d.[46]

The high value of the rupee was fixed in the teeth of opposition from the lone Indian member of the committee. Now the cause was taken up by the Indian business interests. They were opposed to the new rate because it would place the British exporters to India in an advantageous position at a time when they were making a determined bid to recapture a large share of the Indian market, and it would hurt the Indian exports. No sooner was the new parity fixed than the spokesmen of Indian business and industry trained their guns on the government. They attacked the decision in the legislatures, in the currency commission, and in the press. The Currency League was formed to mount further pressure on the government. Initially, Gandhi was not quite convinced that a lower rate of exchange would be in India's interest but he and his followers like Vallabhbhai Patel were eventually persuaded to fall in line.[47] Consequently, in the central legislature the representatives of Indian business and the nationalists put up a common front against the official line. In some of their most powerful speeches, Birla and Thakurdas tore the arguments in favour of a higher parity to pieces, and the Swarajists and Nationalists supported them. So strong was the coalition that the government had to agree to lower the rate to 1s 6d. The concession did not satisfy the Indian members and they voted against the bill *en bloc*. Passed by a slender majority of 3 it would have lost but for the solid backing of the official, nominated, and European members of the house.[48]

Whatever their minor differences, the representatives of Indian business and political factions in the assembly, thus, made common cause against the government on matters affecting Indian economic interests. If the hidden agenda behind the concept of interest representation was to wean the burgeoning industrial class from the rising wave of nationalism, the strategy failed conspicuously. In fact, it produced just the opposite result. The schism between Indian business and the British expatriates, visible in the beginning of the 1920s, widened further as a result of frequent clashes between their respective representatives in the legislature, and repeated attack on the British imperial policy by the business leaders in the course of debates on various issues gladdened the nationalist politicians. The latter's support, in turn, for various concessions for which the industrial leaders were clamouring softened the attitude of even those who, like Purshotamdas Thakurdas, had been sceptical of nationalist intentions earlier. Whatever might have been Gandhi's calculations in opposing the entry into the legislatures, there is no doubt that no other forum could have provided a better opportunity to the spokesmen of economic nationalism on the one hand and those of political emancipation on the other to appreciate each other's respective positions and the basic community of their interests and objectives.

While flouting Gandhi's advice against legislative involvement, a section of Indian business leadership had kept open the line of communication with him. G.D. Birla never failed to take the Mahatma into confidence about his moves and activities through a regular exchange of letters and occasional meetings. The leaders of the Gujarati millowning class – Ambalal Sarabhai, Kasturbhai Lalbhai and others – did not write as many letters, but they met Gandhi frequently. Another method through which they ingratiated themselves with the saint-politician was by donating liberally for his innumerable constructive activities which, though technically unconnected with the Congress, served to expand its mass base. In virtually every alternate letter, Gandhi asked Birla for some amount or other and the Marwari magnate never refused – be it for the khadi programme, Harijan uplift, or publication of journals and magazines. In fact, during the 1920s, Birla emerged as the most important single financier of Gandhi who, in his characteristic humility, regarded the Marwari as one of his 'mentors'. The Mahatma did not need money for himself but other Congressmen, whose material requirements were more pressing, did. By helping them tide over their financial difficulties on several occasions, Birla established a claim on their gratitude and a right to be heard and taken seriously in the corridors of the Congress conclave. At the same time he scrupulously avoided giving any donation to the Congress directly. The Gujarati millowners were less generous with their money but a sense of cultural affinity bound them with Gandhi and Vallabhbhai Patel, his principal lieutenant in the Gujarat region.[49]

Another factor that influenced the attitude of an important section of the Indian business class towards the Congress in the 1920s was the rising tempo of the left-dominated labour movement. Particularly affected were the Bombay mills which witnessed a series of strikes in 1928 and 1929. Cotton manufacturers of the city had faced labour unrest several times before but what they experienced during the closing years of the 1920s was something very different. The leadership of the Girni Kamgar Union, which spearheaded the movement, was now in the hands of 'a group of firebrands who were firm believers in the Communist ideology'. Never before had such a ferocious propaganda been unleashed, not only against the Bombay millowners but also against the capitalist order itself. Never before had the Indian cotton manufacturer experienced such perpetual fear of disruption. Strikes caused dislocation in the Tata Steel Works also around the same time. Dorabji Tata's ill-fated move to form a party of the capitalists was provoked by these events. The more practical among the industrialist leaders, however, concluded that the Congress was a lesser evil under the prevailing conditions, although the Congress was no less active on the labour front. Its pro-labour posture was not always to the liking of the capitalists, but the irritating propaganda of the Congress-controlled All India Trade Union Congress (AITUC) was much less biting than the fear generated by the activities of the leftist unions. Business leaders had no doubt that as long as Gandhi had the commanding voice in the Congress organization, conciliation rather than confrontation would be the guiding principle for the AITUC. The effectiveness of the Gandhian approach to labour-management relations was there for all to see in Ahmedabad. The principal manufacturing centre in Gujarat was not quite free from the symptoms of labour unrest in the closing years of the 1920s, but the arbitration machinery created under Gandhi's inspiration, following the strike of 1918, helped resolve differences between the textile workers and their employers. Industrial relations in Ahmedabad, consequently, continued to be peaceful while Bombay reeled under a prolonged strike.[50]

IV

The 1920s, thus, witnessed a growing congruence of purpose between the Congress and the Indian capitalist class. Despite all their sympathy for the nationalist cause and protests against the discriminatory policies of the government, however, the industrial leaders had no intenion of losing whatever leverage they still enjoyed with the authorities. These contradictory pressures were reflected in their approach to the civil disobedience movement of 1930. Fearing that an open confrontation between the government and the Congress would further hurt their interests at a time when economic prospects were none too bright, they tried to dissuade Gandhi from throwing down the gauntlet. The best way to do this was to convince the Mahatma, who had once again regained his position as the undisputed leader of the Congress, of the usefulness of attending the first Round Table Conference to be convened in November 1930 to resolve the Indian political question. Birla, therefore, pleaded with Gandhi:

> My own impression is that for the present we will not be getting full Dominion Status [which was the demand of the Congress then]. Still we will achieve a great deal just now, leaving the rest to be realized in the course of the next 5-10 years . . . . The sum and substance of all this is that it would be decidedly to our advantage for you to meet the British Cabinet. Let us not miss this opportunity.[51]

He had written this letter after a dinner meeting with Lord Irwin and there is little doubt that Birla's initiative had the blessings of His Majesty's representative in India.

Gandhi, however, ignored the plea. Instead of going to London, he decided to march to Dandi. This was the beginning of the second major agitation Gandhi launched against the British rule. Nothing he or any other political leader had done before had ignited the masses to such an extent as Gandhi's trek to this little known place on the Gujarat coast. Every section of society heeded the call of the Mahatma; no part of the country remained unaffected by the nationalist upsurge. The peasants in the rural areas broke the salt law and challenged the British authority in various other ways; the urban centres witnessed powerful campaigns in support of the boycott of foreign goods.

While the masses gave the fullest possible support to Gandhi, the response of big business was not very different from what it had been to the non-cooperation movement. Little concrete support came from the industrialists. Birla, who continued to remain in close touch with the Mahatma, provided no financial support and his father was a known opponent of the movement.[52] Purshotmadas Thakurdas remained sceptical of Gandhi's methods. Civil disobedience, in his opinion, was 'a very dangerous weapon in the hands of a population, the majority of whom are illiterate'. Distrustful of mass politics in general, he felt that the movement would 'teach the people an extremely dagerous lesson which may greatly inconvenience even a Swaraj Government'. With all his sympathy for Gandhi, Ambalal Sarabhai remaind too preoccupied with his doubt about the constitutionality or otherwise of the movement to do anything tangible.[53] Kasturbhai Lalbhai was among a small group of industrialists who risked a more viable support to the agitation. On the suggestion of G.V. Mavlankar, a prominent nationalist lawyer of Ahmedabad, he had agreed to be the custodian of the funds of a trust associated with Gandhi, out of which the families of the Dandi marchers were being supported. This aroused the ire of the government. His name had 'come into such prominence with the government that they raided our office at Pankore Naka and I had a telephonic message from my friend Lala Shri Ram from Delhi that I was likely to be arrested'. Since the police search revealed nothing incriminating, the Ahmedabad industrialist was left alone.[54]

As on the occasion of the non-cooperation movement, commercial interests – merchants and traders – supported the agitation more enthusiastically than the industrialists. Throughout the 1930s, the latter were repeatedly condemned for their aloofness by the radical elements. Attempts have been made to explain this cleavage in the Indian business classes with reference to their differing perception of the economic distress caused by the depression.[55] It is true that there was much in the boycott movement which seemed to threaten the interest of the industrialists who abhorred violence and the hatred that went with it. It is also undeniable that the Congress propaganda that the economic distress was solely due to the government's fiscal policies made a greater impact on the trading classes. But to explain their respective attitudes to the agitation in the context of their immediate economic interest alone will be misleading for, boycott was no unmixed evil to either group. The industrialists' fear of disrupted production would have been more than counterbalanced by the hope that a depressed demand for foreign goods would augment indigenous production at least at the initial stages when the adverse consequences of the boycott were yet to manifest themselves. And whatever might have been his other calculations, the trader could not have seen a direct and immediate benefit to himself in the disruption of the market for imported goods. Almost up to the onset of the civil disobedience movement, some captains of the Indian industry were expressing their faith in Gandhi's judgement and stressing on self-government as the only solution of India's economic ills.[56] If they became more cautious in their professions and actions after the movement gained momentum and the government adopted a tough attitude, it could not have been due to their immediate economic difficulties caused by Gandhi's call to boycott foreign goods.

The fact of the matter is that the industrial leaders' response to civil disobedience conformed to the set pattern of their behaviour during periods of open confrontation between the government and the nationalist movement. During quieter times, they could shout support for the Congress position on major issues without burning their bridges with the authorities, but when the battle lines were clearly drawn, a more discreet behaviour was called for. Not only did they need the cooperation of the government to run their business, most of them like Birla and Purshotamdas had direct and close links with the highest officials engaged in the political management of the country. They could not have hoped to retain these links if they were to tilt unduly towards the other side in the event of an open conflict. The trading classes, which were socially more distant from the British ruling cirlces and much closer to the masses, had nothing to lose by way of their relations with the authorities and much to gain by falling in line with the general populace.

In view of the congruence of purpose that had developed between the Congress and the industrialists by this time, however, it was not possible for their leaders to remain as indifferent to the civil disobedience movement as they had been to the non-cooperation movement. A complete neutrality would have indirectly helped the government and thus alienated the Congress. What is worse, this would have caused a division among the industrialists themselves for, quite a few of their leaders, particularly Birla and Gujarati millowners whose personal loyalty to Gandhi remained intact, would have certainly resented a do-nothing stance. By way of compromise, as it were, they decided to support the causes for which the Congress was fighting without supporting its agitational tactics. In a resolution conceived by Ambalal Sarabhai and passed at its annual session, the FICCI commended the 11-point programme of Gandhi and declared:

> No constitution will be acceptable to the country including the Indian mercantile community which does not give sufficient and effective power to a responsible Indian government to carry out the administrative and economic reforms indicated by Mahatma Gandhi . . . and which does not vest full economic control in the legslature of India.[57]

The apex organization of Indian business also condemned the police brutalities and refused to participate in the proposed Round Table Conference or even permit any member to participate in his individual capacity. Even Purshotamdas Thakurdas was constrained to resign his seat in the central legislative assembly because of the growing pressure from the 'vast Indian commercial community'.[58] And yet the farthest that the FICCI went in its tangible support for the civil disobedience movement was to recommend the setting up of swadeshi *sabhas* in different regions. Responding to the call, Lala Shri Ram, the then president of the FICCI, organized the Swadeshi Prachar Association, and the Ahmedabad millowners established a swadeshi sabha of their own. The mills accepting membership were required not to use imported material, if Indian-manufactured stores and yarn were available.[59]

Even these steps, signifying only token support for the movement, were not to the liking of a section of big business. The ban on participating in the Round Table Conference created some controversy and even Birla who had welcomed the move in the beginning had to change his mind because of adverse reaction on the part of some members. He pleaded for lifting the ban and the federation responded by clarifying that its resolution was recommendatory rather than mandatory in character and that the member-bodies were free to take their own decision in the matter.[60] Likewise, the move to organize swadeshi sabhas widened the rift between the Bombay millowners and their Ahmedabad counterparts as the latter distrusted the integrity of the former.[61] Notwithstanding these difficulties, the FICCI resolutions, coupled with the rapport that some of its prominent leaders had established with the Congress during peace-time, enabled them to retain their position as honest borkers between the government and the leaders of the movement – particularly Gandhi, who was its supreme arbiter. The following letter written by Birla at the height of the agitation is probably the most clear exposition of both the dilemma and the mission of the Indian industrial class:

> Regarding the present agitation and the result of the Round Table Conference, I agree that we should try our best to get the country out of the present political turmoil. But I do not see my way so far. There could be no doubt that what we are being offered at present is entirely due to Gandhi . . . . This leads one to the conclusion that if we are to achieve what we desire, the present movement should not be allowed to slacken. *We should, therefore, have two objects in view: one is that we should jump in at the most opportune time for a reconciliation and the other is that we should not do anything which might weaken the hands of those through whose efforts we have arrived at this stage*[62] [emphasis added].

This strategy was no more effective in persuading Gandhi to come to terms with the government than it had been in dissuading him from launching the agitation. Birla and others of his line of thinking knew the Mahatma too well to believe that he would easily retrace his steps once he had taken the plunge. Afer he was thrown in jail, there was little possibility of any political dialogue with Gandhi even though Birla continued to correspond with him. The business leaders also believed that they would cut little ice with him as long as the movement was at its height and that any reconciliatory move in the face of the repressive policies of the government would 'unnecessarily irritate people'. They began to see some hope in the closing months of 1930 when there were definite signs that the movement was sagging even though it was still quite potent in some pockats.[63] No less a supporter of the agitation then Jawaharlal Nehru, who was to fret and fume when Gandhi reached an understanding with the viceroy only a few months later, felt in October that 'civil disobedience activities, though still flourishing everywhere, were getting a bit stale . . . . the cities and middle classes were a bit tired of hartal, and processions.[64] Official reports told the same story to the government, and Thakurdas, no enthusiastic supporter of the agitation but an uncanny judge of the situation, felt likewise.[65]

This perhaps was the time for the mediation to succeed. But the Mahatma, still in jail, was perhaps unaware of the change in the mood of the people. Birla, who sought a meeting with his mentor in December would have perhaps apprised him of the situation, but could not see him because Gandhi himself did not show much enthusiasm for a meeting.[66] It was only after he was released in January 1931, as a gesture of goodwill on the part of the viceroy, that he could have realistically sensed the situation. A hasty retreat, however, would have given a serious setback to the Congress. The master tactician must have been looking for an excuse to call off the agitation on his own before it collapsed, as he had done in the case of the non-cooperation movement. The mediation of Irwin's emissaries, Tej Bahadur Sapru, Mukund Ramrao Jayakar and Srinivasa Sastri – back from the Round Table Conference – came handy to him. So did the pleadings of Purshotamdas Thakurdas who had met the viceroy before meeting the Mahatma.[67] Gandhi responded positively and agreed to meet Lord Irwin because he could 'no longer resist the advice' from 'friends whose advice I value'.[68] This paved the way for the Gandhi-Irwin Pact which led to the suspension of civil disobedience. To suggest, however, that 'business pressure played a crucial role' in bringing about this reconciliation[69] or that the Mahatma was won over by the viceroy's charm is to ignore the totality of compulsions impinging on Gandhi's thinking. Neither view does justice to the intelligence of a remarkably astute political strategist.

It can be safely maintained, however, that the policy of equidistance from the government and the Congress, so carefully nurtured by the industrial leaders, was eminently successful during the first phase of the civil disobedience movement. Their leverage with the confronting parties remained unimpaired even though their motives were suspected by a group of Congressmen. As the political storm subsided, the industrialists once again drew closer to the Congress because of their belief that in the impending negotiations for political and economic reform, the cooperation of the Congress would be curcial. This is evident from their role both before and during the second Round Table Conference which began in 1931. Birla was among those who persuaded Gandhi to attend the London conclave, and the FICCI delegation to the conference, particularly Birla and Purshotamdas, followed Gandhi's lead in discussions on economic matters such as the rupee-sterling ratio, commercial discrimination, and financial safeguards.[70] The sole representative of the Congress and those representing Indian big business often made common cause, not only against the government but also against those Indians who were opposed to Gandhi's position. Birla complained bitterly to M.R. Jayakar that Tej Bahadur Sapru in the Federal Structure Committee sided with the government on the question of safeguards and added that 'it is really unfortunate that we could not carry your and Sir Tej's support even on matters in which legitimately we can claim to be heard'.[71] In fact, so closely did the FICCI representatives toe the Mahatma line at London that when the delegation's report was circulated, they were criticized by a number of constituent chambers 'for having tied up our conscience to the apron strings of the Congress'. The only defence that the delegation offered in its favour was that 'it could not fight foreign interest without the weight of the Congress and therefore could not go further than Gandhiji went at the Conference'.[72]

V

When a frustrated Gandhi abandoned the conference and resumed civil disobedience in January 1932, resulting in his reincarceration, Birla and his associates once again reverted to their mediatory role. Though the Marwari industrialist himself refused to participate in the negotiations any further, he persuaded the FICCI to continue to cooperate with the government 'in the framing of a suitable constitution for India' even though a faction led by Lala Shri Ram favoured complete non-cooperation.[73] While the FICCI resolution permitted Purshotamdas to participate in the discussion, Birla himself continued his efforts to bridge the gulf between the Mahatma and the government through his letters to Sir Samuel Hoare, Secretary of State for India, Lord Lothian, Parliamentary Under Secretary of the India Office, and other officers of the government as well as to the leaders of Indian liberals, particularly Tej Bahadur Sapru, and the captains of European business in India. Through these negotiations he kept his lines of communication open and retained his position as a well-meaning mediator acceptable to both parties.[74] His correspondence with Gandhi, of course, never stopped although they could not communicate on political matters very much while the Mahatma languished in jail.[75] The following excerpt from a letter written to Hoare soon after the resumption of civil disobedience is indicative of the role Birla saw for himself after the break-up of the second Round Table Conference. After assuring the secretary of state of the cooperation of big business in bringing about a political settlement he wrote :

> I wish I could convert the authorities to the view that Gandhiji and men of his type are not only friends of India but also friends of Great Britain, and that Gandhiji is the greatest force on the side of peace and order. He alone is responsible for keeping the left wing in India in check. To strengthen his hands is, in my opinion, therefore, to strengthen the bond of friendship between the two countries. But I am afraid in the present atmosphere it is an uphill task to truly explain Gandhiji. Probably the best way to success in this mission is to give you our cooperation as far as possible. And with such 'disqualifications' as I possess, if you think I can be of any use in bringing about happy relations between the two countries, you can always rely on my humble services.[76]

It must have been clear to Birla, however, that his mediation bid had little chance of success until the Indians were willing to water down their demand. One of the issues on which business leaders and the Congress were in complete agreement was the control over Indian finance – 'the crux of the full demand' according to Birla.[77] The government conceded the point in principle, but what it was willing to offer was hedged by so many safeguards that Birla thought that, in practice, ninety-nine per cent of the financial control was going to be vested in the hands of the governor-general.[78] A few other events also indicated to the industrialists that their business interests were not quite safe in an imperial order. For example, the Imperial Economic Conference held at Ottawa in 1932, which was supposed to adopt a tariff agreement 'for the benefit of the trade of both the countries' resulted in the imperial preference system which indirectly offered protection to British industries in the preserved market of the empire. The commercial interests and nationalists alike condemned the agreement as an example of colonial exploitation and found it detrimental to Indian trade and industry. A public meeting held in Bombay under the chairmanship of the well-known financier, Lallubhai Samaldas, passed a resolution denouncing the pact in unequivocal language and its echo was heard in the assembly. So enraged were the business circles that Shanmukham Chetty, who had participated in the Ottawa deliberations as a member of the Indian delegation nominated by the government, had to resign from the executive committee of the FICCI.[79]

Another incident which incensed an influential section of the industrial community was the Mody-Lees Pact of 1933. This resulted from a tripartite conference which discussed ways and means to check the rising imports of Japanese textile goods into India. The British side led by Sir William Clare-Lees conceded that Indian industry was entitled to a 'measure of protection against the imports of United Kingdom yarn and piece-goods', and the Indians were willing to accept the principle of a lower level of protection against the United Kingdom as compared to other countries. Disagreement, however, arose on specific terms. The English products on which the import duty was sought to be lowered were in direct competition with the Ahmedabad mills which had a greater stake in the production of finer counts. To minimize the danger, therefore, Kasturbhai Lalbhai, one of the FICCI representatives, insisted on fixing a ceiling on imports from the United Kingdom and, when this was rejected, walked out of the conference. Sir Homi Mody, who represented the Bombay Millowners Association, signed the pact on behalf of the Indian cotton manufacturers, splitting the Indian millowinging class as no other event had ever done before. Unconcerned, however, the government ratified the agreement.[80]

Coming as they did on the heels of the decision to fix the rupee-sterling ratio at 18d and tie the Indian currency to the British pound, these two events reinforced the doubts of the nationalist-minded industrialists about the intentions of the government. Industrialists, at the same time, did not fail to notice the rising tempo of economic radicalism in a section of the Congress. Ever since the Lahore Congress, Jawaharlal Nehru, the rising star on the Indian political firmament, was veering towards socialist doctrine and was even willing to 'honour and respect the red flag'[81] which was anathema to the Indian capitalist class. Largely because of his influence on the counsels of the Congress the Karachi session, meeting in the last week of March 1931, adopted the famous resolution on the 'fundamental rights and economic programme' which emphasized, among other things, that 'political freedom must include real economic freedom of the starving millions' and 'safeguard the interests of industrial workers'. The resolution also advocated state control of 'key industries and services, mineral resources, railways, waterways, shipping and other means of transport'.[82]

While Nehru's concept of socialism was still rather vague, a band of young enthusiasts, openly wedded to Marxian doctrines, was becoming very vocal in the Congress. The capitalists, however, believed that Gandhi's overarching presence was a foolproof shield against radical propaganda. And the Mahatma was quick to allay their fears at the annual convention of the FICCI which met barely a week after the Karachi session. Reacting to the complaint of the president, Lala Shri Ram, that the Karachi declaration was issued without consulting the business community on their 'vital interests' concerning economic matters, Gandhi declared in his inaugural address that the Congress 'would always be glad to avail of your advice and help'. To assure his listeners still further he added: 'The Congress stands for the industrial prosperity and progress of India. I cannot forget the services rendered by the commercial classes, but I want to go a step further. I want you to make the Congress your own and we would willingly surrender the reins to you. The work can be better done by you'.[83]

A few years later, when Jayaprakash Narayan and others formed the Congress Socialist Party, the working committee expressed its displeasure and Gandhi publicly attacked their programme.[84] He spoke against them even more bitterly in private conversation with Birla. To the latter's way of thinking, the saint-politician was the most formidable bulwark against the tide of leftist propaganda and a very influential section of the Congress leadership was behind the Mahatma in this respect. As Birla put it soon after the formation of the Congress Socialist Party: 'Vallabhbhai, Rajaji and Rajendra Babu are all fighting communism and socialism. It is, therefore, necessary that we who represent healthy capitalism should help Gandhi as far as possible and work with a common object.'[85] Not all capitalists belittled the radical sceptre and a section of them was to raise a hue and cry against the socialist proclivities of Nehru a couple of years later, but for the time being the rise of the leftist tide did not have much impact on the Congress-industry ties. In fact, Birla never lost hope that even if the Congress as an organization was captured by the radical elements, Gandhi would still carry the country with him and isolate them. He always made a subtle distinction between the Congress and its patron saint.[86]

These were the calculations which guided the endeavours of Birla and his associates, after the break-up of the second Round Table Conference, to bring about a rapprochement between Gandhi and the government. They, however, had little hope to cut any ice as long as the Congress continued with the civil disobedience movement and the government with its repressive measures. After his release from jail, however, when Gandhi called off the agitation, ostensibly to enable his countrymen to devote themselves wholeheartedly to the service of the Harijans, Birla saw the opportunity to revive his mediatory role. On the one hand he became more involved in the Mahatma's anti-untouchability drive and cottage industries programme, on the other he continued to press the authorities to create 'mutual appreciation between leaders in the two countries'.[87] Through his contact with Gandhi, he also sensed that the latter would not be opposed to Congress re-entry into the legislatures.[88]

Birla had not wholly succeeded in removing the distrust between the two parties when the British Parliament passed the Government of India Act of 1935, creating a federal structure for India. Based on the principles of a white paper published earlier, the act gave little satisfaction to the Congress or the business interests, and was denounced by both.[89] Gandhi, however, privately felt that the act was capable of producing good results if worked in the right spirit. Birla, with his uncanny business instinct, concluded that it contained the 'seeds which were to germinate, blossom and bear fruit' in full independence for the country.[90] He, therefore, did not want to let this opportunity slip. With Gandhi's blessing, he proceeded to London immediately after the act was passed and established very useful contacts with the principal leaders of both the major political parties in England, including Lord Linlithgow who was to take over as viceroy in 1936 and was thus to oversee the implementation of the new scheme. He used to send long reports on his discussions with the British leaders to Gandhi in order to keep the undisputed leader of the Congress informed of British thinking.[91]

Birla returned to India in September 1935 with the impression that the imperial authorities were serious about the new constitutional arrangement and that the safeguards provided in the act would not be misused to meddle with the Indian administration, once the Indian ministers joined the government. Without losing a moment, he went straight to Wardha to give his mentor 'a first hand report of my impressions'. Gandhi still remained very sceptical because of his feeling that the friendliness that Birla 'experienced in England did not yet prevail in government circles in India', but he agreed to advise the Congress 'to make no new commitment about the reforms' before the arrival of the new viceroy, and 'promised to use his influence to that end'.[92] If the Congress eventually agreed to give a fair trial to the reform act, Birla's behind-the-scene role – to 'interpret Bapu to Britishers and the Britishers to Bapu' – must be given due credit.

VI

The adoption of the new scheme for the governance of the country provided a sort of respite from confrontational politics, even though the Congress continued to be sceptical about the motives of the British government. The ensuing phase of relative tranquillity, particularly after the formation of the Congress ministries in most of the provinces, witnessed once again a growing nexus between the Congress and the industrialists, as had been the case during the mid-1920s, occasional irritants notwithstanding. It was so because the big business depended on the new governments for all sort of concessions and the Congress ministries demonstrated little of that rabid leftism some had feared.[93] The resignation of the Congress governments did not herald a period of real confrontation. The government did not feel unduly threatened by the individual civil disobedience movement launched by Gandhi in November 1940, and did little to suppress it except arresting the individual satyagrahis. And the Mahatma took pains to explain to the authorities that he had no intention to hinder war efforts; his policy was 'to live and let live' and that he could not at once 'swear by non-violence and embarrass England in the hour of her difficulty'.[94]

It was no surprise under these conditions that during the initial phase of the Second World War, the Indian industrialists did not see any contradiction between supporting the war efforts on the one hand and expressing sympathies for the national movement on the other. Not only people like Lala Shri Ram, who according to his biographers 'cooperated with the English rulers and eagerly sought honours from them'[95] but also men like Walchand Hirachand, who invariably invited Congress leaders to preside over the inauguration of his industrial ventures, cooperated in producing goods and services required by the government. Sir Homi Mody, a director of Tata Sons, agreed to serve on the viceroy's executive council with the permission of his house, and G.D. Birla assured the viceroy that 'no man among Indians has worked harder to help him or stood more loyally by him than myself'.[96] And yet Churchill did not hesitate to charge the Indian big business of being behind the Congress. That his suspicion was not entirely baseless was confirmed by G.L. Mehta, the FICCI president, who declared that the 'Indian commercial organizations did not feel apologetic about the fact that they were fully in accord with the essentials of Congress demand for freedom and transfer of power'.[97]

There was a subtle but significant change in this position as Gandhi drew closer to the confrontation of 1942. Just before the adoption of the 'Quit India' resolution by the Congress, Purshotamdas Thakurdas – according to his biographer, he never hesitated 'to throw the full weight of his support' for the British – joined a group of industrialists including G.D. Birla and J.R.D. Tata, the leaders of the two opposite camps, to assure the viceroy of their opposition to a politics of open conflict. 'We are all businessmen', they wrote in their memorandum, 'and therefore we need hardly point out that our interest lies in peace, harmony, good will and order throughout the country'.[98] And during the holocaust that engulfed the country following the arrest of the Congress leaders, they lived up to this assurance. We have no evidence of any material support from the industrial bourgeoisie to the agitators. A few, however, acquiesced in the strikes of the workers in their factories. It is difficult to fathom their motives in the absence of full records, but the following account left by Kasturbhai Lalbhai may provide some clue:

> Indian National Congress Committee met at Bombay in August 1942 and passed the Quit India resolution. I happened to be in Bombay then; so was Khandubhai Desai of the Labour Union. We were returning to Ahmedabad by the Gujarat Mail. We met and discussed our plans in the train. The government was in an ugly mood because the Second World War was at its height and hence they would not be hesitating in imprisoning anyone they thought undesirable. We, therefore, decided that it will be a safe and desirable policy to send away the workers to their villages so that the mills cannot work and no blame can be attached to any particular person. The next morning Ambalal Sarabhai came to see me at my house and said there is going to be three days' strike as a result of the arrests of the national leaders. I said you wait and see. He asked, what I meant. I told him that it is going to be a protracted strike as Khandubhai and I had decided. All the Ahmedabad mills closed down and workers went away to their villages. It attracted attention all over the world as nearly one hundred thousand workers remained on strike, reducing the cloth production vitally required for war. At the end of nearly three months I felt that the mills should be restarted. I got in contact with Khandubhai Desai who was then in jail and obtained his consent.[99]

It appears that the Ahmedabad magnate went along with the proposal of the union leader with a view to avoiding needless confrontation with the workers. Others elsewhere, such as the managements of Mafatlal companies in Bombay and the TISCO in Jamshedpur were guided by similar considerations. It is somewhat significant that Khandubhai Desai did not discuss this move with Ambalal Sarabhai, a stickler for constitutional proprieties, but with Kasturbhai who was much more pragmatic about these things. Whatever their motives, the millowners' acquiescence in their workers' strikes remained a closely guarded secret at that time. They had no intention to incur the wrath of the government.

As the British government's anxiety to placate the Congress became increasingly clear despite the apparent failure of the agitation, the industrialists returned to their dual policy – of benefiting by support to the war efforts and extracting maximum gain from the government on the one hand, and re-establishing a claim on the gratitude of the Congress leadership on the other. They continued to fulfil their obligations under the military contracts and their apex body FICCI agreed to associate itself with the Department of Planning and Reconstruction set up by the government in 1944. At the same time some of them resumed their financial contribution to the Congress. Their political attitude during the days following the 1942 rebellion was best summed by the correspondent of the *New York Times* who after a visit to Ahmedabad in March 1943 wrote : The local millionaires deplored what had been happening in the country and pointed out that their object in life being to make money, like most Indian businessmen, they were keeping one foot in the Congress camp, which they expected to see running the country, and another in the British camp which is running it now and gives them fat orders.[100]

As the possibility that the transfer of power might take place sooner rather than later became more and more distinct, the industrialists' anxiety to draw closer to the Congress became more pronounced. Nothing illustrates it better than their conversion to the concept of economic planning. While it is true that a FICCI president had advised as early as 1934 that 'it would be exceedingly unwise to offer opposition to planning' his organization took no more than 'passing interest in industrial planning and in the work of the National Planning Committee' (NPC)[101] constituted by the Congress in 1938 under Nehru's chairmanship. Despite the fact that some prominent leaders of the FICCI were connected with the committee, the federation refused to contribute even a paltry sum of one thousand rupees, citing budgetary constraints. The NPC could not achieve much in concrete terms, but it was clear to perceptive observers that planning would be an essential component of the economic policy under a future Congress government. It was no surprise therefore that seven prominent businessmen – Purshotamdas Thakurdas, J.R.D. Tata, G.D. Birla, Lala Shri Ram, Ardeshir Dalal, A.D. Shroff, and Kasturbhai Lalbhai – representing all sections of Indian bourgeoisie assisted by John Matthai, a well-known economist close to the Tatas, produced in 1944 what is popularly known as the Bombay Plan.[102] Just a few months earlier Birla had questioned the right of the colonial administration to plan for post-war reconstruction saying: 'Who is going to plan for India, this government or a national government? A promise has been made that after the termination of the war India will get its own government. Will it be right for this government to make any commitments for something which is to be executed by another government?'[103] Now he commended the Bombay Plan to his FICCI colleagues.

He could have as well commended it to the Congress leadership – and with equal success. For the Bombay Plan anticipated in many ways the fundamentals that guided the formulation of the industrial policy of the national government, formed after the transfer of power, and the Five-Year Plans.[104] The authors of the document recognized the need for planned development, emphasized state ownership and control of key industries and concurred with the idea of a central directing authority to ensure successful implementation. Although they assigned a legitimate role to the private sector in the future economic setup, they candidly conceded that it would have to function under tight state direction. They went to the extent of saying that 'practically every aspect of economic life will have to be so rigorously controlled by government that individual liberty and freedom of enterprise will suffer a temporary eclipse'.[105] Much water indeed had flown down the Indus since the FICCI leadership had cried wolf over the Congress resolution on economic policy – a much milder document – passed at its Karachi session not very long ago. Obviously, on the eve of India's independence, the Indian industrialists were anxious to wake up in the new era with as much demonstrated cordiality for the new rulers as possible – a vague reminder of the attitude of the Indian commercial class towards the colonial government before the emergence of Gandhi.

What were the underlying forces that shaped the industrialists' response to the Congress? To say that they were motivated by their class interest is to repeat a truism, but other factors such as their personal equations with the leaders of the national movement as well as the government and the rising tide of patriotism engulfing all segments of society cannot be ignored in our analysis. Eschewing too rigid adherence to consistency, they adopted a pragmatic approach to various issues and developments as they arose from time to time and avoided too pronounced a tilt to any one side – colonial government or the Congress – for fear of alienating the other. With the wisdom of hindsight we may discover a common thread in their response to political developments, but to think that their actions were informed by a well-conceived grand strategy would be an overstatement. A weak and fragmented collectivity, as the Indian industrialists were, can seldom afford such dangerous luxuries.

Notes

* This is a revised and expanded version of a paper published earlier in B.N. Pande and Ravinder Kumar (eds.), *A Centenary History of the Indian National Congress* (Delhi, 1985), vol. II.

1. Bipan Chadra, 'The Indian Capitalist Class and Imperialism before 1947' in *Imperialism and Nationalism in India* (Delhi 1979), pp. 144-70; Claude Markovits, *Indian Business and Nationalist Politics, 1931-39* (London 1985).

2. While Bipan Chandra in the paper cited in note 1 has enunciated the interest-based theory, Rajat K. Ray in his *Industrialization in India* (Delhi 1979), pp. 295 has hinted at the other hypothesis.

3. For a comprehensive discussion see Dwijendra Tripathi, 'Oocuputatiuonal Mobility and Industrial Entrepreneurship in India: A Historical Analysis', *Developing Economics,* IXX (1981), pp. 52-68.

4. A.P. Kannangara, 'Indian Millowners and Indian Nationalism before 1914', *Past and Present,* no. 40 (July 1968), pp. 147-64. Referring to the decision regarding the excise duty, the Bombay Millowners Association observed that 'all things considered the members of the Association have reasons to congratulate themselves that the eventual decision has not been more unfavourable than it is' S.D. Mehta, *Cotton Mills of India, 1854-1954* (Bombay 1954), p.70.

5. N.K. Sinha, 'Indian Business Enterprise: Its Failure in Calcutta (1800-1848), *Bengal Past and Present,* Diamond Jubilee Number (July-December 1967), pp. 112-23.

6. Amalendu Guha, 'Comprador Role of Parsi Seths, 1750-1850' *Economic and Political Weekly, V-48* (28 November 1970) pp. 1933-1936; Dwijendra Tripathi(ed.), *Business Communities of India: A Historical Perspective* (New Delhi 1984).

7. Shirin Mehta, 'Social Background of Swadeshi Movement in Gujarat, 1875-1908', *Viidya,* XIV (1981), pp. 31-46; also see S.D. Mehta, *Cotton Mills*(n.4), pp. 86-8.

8. See for, example, *Bharat Durdasha* of Bharatendu Harishchandra written around 1870 where the poet writes: 'Except that the nations's wealth is diverted abroad, there is allround

prosperity and happiness under the British rule.' Harishchandra is regarded a pioneer of Hindi nationalist poetry. Dalpatram Dahyabhai, a prominent nationalist poet of Gujarat around this period, also expressed the same kind of sentiments. Shirin Mehta, 'Social Background' (n.7), p.32.

9. The writings of these publicists bear this out. See Dadabhai Naoroji, *Essays, Speeches and Writings*, ed. by C.L. Parekh (Bombay 1887); M.G. Ranade, *Essays on Indian Economics* (Bombay 1898); R.C. Dutt, *Speeches and Papers on Indian Questions, 1892-1900* (Calcutta 1904). B.G. Tilak, no admirer of British rule, unreservedly conceded that the 'people were dazzled at first' by the benefits of the British rule. Quoted in G.P. Pradhan and A.K. Bhagwat, *Lokmanya Tilak* (Bombay 1958), p. 72.

10. For the resolutions passed and the speeches delivered at the annual sessions of the Congress, see Annie Besant, *How India Wrought for Freedom*(New Delhi 1975), and Indian National Congress, *Congress Presidential Addresses* (Madras n.d.).

11. Ratna and Rajat Ray, 'European Monopoly Corporations and Indian Entrepreneurship, 1913-1922: Early Politics of Coal In Eastern India', *Economic and Political Weekly*, IX-21 (25 May 1974), pp. M53-M55; Amiya Kumar Bagchi, *Private Investment in India, 1900-1939* (Cambridge 1972), pp. 165-70.

12. Sumit Sarkar, *The Swadeshi Movement in Bengal, 1903-1908* (New Delhi 1977), pp. 117-36; S.D. Mehta, *Cotton Mills* (n.4), pp. 92-3.

13. S.D. Mehta, Cotton Mills (n.4), pp. 90-91; Annie Besant, *How India Wrought for Freedom* (n.10), pp. 528-610; S.K. Sen, *The House of Tatas* (Calcutta 1975), pp. 37-8.

14. For the careers of some of these see S.V. Kirloskar, *Yantrikanchi Yatra* (in Marathi, Kirloskarwadi 1958); G.D. Khanolkar, *Walchand Hirachand; Man, His Times and Achievements* (Bombay 1969); Arun Joshi, *Lala Shri Ram* (New Delhi 1978), B.D. Amin, *The Rise and Growth of the Alembic Chemical Works* (Baroda 1939); Ramkrishna Dalmia, *A short Sketch of the Beginning of My Life and a Guide to Bliss* (New Delhi 1962), N.N. Desai (ed.), *Directory of Ahmedabad Mill Industry, 1929-1956* (Ahmedabad 1957).

15. S.D. Mehta, *Cotton Mills*(n.4), p.106.

16. M.V. Namjoshi, *Chambers of Commerce in India* (Bombay 1967), p. 22.

17. Thomas A Timberg, *The Marwaris* (New Delhi 1978), pp. 166-71; Tripathi, 'Occupational Mobility' (n.3), pp. 62-6; *Bagchi, Private Investment* (n.11), p.216; Verrier Elwin, *The Story of Tata Steel* (privately printed, 1958).

18. For the Congress position see some of the resolutions passed at its annual sessions in Annie Besant, *How India Wrought for Freedom*(n.10), pp. 553-610.

19. Ibid., p.588.

20. Jawaharlal Nehru, *Mahatma Gandhi* (New Delhi 1966), pp. 11-12.

21. For a concise account of some aspects of Gandhian philosophy see B.S. Andholia and D. Tripathi (eds.), *Gleanings from Gandhian Thought* (Jabalpur 1959).

22. G.D. Birla, *In the Shadow of the Mahatma* (Bombay 1968), Introduction, p. xv.

23. While Birla was more active on the political front, Bajaj helped Gandhi in his constructive programme. See Kaka Kalelkar (ed.), *To a Gandhian Capitalist: Correspondence between Mahatma Gandhi and Jamnalal Bajaj* (Wardha 1951); also B.R. Nanda, *In Gandhi's Footsteps: The Life and Times of Jamnalal Bajaj* (Delhi, 1990).

24. A.D. D. Gordon, *Business and Politics: Rising Nationalism and Modernizing Economy in Bombay, 1915-1933* (New Delhi 1978), p. 238.

25. No documentary evidence for Sarabhai's donation is available as it was made anonymously, but his geneorus gesture to Gandhi is common knowledge in Ahmedabad.

26. Dwijendra Tripathi, *Dynamics of a Tradition: Kasturbhai Lalbhai and His Entrepreneurship* (New Delhi 1981), pp. 171-3.

27. Birla, *In the Shadow* (n.22) pp. 8-9, 16-17, 52.

28. Among the bitterest attacks on Gandhian economic philosophy is Jawaharlal Nehru's chapter entitled 'Paradoxes' in his *Autobiography* (London 1936).

29. G.D. Birla quoted in *Sunday*, 26 June-2 July 1983, p. 24.

30. Stanley Kochanek, *Business and Politics in India* (Berkeley 1974), pp. 108-30, 156-96; H. Venkatasubbiah, *Enterprise and Economic Chang: 50 Years of FICCI* (New Delhi 1977), 1-2 Rajat K. Ray, *Industrialization in India* (n.2), pp. 297-309.

31. B.R. Tomlinson, *The Indian National Congress and the Raj* (London 1976), ch. I; S.D. Mehta, *Cotton Mills*(n.4), p. 153.

32. Bagchi, *Private Investment*(n.11), p. 166.

33. G.D. Birla quoted in *Sunday* (n.29), p. 24

34. S. Bhattacharya, 'Cotton Mills and Spinning Wheels: Swadeshi and the Indian Capitalist Class, 1920-22, *Economic and Political Weekly*, II-47 (20 November 1976), pp. 1828-1834.

35. Purshotamdas Thakurdas to N.M. Mazumdar, 7 June 1929. Purshotamdas Thakurdas Collection (hereafter cited as PT collection), Nehru Memorial Museum and Library, New Delhi, file no. 42/II; also see G.D. Birla to Purshotamdas Thakurdas, ibid, 19 June 1929. file no. 42/II; Purshotamdas Thakurdas to G.D. Birla, 30 July 1929, ibid, file no. 42/V. File nos. 24/I and 24/III contain several letters written by businessmen to Purshotamdas Thakurdas against the non-cooperation movement. Also see Jamnadas Dwarkadas, 'Non-Cooperation: A Cry for Halt', *Bombay Chronicle*, 7 June 1920.

36. Kochanek, *Business and Politics in India* (n.30) p. 159.

37. Thakurdas to Sir Henry Craik, 14 September 1920, PT collection, file no. 24/III; Thakurdas to Birla, 11 December 1923, ibid, file no. 42/III.

38. Gandhi to Birla, *In the Shadow* (n. 10) p.586; Birla's speech is reproduced in G.D. Birla, *Path to Prosperity* (Allahabad 1950), pp. 146-53; for the support of others see, *Legislative Assembly Debates*, 14 February 1927, IX-16 (Delhi 1927), pp. 746-85.

43. India: Office of Economic Advisor, *The History of Indian Tariff, 1924-1939* (New Delhi 1940), p. 28.

44. Birla, *Path to Prosperity*(n.40), pp.174-93.

45. Gandhi to Birla, 10 April 1930, in G.D. Birla, *Bapu : A Unique Association* (Bombay 1977), vol. 1, p. 138.

46. Dwijendra Tripathi, 'Silver Qestion, India, and America', *Journal of Indian History*, XLIV (1966), pp. 789-98; K.N.S. Nambudiripad, *A Short History of Indian Currency* (Poona 1955), pp. 144-52.

47. *Legislative Assembly Debates*, 25 January 1927.

48. Birla, *Path to Prosperity*(n.42),pp. 227-42.

49. The correspondence between Birla and Gandhi contained in Birla, *In the Shadow*(n.22) and Birla, *Bapu: A Unique Association* (n.45) 4 vols, provides a good idea of Gandhi's financial demands on the Marwari industrialist. Also see, *Sunday* (n.29), p.25. For the attitude of the Gujarati and Bombay industrialists see Tripathi, *Dynamics of a Tradition* (n.26), pp. 170-90; and Gordon, *Business and Politics*(n.24) pp. 238-9.

50. The Bombay Millowners Association, *Report of 1928* (Bombay 1929), pp. ii-iv; Ambalal Sarabhai to Thakurdas, 5 November 1929 and reply; Naoroji to Thakurdas, 28 March 1930; Birla to Thakurkdas, 3 November, 1929, PT collection, file no. 91; Mazumdar to Thakurdas, 22 May 1929 and Thakurdas to Mazumdar, 7 June 1929; Birla to Thakurdas , 26 April 1929, ibid, file no. 42/II; S.D. Mehta, *Cotton Mills* (n.4), p. 167.

51. Birla to Gandhi, 11 November 1929, in Birla, *In the Shadow,* (n.22), pp,40.-1.

52. Sumit Sarkar, 'The Logic of Gandhian Nationalism: The Civil Disobedience and the Gandhi-Irwin Pact (1930-31), *Indian Historical Review,* III (1976), p. 121; Gordon, *Businessmen and Politics* (n.24), pp. 229-33.

53. Sarabhai to Thakurdas, 17 November 1930, and reply, PT collection, file no. 42/II.

54. Niranjan Bhagat et al. (eds.), *Tribute to Ethics: Remembering Kasturbhai Lalbhai* (Ahmedabad 1983), p. 68.

55. For this interpretation see Gordon, *Businessmen and Politics* (n.24), pp. 200-1. On the possible gain to the mill industry, see Birla to Gandhi, 28 April 1930 in Birla, *Bapu*(n.45),vol.I, pp. 140-2.

56. See, for instance, D.P. Khaitan's address to the Indian Chamber of Commerce, Calcutta, 5 March 1930, *Annual Report for 1930* (Calcutta 1931). Also see Sumit Sarkar, 'The Logic of Gandhian Nationalism' (n.52), pp. 122-3.

57. Federation of Indian Chambers of Commerce and Industry, *Annual Report for 1930* (New Delhi 1931).

58. Thakurdas to Irwin, 31 May 1930, PT collection, file no. 99/II.

59. Arun Joshi, *Lala Shri Ram* (n.14), pp. 223-5; Bhagat et al. (eds.), *Tribute to Ethics* (n.54),p. 69.

60 Venkatasubbiah, *Enterprise and Economic Change*(n.30), pp. 14-15.

61. Bhagat et al. (eds.), *Tribute to Ethics*(n.54), p. 69.

62. Birla to Thakurdas, 16 January 1931, PT collection, file no. 42/VII.

63. Sumit Sarkar, 'The Logic of Gandhian Nationalism' (n.52) has given a brief account of the official reports, pp. 133-4; Thakurdas to Mody (undated but appears to have been written in August 1930), PT collection, file no. 100.

64. Jawaharlal Nehru, *Autobiography* (n. 28)p. 232.

65. Thakurdas to Motilal Nehru, 22 September 1930, PT collection, file no. 104; Thakurdas to D.P. Khaitan, 8 October 1930, ibid., file no. 99/II.

66. Gandhi to Birla, 16 December 1930 in Birla, *Bapu*(n.45) vol. I. p. 148.

67. Gandhi's telegram to Thakurdas in Navjivan Trust, *Collected Works of Mahtma Gandhi* (Ahmedabad 1971), vol. XIV, p. 165; Summit Sarkar, 'The Logic of Gandhian Nationalism (n.52), p. 141.

68. Gandhi to Irwin, 14 February 1931, *Collected Works*(n.67), vol. XLV, pp. 175-6.

69. Sumit Sarkar, 'The Logic of Gandhian Nationalism' (n.52) p. 141.

70. Venkatasubbiah, *Enterprise and Economic Change* (n.30), p.16.

71. Birla to Jayakar, 2 December 1931, in Birla, *In the Shadow,* (n.22), pp.46-7.

72. Venkatasubbiah, *Enterprise and Economic Change*(n.30), p. 17.

73. Birla to Samuel Hoare, 14 February 1932, *In the Shadow*(n.22), p.49; Rajat K.Ray, *Industrialization in India*(n.2), p. 322.

74. For a feel of the nature of Birla's correspondece with some of the key persons see Birla, *In the Shadow*(n.22), pp. 41-67.

75. The correspondence between Birla and Gandhi is contained in Birla, *Bapu* (n.45), vol. I. pp. 140-55.

76. Birla to Samuel Hoare, 14 March 1932, in Birla, *In the Shadow* (n.22), p. 52.

77. Birla to Thakurdas, 28 November 1930, PT collection, file no. 42/VII.

78. Birla to Tej Bahadur Sapru, 31 October 1931, in Birla, *In the Shadow* (n.22), pp. 42-5.

79. Venkatausubbiah, *Enterprise and Economic Change*(n.30), pp. 32-5.

80. S.D. Mehta, *Cotton Mills*(n.4), p. 182; also Tripathi, *Dynamics of a Tradition* (n.26), pp. 179-80.

81. Nehru's statement on 28 January 1930. Jawaharlal Nehru Memorial Fund, *Selected Works*(New Delhi 1973), vol. IV, p.232; Bipan Chandra, *Nationalism and Colonialism in Modern India* (New Delhi 1979), pp. 172-3.

82. Indian National Congress, *Resolutions on Economic Policy and Allied Matters* (New Delhi 1969), pp. 3. 6-9.

83. Arun Joshi, *Lala Shri Ram* (n.14), pp. 226-7.

84. Indian National Congress, *Resolutions* (n.82). See the resolution of 18 June 1934 on pp. 9-10. For the reaction of the Socialists, see P.L. Lakhanpal, *History of the Congress Socialist Party* (Lahore 1946), pp. 44-5.

85. Birla to Thakurdas, 3 August 1934, PT collection, file no. 42/II.

86. Birla to Samuel Hoare, 14 March 1932, in Birla, *In the Shadow* (n.22), p. 51; also see Birla's record of an interview with Sir Henry Craik on 30 June 1935, ibid, p. 145.

87. Ibid., pp. 60-130.

88. Ibid., pp. 128-9

89. Venkatasubbiah, *Enterprise and Economic Change*(n.30), p.18.

90. Birla, *In the Shadow*(n.22),p. 130.

91. Ibid., pp. 157-86.

92. Ibid., p.181.

93. Markovits, *Indian Business and Nationalist Politics* (n.1), pp. 150-78.

94. Birla, *Bapu* (n.45), vol. IV, p.136; P. Sitaramayya, *The History of the Indian National Congress* (Bombay 1957), vol I. p. 278.

95. Khuswant Singh and Arun Joshi, *Shri Ram; A Biography* (Bombay 1968), pp. 8-12.

96. Birla, Bapu (n.45), vol.IV,pp. 190-91.

97. Quoted in H. Venkatasubbiah, *Enterprise and Economic Change* (n.30), p. 41.

98. Frank Moreaes, *Sir Purshotamdas Thakurdas* (n.40). pp. 213, 219.

99. Unpublished Autobiographical Notes of Kasturbhai Lalbhai, courtesy Shrenik K. Lalbhai, Ahmedabad.

100. Venkatasubbiah, *Enterprise and Economic Change* (n. 97), p.42. A note on 'Congress and Big Business' prepared by the Intelligence Bureau of the Home Department, Government of India in 1944 referred to the industrialists' financial help to the Congress. The *New York Times* quotation is from the same source. See Suniti Kumar Ghosh, *The Indian Big Bourgeoisie* (Calcutta 1985), pp. 228-29.

101. Venkatasubbiah, *Enterprise and Economic Change*(n. 30), p. 22.

102. P. Thakurdas et al., *A Brief Memorandum Outlining a Plan of Economic Development for India* (Bombay 1944).

103. Quoted in Venkatasubbiah, *Enterprise and Economic Change* (n. 30), p. 49.

104. This was ably domonstrated by H.V.R. Iyengar in his A.D. Shroff Memorial Lecture delivered in 1967. See, Forum of Free Enterprise, *The Bombay Plan and Other Essays* (Bombay 1968), pp. 1-17.

105. Thakurdas et al., *Plan of Economic Development* (n. 102), p. 48.

4

Indian National Congress and Politics of the Capitalist Class

Bhagwan Josh

The most important characteristic of all the studies which have so far attempted to understand the relationship of the capitalist class, or more precisely the bourgeoisie, with the Indian National Congress (INC) is the assumption that the answer to the following important question already exists: What was the INC before 1947? How is one to conceptualize this institution?

The authors[1] claiming to be Marxists (including the sophisticated ones) have operated with the following definition: The Indian National Congress was a party of the Indian bourgeoisie having links with the liberal landlords,[2] although some have emphasized the multi-class character of the national movement. This definition of the INC was first formulated by the Third International and was later on picked up by R.P. Dutt in his *India Today.* Over time this has become the popular definition of the INC transcending the narrow Marxist circles. This definition is based on the assumption that in a society with contradictory class interests each political party represents the interests of one basic class. Given this framework, the object of research turns out to be to show how in each conjuncture, situation or decision the leadership of the movement, despite its relative autonomy, ultimately ends up doing exactly the same as desired by the basic class which the leaders are supposed to represent ideologically. In other words, the object of this type of research is to 'lay bare' the 'class essence' hidden behind the ideological and political moves or positions of the leaders and depicting the trajectory of their decisions along which they 'fall' towards the *a priori* 'essence' under the pressures, manipulations, threats, financial clouts or ideological hegemony of their basic class.[3]

Throughout the history of the communist movement in India the class character of the Congress has remained one of the most fundamental questions. Various assessments, sometimes contradictory, have been made and discarded from time to time. Even when the communists operated with the above definition, doubts were expressed regarding the correctness of such a conceptualization. For example, during the so-called United Front period (1936-40) the following two contradictory characterizations were attempted. The first, formulated in 1936, stated:

> In so far as the INC represented the class interests of the bourgeoisie up to the present and has played a counter-revolutionary role it might be called a bourgeois counter-revolutionary organisation but in so far as it is an organisation whose membership for the most part consists of the 'people' whose interests are objectively anti-imperialist it might be called a people's organisation. Here again the definition is misleading since it obscures the fact that INC is still for the most part dominated by the bourgeoisie despite the growing disillusionment of the masses with bourgeois leadership. *The facts about INC cannot be stated in these static terms at all*[4] [emphasis added].

It is obvious from the last line in the above paragraph that communists were dissatisfied with this definition formulated in 'static terms'. Their search for a dynamic definition led them to a different conclusion. Their joining the ranks of the Congress enabled them to 'see' within two years that all the 'Congress leaders do not speak the same language'. The fact that 'the left-wing led by the socialists dominated the provincial working committee' of the United Provinces forced the communists to reject the view which projected the Congress as 'an homogeneous whole representing homogeneous class interests and characterised by a uniform ideology'.[5] At this juncture they advanced in 1938 the following dynamic definition of the Congress:

> From a narrow parliamentary platform it (National Congress) has grown into the central mass political organisation of the Indian people ranged against imperialism. The mass struggles of the Non-cooperation days and Civil Disobedience Movement of 1930-32 set a *process of transformation* in motion. With the broadening of the Congress which came about during the course of the struggle and through subsequent developments, the characterisation of the Congress

> as a bourgeois organisation became more and more inadequate. *We failed to understand, anticipate and guide this process* because we isolated ourselves from the mass under Congress influence who participated in this struggle led by the Congress. The formulation that the Congress is a bourgeois organisation and as such unsuitable to be the basis for building the anti-imperialist people's front is wrong in the given situation today[6] [emphasis added].

The point we want to emphasize is that before we explore the relationship between the capitalists and the INC it is necessary to spell out the basic character of the Congress.[7] To do so, a distinction must be drawn between an ordinary political party like the present-day Congress(I) and a people's organization in which various ideological currents contest with each other. Unlike an ordinary party, a mass organization allows various ideological platforms, more radical than the consensus programme, to be preached within its ranks. Not only that, it also keeps open the possibility of such platforms acquiring majority support and becoming dominant within the organization. Thus, unlike the ordinary political party the people's movement is always open to transformation into its opposite. If towards the end of 1947 INC was 'more bourgeois – less socialistic', it was not because it was destined to be so from the very beginning.[8] It was partly due to the manner in which the left currents in the country perceived the INC and played their role inside it or related to it from outside.[9] Given this dynamic conception of the INC, the Indian capitalist class was called upon to evolve a relationship with a political institution which was characterised by a *process of transformation.* It is this process and its anticipated consequences which imparted a sense of ambivalence and complexity to the behaviour of the capitalist class. An analysis of the non-cooperation and civil disobedience movements would bear this out.

I

Because of the specific character of the modern centralized colonial state[10] in India the national movement, over a period, came to evolve two types of opposition to it: constitutional and non-constitutional. By bringing the masses into the national movement Gandhi not only changed the meaning of nationalism but also transformed the Indian National Congress as a political formation. During the non-cooperation movement Gandhi appealed to all the merchants and millowners to desist from dealing in foreign cloth and the use of imported yarn. The emerging mass movement of the Indian people had left the capitalist class with two choices: either they came along (or stayed neutral) or opposed it. But as Gandhi unequivocally stated: '... whether they do [come along] or not the country's march to freedom cannot be made to depend upon any corporation or groups of men. This is a mass manifestation. The masses are moving rapidly towards deliverance, and they must move whether with the aid of the organised capital or without'.[11]

At different points of time there were sections of traders, merchants, and businessmen who supported the national movement while others opposed it. By and large nationalist capitalists fought on two fronts simultaneously – against imperialism and the Congress left wing – upholding nationalist positions along the path of constitutional struggles. Within the ideological spectrum of nationalist opposition, the political perspective of the nationalist capitalists can be located as a delicate balance between liberals (Sapru, Jayakar, etc.) and the Swarajists. The capitalists distinguished their political perspective on the one hand from the liberals' reluctant loyalty to the colonial rulers and on the other the Swarajists' tendency of going over to the position of non-constitutional opposition during the time of mass upsurges. They identified themselves with the objectives and aspirations of Motilal Nehru and C.R. Das but preferred the methods of Sapru and Jayakar. The political perspective of the capitalist class completely overlapped with that of the Congress during the periods of council entry but as soon as the rumblings of the mass movement (i.e. beginning of the non-constitutionalist phase) threatered the horizon and Congress constitutionalists left the councils and joined hands with the Congress non-constitutionalists in the open battle against imperialism, the capitalist class oriented itself towards the liberals who, in the meanwhile had already shifted their political perspective to a relatively more radical posture under the pressure of mass upsurge. The liberals' changed perspective, therefore, coincided with that of the capitalist class. It is common knowledge that during the non-cooperation movement industrialists neither actively participated in the agitation nor contributed liberally to various funds.[12]

Keeping themselves within the bounds of the constitutional path, intelligent capitalists, on the one hand pointed out to the government those forces which believed sincerely in the bonafides of its concern for the 'welfare' of India and, on the other, to those which were telling the masses 'openly and directly that the honesty of the Government of India or of Great Britain is gone'.[13] For a short span of time Sir Purshotamdas Thakurdas was the secretary of the committee leading the anti-noncooperation movement in Bombay. Assuring the government that big business did not support the mass movement he wrote to Sir Thomas Holland: 'The classes that have no stake in the country are mustering strong round about Gandhi. The commercial classes are naturally more thoughtful and more anxious about the wisdom of such action.'[14] The example of anti-noncooperation league was being emulated in other places.[15] It was clear to Thakurdas that 'the policy of noncooperation adopted by the Congress, was 'most dangerous and suicidal'. The Western India National Liberal Association, in active alliance with sections of the capitalists, formed a propaganda committee to explain the real purpose of Gandhi's movement and with this end in view distributed numerous handbills. One of the leaflets stated:

> The last resolution of the Congress Committee called for volunteers to overthrow the state, the creed of Lenin, and the communists and the Moscow international. The method of attack is defiance of the law; the object of the attack is to bring the Government, that is the state or organised society to a stand-still. Stripped of all its verbiage, the creed of Gandhism, in its latest and most definite enunciation comes to nihilism, pure and simple. And it will lead India to the same wretched state that Leninism has taken Russia. Because noncooperation is Leninism – pure and unadulterated.[16]

Thakurdas criticized both the government and the Congress for creating problems in the path of political reforms.[17] The authorities were told that in order to fight non - cooperation successfully government must change its policy: 'Imperial policy will have to be the rule of India for the benefit and best interests of India and the Indian first and the Empire next. Unless this is clearly and practically shown, nothing will inspire confidence from the people in the government. The masses are getting more and more fed up with the policy being followed now'.[18] A little later, on 3 January 1922, seven respected figures convened a conference in Bombay of politicians representing different provinces stating that 'a considerable body of opinion in this country is anxious to see a settlement effected which would make it possible to secure the redress of political grievances and the satisfaction of national aspiration in an atmosphere of peace and harmony'.[19]

With the withdrawal of the non - cooperation movement and the emergence of the Swaraj Party, INC entered into the constitutional phase. Now its political perspective coincided with the political perspective of the capitalist class. Apart from the currency issue, the

Swarajists took up the cause of the capitalist class on many other matters.[20] Sir Purshotamdas, representing the Indian Merchants Chamber, was examined in the legislative assembly on 17 October 1924 by the Reforms Enquiry Committee on a memorandum in which he had urged the abolition of diarchy, the introduction of provincial autonomy and increased responsibility for the central government. He averred :

> If the suggestions made by me are introduced and carried out in the same genuine spirit in which I submit them, I am convinced that the risk from the changes would be, or, in fact, can be small. The stake of the commercial community in the continued good Government of India for ever hereafter is immense. Take away orderly and peaceful government at any time for India, and the first to suffer will be the community dependent on trade and commerce and industry. No adequate safeguard for good government can, therefore, be overlooked by such a community in the demand for constitutional reform at any stage . . . . But in his zeal for the safeguarding of property and person, no Indian can forever stand in the way of constitutional reforms.[21]

Commenting on Sir Purshotamdas's memorandum and its press reports, Motilal Nehru wrote to him:

> I have carefully read the memorandum enclosed in your letter and have seen the report of your viva-voce examination reported in the press . . . . I heartily congratulate you on your success. What is specifically gratifying to me is that you have practically identified yourself and through you the commercial interests of Bombay with the swarajists' demand. It cannot now be said that the swarajists' aims are incompatible with ordered development of commerce and industry and when your evidence is read with the last declaration of the commercial and industrial policy made by the Swarajya party in Calcutta there is little doubt left that commerce cannot have better and stronger allies in the political sphere than the swarajists.[22]

The efforts of Motilal Nehru, Jinnah and Thakurdas brought the three main strands of constitutionalists – liberals, Swarajists and independents led by Jinnah – closer to each other during the years 1923-27,[23] when there was intense cooperation between Swarajists and the capitalist class. In a letter to Sir F.E. Dinshaw, Motilal Nehru wrote to convey his 'need of much larger funds than we did in August last'.[24] He told him, however, that what he had to 'impress upon your Bombay and Ahmedabad friends is the purely business point of view. The cotton Excise Duty Resolution has been duly passed but there is good deal to be done before the duty is actually abolished. Then there are many other commercial problems and it is most essential for effective work in the Assembly to have the strength of the whole country behind us'.[25] The response from Thakurdas was encouraging: 'As far as Bombay is concerned, I think you will command the confidence of a large majority, if not all'.[26]

By 1928, however, the members of the capitalist class were expressing their inability to keep their financial promises. There were two reasons for their changed attitude: economic constraints due to depression and the rise of the left wing within the INC which was actively organizing the working class in Bombay.[27] This left bloc within the INC had played an important role in the demonstrations against the Simon Commission on its arrival in Bombay in February 1928. It was for the first time that the working class was participating in the political movement under a left wing leadership. The first sign of a renewal of radicalization within the Congress was the intervention by the left at the annual session of the INC held at Madras in 1927, where the independence resolution was passed under Jawaharlal Nehru's influence. The coming events showed more definite trends towards the emergence of an embryonic left bloc within the INC.

An important symptom of radicalization was the sharp upswing in the curve of industrial strikes beginning in 1928. In the course of that year the strike wave reached a new intensity, with more workers involved in strikes than at any time since 1921, and with a total loss of working days far exceeding anything previously witnessed – 31 million as against an earlier peak of 13 million in 1925. The strikes in this period were 'bitter and fought with a determination and vigour which were not so much in evidence during the earlier periods'.[28] The biggest strike covered 130,000 workers employed in the textile mills of Bombay. Led by a joint strike committee under the leadership of N.M. Joshi and the Workers and Peasants Party, it started in April and lasted till October 1928.[29] It was a well-planned activity and leaders had carried on vigorous propaganda much before the strike actually started.

The strike divided the capitalist class between those who possessed a political vision and those who, according to G.D. Birla, were apolitical, narrow-minded and short-sighted. Birla condemned the reduction of workers' wages, which was among the causes of the strike, and thought that millowners' 'reactionary attitude in politics has already lost them the sympathy of reasonable people'.[30] Similar sentiments were expressed by Ambalal Sarabhai and Walchand Hirachand.[31] The other group of capitalists led by Dorabji Tata, F.E. Dinshaw and Cowasji Jehangir were thinking of forming a separate political party outside the INC. They also felt that on the Public Safety Bill – primarily directed against the communists – the milloweners should support the government and not the nationalists who were opposed to the bill.

In the early months of 1928 attempts were made by the Congress leaders to establish a much closer alliance between these business interests and the Congress. For this purpose it was decided that Mahatma Gandhi, Motilal Nehru and Dr Ansari should go to Bombay to discuss the matters in detail.[32] The Mahatma, however, informed Dr Ansari from Sabarmati: 'I am in constant touch with the representatives of millowners and so far as I am aware nothing is going to come out of these negotiations. The millowners have decided upon a separate organisation of their own from which they wish to eschew politics altogether'.[33] In a telegram Purshotamdas asked Motilal to communicate with Lalji Naranji as he himself 'cannot say anything'.[34] Motilal was very annoyed with the antics of the millowners and wrote to Lalji Naranji:[35]

> Allow me .... to congratulate you and other millowners of Bombay on the new phase of devotion and loyalty to the government and the banks it controls so rapidly developed after the abolition of excise duty .... I have been thinking over the matter ever since I received your telegram and it is now my considered opinion that the Congress should welcome this change in the attitude of the millowners. An alliance between the Congress and the capitalists who are bent on profiteering by the sufferings of the nation is an impossible one. The more suitable field of work for the Congress is among the workers and not in the owners of the mills. But I was misled by the patriotic talk of some of my personal friends among the millowners. Mahatmaji never believed in an alliance with the latter, and I have now told him that he was right and I was wrong. Our line of action is now clear. We have to deal

> with the enemy within and guard ourselves against it before we can offer battle to the enemy from without.

In a subsequent letter to Purshotamdas he reiterated : 'My opinion about the millowners as a class was not formed in a hurry but is the result of several years' experience of them. There are, of course honourable exceptions which prove the rule.'[36] Dorabji Tata was of the view that a new party was needed to be formed as 'our politicians have rather failed to safeguard the essential economic interests of the country; have failed to stand up against the Red leaders of disruption'.[37] G.D. Birla and Purshotamdas Thakurdas, on the other hand, perceived this move as 'a form of disruption among businessmen in Bombay' and vehemently opposed the attempt to set up an organization of the capitalists with the idea of joining hands with government to fight their 'common enemy' i.e. communism. Dorabji recognized the conflict of interests between the Indian and the English commercial communities in India and agreed with Thakurdas and Birla that as far as 'we are concerned Indian interests predominate'.[38] The strike wave was in full swing till the first half of July 1929, and a section of the capitalist was 'convinced of the necessity of a strong capitalist organisation to combat this poisonous evil'.[39] They did not want to sit with 'folded hands' and leave the serious matter of safeguarding the industry and commerce to politicians who were so 'unhappily divided'.[40] On the question of fighting their 'common enemy' Dorabji advocated a united front of all those who wanted to eradicate the 'communist menace' *irrespective of nationality:*

> . . . . they [European capitalists] are certainly at one with us where the red flag is concerned, and while they are so, can we not use their interest and their motive against the common enemy. . . ? And if looked upon in this light, would it not be better if everyone concerned met together to see how best the campaign could be organised, so that each body in co-operation with others, makes the worth of the whole, all the more effective in dealing with the evil?[41]

What was being debated was the question of the primary and secondary social contradictions. In other words, the question which was being posed was this: who is the main enemy of the Indian capitalist class? The question of struggle for class interests was not irrespective of nationality. This conception of national contradiction being primary and class contradiction being secondary was never lost sight of by Birla and Thakurdas. Explaining his point of view the latter wrote to Dorabji:[42]

> I am . . . . by experience convinced that the *only method* [emphasis added] of co-operation with the European commercial community is when they realise in the Indian commercial community sufficient strength both of character and of means to stand on their just rights and to stand out for the best interests of their motherland. It is pity that at the moment this does not exist in India to the desired extent, but to beat a retreat at this stage and to join hands with the European commercial community without making it clear to them that we are Indians first and merchants and industrialists afterwards, appears to me to be a wrong move.

Thakurdas had voted against the Public Safety Bill.[43] But without advocating a firm stand on the side of the nationalists, he tried his best to impress upon Dorabji that 'the new Association is the surest method of alienating the sympathies of the various political parties in the Assembly, who all agree as to the protection and relief to be given to Indian commerce and industry'.[44] In the opinion of Birla: 'The salvation of the capitalist does not lie in joining hands with reactionary elements . . . . What we capitalists can do towards driving this evil (Bolshevik influence) out of India is to remove the root causes so far as we are concerned and also *co-operate with those who through constitutional means want to change the Government for a national one*'[45] (emphasis added). Most of the capitalists', he added, 'ignore the fact that to some extent they themselves are responsible for breeding communism, and I have not the least doubt in my mind that a purely capitalist organisation is the last body to put up an effective fight against communism'. The logical conclusion of Birla's argument was that communism could be fought only by opposing British imperialism as well as by strengthening the hands of the constitutionalists and right wingers within the INC. As he put it in a letter to Thakurdas:

> Vallabhbhai, Rajaji and Rajendra Babu are all fighting communism and socialism. It is therefore necessary that some of us who represent the healthy capitalism should help Gandhiji as far as possible and work with a common object . . . . I do not think there is the slightest disagreement between us and Gandhiji as regards the representation

> of the commercial community . . . . I do not see any difference between your and my views or between our combined views and the views of Vallabhbhai.[46]

The Indian Merchants Chamber played a very active role by acting as conciliators between the government on the one side and Gandhi and Patel on the other to create an atmosphere for negotiations leading to an honourable settlement of Bardoli question.[47] Birla even suggested that instead of Vallabhbhai businessmen should deposit the excess revenue with the government. 'In this way', he argued, 'while the Government can feel that they had their way Mr. Vallabhbhai in his turn can feel that he was in no way concerned with such payments.'[48] From 1928 onwards, the leaders of the capitalist class actively pursued the policy of mediating between the Congress and the government by constantly remaining in touch with both the sides. The contradictory pulls under which the capitalists were placed demanded of them restraint, calm and poise of a 'tightrope walker'. They were called upon to evolve extreme subtleties of behaviour, of mixing firmness with politeness, threat with cooperation and distrust with apparent trust. The same individual who figured in their 'private letters' to the bureaucracy as 'dear friend' was termed as enemy in their own internal discussions. With one hand they would finance the INC while the other would be extended with friendship towards the bureaucracy.[49]

II

By March 1929, Gandhi was declaring that he fully realized the tremendous consequences of civil disobedience and the no-tax campaign but 'a man who is mad as I am now after freedom has got to take tremendous risks'.[50] Meanwhile the viceroy declared that a round table conference would be called to discuss problems connected with the next constitutional reform. On 1 November, a meeting of important political leaders issued a statement known as the Delhi Manifesto.[51] The Congress leaders wanted an assurance that the proposed Round Table Conference (RTC) would draft a constitution setting up dominion status for India and this constitution would be brought into force immediately. As we have stated earlier, whenever there was some opportunity, the capitalist class considered it its duty to see that a conciliatory atmosphere was created. On the one hand it would impress upon the government through various channels to give concessions to the Congress so as to avoid the Congress falling into the hands of the extremists while on the other it would impress upon the Congress leaders the dangers of starting a mass movement. Birla and Thakurdas had played an active role in framing the Delhi Manifesto.[52] The period between the Lahore session of the Congress (31 December 1929) and the Dandi March (5 April 1930) was full of hectic activity as far as the representatives of the capitalist class were concerned. They immediately jumped into the fray to use the Congress threat of civil disobedience for securing dominion status for India. All their efforts were orientated towards building a bridge between the government and the Congress leadership.

At this stage Birla tried to get Gandhiji to attend the RTC but Gandhi was on the eve of launching the civil disobedience campaign and was deeply preoccupied with it. 'I have *never counselled you on political matters*', wrote Birla, 'but under the present circumstances I have felt it necessary . . . . Let us not miss this opportunity. Even if the conference fails in its purpose, *we shall stand to gain in as much as the left-wingers will come to the fore*. Both ways we stand to gain'[53] (emphasis added). Despite his best efforts Birla could not prevail upon Gandhi to attend the first Round Table Conference.[54] Now it was Thakurdas's turn. Pointing out to a resolution of the Lahore session of the Congress, he wrote to Gandhi:

> The repudiation of debts as approved by the INC at their Lahore session by their resolution No. 10 has had considerable effect on the securities market both in England and in India . . . . I mention this to show what anxiety this resolution of the Congress has created in the minds of the investors in London. To members of the commercial community the depreciation in gilt-edged securities gives enormous anxiety.[55]

Gandhi's reply to this letter was sharp and clear:

> I hope you are not among those who believe that by a mere change of constitution the starving ryots will find themselves in a position to pay a larger revenue than they are paying today. In my opinion the only meaning of swaraj to these people will be an appreciable reduction in the taxes that they are paying directly and indirectly and fixity of tenure. This cannot happen until we, who are partners with the British administrators in the game of the exploitation of

the masses, are prepared to change the angle of our vision even as we expect the former to do.[56]

Thakurdas then pleaded like Birla that Gandhi should first participate in the RTC instead of launching a mass movement:

> If the constitution is not sufficiently changed after the conference in London as to make us masters in our own house i.e. to give Indians complete control over their domestic affairs, I can understand your impatience. But to resort to civil disobedience during the brief intervening period does strike me as being a hasty step . . . . I, therefore, submit with all deference, that the programme which the Indian National Congress resolved upon at Lahore is not conducive to the interests of India, especially in view of the present circumstances in which we are placed'.[57]

The Mahatma's answer was precise and to the point: 'I must not enter into an argument with you, for argument is useless when conviction on either side is deep-seated. I can only give you my assurance that I shall take no hasty step. A risky step need not necessarily be a hasty step'.[58]

Another important capitalist Lalji Naranji was of the view that it was very necessary that the merchant community told the British that the government was responsible for precipitating this serious situation by denying to India the 'real control of the purse of the country' and 'it will be the only solution that will save India from going into further troubles'.[59] At the same time 'we can also tell politicians *including Mahatma Gandhi* that it is *undesirable* [emphasis added] to create a feeling of disregard for authority which will have very disastrous after-effects which no government of swaraj will be able to recover [sic] and bring the country back to normal conditions'.[60] The Bombay Presidency Association, an organization of a section of the Bombay capitalists and liberal politicians, passed a resolution around the same time: 'The Council of Bombay Presidency Association strongly deplores the action of the Indian National Congress in calling upon the country to adopt the goal of independence and to resort to civil disobedience'.[61] With the launching of the civil disobedience movement the Congress was entering into a new phase of transformation.[62] This is how J.K. Mehta, secretary, Indian Merchants Chamber perceived this transformation:[63]

> .... the Congress is fast becoming a party organisation. As constituted formally it had room in it for men of all shades of political opinion and economic views. Rightly or wrongly *it is becoming a labour organisation* [emphasis added]. We need not attack the Congress or try to undermine its position, but we must now recognise that the Congress is also a party organisation and its policies and principles need not be deemed as above criticism.[63]

Interestingly, at the beginning of 1929 when the *transformation process* within the Congress began to be activated, the Indian communists declared that the Congress was a party of the Indian bourgeoisie and it would not lead the Indian people's struggle for freedom against imperialism. They got out of the Congress to form an underground, centralized Communist Party with the aim of creating an alternative mass movement. They also declared that civil disobedience was a sham struggle and refused to participate in the mass upsurge. Later on, however, they conceded that this was a wrong assessment, as has been pointed out earlier.[64] Undoubtedly, their active participation in the movement in the form of left bloc would have further accentuated the transformation process. It was partly due to the communists' policy that the working class did not participate in the movement in Bombay overwhelmingly.[65]

The leading ideologues of the capitalist class were also opposed to the civil disobedience movement. But once Gandhi started the movement they were willing to extend some support to it.[66] Thakurdas wrote to Sir George Schuster: 'I myself believe that if Government does things too late even Mr Gandhi may be disowned by the Congress people and the real mischief-mongers may get the upper hand in the Congress .... Mr Gandhi's agitation is bad but it may prove to be better than some other more vicious agitation to follow, should Government hold out unduly'.[67] In another letter to a member of the House of Commons he stressed the need to grant dominion status to India as soon as possible to 'take the wind out of the sails of the Congress'.[68] As the civil disobedience gained more momentum, he sensed great danger ahead and wrote to Ambalal Sarabhai:[69]

> I myself believe that the civil disobedience movement may not be unconstitutional, but it is certainly a very dangerous weapon in the hands of a population, the majority of whom are illiterate. In fact this is one of the reasons why I have been against the movement

> since last March, and I have all along felt from the very start that this sort of civil disobedience may be suitable to us at the moment, but it might teach the people an extremely dangerous lesson, which may greatly inconvenience even a swaraj Government.

In September 1930, Thakurdas sought the permission of Motilal Nehru to take the initiative to open a dialogue with the government on his behalf.[70] He also informed him that not only in Bombay but throughout the country the merchant community's limits of endurance had been reached.[71] In January 1931 Birla was asking Thakurdas that they should take the initiative and 'try their best to get the country out of the present political turmoil'[72], but at the same time warned against any hasty step.[73] 'Personally', he continued, 'I should not move at all until I am satisfied in my mind that we shall be given unreservedly full and free control over the Indian economics'.[74]

Returning empty handed from the second Round Table Conference, Gandhi resumed the civil disobedience. But this did not deter Birla and Thakurdas from pursuing their conciliation efforts with renewed vigour.[75] Birla in his letters to Samuel Hoare, Lord Lothian and Anderson tried his best to impress upon them that he was the Mahatma's permanent emissary, and that he was ready to help.[76] In May, Birla was painting a gloomy picture of economic conditions in India and pointing out how it was helping the civil disobedience movement. 'We are going to have the greatest trouble', he predicted, and the 'Government is stupid enough not to realise this and everyone will have to pay for it'.[77] While all the leaders were in jail the Congress, according to Birla 'was getting nasty in Bombay',[78] and 'since the businessman was neither a Congressman nor a Governmentman . . . . during the next few years businessmen will have to suffer very much at the hands of the Government and of their own countrymen'.[79] Birla also believed that the government's stern attitude was helping Jawaharlal Nehru.[80] 'The Indian merchants', he wrote to Thakurdas, 'will find great difficulties in dealing with Jawaharlal and that is another point which causes anxiety to the Indian merchants.'[81]

The termination of the civil disobedience movement on 20 May 1934 marked the end of a great wave of national upsurge. In the summer of 1935 Birla went to London with the purpose of establishing contacts between British leaders and the Congress.[82] The essence of his arguments with the British leaders was that unless the government was willing to have some settlement 'a revolution of the bloody type may become an inevitable factor'.[83] Implementing a carefully worked out plan from 1932 onwards, the government, however, knew full well that no such revolution was round the corner.[84] In September 1935 Birla returned to India.

In the meantime, INC after the Bombay session (1934) had once again turned to the constitutional path. The left had opposed the policy of council entry and formation of ministries in the name of developing a revolutionary mass movement. The majority of Congressmen, led by the right wing, had chosen the path of entering the councils and forming the ministries. Meanwhile the Lucknow session (1936) came and went without changing the main thrust of events. Birla, who closely watched the proceedings of the Lucknow session, wrote to Thakurdas: 'I am perfectly satisfied with what has taken place . . . . It could be said therefore that the *things are moving in the right direction* [emphasis added]. The election will be controlled by 'Vallabhbhai group' and if Lord Linlithgow handles the situation properly, there is every likelyhood of the Congressmen coming into office'.[85] With the formation of Congress ministries the right wing of the Congress began to consolidate its forces systematically. In the clash between the left wing and the right wing, during the period 1934-40, the unity of the left wing suffered a serious setback.[86] After the Quit India movement when the leaders were released at the end of 1945, the right wing ideologues within the Congress were fully entrenchad. Within the INC the socialist Nehru stood at the head of an untransformed Congress in which the forces of the right wing could not be ignored.[87] Let it be emphasized that the threat to capitalist interests, real or imaginary, was always perceived from the socialist forces led by Nehru within the Indian National Congress and never from the Communist Party of India.

III

From the evidence presented above one point becomes quite clear that from 1928 onwards, by and large, the capitalists sympathized with nationalist positions and extended support to the Congress-led mass movement, if not whole-heartedly at least to a considerable extent. Nevertheless, at no stage from its initiation to its later development was the capitalist class the driving or decisive force behind the mass movements launched by the Congress leadership. The important role which the representatives of the capitalist class played was that of 'bargaining counters' or 'go-betweens'. There is simply no evidence warranting the assertion that the capitalist class 'played an important part in determining the nature and course of the anti-imperialist movement in India'.[88] The questions regarding the *nature* and *course* of the Indian national movement should be explored in other directions.[89] The recognition of the fact, and it is amply clear from the evidences, that Indian capitalists favoured a certain form of anti-imperialist politics, i.e. constitutionalist forms of struggle over non-constitutional forms, need not be stretched to the assertion that the capitalist class was able to evolve a clear-cut comprehensive strategy and tactics of anti-imperialist opposition.[90] It was during the constitutionalist phase, as we have tried to show, that the political perspective of the capitalist class overlapped with that of the INC. The capitalist class related to the Congress mainly through its conception of anti-imperialist struggle and ideological symbiosis with the right wing leadership.

But had the Indian capitalists developed a class vision? The question is relevant because an otherwise excellent study rejects the view that they had evolved a common platform and can be treated as a class.[91] The unity and internal cohesion of a particular class should however be seen in relation to other social classes and with reference to its capacity to articulate the interests of the class through its leaders in most general form, irrespective of its uneven development and factionalism. So viewed, the formation of the Federation of Indian Chambers of Commerce and Industry and the declaration of the *logic of development* of Indian industries as an inseparable part of the growing national movement must be regarded a watershed in the development of the capitalist class and its slowly evolving political vision.[92] How closely the FICCI represented the general interests of the capitalist class becomes clear from the following comment of J.K. Mehta, secretary Indian Merchants Chamber. In a letter to Thakurdas he wrote:

> It is true that it (FICCI) is a conglomerate body of about forty Indian Chambers and Commercial Associations, the colour of whose politics may and does run into different shades; *at the same time there is the lowest common denomination on which all agree.* Thus for instance, with regard to the four main political issues before the country, I do not think *there is a single Chamber or Commercial Association which has got different views.* These four issues are: (1) The ideal of immediate Dominion Status; (2) Men with nationalist views should capture all the present legislatures; (3) Men of nationalist views should preponderate at the RTC. Legislatures should not

be boycotted. We must go to RTC and utilise it; (4) The public debts should not be repudiated . . . . *The Federation has to draw out the average and express the general view which is uniform throughout the business world*(emphasis added).[93]

This suggests that by the 1930s the unity of Indian capitalists had acquired a degree of class awareness *vis-a-vis* imperialism and other social classes in Indian society, though at times different factions or political shades favoured different *methods* and policies to advance the interests of the class as a whole.

Notes

1. E.M.S. Namboodiripad, *Economics and Politics of India's Socialist Pattern* (New Delhi, 1966); Bipan Chandra, "Indian Capitalist Class and Imperialism", in his *Nationalism and Colonialism in Modern India* (New Delhi, 1979), pp. 144-170. Sumit Sarkar, *Modern India: 1885-1947* (New Delhi, 1985); Ajit Roy, *Indian Monopoly Capital* (Calcutta, 1953); Basudev Chaterjee, "Business and Politics in the 1930s; Lancashire and the Making of the Indo-British Trade Agreement, 1939", *Modern Asian Studies*, XV (1981), pp. 527-573; Aditya Mukherjee, "The Indian Capitalist Class: Aspects of its Economic, Political and Ideological Development in the Colonial Period, 1920-47", in S. Bhattacharya and Romila Thaper (eds.), *Situating Indian History* (New Delhi, 1986), pp. 239-87. In his article "Indian Business and the Congress Provincial Governments, 1937-39", *Modern Asian Studies* XV (1981), pp. 487-526, Claude Markovits follows a similar framework.

2. Many of these authors differ among themselves regarding the 'nationalist potential' and 'feudal linkages' of the capitalist class. But each of them views the INC as a bourgeois party.

3. Two classic examples of this kind of Marxist research are: Bipan Chandra, 'Jawaharlal Nehru and the Indian Capitalist Class, 1936' in his *Nationalism and Colonialism in Modern India* (n.1) and Sumit Sarkar, 'Logic of Gandhian Nationalism : Civil Disobedience and the Gandhi-Irwin Pact (1930-31) *The Indian Historical Review*, III (1976). pp. 114-146. With some additional modifications, Aditya Mukherjee also holds that the Indian capitalist class played an important part in *determining the nature and course of the anti-imperialist movement in India*. Aditya Mukherjee, 'The Indian Capitalist Class: Aspects of Its Economic, Political and Ideological Development in the Colonial Period, 1927-47' (n.1), p.239. According to Bipan Chandra, it was due to this class *determination* that the national movement followed the course of 'pressure-compromise-pressure'. See his 'Continuity and Change' in *Nationalism and Colonialism in Modern India*, (n.1), p.158. However, in his *India's Struggle for Independence : 1857-1947* (New Delhi 1988) Professor Bipan Chadra does not make the distinction between 'Indian National Movement' and the 'the Indian National Congress' as an organisation. The entire multi-class movement is described as being under the "basic hegemony of bourgeois ideology",p.525.

4. *The Communist*, I (9 June 1936), quoted in Bhagwan Josh, 'Nationalism, Third International and Indian Communists' in Bipan Chandra (ed.) *The Indian Left: Critical Appraisals* (New Delhi, 1983) p. 192.

5. *The Communist*, II (11 August 1936).

6. Quoted in Bhagwan Josh, 'Nationalism, Third International and Indian Communists', (n.4), p.197.

7. 'Thesis on the National Congress and the Working Class', *New Age,* V-I (June 1938). Claude Markovits rejects the formulation that INC was the party of the Indian capitalists or, to be more precise, the Indian bourgeoisie. He speaks of the 'links' between capitalists and the INC. While he is able to see the factions and heterogeneity within the capitalist class, he continuously treats the INC as a homogeneous entity. He does not feel the need to divide the INC along ideological lines or at least make the traditional division between left wing or right wing. Claude Markovits, *Indian Business and Nationalist Polities, 1931-39* (Bombay, 1985).

8. Perhaps it would be more appropriate to describe the National Congress as the Congress movement structured as a party which accommodated a whole spectrum of ideologies from liberal shades to socialism as all of them had a common goal – the liberation of the country from foreign rule. The common goal of the contending ideologies opened the all-class national movement to possibilities in which socialists (communists) as well as their opponents could legitimately attempt to hegemonize the movement during the process of strengthening it. For details, see Bhagwan Josh, 'Nationalism, Third International and Indian Communists', (n.4), pp. 154-6.

9. Sashi Joshi, 'The Left and the Indian National Movement, 1920-34 (Ph.D. Thesis, Jawaharlal Nehru University, New Delhi, 1984). Bhagwan Josh, 'The Left and the Indian National Movement, 1934-41' (Ph.D. Thesis, Jawaharlal Nehru University, New Delhi, 1987).

10. The specific nature of the British-Indian colonial state and its implications for the nationalist struggle in India, I have discussed in "The Colonial State and its Enemies", presented at the Indo-German Seminar, Centre for Historical Studies, Jawaharlal Nehru University, New Delhi, 10-12 March 1988.

11. *Young India,* 23 February 1922. Gandhi quoted in S. Bhattacharya, 'Cotton Mills and Spinning Wheels: Swadeshi and the Indian Capitalist Class, 1920-22', in K.N. Panikkar (ed.), *National and Left Movements in India* (New Delhi, 1980), pp. 27-44.

12 In 1921, Gandhi told the millowners: 'Many friends tell me that the nation is not to expect anything from you. They point out the fact that you have not, with one or two honourable exceptions, paid anything for the [Tilak] Swaraj fund'. *Bombay Chronicle,* 6 July 1921.

13. Thakurdas to Sir Thomas Holland, 28 October 1920. Purshotamdas Thakurdas Papers, hereinafter P.T. Papers, file no. 24/II.

14. Thakurdas to Sir Thomas Holland, 16 October, 1920, ibid.

15. 'Our only regret is that we are late in the field and the other side has already sown poisonous seeds which are germinating and which all true well-wishers of the country should eradicate root and branch and bring round the people to sanity and sober commonsense'. A.M. Dalal to Thakurdas, Broach, 19 October 1920, ibid.

16. Leaflet No. 1, January 1922, ibid.

17. 'A short note on the political situation in India' by Purshotamdas Thakurdas enclosed in a letter to Hogg, 8 October 1920, ibid, file no. 24/III.

18. Also note his speech at Surat on 7 November 1920: 'But when in the face of immense scope of constructive and useful work, Mr. Gandhi must launch on a project, which is acknowledged by all to be a short cut to our final goal, may one not despair and at least tell people the advantages of a more cautious and surer, even though considerably slower,

method of acquiring swaraj or whatever you may wish to call it . . . . If after a fair trial of this instalment, Mr. Gandhi and his friends have reasons to urge changes or modifications earlier than fixed by parliament, the country would be more, if not wholly sympathetic to him'. Newspaper cutting in ibid.

19. The signatories to the statement were : M.M. Malaviya, M.A. Jinnah, Purshotamdas Thakurdas, M.R. Jayakar, Ambalal Sarabhai, K. Natrajan and G.M. Bhurgri.

20. For details see Claude Markovits, *Indian Business and Nationalist Politics* (n.7); A.D.D. Gordon, *Business and Politics : Rising* Nationalism and a Modernising Economy in Bombay, 1918-1933, (Delhi 1978), ch.5.

21. Memorandum by Sir Purshotamdas Thakurdas for the Reforms Enquiry Committee (Bombay, 2 October 1924), P.T. Papers, file no. 40/V.

22. Motilal Nehru to Thakurdas, 10 October 1924, P.T. Papers, file no. 40/II.

23. M.A. Jinnah to Thakurdas, 25 May 1925; Thakurdas to Swarajists, 11 November 1924, ibid.

24. Motilal Nehru to F.E. Dinsha, 18 Oct. 1924, *ibid.*

25. Ibid.

26. Thakurdas to Motilal, 11 October 1924, ibid.

27. Sashi Joshi, *Struggle for Hegemony : India, 1920-47* (New Delhi, 1991) vol.I, ch.V, Idem, "Nehru and the Emergence of the Left Bloc, 1927-29", in Bipan Chandra (ed.), *The Indian Left* (n. 4), pp. 45-102.

28. V.B. Karnik, *Strikes in India* (Bombay, 1967), p. 164.

29. Prem Sagar Gupta, *A Short History of the All India Trade Union Congress, 1920-47* (Bombay, 1980), p. 114. The strike was originally directed against certain measures of rationalization, unemployment and a 7.5 per cent cut in wages, but soon seventeen more demands were placed before the millowners.

30. Quoted in Sashi Joshi, *The Left and the Indian National Movement*,(n.9), p.173.

31. Ibid., p. 174.

32. Motilal Nehru to Thakurdas, 8 April 1928; Motilal Nehru's telegram to Thakurdas, 13 April 1928, P.T. Papers, file no. 40/IV.

33. Gandhi to Dr. Ansari, 14 April 1928, in Mushirul Hasan (ed.), *Muslims and the Congress : Selected Correspondence of Dr. M.A. Ansari 1912-1935*. (New Delhi, 1979), p.43.

34. P.T. Papers, file no.40/IV. The telegram is dated 16 April 1928.

35. Ibid. The letter was dated 21 April 1928. A copy of this letter was sent to Purshotamdas Thakurdas, ibid. Four days earlier (i.e. on 17 April 1988), Motilal Nehru wrote to Dr. Ansari: 'The Bombay millowners have proved even worse than I expected. It would have been a wild goose chase to go to Bombay simply to wait upon the pleasure of individual millowners. As you are aware, these millowners reaped a rich harvest during our first intensive campaign for the boycott of foreign cloth. They are evidently expecting the same results by our next campaign. They are mean and selfish lot and in my opinion should be taught a lesson which they are not likely to forget.' Mushirul Hasan (ed.), *Muslims and the Congress* (n.33), pp. 43-44.

36. Motilal Nehru to Lalji Naranji, 28 April 1928, P.T. Papers, file no. 40/IV.

37. N.M. Mazumdar to Thakurdas, 25 May 1929. The letter was drafted by N.M. Mazumdar 'exactly' as Dorabji wished it. Ibid., file no. 40/II.

38. N.M. Mazumdar to Thakurdas, 3 July 1929, ibid.

39. N.M. Mazumdar to Thakurdas, 22 May 1929, ibid.

40. Ibid.

41. Dorabji to Thakurdas, 3 July 1929, ibid., file no. 42/V.

42. Thakurdas to N.M. Mazumdar, 7 June 1929, ibid.

43. *Bombay Samachar*, 5 December 1928. Defending the correctness of his stand, Purshotamdas wrote : 'No person has any sympathy with the activities of the Red Union at all. There has been good deal of cowardly talk going on regarding Public Safety Bill and the attitude taken up by me in the Assembly on the Bill. Believe me the, Public Safety Bill was not intended for the purpose of industrial disputes, but was in reality, a political measure with political aims.' Thakurdas to N.M. Mazumdar, 7 June 1928. P.T. Papers, file no. 42/ II.

44. Thakurdas to N.M. Mazumdar, 7 June 1928, ibid.

45. Birla to Thakurdas, 30 July 1929, ibid., file no. 42/V.

46. Birla to Thakurdas, 3 August 1934, ibid., file no. 42/VI.

47. Birla to Thakurdas, 7 August 1928; Thakurdas to Birla, 28 July 1928; Fakirjee Cowasjee's telegram to Thakurdas, 20 July 1928; Thakurdas to Chunilal, 6 July 1928; Thakurdas to S.T. Sheppard, (Editor, *The Times of India)*, 3 July 1928; Thakurdas to Chunilal, 28 June 1928; K.D. Acharya to Thakurdas, 23 June 1928; ibid.; *The Pioneer*, 22 and 26 July 1928; *The Evening News*, 23 June, 5 and 7 July 1928.

48. Birla to Thakurdas, 25 July 1928, ibid., file no. 74/I. In a letter to Vallabhbhai Patel on 14 June 1928, Purshotamdas wrote : 'I am as anxious as anybody else that you should not get a setback in the stage to which you have got so far, and further that you should get out of this somewhat novel tussle before it gets too late. You will realise that should you eventually be beaten in this struggle, the loss to Gujarat would be incalculable'. Ibid.

49. Such a complex behaviour was certainly beyond the grasp of ordinary members of the bureaucracy. Commenting on the attitude of Indian businessmen, a British official wrote: 'We are often perplexed to find many of these eminent businessmen associating themselves with extreme national economic movements and, at the same time, seeking to retain their positions of power and influence with the government. We do not know as to when these businessmen are sincere, when they flirt with us or when they flirt with the extreme section whose support is necessary for elections to the different public bodies'. A newspaper cutting dated 17 August 1935 in M.R. Jayakar Papers, file no. 196. National Archives of India, New Delhi.

50. D.G. Tendulkar, *Mahatma*, (Delhi, 1951), vol. II, p.473.

51. The prominent leaders were Gandhi, M.M. Malaviya, Motilal Nehru, Jawaharlal Nehru, Subhas Bose and Sir Tej Bahadur Sapru.

52. Birla to Thakurdas, 3 November 1929, P.T. Papers, file no. 91.

53. G.D. Birla, *In the Shadow of the Mahatma*, (Bombay 1953), p. 42. Interestingly, he was not using the left wingers in the Congress as a 'threat' or a 'danger' while arguing with Gandhi.

54. Ibid., p.44.

55. Thakurdas to Gandhi, 30 January 1930. P.T. Papers, file no. 96. G.D. Birla was with him when this letter was dictated by Thakurdas.

56. Gandhi to Thakurdas, 2 February 1930. To this letter, Thakurdas's apologetic reply was : 'You say to these masses swaraj would be welcome only if it led to an appreciable reduction in the taxes which they pay either directly or indirectly. You further say that,

we, who share with the British administrators in this exploitation of the masses, should be prepared to change the angle of our vision towards the masses. I feel that a revolution in India will not improve the position of the masses'. Thakurdas to Gandhi, 6 February 1930, ibid.

57. Thakurdas to Gandhi, 6 February 1930, ibid. The concluding part of the above referred long letter ran as follows : 'I am sure that we are at the crossing of the road, and I strongly feel that whilst one need not approve of most what is prevalent at present, one is hardly justified in taking the risk which the Congress resolution involves. I venture to ask whether the creduality of the masses does not lend itself to exploitation by extremist views, and whether this is not an extremely grave responsibility for any body to take when a large portion of the thinking section of the country is against it'.

58. Gandhi to Thakurdas, 9 February 1930, ibid. The letter is in the Mahatma's own handwriting.

59. Lalji Naranji to Thakurdas, 28 March 1930, ibid. file no. 91. In a letter to Thakurdas Birla wrote : 'He (Motilal) agreed with me that full economic control was the crux of the full demand'. Ibid. file no. 42/VII.

60. Ibid.

61. M.R. Jaykar Papers. file no. 3.

62. It was this transformation process which later on led to the formation of the Congress Socialist Party within the Indian National Congress. Sashi Joshi has discussed this in detail in her *Struggle for Hegemony*(n.27).

63. J.K. Mehta to Thakurdas, 3 February 1930. P.T. Papers, file no. 42/VII.

64. See note 7 above. For the transformation of the Congress in Kerala see Bhagwan Josh, 'Understanding Indian Communists: A Survey of Approaches to the Study of the Communist Movement in India, 1920-47', in Bhattacharya and Thapar (eds.), *Situating Indian History*, (n.1), pp. 288-330. Indian communists made certain choices and acted in one way while they could have made other possible choices equally well and acted otherwise under the same circumstances. Therefore, the historian's task is not only to construct the logic of certain choices as successive links in the emerging chain of inevitability, but also to point out similtaneously the possibility and potential of other available choices which could have been followed but were not.

65. In his presidential address to the All-India Trade Union Congress in 1931 Subhas Chadra Bose observed : 'The Trade Union Congress as a body did not have much to do with the civil disobedience movement last year'. Prem Sagar Gupta, *A Short History of All India Trade Union Congress, 1920-1947* (n.29), p. 185.

66. The Federation of Indian Chambers of Commerce and Industry (FICCI) passed the following resolution unanimously: 'In the opinion of the Committee of the Federation no conference [of the nature of RTC] convened for the purpose of discussing the problem of Indian constitutional advance can come to a solution of the present political difficulty which will be acceptable to the country, unless such a conference is attended by Mahatma Gandhi as a free man, or has at least his approval. For this reason the committee feel it necessary to recommend to the various member bodies of the Federation not to nominate any representatives of Indian commercial interests to RTC unless Mahatma Gandhi is a party to the said conference'. P.T. Papers, file no. 91.

67. Thakurdas to Sir George Schuster, 30 May 1930, ibid.

68. Thakurdas to Major Graham Pole, 19 September 1930, 7 August 1930; Birla to Cambell Rhodes, 6 February 1930: 'India is at the cross-roads. The minimum that we can do with

is complete control in matters domestic at least, barring the political and the military which require further experience and thought. Anything less will not do and is bound to give upper hand to agitators and malcontents'. Ibid., Thakurdas to T.B. Sapru, 8 January 1930 : 'Nothing less than what will make us masters in our own home will do good to the country'. Thakurdas to Irwin, 10 June 1930; Irwin to Thakurdas, 5 June 1930; Thakurdas to Irwin, 31 May 1930; Irwin to Thakurdas, 9 May 1930; Thakurdas to Irwin, 28 April 1930; Thakurdsa to Sir John Bhore, 10 September 1930; Thakurdas to H.R. Gould, Secretary to the Government of Bombay, 16 September 1930, ibid., file no. 99/I.

69. Thakurdas to Sarabhai, 18 November 1930, ibid. file no. 42/VII.

70. Thakurdas to Motilal Nehru, 22 September 1930: 'Reports that I have heard from persons who have lately returned from Simla indicate that the Viceroy may still be able to get the Cabinet's permission to meet you to the fullest extent he can. I do not think it is a question of putting any intermediary between you and the Viceroy. Whosoever works in this matter will work absolutely quietly without any publicity and on such lines as you may privately indicate to Mr. Lalji. In short, the question is whether you can give us any indication of the lines on which to work. If your lines do not turn out to be feasible, your name will not even be mentioned'. Ibid., file no. 104.

71. Thakurdas to Motilal Nehru: 'The commercial community has borne a very substantial part of the brunt involved in this response and they have borne it cheerfully - one may almost say enthusiastically. With the end of this month [September 1930], the movement will have been going on for six months. You will perhaps remember your telling me in Bombay in the third week of June last that you did not expect the movement to have to last for more than three months. That period will expire in 10 days more and I have been admiring how correct a prophet you were regarding the capacity of the commercial community for endurance. Ibid.

72. Birla to Thakurdas 16 January 1931, ibid.

73. Striking a note of caution, he observed: 'It is better that we achieved peace after some time than that we should achieve a patched truce. I would, therefore, ask you not to reduce our demands in our anxiety to bring about peace. Whatever terms are offered should be tested on one point alone, i.e. whether with the powers offered we would be able to increase the productivity and prosperity of the country or not'. Ibid.

74. Ibid.

75. Thakurdas to G.A. Thomas, 21 January 1932, ibid. file no. 104. Apart from Samuel Hoare, Lord Lothian and Willington contacts were established with Benthall, governors of Bombay and Bengal, Reginald Clarke and G.A. Thomas.

76. G.D. Birla, *In the Shadow of the Mahatma*(n.53), pp. 51-2. He wrote to Samuel Hoare: 'He [Gandhi] alone is responsible for keeping the left-wing in India in check. To strengthen his hands, in my opinion, therefore, is to strengthen the bond of friendship between the two countries. If you think I can be of any use in bringing about happy relations between the two countries, you can always rely on my humble services'.

77. Birla to Thakurdas, 16 May 1932. In response to this letter Thakurdas wrote on 28 June 1932 : 'I fully share all your apprehensions in this connection and feel that in the present temper of the Government, we, non-officials, can do jolly little'. P.T. Papers, file no. 107/II.

78. Birla to Thakurdas, 28 June 1932, ibid.

79. Earlier (25 June 1932) Thakurdas had written to him : 'With Congress on one side and the Government on the other, the merely commercial does not know where he stands.' Ibid.

80. Birla to Thakurdas, 28 June 1932 : 'But the Government is stupid in a way and is supporting Jawaharlal indirectly'. In another letter he wrote to Thakurdas on 16 February 1932: 'Government had simply played into the hands of Jawaharlal by arresting Gandhiji'. Ibid.

81. Birla to Thakurdas, 28 June 1932, ibid.

82. Birla, *In the Shadow of the Mahtama,*(n.53), p. 156.

83. Ibid., pp. 145 and 178.

84. Bhagwan Josh, *The Left and the Indian National Movement,*(n.9), ch.II.

85. G.D. Birla to Thakurdas, 20 April 1936, P.T. Papers, file no. 177. The fact that Jawaharlal Nehru stood at the head of the INC and was popularizing socialism in the country alarmed many a businessman. At the beginning of 1936, an all-India Progressive League was formed under the directorship of J.D. Jenkins with the explicit purpose of fighting communism and stopping the left-ward drift in the Congress. Sir Pheroze Sethna, Sir H.P. Mody and Sir Purshotamdas Thakurdas were its members. The pamphlet of the League declared: 'It is now crystal clear that at an early date the bulk of the Indian National Congress, under the leadership of Pandit Nehru, will decide to set aside its modest nationalist pretensions, and advocate instead an out-and-out communist policy. The progressive parties in all the provinces, and the great Indian merchants have until now, not sufficiently realised the extent of the havoc which such a vast organisation as the Congress can bring about in the country, when once it has taken to communism as its final objective. The enemy today is communism'. M.R. Jayakar Papers, file no. 196. Incidentally, the above quotation also clearly points out what could actually pose a real threat to the interests of the capitalists. It was transformation of the Congress towards a left ideology under the leadership of Jawaharlal Nehru.

86. Bhagwan Josh, *The Left and the Indian National Movement,*(n.9), chs. 7 and 8.

87. Nehru's problem within the INC seems comparable to Gorbachov's problems vis-a-vis the conservative Stalinists and Brezhnevites. 'After four years in power', writes a well-known commentator, 'Gorbachov is still surrounded by people, inherited from the past, whom he is unable to remove, and who cannot change their spots though they try hard to pretend otherwise. They want perestroika as a brightly painted new signboard and nothing more'. Dev Murarka, 'Perestroika under Fire', *Times of India,* March 17, 1989.

88. Aditya Mukherjee, 'Indian Capitalist Class' (n.3), p.239. This is the old paradigm dressed in new clothes which had assumed that the bourgeoisie stood at the head of the national movement.

89. This is precisely what has been attempted in Sashi Joshi, *The Left and the Indian National Movement,* (n.9) and Bhagwan Josh, *The Left and the Indian National Movement*(n.9). I have also discussed these questions in my paper : 'The Colonial State and its Enemies, (n.10).

90. Bipan Chandra, 'The Indian Capitalist Class and Imperialism before 1947' in his *Nationalism and Colonialism in Modern India,* (n.1), p.158.

91. Claude Markovits, *Indian Business and Nationalist Politics,* (n.1), p. 182.

92. Purshotamdas received numerous congratulatory letters from different parts of the country referring to his bold address at the second annual meeting of the Indian Chambers of Commerce. R.D. Tata wrote on 1 January 1929 : 'Nothing like it has ever been publicy uttered on behalf of the business community, and in striking an original note you have relieved the whole Indian business world from the meaningless dread

of politics engendered by the widespread interested propaganda. The enemy has tried his best to keep the business and the student aloof by propagating a false belief that polities is something which both of them should avoid going near.' P.T. Papers, file no. 42/VII.

93. J.K. Mehta to Thakurdas, 3 February 1930, ibid.

5

Entrepreneurs and Political Awareness: A Study of Bombay's Business Groups

Gita Piramal

The equations, that business is money and politics is power, have traditionally acquired an almost axiomatic acceptance. But the symbiotic relationship between business groups and politicians in India during the freedom movement taught a new lesson : that business is power and politics money. All the three players in the drama – the business groups, the British government and the Indian nationalists – quickly realized the significance of the new equations.[1] Wooed by both sides, business groups discovered their power and began demanding concessions from both. If the battle-cry of the nationalists was swaraj, in corporate cabins, the bottom-line was economic independence. When Gandhi wove the two strands together in the 1920s, he laid the foundation of the need-based love-hate relationship between business and politics with which we are familiar today.

The process through which the first set of equations changed into the second set is best symbolized in Bombay. As the East India Company gave way to Queen Victoria, and an empire to a republic, during a hundred of India's most tumultuous years, Bombay was frequently the vortex of intense political activity. Naturally the city's entrepreneurs were involved in this dynamic movement. But at what point did their political awareness awaken? Out of Bombay's numerous traders, manufacturers and financiers, who were involved in this political process? And how did they participate? Did they enter directly by standing for elections? Did they finance political parties? Or did they remain content with voicing their opinions through trade associations and lobbies?

These are some of the questions which this paper attempts to address. Unfortunately, all too often there are no clear-cut answers, especially where the financing of political parties is concerned. It is clear, however, that by the turn of the century, the majority of Bombay's business groups had begun to look beyond their companies towards the political environment in general. Even earlier, a few far-sighted entrepreneurs, such as Jamsetji Tata, had started realizing the subtle effects which the British administration had on their businesses, but at the time they were far too weak and dependent on the British to make any demands, Nonetheless, Bombay's entrepreneurs gradually acquired political *savoir-faire,* so much so that during the 1937 provincial elections, Lalchand Hirachand actually stood for – and won as an independent – a seat in the Bombay legislature.

The acquisition of political skills, such as oratory, the ability to organize public meetings and to propagate their views through the media, itself was a notable achievement for Bombay's entrepreneurs. Until Tilak and Gandhi radically altered the fabric of Indian polity, there was virtually no tradition of political involvement, especially among traders from whose roots sprang most of Bombay's business groups. Organizational skills acquired during the course of running their businesses were further honed by participation in various caste and trade associations, and were later put to use for political purposes. As Prakash Tandon recalled his younger days: 'The only public lectures we were used to hearing were the Kathas, religious discourses, and in more recent years, the Arya Samaj sermons, but political lectures were something quite new.'[2]

In Bombay's business environment, political activity tended to cluster around a strong personality and each generation threw up its own forceful personalities. Whenever an issue affected Bombay in particular, or outraged India's citizens in general, it was they who formed the platform or chaired protest meetings. In the 1850s, entrepreneurs such as Jagannath Shankarshet, Sir Mangaldas Nathubhai and Sir Jamsetji Jejeebhoy kept political interest kindled within the commercial community. In the 1900s, political leadership lay in the hands of Sir Manmohandas Ramji, Sir Fazulbhoy Currimbhoy, Sir Vithaldas Thackersey and Jamnadas Dwarkadas. In the radically altered business community of the 1930s, three interest groups developed round the Tatas, Sir Purshotamdas Thakurdas and Walchand Hirachand. During this tumultuous century, the response of Bombay's business community as a class to political events was generally weak. Individually, however, several entrepreneurs from Bombay played meaningful roles in the national freedom movement.

I

In the 1850s, most of Bombay's big business groups remained immersed in their own concerns and demonstrated little political awareness. These were years of opportunity when fortunes could be rapidly made by men of initiative as Bombay transformed itself from a sleepy British outpost into India's major commercial centre. Business interests which occupied most of an industrialist's working day were a serious handicap to political activity. Involved in entrepreneurial pursuits, active on the stock exchange which was just being set up (1864), and engaged in joint-stock companies, the typical businessman or industrialist had little time to devote to politics.

Many of these entrepreneurs were first and second generation immigrants who were drawn to Bombay because the city offered a haven of law and order, in contrast to the troubled areas which they fled. Bombay was perceived as a city where business could be transacted relatively peacefully.[3] This generation looked upon the British with gratitude as symbols of justice and peace, and even their children absorbed the concept that they 'were born to the blessing of the British Raj and accepted them as the natural order of life'.[4]

This was particularly true of the Parsi community from whose ranks were drawn many of Bombay's large business groups of the period. In a letter to *The Times of India,* Jamsetji Nusserwanji Tata (1839-1904), one of the earliest advocates of India's economic independence, wrote :

> Our small community is, to my thinking, peculiarly suited as interpreters and intermediaries between the rulers and the ruled in this country. Through their peculiar position they have benefited more than any other class by English rule, and I am sure their gratitude to that rule is, as it ought to be, in due proportion to the advantage derived from it . . . . Pure Natives, of this country, whenever they venture to criticise the actions of individuals in authority, are liable to have their motives questioned; but in the case of Parsees such doubtful motives must be regarded as non-existent.[5]

Many entrepreneurs had acquired their fortunes through links with the British and depended on them financially.[6] Later, as the cotton textile industry developed, Indian dependence on the British grew rather than diminished. Although most of the mills were owned by Indians, they still dependent on Europeans for skilled labour and technical advice.[7] Thus many Indian fortunes were built on the foundation of British protection and technical skill. The cooperation of European and Indian personnel and capital was one of the unique features of commercial enterprises in Bombay.[8] Because their pre-eminent position had been achieved under the British aegis and to some extent British support, Bombay's business groups as a class preferred any criticism of the Raj to be circumspect and moderate. Thus, to their natural 'timidity' was added a distaste 'to participate in an organization which night be viewed with disfavour by the government' and antagonize their collaborators.[9]

Nor was there even a breeding ground where political ideology could be developed or political thought expressed. Even the university – which later played a major role in Bombay's political awakening – was established only on 18 July 1857. The students of Elphinstone High School, College and Institution, where polity, taught by British professor, was part of the curriculum, were politically more aware, but few businessmen and even fewer of Bombay's industrialists, sent their children to college, though many appear to have contributed to various educational institutions.[10] It cannot be a coincidence that the initial stimulus for the establishment of Bombay's earliest political associations came from Elphinstonians.[11]

Nonetheless, there were a few stray incidents which indirectly indicate the existence of some political awareness among Bombay's businessmen. Between 30 July 1841 and 27 October 1841, eight letters under the pen-name of 'A Hindoo' appeared in the *Bombay Gazette* protesting against various aspects of British colonial policy.[12] The author of these long letters, recently identified as Bhaskar Pandurang Tharkhadkar (1816-47), was an employee of one of Bombay's leading entrepreneurs, Sir Jamsetji Jejeebhoy (1783-1859). The interesting point here is not that these letters probably stimulated Dadabhai Naoroji (1825-1917) to develop his famous drain theory, nor that these letters were probably the earliest form of protest against British rule in western India, nor even that they prompted a lively debate on this subject but the fact that after these letters were published, Jejeebhoy rewarded Tharkhadkar by buying him a house costing fourteen thousand rupees near Kalbadevi. The editor of the *Bombay Gazette* apparently had, however, to relinquish his chair.

Outwardly, Sir Jamsetji Jejeebhoy, a Parsi entrepreneur who made his fortune in the China trade, maintained close links with the British residents of Bombay. He threw lavish parties for them and enjoyed the confidence of the Bombay government. In October 1852 when the Bombay Association decided to send a stiff petition to the British parliament, he resigned his honorary presidentship of the association. Nonetheless, his interest in political activities appears to have been acute. He helped finance the *Bombay Samachar* from the time of its first appearance and he subsequently backed other leading Gujarati papers also. He was, moreover, a founding member of several of the city's political associations.[13]

Table 1 : Major Political Associations of Bombay 1850-90

Bombay Association	(1852)*
Bombay Board of Censors	(1863)
Bombay Branch of the East India Association	(1869)
Ratepayers' Committee	(1871)
Association of Western India	(1872)
Citizens' Committee in Aid of Local Self-Government	(1882)
Bombay Presidency Association	(1885)
Indian National Congress	(1885)
Ratepayers's Association	(1886)

*Figures in parentheses refer to year of foundation
Source : S.M. Edwards, *The Gazetteers of Bombay City and Island* (Bombay, 1885), vol.I, p.455.

Glimmerings of political interest could also be discerned among other Bombay entrepreneurs such as Jagannath Shankarshet (1802-65) and his son Vinayakrao (1831-73), Sir Mangaldas Nathubhai (1832-90)[14] and Damodher Thackersey (1847-93).[15] Many of these were manufacturers and merchants simultaneously. Most were active in caste associations and were leaders of their community. In some families, sons picked up their father's mantle of involvement in public life, thereby starting a dynastic tradition. This was true particularly among the Shankarshets, the Jajeebhoys,[16] the Thackerseys, and the Petits.

As Table 1 shows, Bombay's earliest political organization was probably the Bombay Association formed on 26 August 1852. Though the impetus for its formation apparently came from a small group of Elphinstonians[17] and it was born in the collage itself,[18] its existence and continuance was made possible by the efforts and wealth of Bombay's leading business families, in particular the Jejeebhoys and the Shankarshets.[19] Besides, more than half its membership consisted of businessmen. In fact, soon after its formation, it was remarked in the House of Lords that 'the signatures on a single sheet of the Bombay Association's petition were those of men representing property worth between 2,000,000 and 3,000,000 sterling'.[20]

Given the nature of its membership, it was to be expected that the association's main concerns would be with commercial issues. Until it became morimund after 1879, the association's numerous petitions addressed themselves to problems regarding taxation, administration of justice, encouragement of public works, and the need for better road and rail facilities. The high point of its existence came in 1870 when it called a public meeting which two thousand people attended to protest against an increase in income tax and which was reported in *The Times*, London. But if success were to be measured in terms of actual concessions wrested from the government, the Bombay Association must be reckoned a failure, for the government took little note of its numerous petitions[21] with the single exception regarding the establishment of a university.

The proceedings of the Bombay Association were marked by near unanimity among its members about the beneficial effects of British rule. In his maiden speech at the Bombay Association, Dadabhai Naoroji (1825-1917) said : 'Under the British Government we do not suffer any great *zoolum*. We are comparatively happier under the kind government than we are likely to be under any other.'[22] When its secretariat drew up a list of grievances against the East India Company's administration in a 'Petition to Parliament from the Members of the Bombay Association and other Native Inhabitants of the Bombay Presidency, 1852', it led to a minor exodus.[23] While two of its members, Dr Bhau Daji (1822-74) and Naoroji Furdoonji (1817-85), were both determined to express their views on the political needs of India in 'plain, unmistakable language', another member, Manakji Kharsedji (1807-87) labelled such sentiments as 'suicidal'[24]

For all its timidity, the activities of the Bombay Association show that at least a few of the city's entrepreneurs were in the process of acquiring a smattering of political awareness. For three years following the 1857 uprising, the association almost ceased to exist. The police suspected both its founding president, Jagannath Shankarshet, and Dr Bhau Daji, its secretary, as having some connection with the mutineers, and Shankarshet 'felt it wise to avoid calling the Association together until the trouble died down'.[25] According to one source, Shankarshet in fact was secretly impeached and 'might well have succumbed to the attacks of his accusers'[26], as his guilt was firmly believed in by several influential Englishmen. But Lord Elphinstone, Governor of Bombay(1853-60), considered him non-guilty.

During the 1870s and 1880s, political interest tended to go hand in hand with changes in the government's taxation policies. As Table

1 reveals, new associations came into existence around 1869-71 and 1882-85, both periods which witnessed strong agitation by Bombay's rate-payers. Municipal politics also came of age around this time, with elections being keenly contested.

A few isolated incidents of national importance, such as the Ilbert Bill, also kept political interest simmering in Bombay. In 1883, the viceroy's law member, Sir C.P. Ilbert, sponsored a bill permitting Indian judges to try Europeans in courts outside the presidency towns contrary to the Criminal Procedure Code of 1873. Effectively the bill tried to diminish racial distinction, but a sharp reaction from the Anglo-Indian community forced the viceroy to alter some of the bill's clauses. In Bombay, the agitation was much quieter than in Bengal, perhaps because there were 'few Europeans settled outside the Presidency Town'[27] but a few prominent entrepreneurs led by Sir Jamsetji Jejeebhoy (second baronet, 1811-77), and Sir Mangaldas Nathubhai did get together with Pherozeshah Mehta, Badruddin Tyabji and Dadabhai Naoroji to address a large public meeting at the town hall on 28 April 1883 to discuss the issue.[28]

Dadabhai Naoroji's frequent visits to Bombay from England were also responsible for reactivating the dull political scene in Bombay. The Bombay Presidency Association which he helped found on 31 January 1885 was perhaps the city's first organization 'with a truly political objective'[29] Of its forty-two active members most were professionals, predominantly lawyers. Fourteen members were drawn from the business community, but only one was a millowner (see Table 2). There were, however, a significant number of entrepreneurs who, even if they took only minor interest in the association's proceedings, were prepared to underwrite its programmes and to attend the occasional public meetings to demonstrate their support for its platform.

One of these was J.N. Tata, the Parsi pioneer of the Indian iron and steel industry. In ten years, he attended only four of the council's meetings, but usually could be persuaded to provide financial support when necessary. At the unveiling of a statue of J.N. Tata on 12 April 1912, Sir Pherozeshah Mehta described Tata's contribution to the association : 'Though he could never be induced to appear and speak on a public platform, the help, the advice, and the co-operation which he gave to political movements never ceased except with his life . . . . And not only was Mr. Tata himself the foundation member of the Association but he induced his old father to go and do likewise'.[30]

Table 2 : Occupations of the Forty-nine Active Members of the Bombay Presidency Association

Lawyer	24
Doctor	4
Journalist	2
Educator	1
Engineer	1
Business	7
Merchant	6
Millowner	1
Unidentified	3

Source : R.I. Cashman, *The Myth of the Lokamanya*, (Berkeley 1975), p.154.

Many members of the association were members also of a new political organization which was to sweep through India, the Indian National Congress. Cashman, in fact, goes so far as to suggest that the council of the Bombay Presidency Association was 'the most powerful branch organization of the Congress'.[31] Interestingly, there must have been an informal link between the two organizations through the Tyabji brothers, Badruddin and Amiruddin. Badruddin was president of the third session of the Indian National Congress while Amiruddin was a joint secretary of the council of the Bombay Presidency Association for several years.[32]

The seventy-two delegates of the Indian National Congress held their inaugural session in Bombay from 28 to 30 December 1885 under the presidentship of W.C. Bonnerjee (1844-1906). From almost the beginning, the organization was dominated by Bombay politicians. Bombay provided presidents for nine out of twenty-two annual sessions of the Congress held from 1885 to 1906.[33] Many of these were lawyers for the 'Bombay Bar then was the strongest in India'.[34] Cashman suggests : 'Bombay had a quality and depth of leadership which few other cities could match . . . [and it provided] . . . presidential timber for the annual Congress meetings'.[35]

From its inception, the Indian National Congress was dependent for financial support on Bombay's entrepreneurs. Several millowners of various communities donated small amounts in their private capacity.[36] In 1988, the council of the Bombay Presidency Association entrusted the task of collecting Rs 25,000-30,000 required for the 1889 Congress session to a committee of Bombay's entrepreneurs. This committee included two prominent millowners, Sir Mangaldas Nathubhai and Damodher Thackersey, besides leading mill directors and merchants such as Vijbhookhundas Atmaram, Vassonji Khimjee,

Vundravundas Purshostumdas, Hariprasad Suntokram and Jivandas Moolji.[37]

From all this, it appears that during the period 1850-95, but for a few stray exceptions, by and large there was negligible political interest among Bombay's entrepreneurs. There were scarcely a hardful of industrialists – mainly millowners – who had some political interests. Vishwanath Narayan Mandlik's bilingual newspaper, *Indu Prakash* or *Moonlight* (in Marathi and English), referred to them as 'the upper ten'.[38] Most businessmen like Premchand Roychand (1831-1906) showed no inclination towards politics[39]. Events such as the liquidation of the highly respected firm of Kessowji Naik & Company (towards the end of 1878), agents for four cotton textile mills whose liabilities came to a staggering three crore rupees, drew their attention more easily than did questions about examinations to the Indian Civil Service.[39]

The reluctance of members to pay their annual dues is a good index of the political lethargy of Bombay's business groups – it was not as if they could not afford the payment. The annual membership of the Bombay Association was twenty-five rupees, while that of the Bombay Presidency Association was ten rupees for residents of Bombay and six for non-residents. In his letters to Dadabhai Naoroji, Sir Dinshaw Wacha (1844-1936) frequently complained about arrears accumulated by members of the association despite 'all sorts of dunning'.[41] In 1898, dues amounting to Rs 3,675 had to be realized for the three preceding years and at least half had to be written off as dead loss, according to Wacha.

The political proclivities of Jamsetji Tata can perhaps be presented as typical of active Bombay entrepreneurs of the period. By the time Tata died (1904), he had established one of Bombay's most influential business groups though in actual terms, the group had only three textile mills and one hotel, his other ventures being still on the drawing boards. Nonetheless, in monetary terms, the family was one of the richest in Bombay. In 1901, Tata was described as a millionaire who 'mops up millions in an ordinary year' and had made a fortune of fifty million sterling.[42]

Tata generally tried, successfully, to give the impression that he was far too immersed in his business to take an interest in political questions. But he met Sir Pherozeshah Mehta at least once a week to discuss current events. Some years after Tata's death, Mehta remarked: 'The current notion that Mr. Tata took no part in public life, and did not help and assist in political movements, was a great mistake. There was no man who held stronger notions on political matters'.[43]

As seen already, Tata was a member of the Bombay Presidency Association, and in 1885 he was present at the birth of the Indian National Congress. But his presence was always behind the scenes. He never addressed a political meeting, though once or twice he consented to second a resolution. Moreover, during the first years of its existence, the annual meetings of the Congress were not marked by those stormy scenes which began in the 1920s.

Jamsetji Tata's name is conspicuously absent from the original list of member mills of the Bombay Millowners Association (BMA) founded in 1875.[44] But when excise duty was first introduced on Indian mill-made cloth in 1895, along with Nowrosje Nusserwanjee Wadia (1849-99)[95], Tata submitted an unsuccessful memorial to the finance member on behalf of the BMA. During a business visit to London shortly after this, Tata managed to obtain a private interview with Lord George Hamilton, Secretary of State for India, to try and convince him to remove the excise duty. The unsuccessful visit was followed up by the presentation of a brochure on the 'true average earnings' of Bombay mills, a copy of which was presented not only to Lord Hamilton but also distributed among Indian millowners.[46]

Tata's attitude towards the British and theirs towards him appear confusing. On the one hand is Tata's letter to the *Times of India* (quoted above) expressing Parsi gratitude and loyalty to the British. On the other hand, he secretly financed the publication of a special Indian edition of a book on Indian poverty, *Prosperous British India,* written by Digby.[47]

The British were acutely aware of the influence which Tata's financial power could wield.[48] Many of his contemporaries were knighted, but in Tata's case, honours and distinctions were showered on him after his death.[49] Fifteen years after J.N. Tata's death, Hamilton wrote to his son, Sir Dorab Tata (1859-1932):

> It is by solid work such as your father did, that India will be brought up to a higher standard of comfort and civilization, and as that higher standard develops so will the capacity for self-restraint and self-government increase. I therefore look upon your father and the group of men who are following in his footsteps, not merely from the commercial standpoint, but as political pioneers of the most reliable character.[50]

Yet one of Hamilton's colleagues, Sir John Edge, maintained: 'I cannot see that political assistance in times of difficulty could be expected from men like Mr. Tata'.[51]

II

From about 1890, economic growth in Bombay began to falter after almost forty years of unparalleled progress. The city's potential position as the *urbs prima* in India was jolted by the periodic appearance of the bubonic plague,[52] famine,[53] communal riots,[54] restive labour,[55] and currency fluctuations.[56] Bombay's cotton mills in their infancy had to learn to face external competition from China and Japan, internal competition from upcountry mills and frequent attacks from Lancashire mills through excise levies. Foreign trade was often disrupted.

Disturbed conditions such as these began to foster an aggressive attitude amongst Bombay's otherwise timid and apolitical entrepreneurs. No longer were they quite so willing to accept that British rule was entirely beneficial. This change in attitudes can be seen in expected quarters: for example, the Tatas named their Nagpur mill, founded in 1874, as the Empress Mill, but in 1886, when they bought the old Dharamsi Mill, they renamed it the Svadeshi [sic] Mill.[57]

During this period, Bombay's business groups gradually began to understand the impact of political events on their companies and voice their concerns publicly. Linking the government's silver policies to the falling demand for Bombay's yarn, Sir Sorabji Saklatvala (1879-1948), Jamsetji Tata's nephew and a director of Tata Sons, vehemently protested : 'Never before in the history of modern trade has legislation had a more disastrous and immediate effect on an important and well-established industry'.[58] In the Imperial Legislative Council, Sir Vithaldas Thackersey (1873-1922), one of Bombay's biggest millowners who established the first Indian university for women, attacked British double standard of the free trade principle in a non-free country: 'After the Boer War, when Great Britain levied an import-duty on wheat, there was no question of levying a countervailing excise-duty on the production of wheat in the United Kingdom. I do not know whether at that time this principle of free trade slept; but of course the case in India is different'.[59]

Faced with diminishing profits, Bombay's entrepreneurs started organizing themselves into trade associations to take up issues concerning them with the government. To counter attacks by Lancashire mills, Bombay millowners founded the Bombay Millowners Association (BMA) on 1 February 1875. For lack of space, it is not possible to go into details of the heavy and well-documented warfare between the Bombay and Lancashire mills. It is important to note, however, that the politics of cotton during this period became a major issue between Indian nationalists and the British government, and went far beyond mere competition between Lancashire and Bombay mills.[60]

Though Bombay's business groups began to display some political awareness, they were far too weak and too dependent on British technology to go so far as to give support to the swadeshi movement of 1905-11.[61] In a letter to Sir Dinshaw Wacha, Dadabhai Naoroji pertinently asked: 'I wonder whether Lancashire being boycotted will retaliate by not providing India with machinery for new mills and repairs for old ones. Can India undertake to start factories to prepare the machinery?[62] Mangaldas & Company tried to answer Naoroji's question in May 1906 when it established the Indian Bobbin Manufacturing Company with a capital of seventy-five thousand rupees at Surat.[63] Unfortunately, no further details are available about this venture.

Bombay's business groups were frequently somewhat short-sighted and unpatriotic – as more than one nationalist leader pointed out. During the height of the movement, with a strong demand for Indian cloth, Bombay millowners 'enormously' raised their prices.[64] And when Bal Gangadhar Tilak (1856-1920) wrote to Wacha asking him to exert influence on millowners to supply *dhoties* to the Indian market at moderate rates, millowners refused point blank to comply with this request.[65] They took refuge in maintaining that swadeshi should be a platform on which all could meet – 'official and non-official, European and Indian, the political agitator and the quiet worker'.[66] It must be pointed out, however, that swadeshi-induced demand was for cloth and at that time, most Bombay mills had been erected with the yarn-export market in mind. Compared to its spinning capacity, Bombay's weaving capacity was marginal. Many Bombay mills began adapting to the changing conditions and started utilizing their reserves and available capital for increasing their weaving and finishing machinery.[67]

Smaller industrialists, such as the Kirloskars, responded more positively to Tilak's swadeshi call than the millowners. One of India's top twenty business houses today, at the turn of the century the Kirloskar group's business activities were modest: it had a small foundry at Belgaum which Tilak visited in 1906. Two Kirloskar brothers, Laxmanrao (1869-1956) and Ramchandrarao, were among Tilak's earliest supporters. Ramchandra 'paid his first subscription to [Tilak's]*Kesari* in 1880 and remained a faithful subscriber until his death in 1960 at the age of 103'.[68]

Given the business environment in the 1900s as described by Laxmanrao's son, Shantanu (b. 1903), it is easy to understand why Tilak became Laxmanrao's 'political hero'. Iron ploughs made by Kirloskar Brothers had to compete in a market already flooded by the British ploughs, for which even high-ranking British officials used to act as virtual agents and salesmen. 'Such officials used to hold public meetings in their Districts and ceremoniously presented colourful turbans to farmers who bought British ploughs, thus conferring on those purchasers a social honour in their community which acted as a powerful inducement to buy British products'.[69] Swadeshi sentiments would not only help counter such aggressive salesmanship, but actually promote Indian ploughs.

Though Bombay's business groups were unwilling to lower the price of their *dhotis,* they were perfectly willing to participate in swadeshi money-making schemes. On 11 December 1905, a few entrepreneurs came together to start the Bombay Swadeshi Cooperative Stores Company Ltd for doing business in only swadeshi goods. Established with a capital of two and a half lakhs, the company had four prominent Bombay industrialists as directors : Ratan Tata (1871-1918), Gordhandas Khatau (1873-1916), Sir Manmohandas Ramji (1857-1934), and Dwarkadas Dharmsi,[70] besides a Poona politician, Balasaheb Natu.

Several industrial enterprises were founded during this tumultuous period, the most notable of which was the Tata Iron and Steel Company, India's first steel plant.[71] Indian banking too came of age with the establishment of the Indian Specie Bank[72] and the Bank of India in 1905; the Bank of Baroda, the Indian Bank (Madras), and the Indian Financial Syndicate (Calcutta) in 1907 besides the Central Bank of India (1911) and the Bank of Mysore (1913). The first industrial conference was held at Nagpur in July 1905. These conferences became an annual feature, held at the time of the Congress sessions to discuss economic problems facing the country.[73]

The swadeshi movement also stimulated the establishment of the Indian Merchants Chamber (IMC) on 7 September 1907.[74] Amongst the chamber's founders were Sir Purshotamdas Thakurdas (1879-1961),[75] Sir Dinshaw Wacha, Sir Ibrahim Rahimtoola (b. 1862),[76] Sir Fazalbhoy Currimbhoy (b. 1872),[77] Girdhardas Jethabhai, Sir Manmohandas Ramji, Sir Vithaldas Thackersey and his brother Madhavjee Thackersey (1881-1937). Though ostensibly representing traders and merchants, for over twenty-five years the chamber's leadership lay in the hands of the city's business groups.[78] Basically a trade association, right from the beginning the chamber displayed a keen interest in political matters and emerged as the most vocal lobby of Indian commercial and industrial sentiments.

During the First World War, most groups were too busy working their machines to play a forceful political role. Demand for all types of Indian manufacturs was strong and profitability excellent. At the eighth annual general meeting of the Fazulbhoy Mills its chairman, J.A. Wadia, who later gave evidence before the Indian Tariff Board (Cotton Textile Industry Enquiry), in 1927, told shareholders:

> I beg to congratulate you on the satisfactory result of the last year's earning which is the highest we have obtained in any one year, namely Rs. 9,40,000. Although I gave you a very satisfactory balance sheet for the year 1912, I never anticipated that your profits would be so satisfactory as they have turned out to be. A glance at your balance sheet will show that your paid-up capital is Rs. 18 lacs. Whilst we have earned for you during the last 5 1/2 years about Rs. 22 lacs, and we have given you in the shape of dividends uptill the end of the last year Rs. 6,30,000.[79]

Nonetheless, there were a handful of business groups, such as the Morarjee family, who continued to be keen supporters of the national movement.[80] When M.K. Gandhi landed in Bombay from South Africa on 9 January 1915, Narottam Morarjee (1877-1929), son of Morarjee Goculdas, was among those who received Gandhi and Kasturba on board the ship. Later, when Gandhi approached Narottam for help for the establishment of the Sabarmati Ashram at Ahmedabad, 'a substantial donation was promptly forthcoming'.[81] Both his side of the family and his cousins, Ratansi and Tricamdas Morarjee, were friends of Annie Besant and prominent members of the All-India Home Rule League.[32]

III

From 1919, events such as the Jallianwala Bagh massacre (1919) and the Hunter Commission, the Rowlatt Act (1919), the Khilafat Movement (1920), and the Simon Commission (1927) began to whip up public indignation against the British government. Fanned by Gandhi, these events led directly not only to the advent of mass nationalist agitation but also to a period of rioting and violence.[83] In the face of disrupted conditions in trade, industry and commerce, Bombay's business groups felt themselves caught in a dilemma. Many retreated from political activity.

The changing attitude of Sir Manmohandas Ramji, a Kutchi Bhatia piece-goods merchant, millowner and partner of the Thackerseys, was perhaps typical of the Bombay entrepreneur of the time. An early and active supporter of nationalism during its conventional and constitutional phase, Ramji initially played an energetic political role, working through the Bombay Millowners Association, the Indian Merchants Chamber and the Native Piece-goods Association which were at the forefront of several agitations against the British government. As a municipal councillor for eighteen years, a member of the Bombay legislative council (1910-20), and of the legislative assembly (1921-23), he was a powerful voice in favour of the nationalist cause. But after the advent of agitational politics, Ramji tended to withdraw his participation. For example, he was a member of the All-India Home Rule League, but dropped out when Gandhi converted the league into the Swarajya Sabha in 1920.[84]

Many entrepreneurs, though approving of nationalist aspirations in general, were cautious about endorsing the more aggressive programmes initiated by various political parties. In 1925, for example, Annie Besant (1847-1933), the then general secretary of the National Congress, was preparing a swaraj bill for presentation to Whitehall which she was anxious that Sir Purshotamdas Thakurdas should endorse and sign. When approached, Thakurdas declined. Besant wrote a letter to Thakurdas conveying more than a hint of rebuke: 'I am sorry you will not sign the memorandum claiming Swaraj. You always seem to agree with our politics, and yet you will not help in a definite way. Your signature would be useful because of your weight as a great merchant and as representing Bombay merchants. Why should you not'? In another letter, she apologized to Thakurdas, saying: 'There are many conditions which a great merchant and financier like yourself must consider which do not fetter a knight errant like myself'.[85]

Moreover, during this period the nationalists received virtually no support from the largest Indian business house, the Tatas. Though the founder of the group, Jamsetji Nusserwanji Tata, was one of the earliest nationalist business leaders of Bombay, under the leadership of his sons Dorab and Ratan, the group withdrew from political activity. The suspicions harboured against J.N. Tata by the British precluded his being given a knighthood or baronetcy,[86] but both Dorab and Ratan were knighted. Several top executives of the Tata group were amongst the most active protagonists of the anti-noncooperation movement. In fact, it appears that the Tatas, as a corporate policy, tried to keep aloof from the nationalists and the national movement. This was due to several reasons. First, after the First World War a situation of mutual dependence developed between the Tatas and the British government. The state, directly or indirectly, was the largest buyer of several Tata products, while the Tatas were the only suppliers of steel and rails to government railways and arsenals. Secondly, alone among Indian business groups, the Tatas had cultivated a permanent link with the colonial state through the hiring of retired members of the Indian Civil Service. In fact, on one occasion the volatile and highly entrepreneurial Walchand Hirachand (1882-1953) openly accused the Tatas of having 'a special preference for Europeans as against Indians',[87] even though Walchand also hired retired European army officers to obtain engineering contracts.[88] Many others too were not against hiring European personnel.[89] Also, the Tatas were highly westernized, both in their social mores, and in their management culture. Hence, they probably had less hesitation – or less distrust – in collaborating with the British.

The Tata attitude to the labour situation of the 1920s is a case in point. As the first rumblings of the trade union movement were heard, Sir Dorab Tata proposed the creation of a federation of both Indian and British employers to fight the incipient communist menace.[90] But not all Indian businessmen were happy at the thought of aligning themselves with British businessmen to fight the scourge of trade unionism. Also, the Tatas were grateful to the government for providing protection to their steel mills in 1924, when TISCO was on the verge of bankruptcy. As N.B. Saklatavala, TISCO's chairman, told shareholders in 1931: 'If protection has not paid dividends, it has at least preserved your property'.[91]

The dilemma in which Bombay's business groups found themselves manifested itself in the agitation against the Rowaltt Bills. Under this draconian legislation, introduced in 1919, a person could be detained anywhere, arrested without a warrant and his house searched. Certain offences could be tried in camera and the accused was not entitled to engage counsel. There was no right of appeal from the orders of the special tribunals. In short, the authority of the executive was substituted for that of the judiciary so far as security of property and safety of persons were concerned.

Initially, most of Bombay's entrepreneurs supported the nationalists in their opposition to the 'black acts', but much of this support faded out when Gandhi introduced the new weapon of *hartal* (closure of shops and markets). As riots spread and Gandhi inaugurated the passive resistance campaign, several of the city's most prominent industrialists banded together to sign a manifesto against passive resistance. The signatories included: Sir Dinshaw Wacha, Sir Homi Mody (1881-1969),[92] Sir Cowasji Jehangir and Sir Fazulbhoy Currimbhoy.[93]

Active opposition to Gandhi's campaign had begun to build up earlier. In October 1920, some millowners held a meeting under the chairmanship of Sir Dinshaw Wacha to discuss their attitude to non-cooperation. At this meeting, it was resolved that as non-cooperation would lead to violence, steps should be taken to inform public opinion of the dangers of the movement and lecture committees should be formed for the purpose.[94] Next an Anti-Noncooperation Committee was elected with Thakurdas and Sir Chimanlal Setalvad as honorary secretaries and several industrialists as members. Support from the Tata group was strong – with Homi Mody and Pheroze Sethna giving their open support, and 'anonymous' funds being donated by R.D. Tata(1856-1926) through the mediation of Thakurdas.[95]

If the purse-strings of Bombay's business groups were open for the anti-noncooperation movement, they appeared to have been closed tight for Gandhi. During a visit to Bombay on 2 July 1921, Gandhi addressed himself to the city's millowners: 'Many friends tell me that the nation is not to expect anything from you. They point out the fact that you have not, with one or two honourable exceptions, paid anything for the [Tilak] Swaraj Fund'.[96] The fund was founded by a group of stockbrokers in 1919. The single largest contributor to the fund was probably Ardeshir Godrej (five lakhs rupees), followed by Anandilal Poddar (1874-1940), a Marwari cotton broker who gave two lakhs. Another Marwari cotton broker, Surajmal Hurnandrai Ruia donated sixty thousand.[97]

The retreat of Bombay's business groups from political activity during this period can also be discerned in their cold attitude towards the Federation of Indian Chambers of Commerce and Industry (FICCI), established in 1927. Though FICCI's *raison d'etre* 'was to get a proper foothold before the executive at Delhi, so that the claims of Indian commerce and industry would not be at a disadvantage in comparison with those of European interests',[98] several important Bombay groups such as the Tatas,[99] the Khataus, and the Thackerseys refused to join it. And though Thakurdas succeeded in persuading Sir Dinshaw M. Petit to become FICCI's first president, the BMA refused to join so broadly based an organization. The IMC, however, immediately became a member, and in fact housed FICCI's office for two years until it was shifted to Delhi.[100]

FICCI rapidly became an effective voice in arguing for Indian industrial interests. Soon after its creation, it successfully lobbied for Indians to be permitted entry into the jute trading rooms in London, besides wringing other concession, 'the main beneficiaries being Birlas and Scindias'.[101] Despite such obvious benefits, many of Bombay's entrepreneurs remained indifferent to FICCI. Part of their aloofness lay in their unwillingness to be closely associated with FICCI leaders like G.D. Birla, Shri Ram, Padampat Singhania and Kasturbhai Lalbhai, all of whom were known for their strong nationalist views and pro-Congress sympathies.

Another factor in the withdrawal of Bombay's business groups from political activity was labour unrest. In January 1924 there was a general strike of cotton mill workers during which the communist movement made its first appearance.[102] There were eight major strikes in Bombay between 1922 and 1929, many characterized by a great deal of violence and intimidation. Bombay's millowners, by and large, were unused to dealing with a militant labour force. Workers in Bombay's industries had remained quiescent for years. In 1896, the *Times of India* had exulted over the peacefulness and docility of millworkers: 'Thrice happy Bombay! A large trade emporium with a labouring population full of gentleness and meekness, content to give a full day's labour for the barest necessities of life, and never to presume to question the justice or generosity of their employers'.[103]

Such a state of affairs could not possibly continue, particularly as millowners fought tooth and nail against improvements in working conditions.[104] As Jamsetji Tata had forecast in 1888:

> No doubt, Bombay being the centre of all trade and the port of transit nearest to Europe, a larger number of the unemployed will find their way here. But it should be borne in mind that the older operatives are now getting educated and beginning to have a faint glimmer of their true position in the industrial development. They pretty freely know when to strike and when to demand higher wages.[105]

But as violence spread from one mill to another in the 1920s, and the communist movement strengthened itself, worried millowners drew closer to the British government to fight this new 'menace'. Sir Victor Sasson (1881-1961), one of Bombay's biggest millowners and a member of the royal commission set up in 1929 to investigate labour conditions, dismissed India's aspirations to self-government as clear evidence of the 'Red Hand'[106] 'It is my firm conviction', he declared, 'that the agents of Communism in India are making any grievance, real or imaginary, the excuse for the further spread of Moscow doctrines, the industrial agitation being but a cloak for a wider and more sinister motive'.[107]

From the millowners' point of view, the alliance with the government was highly successful. By 1930 most unions in Bombay were virtually broken up. There was a marked decline in labour unrest for almost a decade.[108] And in the process they managed to wrest some relief from the cotton excise duty by linking wage reductions to the duties.[109]

IV

Towards the end of the 1920s and the beginning of the 1930s, there was a noticeable change in the relationships which Bombay's business groups had with the British government and with the Congress. Amongst millowners, the change was largely due to greater pressure on bottom lines as Japanese competition became keener and the depression set in. Millowners wanted the government to help stanch the flow of red ink but the government did not appear unduly concerned. On the contrary, the government obstinately refused to devalue the rupee in spite of an active campaign for devaluation launched by Indian business circles. The government also rejected the recommendation in the 1927 report of the Indian Tariff Board for a rise in the duty on imported cotton goods. In February 1930, this was followed by the Cotton Industries Protection Bill which created differential duties on British and non-British cotton goods, an issue which led to the resignation of G.D. Birla (1894-1983) and Thakurdas from their seats in the legislative assembly. As Claude Markovits points out, relations between big business and the government were at 'their lowest ebb for many years'.[110]

In the circumstances, the anti-government feelings of Bombay millowners were converted into a pro-Congress attitude almost as a natural corollary. With its boycott programme and swadeshi ideals, the Congress offered a way out of dealing with heavy inventories of unsold stock. Gandhi was well aware of this change of attitude among businessmen and took great care to include in his 'Eleven Points' most of the issues which were closest to the hearts (and balance-sheets) of Indian businessmen.[111]

Moreover, the communist threat which had loomed so large during the 1928-29 strikes, gradually retreated, paving the way for a better understanding with the nationalist leaders.

The emergence of several new business groups was another factor in the increased political interest of Bombay's entrepreneurs. The 1930s were years of profound change, with many of the pioneer groups being liquidated and new groups taking their place. One of the biggest groups to be wiped out during this period was that of the Currimbhoys. Along with Sassoons (Jews from Baghadad), the Currimbhoys (Khojas from Kutch) between them controlled 'about half the paid-up capital of the Bombay mills and 2/7 of the looms and spindles'.[112]

The failure of the Currimbhoy group with thirteen mills brought into sharp focus the depression in the Bombay textile industry. This group, more than any other, was particularly vulnerable to bankruptcy as it had not diversified. When the industry displayed signs of chronic sickness from 1924 onwards, so did the Currimbhoy mills. Currimbhoys had long ties with East Asia,[113] and their dependence on the China and east Asian markets, which had begun to dwindle, worked against them. And at a time when skilful management was badly needed, the new generation of Currimbhoys had acquired a taste for the good life and simply did not have the ability to manage their unwieldy empire effectively.[114] The political impact of the liquidation of the Currimbhoy group was that it removed from Bombay's political scene a highly westernized family of conservatives.

The political consequence of the changes in the capital structure of Bombay's society was that many promoters of the new groups were formerly merchants who held nationalist and pro-Congress views, while the older groups had followed a moderate stance. Some made the transition from trade to industry by buying out the bankrupt concerns of the pioneer groups. Other merchants became industrialists by setting up new concerns in industries which were given protection, such as the Walchand and Bajaj groups. These groups possessed a strong tradition of political involvement from their earlier merchant days when many of them had participated in the *hartals* which frequently closed Bombay markets. Investing in the profitable sugar industry, these groups now had greater financial resources to pour into the freedom movement.

The revived pro-Congress attitude of Bombay's big business was reflected in its support, admittedly limited, to Gandhi's call for civil disobedience after the December 1929 Congress session in Lahore. Markovits suggests that business support – which took the form of both financial help and participation in the boycott of foreign cloth – was an important factor in the overall success of the first phase of civil disobedience (March 1930-March 1931).[115] The only open condemnation of the agitation in Bombay came from a Tata director, Pheroze Sethna, which Thakurdas thought was a 'hasty step'.[116]

Support for the Congress from Bombay's business groups was evident from the swadeshi pledges of several millowners. In August 1930, after over two years of deliberations, the Congress Working Committee published a list of fifty-six mills to be boycotted, twenty-four of which were located in Bombay. These 'non-swadeshi' mills were so designated after consultation with the Swadeshi Sabha and 'under strong influence from the Bengal Provincial Congress Committee'.[117] To be classified as swadeshi, mills were not to weave or spin lower than 18s counts (so as not to compete with the handloom industry); they were not to use foreign yarn or silk; they were not to have more than 25 per cent foreign directorship or capital; and they were to insure with Indian companies. Millowners, moreover, were called upon to sign a pledge identifying themselves with national aspirations.[118]

In its narrow definition, boycott could mean the banning of all goods of certain description manufactured entirely outside India. Reeling under the impact of depression, with godowns full of unsold stocks, very few Indian industrialists argued with this interpretation – or its corollary, the swadeshi movement. But it could also mean (a) the boycott of firms which had either foreign management or used foreign capital even though they produced or supplied commodities within India, and (b) the boycott of capital goods or components used for manufacturing in India. The Indian capital goods industry was almost non-existent and most components for manufacturing operations had to be imported, often from different countries. Thus a simple declaration of boycott of foreign goods or firms still left a host of unanswered questions. What percentage of foreign management and capital constituted a foreign firm? How was a foreigner to be defined? Should all components be manufactured in India and could firms import capital goods? Other questions of importance related to the ability to replace the boycotted product at a reasonable price and to the security of jobs and capital of those Indians involved in foreign firms and in importing foreign goods.

The Congress had no clear-cut boycott policy that answered these questions. In reply to a query from Rameshwardas Birla (1892-1973), G.D. Birla's brother, about Indian-manufactured cloth, Gandhi wrote back: 'I am convinced that the boycott will be successful only through khadi. This, however, does not mean that mills have no place in the scheme at all. The mills can have their deserved place by recognizing the worth of khadi. The conception of God envelops all Gods'.[119] Such uncertainty left the boycott open to criticisms of all sorts, such as misuse of the boycott for purposes of purely domestic business competition, creating high prices, and throwing both businessmen and labourers out of work. In fact, such abuses did occur in Bombay, but not to the extent to which the opponents of the Congress claimed.[120]

The dilemma posed by the boycott became apparent almost immediately. The banning of twenty-four Bombay mills directly affected fifty-one thousand labourers, well over a third of the mill labour force, and an aggregate investment by Indians of over Rs 18,035,500 – not to mention the annual consumption of 342,000 bales of cotton. Apart from the millowners, this naturally caused concern amongst a wide section of the city, including those who held shares in the mills. The honorary secretary of the Bombay Shareholders Association, J.J. Kapadia, wrote to the secretary of the boycott committee of the Bombay Provincial Congress Committee (BPCC) pointing out that Indian shareholders owned approximately 30 per cent of the total paid-up share capital in seventeen European-controlled mills.[121] Several mills managed by non-Indian interests at first refused to comply with the clauses drawn up by the Congress, 'but a boycott by traders and consumers soon brought them to their senses'.[122] The remaining boycotted mills promptly started to negotiate through the Bombay Millowners Association with the BPCC, which waived the proviso concerning foreign directors, thus lifting the ban on mills in the Brady group.

Included at first in the list of boycotted concerns was the Toyo Podar Mills, managed by the Marwari cotton brokers, the Podars, in partnership with a large Japanese trading house, Mitsui & Company. To forestall being classified as a non-Indian mill, more members of the Podar family were taken on the board. Just before the outbreak of the Second World War, Mitsui snapped its links with Indian collaborators and the Podars gained full control of the mill which was then renamed the Podar Mills. Interestingly, the fortunes of the Podars had been made on exports of Indian cotton to Japan but they were one of the largest donors to the Tilak Swaraj Fund floated by Gandhi in 1921.[123]

The Sassoon group posed, however, the most serious trouble. Consisting of the larger and original David Sassoon & Company and the smaller break-away firm, E.D. Sassoon & Company, this Jewish group together controlled thirteen mills, employing twenty thousand workers, which accounted for nearly 25 per cent of Bombay's total cotton textile production. Most of the workers were Indian, and they had thousands of Indian shareholders, but the family preferred to consider itself European rather than Indian or Baghadadi.[124] The larger group at the time was headed by Sir Victor Sassoon, a member of the legislative assembly (1926-29). Bedevilled by factory strikes and boycotts, he came to be regarded at Viceregal Lodge and in the assembly 'as a last-ditch reactionary', impatient with even the hints of dominion status.[125] When the Congress showed no change of heart, Sir Victor's temper, 'always at low boiling point, became more violent with every turn of Gandhi's hand loom'.[126] He became even more intractable when demonstrations started at his mill gates. In Shanghai, he was used to playing the mandarin. Here in Bombay, where his great grandfather had settled a century before, he resented being denounced as 'foreign' exploiter of labour.[127] An attempt was made to remove the Sassoon mills from the boycott list by altering the use of artificial silk clause. After the BPCC was declared illegal, some of its members formed a joint committee with a few millowners in order to determine whether the Bombay mills should be allowed to use imported artificial silk. The outcome was the so-called Artificial Silk Agreement whereby the Sassoon mills were to be admitted to the swadeshi ticket. Subsequently, however, the Congress disowned the agreement and the Sassoons remained on the boycott list.[128]

The price of a ten-rupee deferred share of the largest mill in the Sassoon group, the E.D. Sassoon United Mills, crashed to one rupee. Without the goodwill of workers, the mills could not be well managed and red ink started spreading over the ledgers of Sassoon companies. Both Sassoon groups began liquidating their Indian assets. David Sassoon & Company quietly transferred its assets from Bombay to Shanghai and Hong Kong, to be absorbed in a vast estate development and in the E.D. Sassoon Banking Ltd. The smaller E.D. Sassoon & Company also sold its Bombay properties but poured these funds into international trading.[129]

By mid-1931, with his preparations completed, Sir Victor Sassoon announced his decision to leave Bombay and make Shanghai his headquarters. The disclosure came as a shock to many, but not to the Bombay Stock Exchange which was 'aware of the steady transfer of assets and the significance of the new Company registered in Hong

Kong'.[130] On 17 July, Sir Victor Sassoon crisply explained why he was leaving the country: 'There will be less scope in India for a foreigner in the future because of the cut-throat competition with Indian firms, who have less overhead charges, and because of the anti-foreign prejudice. It looks as if India under Swaraj will have a great deal of internal trouble'.[131]

The net result of the boycott of the Sassoon group was not particularly beneficial for the nation. The Sassoons lost interest in maintaining their mills and gradually much of the machinery became obsolete, and administration far from efficient. Between 1943 and 1949, they sold six of their mills. The buyers came from disparate backgrounds: three mills were sold to Marwaris (the Apollo Mills to the Bangurs, the E.D. Sassoon Mills to Agarwal & Company, Edward Textiles Ltd. to Puranmal Radha Kishan & Company); two mills to Gujaratis (Elphinston Mills to C. Mulraj & Company belonging to the Khatau Group who were Bhatias, and Sassoon Spinning & Weaving Company to the Mafatlals who were Patels).[132] These sales implied flight of scarce capital – one of the mills was reportedly sold for the then incredibly high figure of Rs.4.80 crore[133] – although they heralded the process of Indianization, a movement which gathered momentum in the 1940s and 1950s.

Meanwhile, the boycott negotiations continued with boycott committees issuing different lists of mills from time to time. But the position was still unclear even as late as October 1931, when mills were still being brought on or off the boycott list since the original criteria were not rigidly followed. None of this helped to foster a sense of security in the mill industry during a time of depression. Nonetheless, probably thirty-five Bombay mills at least must have signed the pledge. Their signing of such a pledge had a symbolic value which neither the British nor the nationalist leaders missed – it appeared as an act of allegiance to the Congress and thus had a big moral impact. Corporate advertising reflected the change in the business environment. An advertisement, after listing the four mills under the management of Thackersey Mooljee and Company, proclaimed in bold letters 'Capital, Labour and Management – 100% Swadeshi'.

The enthusiasm for the Congress displayed by Bombay's business groups began, however, to peter out by 1932, as did their financial support.[134] It diminished sharply when the Congress chose to resume civil disobedience on 4 January 1932. It ebbed further with Jawaharlal Nehru's increasingly Marxist speeches. It reached rock bottom with the decline in the city's main industrial activity, textiles, as the Great

Depression inexorably reached Indian shores. With the government's half-hearted stand providing only minor relief, millowners now took things into their own hands and concluded their own separate agreement with Lancashire mills – the Lees-Mody Pact of October 1933.

The pact took its name after Sir Homi Mody, a Tata director and chairman of the BMA, and Sir William Clare Lees, leader of a delegation of Manchester millowners (the British Textile Mission) who came to India to meet the BMA to work out an understanding with each other. Under the agreement, Bombay mills were granted limited protection against British textiles, but strong protection against those of other countries, especially Japan. Bombay mills agreed to accept a reduction in import duties on yarns and piece-goods made from artificial silk, and promised not to press for new duties on British imports. In return, British millowners would allow Indian mills to share in British quotas to countries where India did not have independent quotas. Manchester would also help bring Indian manufacturers and importers together in markets where India did not have good marketing arrangements, and to popularize the use of Indian cotton by British firms.[135]

The pact provoked controversy on two counts. Indian millowners outside Bombay did not see any advantage in it for the Indian industry. Nationalists equated it with the unpopular Ottawa Trade Agreement of 1932 and singled out Mody for 'selling out' to the British. Jawaharlal Nehru believed that this agreement was tantamount to treason and wrote in his autobiography: 'the Bombay mill industry in a body, during the continuance of civil disobedience and when we were preaching the boycott of British goods, had the temerity to conclude a pact with Lancashire. From the point of view of the Congress, this was a gross betrayal of the national cause'.[136]

Thus strained, the relationship between Bombay's business groups and the Congress almost splintered during Nehru's visit to the city in May 1936. Fears about his Marxist thinking among Bombay's business groups had been building up throughout the 'Indian summer of his leftism' which started in 1933.[137] Alarmed by the socialist content of his presidential address to the Lucknow Congress in April 1936, twenty-one 'mercantile leaders' of Bombay issued a manifesto against Nehru which appeared in the, *Times of India* and the *Tribune* on 20 May 1936. Since N.B. Saklatvala, A.R. Dalal, Homi Mody, Cowasji Jehangir, Pheroze Sethna and A.D. Shroff – all associated with the Tata group in one way or another – were signatories to the manifesto, there was 'good reason to think that the House of Tatas played an important role in the whole affair'.[138] Thus during the 1930s, the

Congress alienated two of Bombay's biggest business groups: the Sassoons and the Tatas.

Table 3 : Signatories to the May 1936 Manifesto against Nehru

1.	Sir N. Saklatvala	12.	Mr. Chunilal B. Mehta
2.	Sir Purshotamdas Thakurdas	13.	Mr. K.R.P. Shroff
3.	Sir chimanlal Setalvad	14.	Mr. Ratanji Hirji Govindji
4.	Sir Pheroze Sethna	15.	Mr. Ranchoddas Jethabhai
5.	Sir Cowasji Jehangir	16.	Mr. Khimji Vishram
6.	Mr. V.N. Chandavarkar	17.	Mr. Haridas Madhavdas
7.	Sir Shapoorji Billimoria	18.	Mr. Dharamsey Mulraj Khatau
8.	Mr. Walchand Hirachand	19.	Mr. Ishwardas Lakhmidas
9.	Mr. Mathuradas Vissanji	20.	Sir Homi P. Mody
10.	Mr. A.R. Dalal	21.	Mr. A.D. Shroff
11.	Mr. R. Chinoy		

Source : *Times of India*, 20 May 1936.

An uneasy truce was cobbled together by G.D. Birla almost immediately, and a contrite Walchand Hirachand promptly contributed one lakh rupees towards the Faizpur Congress session,[139] though Thakurdas pointedly refused to contribute.[140] A partial rapproachement between the Tatas and Nehru was arrived at within a couple of years. In 1939, faced with a strike at Jamshedpur, the Tatas accepted Nehru's mediation and in a letter dated 10 August 1939, J.R.D.Tata (b.1904) thanked him for his efforts.[141]

In the meantime, the provincial elections of February 1937 were held. In Bombay the Congress made substantial gains and formed the ministry. Several of the city's entrepreneurs contested these elections. Two notable winners were S.B. Saklatavala, a cousin of J.R.D. Tata, and Lalchand Hirachand (b.1904), Walchand's brother. The participation of Bombay's business groups in these elections brought home the awakening of their political awareness. The canvassing and winning of elections proved that their political tutelage was over and that Bombay's business groups had come of age in the political arena. In the process, they learnt that politics was power. This realization combined with the Congress's need for their money, enabled them to grasp a new equation - that business could be power as well.

Notes

1. In a letter to G.D. Birla Gandhi wrote: 'I am ever hungry for money'. Gandhi to Birla, 9 October 1927, in G.D. Birla, *Bapu: A Unique Association*, (Bombay 1977), vol. I, p.72.

In a 'most secret and personal' communication, Lord Linlithgow, Viceroy of India from 1935-1943, wrote: 'I am anxious that every possible step should be taken to trace and bring home to those concerned the part played by 'Big Business' in the recent disturbances'. Linlithgow to all Provincial Governors, 2 November 1942, in G.D. Birla, *Words to Remember* (Bombay 1983), p.116.

2. Prakash Tandon. *Punjabi Saga* (Calcutta 1988), p.112.

3. That this attitude was widespread is clearly highlighted in several autobiographies and biographies, such as those of members of the Podar family: 'A Brief Biography of Raja Ramdeo Anandilal Podar (Nawalgarh)', unpublished typescripts in the Podar family archives, n.d.; the Walchand Hirachand group: G.D. Khanolkar, *Walchand Hirachand: Man, His Times and Achievements* (Bombay 1969); and the Thackersey group: Chhagunlal Jamnadas, *The Life of Late Shett Damodher Thackersey Mooljee, J.P.* (Bombay 1895). See also R.H. Jalbhoy, *The Partrait Gallery of Western India* (Bombay 1886).

4. Tandon, *Punjabi Saga* (n.2), p. 112; Bipan Chandra, 'The Indian Capitalist Class and Imperialism Before 1947', in his *Nationalism and Colonialsm in Modern India* (New Delhi 1979), p. 154.

5. Quoted in S.K. Sen, *The House of Tata, 1839-1939* (Calcutta 1975), p.24.

6. D.E. Wacha, *Shells from the Sands of Bombay: Being My Recollections and Reminiscences, 1860-1875* (Bombay 1920), p. 98.

7. S.M. Rutnagur, *The Bombay Industries: The Cotton Mills* (Bombay 1927), p. 288.

8. Government of India, *Report of the Indian Industrial Commission, 1918* (Calcutta 1918), p. 73.

9. Richard I. Cashman, *The Myth of the Lokamanya: Tilak and Mass Politics in Maharashtra* (Berkeley 1975), p. 166.

10. In their reports for 1870-71, the principals of the Elphinstone College and the Deccan College mentioned that the majority of their pupils came from poor families. In an editorial of 31 August 1873, the *Native Opinion* added: 'The plain truth is that higher education has been made available only to the favoured sons of wealth and fortune. Unfortunately they have not acquired a taste for learning'.

11. One of Elphinstone College's most famous students was Jamsetji Tata who studied there from 1856 to 1858 as a 'free student'. Tata was later to become a founding member of both the Bombay Presidency Association and the Indian National Congress. See Frank Harris, *Jamsetji Nusserwanji Tata: A Chronicle of His Life* (Glasgow 1958). Three of the six boys of Tyab Ali, a leading trader of the early nineteenth century, went to the Elphinstone Institution. Two of these, Badruddin (1844-1906) and Amiruddin, became lawyers and were active not only in Muslim associations such as the Anjuman-i-Islam, but later also in the Bombay Presidency Association and the Indian National Congress. See Husain B. Tyabji, *Badruddin Tyabji: A Biography* (Bombay 1952).

12. These letters, though appearing under the heading of 'Correspondence' in the *Bombay Gazette*, were fairly long and were more in the nature of lead editorials. Each letter centred on one of eight subjects: (a) The odious nature of British rule in comparison with other powers; (b) treatment of Indian princes; (c) the Company as ruler; (d) economic drain; (e) law and justice; (f) education; (g) religious policy; (h) British historiography in India. For more details about these letters, see J.V. Naik, 'An Early Appraisal of the British Colonial Policy', in *Journal of the University of Bombay*, XLIV & XLV, new series (1975-76), pp. 243-70.

13. J.R.P. Mody, *Jamsetjee Jejeebhoy, The First Indian Knight and Baronet, 1783-1859* (Bombay 1959).

14. A Kapol bania, Nathubhai was a wealthy banker, landlord and millowner. He was not only a social reformer but as president of the Bombay Association from 1867-71, played an active part in local politics. Along with Morarji Goculdas, a prominent Bhatia millowner, Nathubhai organized several meetings to protest against the government's cotton textile policy in 1879. The *Times of India*, 6 May 1879. See also Jalbhoy, *Portrait Gallery* (n.3), pp. 20-21.

15. The biggest Hindu millowner in Bombay with four mills under his management, Damodher Thackersey, played a prominent role in local politics especially in the ratepayers agitation of 1871. See G. Piramal, 'Industrial Entrepreneurship in Historical Perspective: A Case Study of the Thackersey Group, 1873-1939', (unpublished Ph.D. thesis, Bombay University, 1988).

16. In December 1863, Rustomji Jamsetji Jijeebhoy (1824-72), second son of the first baronet, founded a trust of Rs. 150,000 enabling five Indians to study law in Europe. The proposal was open to a Parsi, a Hindu and a Portuguese in Bombay, and a Muslim, a Hindu or east Indian from Calcutta or Madras. Two of the first beneficiaries of this trust were Pherozeshah Mehta (1845-1915) from Bombay and W.C. Bonnerjee (1844-1906) from Bengal, both of whom were later to play crucial roles in Indian politics. Tyabji, *Badruddin* (n.11), p.21.

17. Christine Dobbin, *Urban Leadership in Western India Politics and Communities in Bombay City, 1840-1885* (London 1972), p.78.

18. Mody, *Jamsetji Jeejibhoy* (n.13), p.40.

19. B. Martin, *New India, 1885* (Bombay 1970), p. 48.

20. Proceedings of the Second Annual General Meeting of the Bombay Association, 1855 quoted in Dobbin, *Urban Leadership* (n.17), p. 83.

21. Martin, *New India* (n.19), pp. 2-3.

22. Quoted in Mody, *Jamsetji Jeejibhoy* (n.13), p. 40.

23. Dobbin, *Urban Leadership* (n.19), p. 82.

24. Interestingly, Dr. Bhau Daji, a well-known Indologiest, was a graduate from the Grant Medical College and Naoroji Furdoonji was a translater at the Bombay High Court. Manakji Kharsheji, the son of a leading member of the Parsi Panchayat who lost his money in the crash of 1865, was an assistant collector at Bombay's Customs House. S.P. Sen, *Dictionary of National Biography* (Calcutta 1973), vol. II, pp. 382-4; and vol. III, pp. 223-4; Dobbin, *Urban Leadership* (n.19), p. 26.

25. Dobbin, *Urban Leadership* (n.19).

26. S.M. Edwardes, *The Bombay City Police: A Historical Sketch, 1672-1922* (London 1923), p. 45.

27. Dobbin, *Urban Leadership* (n.19).

28. See Tyabji, *Badruddin* (n.11), pp. 129-42, for a graphic description of events leading up to the 28 April meeting as well as newspaper reports on the controversy.

29. A. Tikekar, 'The Ferment: Political Activities Before 1885', in R. Zakaria (ed.), *100 Glorious Years: Indian National Congress 1885-1985* (Bombay 1985), p. 20.

30. D.E. Wacha, *The Life and Life Work of J.N. Tata* (Madras 1915), p. 110.

31. Cashman, *Myth of Lokmanya* (n.9), p. 153 and p. 160; Harris, *Tata* (n.11), p. 248, says that the Bombay Presidency Association 'provided the local machinery for Congress'.

32. Three sons of Tyabji Ali, Badruddin, Amiruddin and Camiruddin, came to be recognized

as heads of the Muslim Suleiman Bohra community by virtue of the extensive business fortune acquired by their father, who established commercial houses in London, China and Karachi. Jalbhoy, *Portrait Gallery* (n.3), p. 58.

33. The Bombay presidents of Congress were:

    1886 Dadabhai Naoroji

    1887 Badruddin Tyabji

    1890 Pherozeshah Mehta

    1893 Dadabhai Naorji

    1986 Rahimtoola Sayani

    1900 Narayan Chandavarkar

    1901 Dinshaw Wacha

    1905 Gopal Krishna Gokhale

    1906 Dadabhai Naorji

34. Tyabji, *Badruddin* (n.11), p. 28.

35. Cashman, *Myth of Lokmanya* (n.9), p. 160.

36. For example, in 1886 Damodher Thackersey donated three hundred rupees as a personal contribution to the Indian National Congress.

37. D.E. Wacha to Dadabhai Naorji, 9 July, 1 November and 15 November 1889. Quoted in Cashman, *Myth of Lokmanya* (n.9), p. 158.

38. *Indu Prakash,* 9 February 1885.

39. Premchand Roychand, sometimes called the uncrowned king of speculators, was one of Bombay's richest citizens until the crash of 1865 wiped him out. See D.E. Wacha, *Premchand Roychand: His Early Life and Career* (Bombay 1913).

40. J.R.B. Jeejeebhoy, *Bribery and Corruption in Bombay* (Bombay 1952), pp. 250-2.

41. Wacha to Naoroji, 7 September 1904, quoted in Cashman, *Myth of Lokmanya* (n.9), p. 166.

42. Sen, *House of Tata* (n.5), p. 25.

43. Speech of Sir P. Mehta, quoted in Wacha, *J. N. Tata* (n.30).

44. Millowners Association, Bombay, *Centenary Souvenir, 1875-1975* (Bombay 1979), annexure A, p. 73.

45. The founder of the Bombay Dyeing & Manufacturing Co. Ltd. See *Diamond Jubilee of the Bombay Dyeing & Manufacturing Co. Ltd. 1879-1939* (Bombay 1940); *Bombay Dyeing: The First Hundred Years 1879-1979* (Bombay 1979).

46. Wacha, *J. N. Tata,* (n.30), p.5.

47. In May 1903, Curzon informed Hamilton: 'Tata had a good deal to do with the publication of Digby's book on Indian poverty, and that he paid for a special edition of the work which has been circulated throughout India'. Quoted in Sen, *House of Tata* (n.5), p.35.

48. Hamilton apparently once remarked that Tata's great wealth 'must have ultimately a very mischievous social effect'. Quoted in ibid., pp. 25-6.

49. Hamilton proposed to give him some appropriate distinction in 1899 after Tata had made a gift of two million sterling as an endowment to Scottish universities. But apparently nothing was done at the time. Hamilton to Curzon, 6 September 1899 and 6 June 1901, quoted in ibid., p. 21.

50. Hamilton to Dorab Tata, 25 June 1920, quoted in Harris, *Tata* (n.11), p. 249.

51. Quoted in Sen, *House of Tata* (n.5), p. 26.

52. As many as 22,000 people died during one of its worst visitations in 1896-27 and plague accounted for altogether 114, 506 deaths between 1896-1906. *Census of India, 1911, vol. VIII, part I: Bombay Town and Island* (Bombay 1912), P. 9.

53. From 1896 to 1906, Bombay Presidency suffered an almost unbroken chain of major and minor famines. Such calamities brought untold hardship for the working class; for the city merchant they meant disruption in trade, especially in the export of wheat and other foodstufs which had gained in importance with the sharp reduction of opium trading after the Treaty of Nanking (1842). See B.M. Bhatia, *Famines in India, 1860-1965* (Delhi 1967); and 'Trade in India' in *The Cyclopedia of India* (Calcutta 1909), vol. III, p. 106.

54. June 1832 saw the first Hindu-Parsi riot. These were repeated in October 1851 and again in February 1874. At the time of Muharram, Hindu-Muslim riots became an almost regular occurrence, but in August 1893, 1911 and 1929, they affected the city seriously. A. Tikekar, *The Cloister's Pale* (Bombay 1984), p. 64.

55. Bombay's first trade union, the Bombay Millhands' Association, was established in 1896.

56. In 1893 the mints were closed for the free coinage of silver, the first step in moving away from the silver standard. It created a currency muddle whose immediate impact was a drastic curtailment of Bombay's yarn exports to China and Japan. See S.D. Mehta, *The Cotton Mills of India* (Bombay 1954), pp. 64-5. In the case of the Hindoostan Spg & Wvg Mills Ltd., for example, exports which were of the order of Rs. 206,029 in 1893 immediately halved the next year to Rs. 191,763. *Annual Report of the Hindoostan Spg & Wvg Mills Ltd.* for the years ended 30 June 1893 and 30 June 1894.

57. Harris, *Tata* (n.11), pp. 29, 47.

58. Sir S. Saklatvala, 'The Indian Cotton Textile Industry', in *Indian Textile Journal: Jubilee Souvenir, 1890-1940* (Bombay 1940), p. 19.

59. Sir V. Thackersey, 'Speech on the Abolition of the Countervailing Excise Duty on Indian Cotton Goods', 9 March 1911, in H.L. Kaji, *The Life and Speeches of Sir Vithaldas Thackersey* (Bombay 1934), p. 351.

60. The feeling that the British government would always look after Lancashire interests over those of Bombay became clear to Bombay millowners almost from the inception of the industry. In1879, Sir Mangaldas Nathubhai and Morarjee Goculdas, two prominent millowners, wanted to organize a public meeting to discuss the question of import duties. Permission was denied to them to use the town hall and the venue was shifted to the Framji Cowasji Institute where on 3 May 1879 a petition was read out and charges of 'the gravest nature, including instructions disobeyed, pledges broken, sacred trusts violated, revenues misappropriated and the first principles of economy ignored' against the government were made. *Times of India*, 6 May 1879; Tyabji, *Badruddin* (n.11), p. 128.

61. Officially launched when Lord Curzon announced the partition of Bengal, the swadeshi movement was the response by some Indian nationalists to fight British imperialism with its own weapons of trade and commerce. Bipan Chandra, *The Rise and Growth of Economic Nationalism in India* (New Delhi 1982), p. 746.

62. Dadabahi Naoroji to Sir Dinshaw Wacha, 19 October 1905, quoted in Mehta, *Cotton Mills* (n.56), p.92.

63. *Indian Textile Journal*, (n.58), p. 340.

64. Ibid.

65. Cashman, *Myth of Lokmanya* (n.9), p. 175.

66. *Kaiser-i-Hind,* 23 December 1906.

67. From 1900 to 1914, the number of spindles in Bombay increased from 2.5 million to 3 million, but the number of looms more than doubled from 22,000 to 48, 000.

68. S.L. Kirloskar, *Cactus and Roses* (Pune 1982), p. 55.

69. Ibid., p. 56.

70. A millowner who subsequently fell on hard times. His son, Jamnadas Dwarkadas, an importer of mill dyes, was one of the earliest members of the Home Rule League and played an important role in the boycott committees of the 1930s.

71. See V. Elwin, *The Story of Tata Steel* (Bombay 1958).

72. See G. Piramal, 'Industrial Entrepreneurship in Historical Perspective' (n.15), and Kaji, *Life and Speeches* (n.59).

73. Later they were merged into the Federation of the Indian Chambers of Commerce and Industry.

74. Indian Merchants' Chamber, *Platinum Jubilee Commemoration Volume, 1982* (Bombay 1982), p. 14.

75. A cotton merchant, Thakurdas played a pivotal role in national politics, through his position as a member of the Council of State and the Central Legislative Assembly; through the Federation of Indian Chambers of Commerce and Industry (FICCI) and the IMC; and through his prolific correspondence with almost all the major players of the day. See Frank Moraes, *Sir Purshotamdas Thakurdad* (Bombay 1967).

76. A merchant, millowner and landlord, Rahimtoola became a central figure in the political firmament because of his great influence with various governors. A.D.D. Gordon, *Businessmen and Politics: Rising Nationalism and a Modernising Economy in Bombay, 1918-1933* (New Delhi 1978), p. 247.

77. The Currimbhoy Group was one of Bombay's largest with thirteen mills, controlling 13,000 looms out of the city's total of 71,000 looms. *Report of the Indian Tariff Board: Cotton Textile Industry Enquiry, 1927* (Bombay 1927), vol. IV, p. 80.

78. *Times of India*, 11 November 1932 described the chamber as representing 'the largest amount of capital and enterprise in western India'.

79. *Bombay Chronicle*, 19 April 1913.

80. The founder of the group, Morarjee Goculdas (1833-80) was one of the earliest to get into the cotton textile industry. A large family and well connected to other Bhatia millowners, the Goculdases promoted several industrial concerns - the Sholapur Mills, the Dharamsi Morarjee Chemical Company, the Scindia Steam Navigation (along with Walchand Hirachand and the Khataus) - besides the Morarjee Goculdas Spg & Wvg Mills. See G. Piramal 'A History of the Morarjee Goculdas Spg & Wvg Mills 1871-1934 (unpublished M.A. dissertation, Bombay University, 1981).

81. N.G. Jog, *Narottam Morarjee: Architect of Modern Indian Shipping* (Bombay 1977), p.13.

82. Gordon, *Businessmen and Politics* (n.76), p. 158.

83. Almost throughout the inter-war period, sporadic violence continued to be a problem. The Thackersey-managed Indian Manufacturing Co. Ltd. first took out riot insurance in 1923 and this form of insurance became an almost regular item in the annual reports of the company after that, the premium rising steeply in 1933 and again in 1942. *Annual*

Reports of the Indian Manufacturing Co. Ltd, for the years ended 31 March 1923, 1933 and 1942.

84. Hindoostan Mills, *100 Years*; Chairman's Statements, at the annual general meeting of the Indian Manufacturing Co. Ltd, 10 August 1935; Gordon, *Businessmen and Politics* (n.76), p. 158; Rutnagar, *Bombay Industries* (n.7), p. 722.

85. Moraes, *Purshotamdas*, (n.75), pp. 109-10.

86. See section I.

87. Khanolkar, *Walchand Hirachand* (n.3).

88. Ibid., p. 114.

89. In 1913, Dewan Bahadur K.P. Puttana wrote to Sir Vithaldas Thackersey asking him whether he should appoint European or Indian as a manager to the New Bank of Mysore which was going to be floated. Thackersey wrote back: 'The Bank is a commercial undertaking and it will be the pride of the Manager to make the Bank as great a success as possible. There is no political question involved'. Sir V. Thackersey to Dewan Bahadur K.P. Puttana, 9 April 1913, quoted in Kaji, *Life and Speeches* (n.59), p. 146.

90. Sir Dorab Tata's proposal is mentioned in a letter from a Tata executive to Thakurdas, 3 July 1929. Quoted in Claude Markovits, *Indian Business and Nationalist Politics 1931-1939: The Indigenous Capitalist Class and the Rise of the Congress Party* (Cambridge 1985), p. 30.

91. Quoted in Rajat K. Ray, *Industrialization in India: Growth and Conflict in the Private Corporate Sector, 1914-1947* (Delhi 1979), p. 83.

92. Closely associated with the Tatas, being a director both of TISCO and Tata Sons, Mody was a Parsi lawyer and was twice president of the BMA.

93. Gordon, *Businessmen and Politics* (n.76), p. 157.

94. Ibid., p. 159.

95. Ibid.; Markovits, *Indian Business and Nationalist Politics* (n.90), p. 37. The son of Dadabhai Tata, and Jamsetji Tata's brother-in-law, R.D. Tata became a partner of Tata Sons in 1907, and was chairman of TISCO in 1922. Father of the present head of the Tata group, J.R.D. Tata.

96. M.K. Gandhi, 'Appeal to the Millowners', *Bombay Chronicle*, 6 July 1921.

97. 'A Brief Biography of Seth Anandilal Podar' (n.3), p. 21.

98. Thakurdas, quoted in Stanley Kochanek, *Business and Politics in India* (Berkeley 1974), p. 159.

99. Except for a brief period in the late 1930s when through the persuasion of Lala Shri Ram, A.R. Dalal joined the FICCI committee, the Tatas stayed out of FICCI. The Tata representative dropeed out of the organization on the eve of the 1939 crisis between the Congress and the British government. Ibid., p. 161.

100. Khanolkar, *Walçhand* (n.3), p. 338.

101. Moraes, *Purshotamdas* (n.75), p. 44.

102. M.R. Masani, *The Communist Party of India* (London 1954), p. 35; *Bombay Chronicle*, 'Strike at the Gold Mohur Mills', 17 August 1924; 'Echo of Mills Riots', 2 November 1924.

103. *Times of India*, 28 March 1896.

104. As a member of the Indian Factory Labour Commission of 1907, Sir Vithaldas

Thackersey stressed that labour legislation for a twelve-hour working day 'would endanger the future of Indian factories'. Sir V. Thackersey, 'Speech on the Factory Bill' in the Imperial Legislative Council, 21 March 1911, in Kaji, *Life and Speeches* (n.59), p. 354.

105. Quoted in V.B. Kulkarni, *History of the Indian Cotton Textile Industry* (Bombay 1979), p. 326.

106. S. Jackson, *The Sassoons* (London 1968), p. 215.

107. Ibid.

108. T.V. Baddeley, 'Industrial Disputes and Their Settlement', in the *Indian Textile Journal* (n.58), pp. 281-3.

109. *Bombay Chronicle*, 17 August 1924.

110. Markovits, *Indian Business and Nationalist Politics* (n.90), p. 68.

111. The Eleven Points first appeared in *Young India* on 30 January 1930 under the headline 'Subsistence of Independence'. They were:

1. Total prohibition,
2. Reduction of the ratio to 1s 4d,
3. Reduction of the land revenue to at least 50% and making it subject to legislative control,
4. Abolition of the salt tax,
5. Reduction of the military expenditure to at least 50% to begin with,
6. Reduction of the salaries of the higher grade service to one half or less so as to suit the reduced revenue,
7. Protective tariff on foreign cloth,
8. The passage of the Coastal Traffic Reservation Bill,
9. Discharge of all political prisoners save those condemned for murder or the attempted thereat by the ordinary judicial tribunal, withdrawal of all political prosecutions, abrogation of Section 124A, the Regulation of 1818 and the like, and permission to all the Indian exiles to return,
10. Abolition of C.I.D. or its popular control,
11. Issue of licences to use fire arms for self-defence subject to popular control.

112. *The Report of the Indian Tariff Board* (n.77), p. 88.

113. The legacy of these ties can still be noticed on their coat-of-arms. In the central part of the decoration, there is a Chinese junk sailing on the sea, along with a crescent (to show their religion) and a lotus (to show their Indian origin). *Debrett's Illustrated Baronetage* (London, 1976), p. 1543.

114. Asif E. Currimbhoy in a letter dated 21 February 1984 to the author.

115. Markovits, *Indian Business and Nationalist Politics* (n.90), p. 71.

116. Ibid., pp. 70, 74.

117. Gordon, *Businessmen and Politics* (n.76), p. 208.

118. See B. Pattabhi Sitaramayya, *History of the Indian National Congress* (Bombay 1946), vol. I, appendix V, p. 652 for the complete pledge forms which mills had to fill.

119. Gandhi to Rameshwardas Birla, 28 April 1930 in Birla, *Bapu: A Unique Association*, vol. I, p. 139.

120. Gordon, *Businessmen and Politics* (n.76) p. 208; Mehta, *Cotton Mills* (n.56), p. 177.

121. Markovits, *Indian Business and Nationalist Politics* (n.90), p. 24; Gordon, *Businessmen and Politics* (n.76), p. 209.

122. Mehta, *Cotton Mills* (n. 56), p. 177.

123. G. Piramal, 'Entrepreneurship in Bombay', *Economic Times*, 18 February 1984.

124. Jackson, *Sassons* (n.106), p. 214.

125. Ibid.

126. Ibid., p. 215.

127. Ibid.

128. Gordon, *Businessmen and Politics* (n.76), p. 210.

129. Jackson, *Sassoons* (n.106), p. 218.

130. Ibid., p. 225.

131. Quoted in ibid., p. 225.

132. Compiled from ibid.; M.L. Kothari, *Industrial Combinations* (Allahabad 1967); Mehta, *Cotton Mills* (n.56).

133. Mehta, *Cotton Mills* (n.56), p. 208.

134. Kochanek, *Business and Politics* (n.98), p. 162.

135. Kasturbhai Lalbhai, 'Trade Treaties and Pacts', in *Indian Textile Journal*, (n.58), pp. 24-5.

136. Cited in Kochanek, *Business and Politics* (n.98), p. 162.

137. Bipan Chandra, 'Jawaharlal Nehru and the Capitalist Class, 1936', in *Nationalism and Colonialism in Modern India* (n.4), p. 171.

138. Markovits, *Indian Business and Nationalist Politics* (n.90), p. 111.

139. Khanolkar, *Walchand* (n.3), p. 342.

140. Markovits, *Indian Business and Nationalist Politics* (n.90), p. 120.

141. J.R.D. Tata to J. Nehru, 10 August 1939, quoted in ibid., p. 149.

6

Congress and the Left Critics

B.R. Nanda

The eighteen accused in the Meerut Conspiracy Case, who included the founding fathers of the Communist Party of India, in their long statement before the court, declared that Gandhi's civil disobedience campaigns were a means of sabotaging 'revolutionary movements', that the Indian National Congress under his leadership shied away from violence as it did not want to overthrow foreign rule, and that Gandhi was really working for a compromise in the interest of the Indian bourgeoisie.[1] This statement was in accord with the thesis presented to the Second Communist International by M.N. Roy in 1920, and his subsequent commentary on the non-cooperation movement. Roy made a pointed reference to the instinct of 'preserving property rights [which] betrays the class affiliation of Gandhi in spite of his pious outbursts against the sordid materialism of modern civilization'.[2]

Young Roy had left his country during the First World War. He had little first-hand information about the conditions in India in the early 1920s; nor had he met Gandhi. But his thesis of a direct nexus between Gandhi and Indian capitalists became a leftist dogma which was taken up, elaborated and propounded by numerous writers to our own day;[3] it has inspired at least two beliefs which have had an astonishingly long life. One of these is that the capitalists kept Gandhi and the Congress flush with funds; the other is that, as a *quid pro quo*, Gandhi astutely checked the revolutionary aspects of his struggle against the Raj to suit the vested interests of the capitalists.[4] From these beliefs has stemmed the leftist thesis that there was an alliance between Gandhi and Indian capitalists and that he regulated the intensity of his satyagraha against the British at their bidding and in their interest.[5]

A balanced evitique of the leftist thesis would require a close examination of these beliefs and this is what, this paper seeks to do.

I

The financial position of the Congress in the years before the First World War was, in the words of the historian of the Indian National Congress, 'never very sound'.[6] The irony of the situation, as a Poona journal put it, was that 'those who can and ought to pay for the Congress have not the will, while those whose heart is in the movement are most of them too poor to pay'.[7] The main expenditure in those early years was on the holding of annual sessions which had to be met from the delegates' fees, supplemented by donations. The Congress was rarely able to meet its commitments to its branch in London, the British Committee of the Congress, whose chairman Sir William Wedderburn, while complaining of 'the want of pence', met the deficit from his own and his friends' pockets.[8]

From 1920 the Congress was dominated by the personality of Gandhi. Despite his indubitable charisma, and the great reverence in which he was personally held by all sections of society, it is significant that hardly any capitalist, with the exception of A.D. Godrej, Omar Sobhani and Jamnalal Bajaj, contributed to the Tilak Swaraj Fund. Not a single industrialist signed the satyagraha pledge against the Rowlatt Bills in the spring of 1919. So, far from supporting Gandhi, the prominent industrialists of Bombay banded together to form an Anti-noncooperation Committee, with Purshotamdas Thakurdas and Chimanlal Setalvad as secretaries, and the Tatas as financiers. Gandhi knew some of the industrialists, and treated them – as he treated everybody else – with courtesy, but he had no illusions about them. In a letter 'To the Millowners' published in the *Bombay Chronicle*, he wrote that the merchants, whom he was urging to boycott the sale of foreign cloth, had 'frightened me by saying that the result of their response will simply mean that you millowners will immediately send up the prices and fling up in the face of the nation the law of supply and demand in support of the inflation of price'.[9]

Gandhi's appeal to the industrialists 'to conduct their business on national rather than on purely commercial lines' fell on deaf ears. He discovered that the industrialists were not susceptible to such appeals; they were hard-headed men, not easily swept off their feet by patriotic slogans. Some of them, such as the Tatas in Bombay and the Mukherjees of Martin Burn in Calcutta, were socially integrated with the European business community, and were dependent upon official patronage for orders from the railways and other government departments, and for access to markets abroad. Then, there were men like Sir Purshotamdas Thakurdas, 'the cotton king of Bombay' and Lala Shri Ram, the Delhi industrialist, who were 'moderate nationalists', to whom Gandhi's methods of satyagraha and civil disobedience were anathema. Finally, there were industrialists like G.D. Birla, whose nationalist sentiment was heightened by their sense of resentment at British discrimination against Indian trade and industry. Birla was perceptive enough to see that Gandhi's struggle would ultimately weaken the Raj and help to loosen the grip of British capital on the Indian economy. He sincerely wished Gandhi and the Congress to succeed in wresting power from the Raj, but he did not want to get himself embroiled in the struggle.

Birla and his friends stayed out of the non-cooperation movement; in the mid 1920s they sought the support of the Congress Swarajists, led by Pandit Motilal Nehru, in the central legislative assembly to extract concessions from the government. This support was willingly given. Motilal was glad to extend a helping hand in the fight for protection for nascent Indian industries against foreign competition as well as for an equitable rupee-pound ratio. What Motilal saw of the cynical opportunism of the Indian capitalists in these years deeply shocked him. He found that their patriotic fervour cooled off as soon as their immediate objectives were attained. They had the temerity to suggest a meeting with top leaders of the Congress before they made any contributions to the funds of the Swaraj Party for the forthcoming elections. Motilal turned down their suggestion with withering scorn. In a letter to a Bombay millowner, Lalji Naranji, he wrote on 21 April 1928:

> It is very kind indeed of Sir Fazulbhoy Currimbhoy and Mr Stones to condescend to see the Mahatma, Dr Ansari and myself and hear what we have to say. Please tell them with my compliments that on the conditions mentioned by you, we have no alternative but to decline the honour. Allow me, however, to congratulate you and other mill-owners of Bombay on the new phase of devotion and loyalty to the government and the banks it controls, so rapidly developed after abolition of the excise duty and the fight for 1/4 [1s 4d]. I have been thinking over the matter ever since I received your telegram, and it is now my considered opinion that

> the Congress should welcome this change in the attitude of the mill-owners. An alliance between the Congress and the capitalists, who are bent on profiting by the sufferings of the nation, is an impossible one. The more suitable field of work for the Congress is among the workers and not the owners of the mills. But I was misled by the patriotic talk of some of my personal friends among the mill-owners. Mahatmaji never believed in an alliance with the latter, and I have now told him that he was right and I was wrong.[10]

Three days later, Gandhi himself confided to Jawaharlal Nehru (who was in Europe at the time) that the Bombay millowners 'wanted to do a deal with the Congress. But I am not sorry for the abortive negotiations. They have cleared the atmosphere'.[11] And Nehru himself has discounted, in his *Discovery of India* written in 1944, the 'frequent assertion' that the Indian National Congress was heavily financed by the big industrialists:

> This is wholly untrue and I ought to know something about it, as I have been general secretary and president of the Congress for many years. A few industrialists have financially helped from time to time in the social reform activities of Gandhiji and the Congress, such as, village industries, abolition of untouchability and the raising of depressed classes, basic education, etc. But they have kept scrupulously aloof from the political work of the Congress, even in normal times, and much more so, during periods of conflict with government. Whatever their occasional sympathies, they believed, like most sober and well-established individuals, in safety first. Congress work has been carried on almost entirely on the petty subscriptions and donations of its large membership.[12]

Gandhi prided himself on the fact that while Madan Mohan Malaviya knew how to secure donations from the princes, he himself specialized in collecting contributions from the poor. The Mahatma valued the coppers of the poor as much as the magnificent gifts from the rich. He was sometimes disconcerted by the niggardliness and cynicism of the richer donors. In 1940 he issued an appeal over his own signature for five lakh rupees for erecting a memorial to that great Christian friend of India, C.F. Andrews. After about a month he found that only a small sum had come in. He issued another appeal. Again a few thousand rupees trickled through. Gandhi then talked to Vallabhbhai Patel, who told him that money could not be collected for memorials even by a Mahatma by merely issuing appeals in the press. He suggested that Gandhi should go to Bombay and stay there for a week. Much against his will, Gandhi went to Bombay in response to Patel's invitation, and was able to collect five lakhs. But after that he never issued any appeal for funds to erect memorials. 'I have had a very sad experience about C.F. Andrews' memorial', he told Shriman Narayan, Jamnalal Bajaj's son-in-law, 'I am not prepared to burn my fingers once again'.[13]

Gandhi never expected much from the Indian capitalists and preferred the Congress funds to come from its supporters at the grassroots. The idea that a central organization, such as the All-India Congress Committee (AICC), should finance provincial or district congress committees seemed to him utterly wrong. On the contrary, it was for the district committees to finance the provincial committees, and for the latter to contribute funds to the functioning of the All-India Congress Committee. Above all, the strictest economy was essential in disbursing public funds. Gandhi felt:

> We may not build a pucca building when a thatched cottage would do. We may not use a motorcar when a bullock cart would serve the purpose, and we must avoid the bullock cart when the journey can be made on foot. Similarly the rigidest economy should be exercised in regulating the expenses of feeding workers.[14]

The fact of the matter is that the support which the national movement drew from the business class came largely from small merchants and petty shopkeepers who closed their shops when *hartals* were declared, occasionally attended public meetings addressed by Congress leaders and openly or secretly contributed their mite to Congress funds. As for the big merchants and the industrialists, their watchword was 'safety first'. In 1921 they ostentatiously refrained from contributing to the Tilak Swaraj Fund; if the target of one crore was finally attained, it was not through the donations of a few tycoons, but by a massive campaign to rope in thousands of small merchants and professional men and farmers and workers in towns and villages. According to Hare Krushna Mahtab, the veteran Congress leader of Orissa, the contribution of twenty-three thousand rupees from that province to the Tilak Swaraj Fund was made by 'door to door collections in all the districts. Even the copper pice were accepted. Everywhere there were small collections. There were no donations say of even Rs. 100'.[15] The experience of most provinces was probably the same, except that of Bombay and Bengal. But even in these two provinces it was the merchants rather than the industrialists who loosened their purse-strings to help complete the quotas of collection fixed for these provinces.

The bulk of the Tilak Swaraj Fund was spent – as it had been meant to be spent – on the non-cooperation movement, on subsistence allowances to lawyers who had given up their practice, on national schools, and on the promotion of khadi and other planks in the Congress programme.

By 1927 the Tilak Swaraj Fund was dwindling and the general secretaries of the Congress were stressing the urgency of collecting money for the efficient running of the central office of the AICC.[16] Among the steps suggested by them were the raising of the fee for the Congress delegates to the annual sessions from one rupee to ten rupees, and the levy of a fee on members of the AICC, besides contributions from provincial Congress committees. But no substantial improvement took place in the financial position of the Congress. All it was able to do was to arrange its annual sessions with the customary eclat. The AICC and the provincial Congress committees operated on shoe-string budgets.

In 1936 the AICC through its travelling inspectors compiled some information about the offices of the provincial Congress committees which makes interesting reading. The Maharashtra Congress Committee paid Rs 15 a month as rent for its office, and employed a secretary for Rs 60 a month and an accountant for Rs. 30;[17] its total assets were Rs 2,892. Some of the other provincial committees were much worse off. The Central Provinces Congress Committee at Nagpur paid a monthly rent of Rs 5, it had no paid staff, and its assets amounted to Rs 406.[18] The Kerala Congress Committee at Cochin had free accommodation for its office, and employed an office secretary at Rs 20 a month; its cash balance was Rs 49. The Karnataka Congress Committee at Dharwar paid Rs 15 a month as rent for its office, and boasted of Rs 21 in the bank, besides a cash balance of Rs 4. Incredible as it may seem, in March 1937, Jawaharlal Nehru, the Congress president, was hard put to it to finance the Bombay branch of the Civil Liberties Union, which was under the charge of his brother-in-law, Raja Hutheesing. Nehru expressed his anguish to a friend in Bombay:

> It is a standing wonder to me how a person will gladly spend a hundred rupees or more in entertaining me, and many thousands of rupees on a marriage function or another, and yet be averse to give a small donation for public work. Can we not get a number of people to give a small subscription of Rs 10 or 15 a month for this Union?[19]

A year earlier, Govind Ballabh Pant had confided to Rajendra Prasad, one of the three members of the Central Paliamentary Committee, that the prospects of securing funds for provincial elections in the United Provinces locally were dismal.[20] The letter was intercepted and brought to the viceroy's notice. Lord Linlithgow's comment was: 'Finance in all probability is going to be the limiting factor for the electoral and agrarian activities of the Congress. We ought to watch their moneybags with constant attention'.[21]

About the same time Bhulabhai Desai, who had borne the brunt of organizing the elections campaigns for the central assembly in 1934, was entertaining the liveliest scepticism about support from the industrialists. Desai told Birla that the provincial elections in the subcontinent on an extended franchise would need at least ten lakhs, and that it was 'the duty of the upper middle classes, the businessmen and the industrialists to provide it'. Desai complained that though the Indian industrialists had profited from the swadeshi movement, they had 'hardly any sense of shame which would make them feel small that they are in no way interested or helpful in any patriotic work at all'.[22] Birla was clearly of the view, as Desai noted in his diary on 20 February 1936,'that the upper middle class and the industrialists are not at all taking their share of the burden of India's freedom. If others could be persuaded, Mr Birla is willing to bear his share of the burden . . . . He agreed it should be a voluntary contribution and not a matter of begging for favours'.[23] A few days later, when the captains of Indian industry, Walchand Hirachand, Purshotamdas Thakurdas, Padampat Singhania, Kasturbhai Lalbhai and others, assembled at Bombay for a meeting of the Federation of Indian Chambers of Commerce, all that Bhulabhai could secure from them was the promise to contribute ten to twelve thousand rupees to offset partially the deficit of twenty-five thousand incurred by the Congress in the central assembly elections two years earlier.[24]

The fact is that the reluctance of the capitalists to contribute to

Congress funds, at least until 1937, was based on careful calculations. The political and economic programme of the Congress, however conservative it might have seemed to its socialist and communist critics, struck the princes, landlords and capitalists – whose interests were tied up with the status quo of the Raj – as much too radical. It is significant that in the provincial elections in 1937, the Congress won only four out of the thirty-seven seats reserved for landholders, and of the fourty-six seats for commerce and trade organizations only three seats went to the Congress. In the 1920s and 1930s – indeed even in the early 1940s – the result of the conflict between the Indian National Congress and the British government was by no means a foregone conclusion. Those who joined the Congress camp, did so with their eyes open; they knew they were incurring the displeasure of the authorities and might have to pay a heavy price for it.

II

The hard choice which confronted big businessmen during the turbulent years can be best illustrated by contrasting the careers of Ghanshyam Das Birla and Jamnalal Bajaj, both Marwaris, and in their own ways close to Gandhi.

Bajaj had plunged into the political arena at Gandhi's instance in 1920, and never looked back again. His supreme loyalty was to Gandhi and the causes which he espoused from time to time. Jamnalal's resources were smaller than those of the great magnates of Bombay and Calcutta, but he made substantial contributions to the funds of the Congress and to Gandhi's social reform activities. As a member of the Congress Working Committee, and indeed its treasurer, Jamnalal took full responsibility for its policies, and repeatedly courted imprisonment in 1923, 1930, 1932,1939 and 1940.

In contrast, G.D. Birla's attitude towards Gandhi and the Congress was ambivalent. In the evening of his life Birla recalled:

> There was not much in common between us so far as our mode of life went. Gandhiji was a saintly person, who had renounced all the comforts and luxuries of life. Religion was his main absorption and this interest drew me irresistibly towards him. His outlook on economics, however, was different. He believed in small-scale industries – charkha, *ghani* and all

> that. On the other hand I led a fairly comfortable life and believed in the industrialisation of the country through large scale industries . . . . He not only tolerated my independence of thought, but loved me all the more for it, as a father would his child.[25]

Birla had started his life as a jute and gunny broker; he lived to found one of the largest industrial empires in independent India. As a young entrepreneur in Calcutta, he was a protege of Lord Ronaldshay, the Governor of Bengal, who nominated him to the Bengal legislative council in the hope that he would have a sobering influence on the younger members of the Marwari community with nationalist proclivities.[26] Birla came nowhere near the non-cooperation movement. He did not allow politics to deflect him from his onward march in the field of trade and industry. In 1924, he explained to Jamnalal his reasons for abstention from active politics:

> I am enmeshed in business. My revered father and elder brother do not like my abandoning business. I do everything to please them. This is also my *dharma* . . . . However, if any financial help or personal service is required by Mahatmaji, I shall be happy to render it. My situation is peculiar: I want one thing and do another.[27]

In the late 1920s Birla entered the central legislative assembly, not as a member of the Congress Party, but of the Nationalist Party, led by Lajpat Rai and Malaviya. He remained in the good books of the government, and was nominated to the Indian Fiscal Commission, the Royal Commission for Labour, and the International Labour Conference. At the same time, he was in intimate touch with the nationalist leaders, especially Gandhi, to whose 'constructive' activities he made generous contributions. When, however, Gandhi launched the Salt Satyagraha in 1930 Birla steered clear of it. Lord Willingdon once described Birla as 'one of those men who would only do anything, if it suited his own pockets'.[28] This was a grossly unfair judgement, because Birla sought to safeguard not only the interests of his own family, but those of Indian trade and industry as a whole. For decades the scales had been loaded in favour of the British-owned companies in India, who formed the Associated Chambers of Commerce in 1921. Birla played a leading part in building up a rival body, the Federation of Indian Chambers of Commerce, which came into existence in 1927.

It was part of Birla's strategy to alienate neither the Congress nor the government. He cultivated contacts with high-ranking British officials in India and Britain; this was not difficult for him because of his known proximity to Gandhi. In his correspondence with British statesmen he made it a point to disavow any connection with the Congress. He claimed that he was 'not a Congressman but a Gandhi man'.[29] He shrewdly played upon the hopes and fears of the British viceroys and secretaries of state. He told them that Gandhi was their best bet for a peaceful solution of the Indian problem: he alone stood between order and chaos.[30] Birla even made a distinction between Gandhi and the Congress, and floated the idea that if the Congress became too radical a body, the British might be able to do business with Gandhi. This was a fatuous distinction, because Gandhi would never have been a party to the destruction of the Congress which he had built up as an instrument of the nationalist struggle against foreign rule.

We get an insight into Birla's strategy in a letter he wrote to Sir Samuel Hoare, the Secretary of State for India, a few weeks after the British government had clamped down upon the Congress and locked up its leadership in jail:

> I should like you to know me as I really am. I need hardly say that I am a great admirer of Gandhiji . . . . I have liberally financed his khadi production and anti-untouchability activities. I am also a believer in khadi as a supplementary occupation for the Indian masses. I have never taken any part in or financed the civil disobedience movement. But I have been a very severe critic of the financial policy of the government and so have never been popular with them.
>
> Even today I do not see eye to eye with the policy of the government.[31]

Birla offered his cooperation to the government, if it was prepared to revise its fiscal and economic policies to suit indian industry. He even hinted that the fact that the Congress had been outlawed was no bar to cooperation between the British government and 'progressive opinion not identified with the Congress'. He suggested a dialogue between Indian and British businessmen. 'So far as we are concerned' he told Sir Samuel, 'you will find us always ready to work for the economic interest, leaving aside sentiments and politics'.[32] 'Never had' says Claude Markovits, 'such a clear offer of collaboration been extended by Indian big business to the government and this while Gandhi and the entire Congress leadership were in jail'.[33] No wonder that a few months later, the liberal leader Srinivasa Sastri was asking Kodanda Rao: 'Has Birla been turned away from Gandhi's policy? That is a shrewd blow'.[34]

This was the time of the Ottawa and Modi-Lees pacts when Indian capitalists were bending over backwards to placate British business for temporary gains which would help them to get out of the economic depression.

Jamnalal Bajaj had a first-hand experience of Birla's astute diplomacy during the Jaipur State imbroglio in 1938. When the tension between the state authorities and the Praja Mandal was building up, and Jamnalal, on the advice of Gandhi and Vallabhbhai Patel, was planning a struggle for the assertion of elementary political rights in the state, he sought the assistance of Birla, who also claimed to be a native of Jaipur State and professed to take an interest in its welfare. Birla offered to use his influence with Sir Bertrand Glancy, the political adviser to the viceroy, and with Young, the inspector-general of police in Jaipur, to arrive at a *modus vivendi,* and advised Jamnalal to be patient and not to precipitate a crisis by defying the orders of the state authorities.

The movement, which had started on the issue of the recognition for the Praja Mandal, in the meantime, became a part of the wider struggle for the people's rights in princely India under the aegis of Gandhi and the Congress. Birla took no part in this struggle. It is doubtful if he had any real influence with the officers of the political department. It is surprising that Jamnalal could not foresee that Birla, who had kept clear of satyagraha struggles in British India, would not burn his fingers in princely India. After the worst was over, Jamnalal approached Birla to join the executive committee of the Jaipur Praja Mandal. Birla's response was an unequivocal refusal: 'You have written to me that I or my son Lakshmi Niwas should join the executive committee of the Praja Mandal. This advice is ill-conceived. This work is against my nature and I do not want to put my foot into something for which I have no natural enthusiasm'.[35]

Birla was aware that Jamnalal was acting in the Jaipur affairs in consultation with Gandhi, but he did not take his cue in politics from Gandhi or from anybody else. In Birla's scheme of things, economics took precedence over politics. Gandhi and the Congress might be interested in the primacy of Indian self-government, but Birla's eyes were riveted on the short and long-term prospects of Indian industry. This was so even when the Second World War took a critical turn, and a political crisis of the first magnitude loomed large. Birla wrote to his friend Purshotamdas Thakurdas:

> We should watch one thing very carefully. In the name of War Industrialization we should not allow the government to do anything to put up new industries under the control of British interests. I fear this might be the result. Already I have heard that aeroplanes and motor cars may be manufactured, but perhaps not by Indians but by Englishmen.[36]

In fairness to Birla, it must be acknowledged that in his calculating attitude towards the nationalist movement he was not alone. Most capitalists in India, in keeping aloof from the national movement, were governed by a concern for their family fortunes. It must also be conceded that he was playing not only for his own hand, but for Indian trade and industry as against foreign capital; and even though he did not finance the political activities of the Congress, he gave generous support to the Mahatma's non-political work. Birla was shrewd enough to project the interests of the entire capitalist class in India. He had access to some of the top leaders of the Congress, including Gandhi, but he knew that there was no question of buying up, manipulating or pressuring the national leaders.

Some other industrialists were infinitely more cynical and opportunistic in their outlook. Ramkrishna Dalmia, who was building up his commercial empire in Bihar, contributed twenty-seven thousand rupees to the election fund of the Congress in that province in 1937. But as a *quid pro quo* he insisted on having a say in the selection of Congress candidates, expected Congress support for his own election without standing on a Congress ticket, and financed clandestinely some candidates who were opposing the Congress.[37] In so far as Dalmia perceived a chance of acquiring political influence by contributing to election funds in 1937, he was more prescient than most of his fellow capitalists, but he did not really tilt towards the Congress until 1945 when the liquidation of British power was in the offing.

III

Gandhi had no illusions about the motives of Indian capitalists, with some of whom (such as G.D. Birla, Ambalal Sarabhai and Kasturbhai Lalbhai) he had cordial personal relations. He used them, as in the Round Table Conference in London in 1931, to spike the guns of British capitalists and financiers. Birla appointed himself as the Mahatma's spokesman in discussions with British officials in India and in England, but they did not take long to discover that the Marwari industrialist was not as influential in shaping Congress policies. His published correspondence gives an exaggerated impression of his actual role in political developments. He certainly had access to Gandhi, and his influence was always cast in favour of restraint, of avoiding a confrontation with the British Raj, or of seeking a truce. But there were powerful Congress leaders, such as Jawaharlal Nehru, and Congress socialists, such as Jayaprakash Narayan, who brought a contrary pressure to bear on Gandhi. The fact is that every possible point of view, from the most conservative to the most radical, was represented in the All India Congress Committee, and even in the Congress Working Committee. Gandhi listened to everybody but made up his own mind; on what appeared to him as fundamental issues, he did not hesitate to strike out a line even against his closest colleagues.

Some historians have been misled by the fact that Birla and his fellow capitalists wrote letters to Gandhi or pleaded in person for a particular course of action at a certain time. This does not prove that Gandhi acted at their bidding; he took his own decisions on critical issues such as the launching of non-cooperation in 1920, the withdrawal of civil disobedience in 1922, the signing of the Gandhi-Irwin Pact in 1931, the withdrawal of civil disobedience in 1933, the acceptance of office in 1937, and the Congress policy during the Second World War. In 1938 the Mahatma told off Birla, when he sought his support for a bargain with Lancashire for its supposed advantages in economic terms: 'What you say is correct from the economic point of view. But I look at it, and I ought to look at it, as a national political issue. We cannot enter into any agreement with Lancashire, which will bind us to buy their cloth'.[38]

The fact that Birla was Gandhi's host in Delhi or Calcutta does not prove anything. The attitude of the Birla family towards Gandhi was one of respect and affection, which were reciprocated by the Mahatma, who maintained his personal links with individuals irrespective of political or social differences. When Kanji Dwarkadas wrote to Gandhi not to stay with Birla, Gandhi told him that his political views were not affected by his personal relations with people. This indeed was true.

There is little evidence to indicate that Birla or his friends were able to get in Gandhi's lifetime any substantial economic gain because of their association with him. Indeed, in the framework of the imperial rule until 1947, Gandhi had no patronage to dispense. The Indian industrialists certainly gained (for example, in protective tariffs) from the nationalist pressure against foreign capitalists and financial interests in India; but this was an inevitable byproduct of the nationalist movement.

Notes

1. B.R. Nanda, *Gandhi and His Critics* (Delhi 1987),pp.131-2.
2. Sibnarayan Ray (ed.), *Selected Works of M.N. Roy* (Delhi 1987), vol.I, p.370.
3. Hiren Mukherjee, *Gandhiji: A Study*, (New Delhi 1978), p.183.
4. E.M.S. Namboodiripad, *The Mahatma and the Ism* (New Delhi1958), p.111.
5. A.R. Desai, *Social Background of Indian Nationalism* (Delhi 1976), p.368.
6. S.R. Mehrotra, *Towards India's Freedom and Partition* (Delhi 1979), p.77.
7. Ibid.
8. B.R. Nanda, *Gokhale, Indian Moderates and the British Raj* (Delhi 1977), p.158.
9. *Bombay Chronicle*, 6 July 1921.
10. Motilal Nehru to Lalji Naranji, 21 April 1928, Purshotamdas Thakurdas Papers, hereinafter P.T. Papers, file no. 40/IV, Nehru Memorial Museum and Library, New Delhi.
11. Gandhi to Jawaharlal Nehru, 24 April 1928, Navjivan Trust, *Collected Works of Mahatma Gandhi* hereinafter C.W.M.G. (Ahmedabad 1958), vol. XXXVI, p. 258.
12. Jawaharlal Nehru, *Discovery of India* (Calcutta 1946), p.589.
13. Shriman Narayan, *Window on Gandhi and Nehru* (Bombay 1971), p.19.
14. C.W.M.G., (n.11), vol.XLVI, p.160.
15. Interview with H.K. Mahtab, Oral History Transcripts, Nehru Memorial Museum and Library, New Delhi.
16. Annual Report for the year 1927, presented by the general secretaries to All India Congress Committee in A.M.Zaidi and S.G.Zaidi, *Encyclopaldia of the Indian National Congress* (New Delhi, 1976), vol. IX, p. 323.
17. A.I.C.C. Papers, file no. 46, Nehru Memorial Museum and Library, New Delhi.
18. Ibid.
19. Jawaharlal Nehru to J.A.D. Naoroji, 27 March 1937, Jawaharlal Nehru Papers, Nehru Memorial Museum and Library, New Delhi.
20. Govind Ballabh Pant to Rajendra Prasad, 11 May 1936 in Home Political, file 4/45-1936, National Archives of India, New Delhi.
21. Ibid.

22. Bhulabhai Desai Diary, entry of 2 February 1936, Nehru Memorial Museum and Library, New Delhi.

23. Ibid., 10 February 1936.

24. Ibid., 25 February 1936.

25. G.D. Birla, *In The Shadow of the Mahatma* (Calcutta 1953), p. xv.

26. Lord Ronaldshay, Governor of Bengal to Secretary of State Montagu, 6 January 1921, Montagu Papers, India Office Library, London.

27. G.D. Birla to Jamnalal Bajaj, 27 October 1924, in Ramkrishna Bajaj (ed.), *Patra Vyavahar,* Jamnalal Bajaj's Correspondence in Hindi (Delhi 1958), vol. I, p.68.

28. Lord Willingdon to Sir Samuel Hoare, 21 March 1932, Templewood Papers, India Office Library, London.

29. Lord Linlithgow's note of interview with G.D. Birla, enclosed with his letter to Secretary of State Zetland, 10 August 1936, Linlithgow Papers, India Office Library, London.

30. Linlithgow to Zetland, 10 August 1936, ibid.

31. G.D.Birla to Sir Samuel Hoare, 14 March, 1932, Templewood Papers, India Office Library, London.

32. Ibid.

33. Clande Markovits, *Indian Business and Nationalist Politics, 1931-1938* (Hyderabad 1985), p.33.

34. Srinivass Sastri to Kodanda Rao, 10 Oct. 1933, Kodanda Rao Papers, Nehru Memorial Museum and Library, New Delhi.

35. G.D. Birla to Jamnalal 20 April 1940, Bajaj (ed.) *Patra Vyavahar*, (n.27), vol. VIII, pp. 105-6.

36. G.D. Birla to Purshotamdas Thakurdas, 25 June, 1940, P.T. Papers, file no. 177.

37. B.R. Tomlinson, *The Indian National Congress and the Raj, 1929-42*, (London 1976), p.83.

38. Gandhi to G.D. Birla 17 April 1938, *C.W.M.G.* (n.11), vol. LXVII, p. 31.

7

The Marxist Discourse on Gandhi

Bhikhu Parekh

On the face of it Gandhi's economic thought appears strange, even self-contradictory, and not easy to classify. He revolted against modernity, advocated self-contained villages and a simple and austere life, and seems 'feudal'. But the Indian National Congress under his leadership pursued policies that laid the foundations of the bourgeois-liberal state. Yet he denounced capitalism including the very institution of private property, advocated cooperative living and thus appears to be a socialist! Like his thought his practice too seems contradictory. He championed the cause of the poor, lived like one, and was one of the first to place their economic and social uplift on the national agenda. He also, however, enjoyed close relations with some of the biggest capitalists, and depended on them not only to finance the Congress and the independence movement but also his constructive programme.

It is, therefore, hardly surprising that the Marxist commentators on Gandhi have had considerable difficulty in coming to terms with him. For M.N. Roy, his first Marxist commentator, he was a 'reactionary' leader, a champion of a 'patriarchal or feudal civilization' hankering after a historically superseded hierarchical and rurally based social order. In Roy's view Gandhi was not unique to India; 'there are Gandhis in every country' embarking on the path of industrialization.[1] He agreed that Gandhi was genuinely concerned about the poor and the oppressed, but insisted that his preferred society was inherently incapable of promoting their interests. As he put it:

> Gandhism is nothing but petty-bourgeois humanitarianism hopelessly bewildered in the clashes of the staggering forces of human progress.

> The crocodile tears of this humanitarianism are shed ostensibly for the undeniable sufferings of the majority in capitalist society, but they are really caused by grief over the end of the old order, already destroyed or about to be so. It pines for that ancient golden age when the majority were kept in blissful ignorance in order that a few could roll in idle luxury, undisturbed by the revolt of the discontented, the spiritual culture of which was based on the barbarism of the people at large, the simplicity of which was the sign of its backwardness. This longing glance backwards is due, in some cases, to the consummate intrigues of the forces of reaction, and in others, to voluntary subordination to the influence of the same agency. Its tendency towards a sort of religious or utopian socialism proves that Gandhism, as well as its source Tolstoyism, belongs to the latter category. Or in other words, the services rendered by it to reaction are involuntary.[2]

Roy thought that Gandhi, a great mass mobilizer, had released new forces which his reactionary ideas would not be able to control and which would eventually devour him. 'The imminent collapse of Gandhism . . . will demonstrate that a socially revolutionary movement cannot be influenced by reactionary forces', Roy predicted.[3]

The Comintern and its Indian allies were more damning but less clear. For them Congress under Gandhi was 'a class organization of the capitalists' working against the interests 'not only of the workers and peasants but also of wide sections of the town petty bourgeoisie'.[4] The Indian capitalists were not really bothered about independence because their interests were tied up with those of 'both British imperialism and Indian feudalism'. As their spokesman Gandhi was 'an agent of imperialism', indeed 'a police agent of British imperialism in India'.[5] Following the Popular Front strategy of the Comintern, the communists did a somersault in the mid-1930s. They now admitted their 'left sectarian error' and agreed that Congress represented 'the united front of the Indian people in national struggle'.[6] Though conservative in its orientation, it was capable of transformation by internal pressures from left-wing forces. Rather than avoid it, the communists were enjoined to join or at least work in close cooperation with it. Gandhi was now called a great nationalist leader who had played a 'progressive role' in turning the Congress into an anti-imperialist movement. Though he still remained an 'ally' of the capitalists and exerted a reactionary economic and social influence on the Congress, his political and historical influence was warmly commended. Once, however, the Second World War became 'people's war', the communists advanced yet another view. Gandhi and the Congress were now condemned for not collaborating with their imperialist rulers, and declared feudal, unprogressive, narrow and anti-people. The Congress was dubbed as a Hindu body mainly representing a coalition of feudal and capitalist interests, and the Muslim League was considered entitled to a separate state to protect Muslim interests.

In Why Socialism? written during his Marxist days, Jayaprakash Narayan offered a somewhat different analysis of Gandhi. Unlike Roy, who could not make up his mind whether Gandhi's thought was feudal or petty-bourgeois and dismissed it as reactionary, Narayan thought it was 'reformist' and represented the interests of the big bourgeoisie. In his view the 'essence' of Ghandhi's 'curious philosophy' consisted in such ideas as class collaboration, rejection of radical social transformation, an ineffective theory of trusteeship and social and economic inequality. These reformist doctrines had long been advocated in the west by 'smug bourgeois professors, thinkers and churchmen', and were neither uniquely Indian as Gandhi claimed nor original to him. Gandhi was not interested in securing social justice but in 'covering up the ugly fissures of society', and gave his 'open and avowed' approval to the 'large-scale, organized theft and violence' inherent in capitalism. Narayan observed: 'Gandhism may be a well-intentioned doctrine. I personally think it is. But . . . it is . . . a dangerous doctrine. . . . because it hushes up real issues and sets out to remove the evils of society by pious wishes. It thus deceives the masses and encourages the upper classes to continue their domination'.[7]

A.R. Desai in his *Social Background of Indian Nationalism* took a slightly different view of Gandhi. He saw Gandhi as a spokesman not so much of a specific bourgeois faction as of the capitalist mode of production. He observed:

> The bourgeois consciousness of Gandhi should not . . . be confounded or identified with the sordid consciousness of an ordinary bourgeois. Gandhi was a bourgeois only in the sense that he sincerely believed in the validity of the existing society based on capitalist property system, alternative to which he saw social chaos. Gandhi recognised and denounced in burning words the barbarities of capitalist exploitation but could not transcend his essential bourgeois outlook. Gandhi loved the masses but also believed in the bourgeois social system.[8]

Later Marxist commentators such as Hiren Mukerji, E.M.S. Namboodiripad and B.T. Ranadive have broadly endorsed Desai's view. In recent years Marxist scholars have adopted a much more sophisticated approach. They have concentrated on the entire body of Gandhi's thought rather than his early *Hind Swaraj*, paying close attention to the way he changed his early ideas in response to the exigencies of the nationalist struggle. They have also seen Gandhi's ideas not as a homogeneous whole but as a cluster of different and sometimes contradictory tendencies. They have paid far greater attention to his actions than did the earlier generation of Marxist commentators, and examined his programmes and policies, the groups he favoured, his stands or silence on controversial matters and the overall political role of his ideas in the consolidation of the nationalist movement. Partha Chatterjee's recent work is one of the best examples of this new approach.[9]

Chatterjee's argument is articulated at several different levels and not easy to follow. He agrees with M.N. Roy that Gandhi's *Hind Swaraj* idealized pre-capitalist economic and social relations and represented a backward-looking petty bourgeois utopia, but insists that it was not the 'fundamental core' of what he calls 'Gandhism'. Gandhi's economic ideas changed over time; they are inextricably tied up with and can not be examined in isolation from his moral theory, especially his doctrines of nonviolence and moral purity; and they need to be understood not merely in terms of his subjective intentions but also the way they were objectively interpreted and appropriated by the Congress.

For Chatterjee the Indian nationalist movement was dominated by the champions of the bourgeoisie and furthered the latter's interests. It had no hope of defeating the colonial rulers without mobilizing the masses especially the peasantry, the largest single class in India. The unique historical role of 'Gandhism' consisted in achieving this vital task. It articulated the views and forms of consciousness of the peasantry, and mobilized and brought it within the nationalist movement. Though Gandhi claimed to have radicalized and empowered the masses, in fact he did no such thing.Thanks to his emphasis on nonviolence and the concomitant moral elitism, he organized the peasantry on a local and not national basis, concentrated on its specific grievances rather than questions of property rights, and prevented it from developing its own organization and leadership. Under Gandhi the peasantry, therefore, played an active but subordinate role within a struggle 'wholly conceived and directed by others', and subserved bourgeois interests. It was true that Gandhi was critical of capitalism, the modern state, the bourgeois representative democracy and so on, but since he had no viable alternatives, he kept compromising with them and allowed them to develop and acquire legitimacy. Chatterjee observes:

> It is only by looking at it in that historical context that it becomes possible to understand the unique achievement of Gandhism: its ability to open up the possibility for achieving perhaps the most important historical task for a successful national revolution in a country like India, viz., the political appropriation of the subaltern classes by a bourgeoisie aspiring for hegemony in the new nation-state. In the Indian case, the largest popular element of the nation was the peasantry. And it was the Gandhian ideology which opened up the historical possibility for its appropriation into the evolving political structures of the Indian state.[10]

He goes on:

> While it was the Gandhian intervention in elite-nationalist politics in India which established for the first time that an authentic national movement could only be built upon the organized support of the whole of the peasantry, the working out of the politics of non-violence also made it abundantly clear that the object of the political mobilization of the peasantry was not at all what Gandhi claimed on its behalf, 'to train the masses in self-consciousness and attainment of power'. Rather the peasantry were [sic.] meant to become willing participants in a struggle wholly conceived and directed by others.[11]

My intention in this paper is not to comment on these and other Marxist interpretations of Gandhi, nor to trace the significant methodological, epistemological and other shifts in the Marxist discourse on him, but to assess the validity of the central Marxist thesis. It is that although Gandhi passionately championed the cause of the poor and the oppressed and mobilized the masses on a scale uprecedented in Indian history, both his ideas and especially his actions reinforced the bourgeois hegemony of the nationalist movement and helped consolidate the capitalist mode of production. He may or may not have intended the outcome, but its roots lay deep in his thought and actions. His hopelessly unrealistic alternative to capitalism, his theory of nonviolence, his largely impotent theory of trusteeship and his naive belief in class harmony not only undermined his criticisms of capitalism but allowed it to flourish without a serious challenge. His failure to organize the peasantry on an all-India basis and challenge the bourgeois hegemony of the nationalist movement meant in effect that the Congress and the new Indian state were taken over by the bourgeoisie.

Since the Marxist thesis appeals to Gandhi's ideas and actions, I shall discuss them in that order in the first two sections. In the third, I shall analyse the ideologically and organizationally complex structure of the Congress under Gandhi's leadership, and then assess the validity of the Marxist thesis.

I

For Gandhi capitalism, socialism, communism and all such 'economically' orientated ideologies were unique products of modern civilization resting on the 'materialist' view of man.[12] In this view man was equated with the body and seen as an essentially self-centred being who found his fulfilment in the gratification of his ever-increasing and inherently insatiable wants. Capitalism was based on the belief that most men were most likely to satisfy most of their desires most of the time under a system of private property. Communism rested on the opposite belief that such a goal could only be realized in a state-controlled economy. For reasons too well known to need reiteration, Gandhi rejected the 'materialist' view in favour of a 'spiritual' view of man. Since capitalism and communism rested on a dubious philosophical anthropology, he insisted that they were both fatally flawed.

Gandhi also advanced two other objections against capitalism. First, the concept of private property lying at its base was logically incoherent. For Gandhi, there was no logical basis on which a man could claim exclusive ownership of the products of his labour. He owed his existence, survival, intellectual and moral capacities, character, skills, ambition, motivation – in short his very humanity – to others. Since these were all socially derived and formed a social trust to be used for the well-being of others, their products could not be his private property to be used as he pleased. Furthermore, the efforts of countless men and women flowed into one another to produce an object, rendering it impossible to demarcate the distinctive contribution of each. Their cooperation occurred within the context of the established social order whose silent and unnoticed but vital contribution could not be ignored either. Even as an event was caused by a number of factors operating against the background of a given set of conditions such that none of them could be arbitrarily abstracted and called its cause; no direct relationship could ever be established between the specific activity of an individual and a specific result. There was, thus, no logical basis on which he could claim a specific reward. Many an Indian philosopher had advanced the argument to reject the concept of causality. Gandhi used it to attack the idea of private property as well.

Second, for Gandhi capitalism was an exploitative system propelled by greed and based on the survival of the fittest. Not surprisingly, it caused enormous moral havoc in society. It created large-scale unemployment and condemned millions to miserable lives. Even the employed were poorly paid, worked under inhuman conditions, found neither joy nor fulfilment in their jobs and were constantly haunted by the fear of unemployment and poverty. Since they were treated and even referred to as commodities, they behaved and lived like one, and developed neither self-respect nor self-discipline. They were rightly consumed by anger and hatred against their employers and seethed with the spirit of revenge and violence. In Gandhi's view capitalists led equally empty and inhuman lives devoted to the pursuits of mindless pleasures and devoid of nobility and idealism. Fearful of losing their privileges and actually aware of the smouldering violence of their victims, they remained anxious and tense and depended on the heavily armed state for their protection and security. As Gandhi put it, no man could degrade another without degrading himself and there were no winners in an exploitative relationship. Since human beings generally found it difficult to live in the midst of poverty and degradation – especially when they were its cause – without somehow convincing themselves that they were right to do so, capitalists generally argued that the poor and the oppressed belonged to an inferior and flawed species and deserved their predicament. For Gandhi, the central moral defect of a class-divided society was its inescapable tendency to divide mankind into two different species, and to ignore the fundamental fact that no man could flourish and realize his humanity at the expense of another.

Gandhi did not think much of communism either. Like capitalism it was based on the materialist view of man and did not represent a new or higher civilization. It was really the twin of capitalism and only claimed to offer more of the same. It also had other fatal defects. It represented a statist approach to social problems, treated men as mere resources to be exploited as the state deemed proper, and dried up all sources of initiative and energy in society. By combining both the economic and political power in the hands of the state, communism posed a grave danger to human freedom and dignity. It needed a violent revolution to establish it and, as history amply demonstrated, all such revolutions led to greater evils than those they were designed to eradicate. Since communism was based on the belief that anyone standing in the way of the desired goal could be justifiably eliminated, it sanctioned massive violence and had a deep anti-human orientation. Gandhi acknowledged that the communist society eliminated poverty, discouraged greed and ensured every citizen a right to work, but he was convinced that its moral deficiencies far outweighed its strengths.

Gandhi thought that in addition to being inherently unacceptable, capitalism, communism and all such want-based and self-centred western ideologies were incompatible with India's 'essentially spiritual' civilization. Rather than copy the west or indigenize imported ideologies. India had to evolve its own 'humane' and 'spiritual' economy expressing and sustaining man's moral being. Gandhi's spiritual economy rested on the following principles.[13]

First, every man had a right to work. Man needed to work in order to acquire such basic human qualities as a sense of self-respect, dignity, self-discipline, self-confidence, initiative and the capacity to organize his energies and structure his personality. Welfare payments by the state sustained the body but impoverished the soul and dehumanized him. Furthermore, since the social order was sustained by the spirit of *yajna* or spontaneous cooperation of all its members, an individual lacking the opportunity to work was denied the privilege of participating in it, and this cut him off from the moral and spiritual life of his community and involuntarily reduced him to the demeaning status of a social parasite.

Second, economic life had to be in harmony with and create conditions necessary for man's moral and spiritual development. For reasons we need not consider here, Gandhi thought that men could only realize their full moral potential in small, relaxed, self-governing and interdependent communities. Since the latter lacked vitality without an autonomous economic base of their own,he argued that production should be decentralized and each community become relatively self-sufficient in its base needs. As he imagined it, the village land was to be owned in common, farming done on a cooperative basis, the produce equitably divided, and only the surplus land was to be used for cash crops. The villages were to encourage locally based industries and crafts, and to import only what they could not themselves produce. Full employment or the right to work was the necesary requirement of man's spiritual nature, and Gandhi could not see how it could be ensured except in such self-sufficient communities.

Third, since village communities were to form the basis of the Indian economy, the nature, pace and scale of industrialization were to be determined by and subordinated to their requirements. Large-scale industries were necessary, but they had to be restricted to the minimum, located in the cities, and only allowed to produce what the self-sufficient communities themselves could not. Since competition between the two necessarily led to the latter's destruction, a national plan was to be prepared laying down what share of the market was to be reserved for each, what should be produced locally, and how it could be done more efficiently. That was the only way to avoid the rise of huge and inhuman cities and the urban exploitation of the countryside.

Fourth, the means of production of the basic necessities of life had to be collectively owned. They affected man's very survival and could easily become instruments of the most dangerous forms of exploitation. Industries of vital national importance had also to be owned by the state, which it had to either set up itself or nationalize 'without compensation', for 'if you want the government to pay compensation it will have to rob Peter to pay Paul and that would be impossible'. Fifth, since all socially useful activities were equally important, their wage differentials needed to be reduced to the minimum. And finally, since a healthy moral community was impossible in a grossly unequal society, the state had to embark on a programme of levelling up the poor and the oppressed and levelling down the rich. The resources needed to help the poor were to be raised by taxing the rich at a 'much higher figure' than the 70 per cent then obtaining in Britain.

Concerning the form of ownership, Gandhi proposed his well-known theory of trusteeship, an economic extension of his philosophical concept of man as a trustee of his capacities. The theory was intended to avoid the evils and combine the advantages of both capitalism and communism, and aimed to socialize property without nationalizing it. As he imagined it, every industrialist employing more than a certain number of workers was to look upon his industry not as his property but as a social trust. He was to work along with his employees, to take no more than what he needed for a moderately comfortable life, to look upon them as 'members of his family' and jointly responsible with him for the management of the industry, and to provide healthy working conditions and welfare schemes for them and their families. Part of the moderate profit he made was to be devoted to the welfare of the community, the rest used to improve the industry. The owner was free to bequeath his industry to his children or whoever he liked *only if* the latter agreed to run it in the spirit of trusteeship.

Gandhi admitted that none of his capitalist friends had become a trustee, the only exception being Jamnalal Bajaj who 'came near, but only near it'. Asked what should be done to get them to become one, he replied that the sustained pressure of the educated and organized public opinion including satyagraha was the best way. If that did not work, he was reluctantly prepared for the state to impose trusteeship by law. It would prescribe the amount of remuneration to be paid to the trustee 'commensurate with the service rendered and its value to society'. The trustee was free to choose his heir, but the choice had to be 'finalized' by the state. Gandhi thought that such a cooperative decision checked both. The trustee retained formal ownership of his property, but his use of the profit, his income and choice of heir were subject to state control. As Gandhi put it, 'I desire to end capitalism almost if not quite as much as the most advanced socialist and even communist. But our methods differ, out languages differ'.[14]

Professor Dantwala and other socialists had a long discussion with Gandhi regarding the nature and implications of his theory of trusteeship. They summed up his views in a draft which he endorsed after making a few changes, all designed to strengthen its egalitarian thrust. The final version read as follows:

1. Trusteeship provides a means of transforming the present capitalist order of society into an egalitarian one. It gives no quarter to capitalism, but gives the present owning class a chance of reforming itself. It is based on the faith that human nature is never beyond redemption.
2. It does not recognise any rights of private ownership of property except insofar as it may be permitted by society for its own welfare.
3. It does not exclude legislative regulation of the ownership and use of wealth.
4. Thus under *state-regulated trusteeship* an individual will not be free to hold or use wealth for selfish satisfaction or in disregard of the interests of society.

5. Just as it is proposed to fix a decent minimum living wage, even so a limit should be fixed for the maximum income that would be allowed to any person in society. The difference between such minimum incomes should be reasonable and equitable and variable from time to time so much so that the tendency would be towards obliteration of the difference.
6. Under the Gandhian economic order the character of production will be determined by social necessity and not by personal whim or greed.[15]

The draft was a fairly accurate statement of Gandhi's mature economic views. Since the early 1930s he had increasingly begun to turn radical, partly in response to the political pressure of the discontented groups, partly because of his experiences with the Indian capitalists, and partly because he saw more clearly than before the economic implications of his moral and political thought. He insisted that a fundamental revolution in property relations was both necessary and inescapable. 'Without a material revision of vested interests', he observed, 'the condition of the masses can never be improved'.[16] He was concerned that the exploited masses lacked an awareness of their rights, and wondered how to radicalize them without letting them turn violent. 'Land and all property is his who will work for it. Unfortunately the workers are or have been kept ignorant of this simple fact'.[17] He was convinced that if nothing was done in time the desperate 'peasants would take the land. We would not have to tell them to take it'.[18]

Gandhi appreciated more than ever before the redistributive role of the state and assigned it a wide range of functions. He was prepared to impose trusteeship by law, raise the level of taxation, nationalize vital industries and establish a programme of positive discrimination for the poor and the oppressed. He repeatedly warned the Indian bourgeoisie of the 'inevitable' violence of the workers and peasants, and urged the latter to stand up for their rights including launching satyagrahas. He announced that after independence he might himself lead satyagrahas against the vested interests, which were likely to be 'more bitter' and protracted than those against the British. Though he was opposed to violence, he was prepared to put up with the 'defensive', 'legitimate' and 'pardonable' violence of the 'desperate' and 'frustrated' masses. In 1942 he gave several important interviews to Louis Fischer in the course of which he conceded that if the peasants stopped paying taxes and seized the land in protest against the landlords' oppression, it might lead to violence, but asserted that the peasants' action would add to their confidence for independent action; the resultant chaos could be soon brought under control.[19]

Gandhi's ideal society then was semi-industrialized, economically more or less self-sufficient, substantially egalitarian, based on cooperative production and ruled out extensive international trade. It involved medium size agro-industrial residential units,nationalization of basic industries, heavy taxation, death duties, state regulation of ownership, and workers' participation in the management of industries. Needless to say,Gandhi's society is neither communist nor capitalist and has a wholly different orientation and basis. The centrality of the state, extensive government control of the economy, large-scale industrialization, bureaucracy and so on, which characterize communism, are absent in Gandhi's society. The pursuit of profit, the more or less unlimited right to acquire and dispose of property, competition, integration of the national economy into the world market, unregulated mechanization and the ever-increasing scale of production, which constitute the basic preconditions of the capitalist economy, are also absent. So far as Gandhi's economic thought and ideal social order are concerned, he was not a champion of feudalism, capitalism or communism; he was a class by himself.

II

Having briefly considered Gandhi's economic ideas, we shall now examine his actions, decisions, and the groups he favoured, ignored and opposed to see if they support the Marxist thesis.

When Gandhi became the unquestioned leader of the Indian independence movement, he had to work out a coherent strategy of struggle. He was convinced on the basis of his South African and Indian experiences that moral appeals, petitions and constitutional pressures upon which the Congress had hitherto relied were impotent against a determined government. He also ruled out the method of violent agitation advocated by the terrorists and their sympathizers, on the grounds that it was morally unacceptable and politically ineffective in the context of a divided, disarmed and demoralized nation facing a united and well-armed government. As we shall see later, he was also worried that once violence became respectable and organized, the masses were likely to want to use it against their native exploiters, thereby dividing the nationalist movement and playing into the hands of the colonial rulers. In his view the method of satyagraha, as he had developed and tried out with some success in South Africa, offered the only realistic hope of securing independence.

Gandhi's satyagrahic method of struggle, which he more or less successfully persuaded the bulk of the Congress and even the country to accept, determined the nature and limits of his political praxis. It required that the Congress should cease being a merely debating body and become an effective tool of collective action with an extensive national network, linked to the central leadership by a clearly established chain of command. Accordingly, Gandhi set up Congress branches all over the country, introduced a system of public accountability, vetted and trained local and regional leadership, established a clear structure of authority stretching right down to the villages, and turned the annual Congress session into something like a national parliament of delegates representing regional interests and views. The Nagpur session of 1921 had a distinctly Gandhian look not only in its dress, language and manner of conduct but also in its agenda and political self-confidence.

The satyagrahic method also required mass participation for its success. When Gandhi appeared on the scene a large number of social groups were outside the Congress and available for recruitment – for example, the poor, the unemployed, the different strata of peasantry, landless labourers, industrial workers,merchants, traders, sections of big bourgeoisie, rising industrialists, women and the untouchables. He selected and set about cultivating some of these but not others. This was not an accident,nor a matter of his personal political preference,nor a question of their political accessibility, but inherent in his satyagraphic method of struggle. That method could only succeed if those participating in it satisfied certain conditions. Gandhi, therefore, recruited and mobilized those social groups that did, and ignored those that did not, satisfy them.

First, satyagraha involved *hartal*, boycott of foreign cloth, and above all non - cooperation with the government, defined widely to include not only withdrawal of essential services without which it could not function but also refusal to pay land revenue and taxes. This meant that only those groups were capable of contributing to its success who owned shops, traded in foreign cloth, provided services essential to the conduct of government and paid taxes.

Second, satyagraha involved adherence to nonviolence even under grave provocation. Those social groups who had a tradition of nonviolence or stood to gain from it were, therefore, ideal whereas those with a high propensity to violence were risky. Third, satyagraha invited government repression and brutality, which the participants could not bear for long unless alternative sources of moral and social pressure were available to strengthen their resolve, to dissuade the waverers from capitulating and to sustain a spirit of mutual help. Well-organized and long-established social groups bound by strong moral and social bonds were obviously better equipped to undertake it than those of relatively recent origin or held together by tenuous ties. Fourth, satyagraha required mass mobilization, concerted action and effective local leadership. Those groups that had a tradition of organized action, readily available channels of communication and a well-established network of leadership were likely to prove more effective than those without them.

Fifth, satyagraha involved suffering and sacrifice, and people were unlikely to want to engage in it unless they found protest more to their advantage than acquiescence. Those groups who had grievances against the government, or suffered from its policies, or were forced to bear a disproportionate share of the economic burden of colonial rule were, therefore, its ideal constituency. By contrast those pampered by or privileged under the Raj, standing in an ambiguous relationship with it, or confident of looking after themselves under foreign or native rule would either not participate in satyagrahas or remain unreliable allies.

These and other related considerations explain why Gandhi recruited merchants, traders, the middle and upper strata of peasantry, especially those belonging to common castes and forming stable communities, and the professional classes. Surprising as it may seem, he attached considerable importance to the morally and politically regenerative role of the last group. Though the professional classes suffered from the disadvantage of being culturally alienated from the masses, they had the great advantage of having imbibed such progressive western ideas and values as the scientific spirit, social service, concern for the poor and the capacity to take a fresh and critical look at their society. Once they were persuaded out of their 'infatuation' with the modern civilization, they represented a happy 'synthesis' of western and Indian values and were capable of acting as a powerful social catalyst. Gandhi, an English-trained lawyer, saw himself in that light.

Unlike the above-mentioned groups, the poor, the unemployed, the landless labourers, the industrial workers, big business, the industrial bourgeoisie and the large landlords – in short, major groups at either end of the economic spectrum – were least equipped to participate in the struggle for independence as Gandhi conceived and conducted it.

The first four did not pay taxes to the government nor render it vital services, nor own shops or use foreign cloth. Since they had, therefore, little to contribute to the nationalist struggle, Gandhi had no political use for them. He was also acutely aware of their propensity to violence and deeply afraid of mobilizing them. They lacked organized communities, well-established structures of discipline and effective leadership, and had little stake in society. As he repeatedly pointed out, they had long been oppressed and brutalized and were 'rightly' anxious to settle old scores. He knew from experience how easily they tended to resort to violence and diverted the independence movement into a struggle against local landlords, moneylenders and employers. The Chauri Chaura incident convinced him that a 'prematurely' launched and centrally uncontrolled non-cooperation movement was likely to prove a 'Himalayan blunder'. The peaceful agitation led by the U.P. Kisan Sabha turned violent in January 1921 when a large number of low-caste peasants looted the property of their landlords and moneylenders. When the Congress leaders called off the civil disobedience movement in Midanpore and Hughli districts of Bengal after the Gandhi-Irwin pact of 1931, the poorer peasants turned their agitation against the zamindars and the police had to intervene.[20]

Not surprisingly, almost all of Gandhi's satyagrahas took up only local issues, avoided explosive questions of land-ownership and control, were led by his trusted lieutenants, and withdrawn when they threatened to become violent. This was not because he was uninterested in removing social and economic injustices, for he constantly kept attacking them in the strongest possible terms. Rather, he felt that since the unjust Indian society was seething with discontent and since violence was just below the surface, the solution of economic and other problems had to be delayed until after independence.

Just as Gandhi's satyagrahic struggle for independence had no effective role for the poor, the unemployed, the landless labourers and the industrial workers, it had little political role for those at the other end of the economic spectrum. He knew that the interests of some sections of the big bourgeoisie and large landlords were tied up with those of the colonial government or foreign capitalists, and that they had only a limited and essentially instrumental interest in independence. He also knew that most of the rest were anxious not to alienate the government, which had the power to damage their commercial interests by such means as the exchange rate, taxes, trading arrangements and the import policy.

That was why they scrupulously followed the policy of equidistance between the government and the Congress and were unavailable to Gandhi. He knew too that they generally disapproved of his satyagrahas both because these created an economically harmful climate of uncertainty, and because by mobilizing the masses they raised the expectations of and gave the latter a sense of power. That was why they preferred the Swaraj Party's policy of council entry and had even encouraged it to take over the political leadership of the Congress, leaving Gandhi with his humanitarian programme. That was also why they had brought pressure on him not to launch the civil disobedience movement, to settle it quickly after it had begun and to attend the Round Table Conference, and had even tried to subvert its second phase.

Though Gandhi, thus, neither needed nor expected the active political support of the bg bourgeoisie, he needed their money to run the Congress organization, to help those who had suffered in satyagrahas and, above all, to finance his constructive programme. To be sure, his financial needs were not very large. The Congress did not have a large bureaucracy and was mainly manned by volunteers. The constructive programme was run by dedicated volunteers, many of them middle-class women brought into public life for the first time. It was striking that the Indian capitalists were unwilling to meet even the limited Congress expenses. Most contributed nothing or very little, or did so on an on-off basis. When asked by Gandhi to raise money from the caste Hindus to provide higher education for Harijans, G.D. Birla replied:

> In Delhi I walked from door to door for two days and I got only Rs. 1500 after great difficulty. One big contractor, who, is supposed to be a great reformer and a Congressman, . . . promised to pay, but never paid. Ahmedabad is also helpless. In Bombay four Marwari firms, after having promised subscription, are withholding payment. I do not think this is because people do not like the work. But everybody wants to evade payment, if it is at all possible. . . . I confess that I cannot bring money from others.[21]

Only a few such as Birla, Bajaj and Ambalal Sarabhai were generous with their help. Even that was irregular and modest, and Gandhi often had to write plaintive letters to Birla to help out organizations threatened with bankruptcy. Birla made sure that none of the money went to finance Gandhi's political work. Some of the indian capitalists were so timid that they kept their contributions secret and sometimes withdrew them under government pressure. Even Birla felt the pressure when Lord

Linlithgow, whom he had diligently cultivated, cut him off from his social circle for supposedly financing the independence movement in 1940. Birla reassured the viceroy's secretary that he was a 'Gandhi-man' not 'a Congressman', but to no avail.[22] He sadly moaned, 'this brings to an end my relations with the Viceroy. What wooden minds these men have got'.[23]

The meanness of the capitalists was not lost on a man as shrewd as Gandhi. He knew that they were only interested in their profits, had no social conscience, and used him and the Congress to extract economic concessions from the government. He knew too that during the two world wars, especially the second, they had created artificial scarcity of consumer goods, engaged in black market and used the emergency regulations to repress their workers. What Gandhi really thought of the Indian capitalists is evident in his attitude to Birla, who was like a son to him and whose relations with him have aroused strong Marxist suspicions.

In spite of their close friendship and the considerable help he had secured from him, Gandhi remained deeply suspicious of Birla and said so both in private and public. He regretted that Birla had taken no steps to become a trustee of his property and had let him down. When Birla set up a mill in the princely state of Gwalior, the government obtained the land for him without paying adequate compensation to its poor owners. Gandhi pursued the matter with him in a series of letters, and told him to drop the project rather than harm the 'just and legitimate interests of the poor'. When Gandhi received complaints about the mill, he asked Birla for an explanation. Birla blamed the local 'agitators' for stirring up the trouble. Gandhi wrote back: 'The dispossessed class is today full of rancour. There is no denying the fact that they have been sinned against and as a class we have a lot to expiate for, not necessarily our sins but of the system with which we are identified'. The attempt to exonerate Birla as an individual but to inculpate him as a member of his class was typical of Gandhi. He asked Birla to show understanding and generosity 'not in a spirit of virtue but as a simple discharge of a debt overdue'.

When Tata, Birla and Kasturbhai Lalbhai led an industrial delegation to Britain just before independence, Gandhi feared that they might compromise India's vital interests by establishing unacceptable links with their British counterparts. He issued a public statement warning them against a 'shameful deal'. Birla was most upset and cabled Gandhi from Cairo asking why his integrity and patriotism were doubted. Gandhi reiterated his view in a telegram and, to rub salt in the wound, blessed him in the name of 'famishing and naked India'. He followed it up with a letter saying that Birla and his associates had no reason to be upset 'provided they are sincere in their protestations of injured innocence', and pouring scron on Tata's alleged concern for the poor. The distraught Birla assured him that Tata was a 'genuine article', and asked to know once again why his patriotism was impugned. Gandhi's reply is not traceable.[24]

III

The Congress under Gandhi's leadership, then, was a middle-class organization enjoying the support and loyalty of small traders, merchants, the middle and upper peasantry and the professional classes. They were at the centre of the struggle for independence, went to jail, shed their blood, lost their property, suffered domestic and other privations, and in general formed Gandhi's 'army for swaraj'. They constituted its social basis, shaped its ethos, ideals, language of discourse and manner of debating and resolving differences, and created and sustained a distinct Congress culture. The big bourgeoisie at one end of the economic spectrum and the poor, the unemployed and the rural and urban proletariat at the other were not an integral part of the Congress. They neither shared its dominant ethos nor thought of it as 'their Congress' or political home, and some of them had their own separate organizations and parties.

Gandhi, however, did not and indeed could not afford to ignore these groups. The Congress was a national party, aiming and claiming to present all Indians and confronting the colonial government in their name. He knew too that by ignoring them, it risked driving them into the arms of the government all too willing to 'divide and rule' its subjects. He was also anxious to evolve a broad national consensus among the country's different groups and communities in order to give the independence movement a broader social and ideological basis and to bequeath independent India a measure of ideological coherence. Since the Congress under him had captured and consolidated the middle ground of Indian politics, he thought it was well-equipped to mediate between the social and economic extremes. It could provide a public forum where all the major groups could meet under its stewardship, debate their differences, get to know one another and evolve a widely acceptable consensus.

Without losing its distinct social basis, the Congress under Gandhi's leadership, therefore, sought to become a broad-based anti-imperialist movement and evolved a complex network of relationships with the groups falling outside it. Though it did not mobilize and recruit them, it maintained a constant dialogue with them. It invited them to make representations to it on important issues, sometimes succeeded in persuading their spokesmen to join it, and in general remained a relatively open organization. Such an arrangement also suited them as it enabled them to influence Congress policy without risking government displeasure, compromising their ideology or losing their political independence. They, therefore, took full advantage of it, with the result that no major social group was without its sympathizers in the Congress.

Over time the Congress became a broad 'church' accommodating individuals and organizations representing a wide variety of views and interests. The Swarajists occupied important positions within it and were allowed to speak in its name. Until they were barred from holding office in 1945 because of their position on the 'people's war', the communists participated in its elections at all levels and held high offices including membership of the All India Congress Committee (AICC). For years the Socialist Party functioned as a ginger group within the Congress, and Gandhi went out of his way to ensure that its views were heard and its members adequately represented at various organizational levels

In all this Gandhi played the skilful role of a head of the 'national family'. He presided over the internal debates within the Congress, often acting as a kind of conduit through which different groups spoke to one another. He sensitized peasants and landlords, capitalists and workers, intellectuals and illiterate masses, communists and conservatives, caste Hindus and untouchables to each other's expectations, hopes and fears, and urged them to settle their differences in the spirit of justice and goodwill, befitting the members of a 'common family'. He threw his weight behind different groups at different times and ensured that none felt neglected. He repeatedly attacked Indian capitalists, held them under check on many occasions, made sure that they did not take over the Congress, alerted the country to their machinations, and instilled in it a healthy suspicion of them. While pleading the cause of the poor and keeping them before the national consciousness, he chided them for being impatient, undisciplined and immoderate in their demands and language. He insisted that India's independence was fragile without its social and economic regeneration and advanced a broad-based concept of swaraj. Though the constructive programme was a woefully inadequate answer to India's appalling problems and had an extremely limited practical impact, its symbolic and pedagogical value was considerable. It stressed the interdependence of political and economic issues, encouraged a sense of solidarity with the poor, helped create a dedicated group of grassroots workers capable of mobilizing the masses, and fostered a tradition of social service.

Though organizationally the Congress had a narrow social base, its ideological and political orientation was much broader. That was why it could legitimately claim to be and was widely accepted as a national organization entitled to speak in the name of all or at least most Indians. M.N. Roy felt compelled to conclude on the basis of his assessment of the communist experience between 1920 and 1934 that 'no movement can be organized separately and in opposition to the movement led by the Congress'.[25] As B.T. Ranadive put it recently, all those who pitted themselves against it were inevitably routed.

The Congress under Gandhi then had an intricate and ingenious structure. It had a middle-class or 'petty-bourgeois' core, around which it gathered a wide variety of groups. It offered its hospitality to different views and interests, but it was a home only for the middle classes. It provided a public forum for and sought to arbitrate between all Indians, but it had a definite structural, ideological and social bias that set limits to its national character and to the kind of consensus it evolved. Basically, it was wedded to the politics of accommodation and compromise, avoided extremes of all types, and sought to occupy the middle ground. It was concerned about the poor and informed by a spirit of social service. But it remained deeply fearful of their 'extremism' and propensity to violence, and did not actively involve them in, let alone allow them to, lead the movement for their liberation. It had a healthy suspicion of the rich and was critical of the evils of capitalism, but it was committed to the defence of private property. Thanks to this distinct bias, it had a fuzzy but fairly firm identity, an inner point of balance, a measure of autonomy and resilience which saved it from being hijacked by either the right or the left. From time to time it did swing from one extreme to the other, but always within a limited range and eventually returned to its normal state of accommodation and compromise.

The Congress had a middle-class social basis and bias. But it also aspired for a truly national consensus reconciling the interests of all major social groups. The hiatus between its composition and aspirations, its social base and ideological consciousness created problems. The excluded groups had to rely on their sympathizers within the Congress and access to its influential leaders, above all Gandhi, to ensure that their interests received equal attention. Though, as we saw, all major groups had these advantages, the big bourgeoisie had a considerable edge over the rest. They were politically more skilful. They had their regular professional lobbyists within the Congress. Some of them controlled, and many of the rest enjoyed unhindered access to, the media. Some of them had social and familial ties with the Congress leadership. There was a broad similarity of views between them and many a middle-class group active within the Congress. Some industrialists acted as intermediaries between the Congress and government and were politically important. Some of them financially helped out Congress leaders – as when Birla regularly sent *hundis* to Rajaji, Dalmia financed the provincial elections in Bihar and several industrial houses offered investment and other opportunities to politically friendly leaders. The poor, the industrial workers, the agricultural labourers, the poor farmers and others had no such ideological, political, financial, organizational and other advantages. They had largely to rely on periodic riots and agitations and the socially conscious sections of the middle, especially professional, classes to ensure that they were not forgotten.

Not surprisingly the Congress, which intended to be and generally remained a more or less evenly balanced coalition of classes and interests under middle-class leadership, tended on several occasions and in several important areas to tilt towards the big bourgeoisie. Though Gandhi's 'simple but vital' eleven-point programme presented to the viceroy before the civil disobedience movement in 1930 included such items as reduction of land revenue by half and abolition of the salt tax, it included several others specifically designed to promote the interests of the Indian bourgeoisie. The Gandhi-Irwin Pact had a similar thrust. Gandhi knew that the constructive programme was desperately starved of resources, but did little save rebuke the rich for their meanness. When he saw the condition of the *dublas* and *hali* labourers in Bardoli, he bitterly accused the Patidars of 'swadeshi dyerism' but, again, did not launch a movement against them. In the 1930s he pressurized the government to protect Indian textile industries against Japanese competition, but did not demand then or on similar other occasions that the industrialists in return support his pro-poor causes.[26]

Gandhi could have avoided the periodic Congress tilt towards the big bourgeoisie and developed a truly national consensus by mobilizing the weaker sections of society and giving them an effective political presence within it. There were several reasons why he did not do so, two of the most important being his theory of reform and the inescapable constraints of the independence movement.

In its basic philosophy and ethos, Gandhi's campaign against poverty bore an uncanny resemblance to that against untouchability. As I have argued at length elsewhere, he took a religious view of untouchability and made its eradication an exclusively Hindu responsibility.[27] While this focused attention on the centuries of Hindu oppression, it had the great demerit of treating the Harijans as passive objects helplessly waiting for their masters to get off their backs. Like the cow, they were a 'poem of pity', a tragic symbol of Hindu tyranny about which they were themselves expected to do little. They were, therefore,never involved in the struggle for their liberation and failed to develop a collective organization, a corporate identity, an indigenous leadership, a tradition of struggle, and memories of collective action. It was striking that Gandhi's campaign threw up extensive Hindu literature *about* them but little *by* them. Gandhi spoke for them, but did not encourage them to speak for themselves. Thanks to his mistaken strategy, his love kept them almost just as dumb as had the centuries of humiliation.

The lack of active Harijan involvement in the Congress and other organizations had unfortunate consequences. In the absence of an organized and vocal Harijan presence, Gandhi remained surrounded by caste Hindus enjoying direct and constant access to him. Subjected to their daily pressures and skilful manoeuvres, he exaggerated their fears and anxieties and was insufficiently sensitive to Harijan feelings and opinions. He could not rely on the organized power of the Harijans to counter the caste lobby, and not having encouraged their mass movement, he was unable to mobilize the grassroots pressure either. His daily mail, too, brought scores of letters from angry and bitter caste Hindus, but almost none from the illiterate Harijans. Gandhi, therefore, tended to take the latter for granted and spent most of his time and energy reassuring caste Hindus.

Gandhi's approach to the poor, the landless labourers and others had a similar thrust and remained inadequate for three related reasons. First, even as he called the untouchables Harijans (God's people), he called the poor *Daridra-narayan,* manifestations or incarnations of God. They were tragic symbols of the greed and inhumanity of the rich. Just as it was the responsibility of the educated and morally conscious caste Hindus to fight against the orthodox and purge their religion of the 'evil blot' of untouchability, it was the responsibility of the middle classes, especially the socially conscious professional classes, to fight against capitalist exploitation. Since the poor were not to be involved in their emancipation, Gandhi made little attempt to mobilize and radicalize them. Once his faith in the middle classes turned out to be ill-founded, the poor were left in a political limbo.

Second, Gandhi knew well that the poor were angry and frustrated and seething with the 'spirit of violence'. He was also aware of their role in the Russian and Chinese revolutions, to both of which he was a contemporary witness. He was, therefore, deeply afraid that once they were mobilized and their expectations aroused, large-scale violence was bound to result which neither he nor the Congress was likely to be able to control. That was why he strongly disapproved of their spontaneous movements and did not allow even the Congress to lead and organize their campaigns beyond a certain point and without his consent.

Gandhi, therefore, decided to proceed with extreme caution. He repeatedly warned and attacked the rich in the hope of encouraging a conciliatory attitude. He urged the middle classes to take up the cause of the poor and provide a 'responsible' leadership. And while championing the cause of the poor, he constantly urged them to be patient and eschew violence. He hoped in these and other ways to create a moral and political climate in which independent India could embark upon an effective anti-poverty programme. Until the country became free, he was not prepared to risk social violence. He was convinced that once it was free, the poor and the oppressed would 'justifiably' launch satyagrahas in a more propitious climate and with greater chances of success. As we saw, he was not totally opposed to violence either. He was prepared under certain circumstances to put up with the 'defensive' and 'understandable' violence of the poor. And as he told Louis Fischer, he did not mind 'fifteen days of chaos' and was fully confident that the government of independent India would successfully cope with the violence of the rich. In other words, Gandhi's theory of nonviolence did not undermine or emasculate his economic radicalism as his Marxist commentators have argued. Rather he was not prepared to permit violence during the course of the struggle for independence.

Third, as we saw earlier, the poor had no real part to play in the struggle for independence as Gandhi conducted it, and were not recruited into the Congress. Not surprisingly, they were barely visible within it. Hardly any of them was ever elected or appointed to a local or regional Congress committee, let alone to the AICC or as Congress president. Thanks to Gandhi, they were a pervasive *moral* presence within the Congress but, since they lacked an organized and effective voice of their own, they had no *poitical* presence. Being nowhere near its centre of power, they were not involved in shaping its agenda and priorities. Unlike the middle classes and the spokesmen of the big bourgeoisie, they lacked constant access to him and were unable to put moral and political pressure on him. The largely westernized middle-class radicals led by Jawaharlal Nehru were the only spokesmen the poor had within the Congress. Though they were generally sincere, their pressure lacked urgency, passion, defiance and tenacity. And they spoke in an abstract and theoretical language to which Gandhi found it difficult to relate. Within such a politically unbalanced context, for creating which he was himself partly responsible, his deep moral concern for the poor and the oppressed could not find adequate institutional articulation.

IV

In the light of our discussion, it follows that the Marxist interpretation of Gandhi contains important and valid insights but is oversimplified, and that the picture is complex and messy. The Congress under his leadership was *not* a party of the big bourgeoisie, nor committed to capitalism. It was essentially a middle-class party constantly reaching out to new groups and interests on both sides of the economic spectrum, and aiming to evolve a broad and fluctuating economic consensus that was neither wholly capitalist nor fully socialist. Right-wing and left-wing ideas grew up around its 'petty-bourgeois' core and both shaped and were in turn shaped by it. Nehru put the point well: 'Even our more reactionary people are not so rigid in their reactions as they are probably in Europe and America. And even our most advanced people are somewhow influenced by Gandhiji. He created connecting links between conflicting interests'.[28]

The flow of political influence and the process of moral sensitization between the different groups proceeded in both directions. The big bourgeoisie did influence the Congress and enjoy a measure of political power as the Marxists argue, but they were also made aware of the anger, frustrations and legitimate demands of the poor and oppressed and their own social responsibility. The middle and upper peasantry did from time to time link up with the big bourgeoisie, but it also retained its independence, threw up leaders of status and class loyalty, and influenced Congress policies on important matters. Many of these leaders were not created by or in any way indebted to the big bourgeoisie, and had come to power on the basis of their sacrifices and peasant struggles. They had a constituency which they could not lightly ignore and whose interests they could not subordinate to those of some other class. The Marxist commentators are, therefore, wrong in arguing that Gandhi delivered the peasantry to the capitalists. The rural and urban poor had their spokesman at the highest level and their interests were not ignored either. Since, however, Gandhi did not organize and recruit them to the Congress, their political power remained relatively weak and failed to provide an effective counterweight to the big bourgeoisie.

Thanks to the logic of the nationalist movement and Gandhi's interpretation of it, the Congress contained mutually regulating pro-bourgeois as well as pro-poor, pro-industrialist as well as pro-peasantry tendencies within its overall middle-class framework. Since Gandhi failed to mobilize the poor, the pro-capitalist tendency was stronger; but the anti-bourgeois tendency was neither absent nor too weak to offer strong resistance. Thanks to its middle-class bias, the Congress did not allow itself to be taken over by either tendency. From its relatively secure and autonomous ideological point of balance, it arbitrated between them. It knew that it could not pursue pro-capitalist policies for long without feeling morally troubled, provoking internal resistance, and losing its inner point of balance. As Bipan Chandra puts it: 'Indian National Congress was a popular, multi-class movement. It was not a movement controlled by the bourgeoisie, nor did the bourgeoisie exercise exclusive control over it'.[29]

Though the Marxist commentators are right in pointing out that Gandhi did not provide a viable *alternative* to capitalism, they are wrong not to appreciate that his thought had enough resources to offer a coherent and practical *critique* of it. Such ideas as legally enforced trusteeship, nationalization without compensation, the minimum possible wage differential, a heavy death duty, rural uplift and a comprehensive programme for levelling up the poor went a long way towards changing the inner structure of capitalism. Thanks to the constraints of the nationalist struggle, Gandhi did not fully exploit the radical tendencies of his thought. No such constraints existed in independent India. Had any of his followers mobilized these tendencies and mounted a carefully planned campaign of peasants' and workers' satyagrahas as he had urged, or had the Nehru government shown greater skill and determination in harnessing the anti-bourgeois component of his complex legacy, the Marxists would most certainly have seen Gandhi in a very different light.

Notes

1. Sibnarayan Ray (ed.), *Selected Works of M.N. Roy* (Delhi 1987) vol. I, p. 348.

2. Ibid., p. 347.

3. Ibid., 346.

4. 'Draft Platform of Action' in Democratic Research Service, *Indian Communist Party Documents, 1930-1956* (Bombay 1957) pp. 1-21.

5. See Jairus Banaji, 'The Comintern and Indian Nationalism', in K.N. Panikkar (ed.), *National and Left Movements in India* (Delhi 1980) pp. 213-65.

6. Gene D.Overstreet and Marshall Windmiller, *Communism in India* (Berkeley 1960), p. 158.

7. J.P. Narayan, *Why Socialism?* (Varanasi 1936), p. 47.

8. A.R. Desai, *Social Background of Indian Nationalism* (Bombay 1948), p. 148.

9. Partha Chatterjee, *National Thought and the Colonial World: A Derivative Discourse?* (Delhi 1987), ch. 2.

10. Ibid., p. 100.

11. Ibid., p. 124.

12. For a good discussions of Gandhi's relations with the Indian bourgeoisie, to which I am indebted but which takes a somewhat different view, see Claude Markovits, *Indian Business and Nationalist Politics, 1931-1939* (Canbridge 1985)

13. *Young India*, 13 October 1921; 27 October 1921; and 26 October 1924.

14. *Harijan*, 16 December 1939.

15. *Young India*, 16 April 1931 and 17 September 1931.

16. Narajivan Trust, *Collected Works of Mahatma Gandhi* (Ahmedabad 1958), vol LV, p. 42.

17. Ibid., vol. LXIV, p. 192; vol. LXXVI, p. 367.

18. Ibid., vol LXXVI, pp 437, 445f.

19. Louis Fischer, *The Life of Mahatma Gandhi* (Bombay 1983), pp.421f.

20. For a useful discussion, see David Hardiman, *Peasant Nationalists of Gujarat: Kheda District, 1917-1939* (Delhi 1981), pp. 250f.

21. G.D. Birla, *In the Shadow of the Mahatma* (Bombay 1968), p. 101.

22. Ibid., p. 277.

23. Ibid., p. 278.

24. G.D. Birla, *Bapu: A Unique Association*, (Bombay 1977), vol. IV, pp. 361f, 364, 368, 370, 377-78.

25. Ray (ed.) *Selected Works of M.N. Roy* (n.1), vol. I, p. 487.

26. D.N. Dhanagre, *Peasant Movements in India* (Delhi 1983), pp. 91-92.

27. See Bhikhu Parekh, *Colonialism, Tradition and Reform* (New Delhi 1989), ch. 7.

28. Tibor Mendus, *Conversations with Mr. Nehru* (London 1957), p. 140.

29. Bipan Chandra et al., *Iindia's Struggle for Independence, 1857-1947* (New Delhi 1988), p. 26.

8

The Politics of Business Interest Groups: Colonial Madras

Raman Mahadevan

In the literature on the relationship between business and politics, business associations are largely perceived as homogeneous entities in terms of the interests they articulate and represent. The characterization of business, commercial and industrial associations as pressure groups also falls short of capturing the complexities inherent in the process of interest-group alignment. For, implicit in this characterization is the assumption that the business associations in colonial India were essentially forums for extracting concessions from the state. In short, by overemphasizing this bipolar situation, it tends to oversimplify what was in fact a highly complex structure of relationships, involving the Congress-led national movement, the other political parties, labour, and the state.

Business associations and interest groups, though very important for exercising influence on the state, were not the only channels. Leading businessmen were also able to establish direct contact with the colonial government, its bureaucracy and the nationalist movement. Above all, the politics of businessmen was to a large extent conditioned by their immediate economic and commercial considerations. It is, therefore, necessary to study more closely the politics of interest groups in the light of the changing structure of investments. This paper seeks to explore the growth and articulation of the principal interest groups in a particular region.

While the European business interest groups were not unimportant, for the sake of convenience and constraints of space, it is proposed to concentrate on some of the major Indian commercial and industrial interest groups only. This paper also does not discuss the dynamics of the growth of the innumerable mofussil trade associations, representing the interests of small capital, though these were significant. The focus of this paper lies in relating the role of the pressure groups to the changing politico-economic environment in colonial Madras. It also attempts to throw light on the process of control exercised by businessmen over these interest groups.

I

It is well acknowledged that the Madras region, as compared to the Bombay and Bengal presidencies was, both industrially and commercially, relatively backward. The initial and prolonged lag between Madras and other regions was the outcome of complex factors. Among these two were of crucial importance. The near dominance of European capital in the organized sector, including trade, banking and industry acted as a constraining influence on the entry of Indian capital into industry which was consequently delayed. The other crucial difference lay in the initial position, size and strength of the entrepreneurial class in south India. Given the dominance of European capital over the channels of trade and commerce, they took the initiative to establish commercial associations in order to protect and promote their own mercantile interests.

The Madras Chamber of Commerce came into being in 1936.[1] Almost all the leading European agency houses were represented in the chamber and included prominent firms like the Arbuthnots, Binnys and Parrys.[2] Both Binnys and Parrys, the two major European business houses, had very close connections with the chamber.[3] The Madras Trades Association, set up in 1856 was also exclusively a European-dominated body.[4] There was considerable overlap in the membership of the chamber and the association. Towards the end of the nineteenth century there came into being the first major sectional association, again the outcome of European initiative. The United Planters Association of South India, set up in 1893, was a powerful body of European estate-owners in the Nilgiris and adjacent areas.[5] It is not quite surprising that the initiative for promoting the first industrial association also came from the Madras-based European textile interests.[6] They virtually controlled the textile industry in southern India, at least until the 1920s.[7]

Ironically, the beginning of the new trend towards the organization of exclusively Indian commercial interests, as distinct from European, can be traced to south India. The first such 'native merchants chamber' was established in Coconada in 1885.[8] This was later renamed the

Godavari Chamber of Commerce. Paradoxically, however, for the next quarter century there was almost a virtual lull in terms of any significant crystallization of indigenous entrepreneurial interests. That this was so is not entirely surprising given the structure of private capital in south India. Apart from being relatively weak and small in size, it was largely confined to the unorganized credit and trade sector. From around the late nineteenth and early twentieth century a small portion of this capital was beginning to seek outlets in the modern manufacturing and commercial sector.

This capital was differentiated as a consequence of the variations in the channels and process of accumulation. While at one end of the spectrum were sections of the Nattukottai Chettys (the traditional business community of south India) who by exporting part of their capital to the newly opened up colonies managed to sustain a relatively high rate of accumulation, others had to operate within a relatively more restricted area of investment and, thus, had a much narrower base for accumulation. This latter group included the Komati Chettys (from the Andhra region, who were involved as middlemen in the import-export trade and as financiers of the trade in rice and other produce), the Muslim traders (in and around Madras and the North Arcot region, with investments in exports and manufacture of tanned hides and skins) and the Nadar merchants (financing the jaggery and cotton trade). Other social groups from within which certain sections were beginning to develop significant commercial interests around the turn of the century included the Kalladaikurichi Brahmins, the capitalist farmers of Coimbatore and the Saurashtrians of Madurai. This is by no means a comprehensive list of the social groups which at varying points of time together provided the source for commercial and industrial entrepreneurship of south India.

The process of the formation of such a class should necessarily take cognizance of the differentiation with the class and the consequent variations in the size of the class. The relatively smaller size of the local capital was also reflected in the fact that with some exceptions there was very little spatial spread of the capital within south India. In short, the accumulation process itself was spatially very narrowly based and confined largely to the initial area of domicile. This spatial fragmentation had implications for the growth of large intra-regional, sectional and commercial associations and should to some extent explain the delayed growth of such formations.

By the turn of the century, there were clear signs of a certain buoyancy in indigenous entrepreneurial activity in the Madras region as reflected in the promotion of several joint-stock ventures, including quite a few industrial undertakings. The impact and influence of the swadeshi movement in creating a more congenial climate for private industrial investment was crucial.[9] Contemporary reports observed the significantly 'greater demand for a number of locally made articles in the Presidency' and along with it, 'an increasing desire to support and patronise local industries'.[10] The merchants and traders were quick to perceive the advantages arising out of this new situation. The swadeshi ethos also provided the necessary impetus for the crystallization of a certain broad unity of interests among the nascent commercial and industrial interests of Madras.

A clear reflection of this process was the establishment in 1906 of the National Fund and Industrial Association (NFIA) and the Chennai Jana Sangham in 1908. The former had set before itself the ambitious task of 'fostering and improving indigenous industries, the promotion of scientific and technical education and diffusion of knowledge on industrial matters among the people'.[11] It also intended to set up 'a bureau of information relating to the industries and commerce in India'.[12] While a number of leading traders and merchants of Madras came to be associated with this body in the initial stages, it was severely handicapped by paucity of funds, which restricted the scope of its activities.[13] All the same, the importance of such an association as a platform for indigenous commercial interests to discuss problems of mutual concerns should not be overlooked.

In this context the deliberation of the meeting of the NFIA held in 1919 is particularly noteworthy. Present on this occasion were a large number of leading commercial personalities of Madras together with the director of industries. This provided an occasion for a free discussion of a wide range of issues pertaining to the possibilities of industrialization in Madras province, and in particular the role of the state in assisting this process.[14] The notion that capital in Madras was inherently shy, a position taken by the director of industries, was challenged by the merchant members of the association. They argued that it was the lack of the basic infrastructure, including an institutionalized system for dissemination of vital economic, scientific and technical data, which rendered investment a highly risky proposition and hence local capital tended to be more cautious. As one of the commentators observed, 'we want expert knowledge, a laboratory of industrial chemistry . . . on which we can act . . .; if we have that most people will come forward with the capital'.[15]

The Chennai Jana Sangham, established in 1908, had more or less similar aims and objectives as those of the NFIA, the only difference being its overtly weightier political overtones, namely, 'the furtherance of nationalism in the city, by delivering lectures on Swadeshism and boycott of foreign goods'.[16]

Underlying the swadeshi ethos were the growing and sharpening contradictions between sections of Indian and foreign capital, which in turn reflected the relative growth of local capital and its need to carve out an autonomous space for itself. The first concrete or overt manifestation of the conflict appeared in the sphere of banking or the organized credit market. The establishment of the Indian Bank in 1907 was, in a sense, an articulation of this contradiction. Specifically, the collapse of the Arbuthnots in 1906, a leading European business house of Madras with a large banking establishment, and the near-collapse of the firm of Binnys, which gave a severe jolt to the money market in Madras, prompted some prominent merchants and public men to initiate action in this matter.[17] The bank was to provide banking and credit facilities to Indian merchants and entrepreneurs and 'to serve as a channel of safe investments for the middle class'.[18] It was decided to enlist the support of some of the leading Nattukottai Chetty bankers – to generate confidence among investors – and it was asserted by the end of 1907 that two-thirds of the subscribed capital of Rs 1,775,000 was contributed by the Chettys.[19] The large investment of the Chetty capital in the Indian Bank needs no elaboration. Control over the bank would provide them access to relatively cheap credit and thus considerably augment the flow of funds into their resource pool.

The spirit of coalescence which found its initial expression in the founding of the Indian Bank was soon extended to a higher plane, when sections of south Indian commercial interests decided to institutionalize their broad unity of interests. The swadeshi movement and its ideals may have in a broad sense provided legitimacy to the coalescence of indigenous commercial interests, but it was the prospects of a 'new reform scheme' and a legislative council that triggered off the move to form a commercial association with a view to extracting vital concessions from the colonial state.[20] Thus came into being the Southern Indian Chamber of Commerce (SICC) in May 1909 with 'over one hundred of the best businessmen of Madras, representing the trade, manufacture and commerce of this presidency'[21] among its members. The basic character of the SICC, however, at least until the 1920s was predominantly mercantile. With the exception of the local Muslim entrepreneurs, associated with the tanning industry and trade and a few representing the textile industry, the bulk of the members belonged to local merchant groups. Numerically, the Muslim entrepreneurs were the largest, followed by the Komatis.[22] There is no evidence, at least for the initial period, of significant participation by the Nattukottai Chettys in the chamber's activities.[23] During 1910-11 only eight out of 110 members were Nattukottai Chettys[24] and the Annamalai Chetty group, supposed to have exercised a dominating influence over the chamber's politics from the outset, were not even represented in it.[25] In fact, Annamalai Chettiar was, ironically enough, one of the two Indian members of the European-dominated Madras Chamber of Commerce.[26] For, with his vast interests in Burma and Ceylon he did not consider it prudent at this stage to identify himself with a body so avowedly nationalistic in its aims.

A strong critic of the colonial government, the SICC repeatedly demanded fiscal autonomy and protection for indigenous industries from foreign competition and concerted state intervention for the promotion of indigenous industrial investment. Articulating forcefully the ideological position of the chamber, the president, P. Thyagaraja Chetty, emphasised that the 'economic independence of India must be ensured. Not until then will India materially prosper'. Of crucial importance and one that was 'an imperative necessity', he added, 'is the freedom to settle our own commercial, industrial and economic questions, in our own interests, without any subordination of such interests, to those of any others'.[27]

II

The relative weakening of the colonial-metropolitan nexus during the First World War, characterized by a sudden contraction of foreign trade, provided a stimulus for indigenous investment and local enterprise. The pent-up pressure for industrial growth found its release only after the war, owing to difficulties in securing mill machinery earlier. But in view of the heavy annual demand of the imperial treasury on Madras and also on account of the exigencies of the situation arising out of the war, the Madras government was called upon to find ways and means to increase its revenue. There were substantial increases, thus, in excise, customs dues and income tax during this period [28] which to a large extent hit the rising entrepreneurial class. Together with this, the prospects of further constitutional reforms and the enlargement of franchise, provided impetus for sectional interest groups to multiply.

The Southern Indian Skins and Hides Merchants Association (SISHMA) and the Nattukottai Nagarathar Association (NNA), formed in 1917, were among the most prominent of the new associations.

Dependent on an inherently fluctuating and unstable overseas market, the tanned hides and skin trade suffered from periodic crises. The situation was particularly critical following the dislocation of the hides and skin trade during the war.[29] In addition, the traders had to bear with endless restrictions on their trade, unfavourable exchange ratio and the lack of sufficient protection.[30] The cumulative effect of these disincentives was that it tended to turn them into strong critics of the colonial government, and in course of time they were drawn into the nationalist agitation against colonial rule. Their anti-imperialist sentiment found concrete expression in the support they extended to the Home Rule Movement in Madras.[31] As Abbas Hussain, a contemporary observer noted: 'They [the hides and skins merchants] came to know that commerce was inter-allied with politics and that the greater the measure of political freedom they enjoyed, the greater would be the scope and prosperity of the industry'.[32] The formation of SISHMA did not mean the withdrawal of Muslim entrepreneurs from the SICC. On the contrary, they utilized both these forums to further their interests. Jamal Mohammed, the spokesman of the hides trade, was equally active in the SICC in articulating the economic interests and championing the cause of Indian entrepreneurs.

The rationalization of the tax structure in 1916 affected a large number of Nattukottai Chetty bankers and trade merchants, especially those of the upper strata, who had vital stakes in Madras and overseas. This provided the immediate provocation for the establishment of the NNA. Because of their overseas investments and their dependence on the British government for protecting their interests, some Chettys tended to be cautious and maintained a distance from the rising national movement. This may perhaps also explain their relative lack of involvement with the SICC. There were instances, however, of more strident expression of Chetty resentment over the rigorous tax structure and the financial monetary policy of the government. The clearest expression of this contradiction was the large measure of support extended by a number of prominent Chetty bankers and traders to the Madras Presidency Association and the Home Rule Movement.[33]

The early 1920s witnessed the rise of some of mofussil chambers of commerce which were in a sense a reflection of the accretion of capital following the phenomenal growth of internal commerce during and after the war. The Indian Chamber of Commerce, Tuticorin and the Madura Ramnad Chamber of Commerce were essentially attempts by small capitalists to foster their interests. The available evidence, limited though it is, would seem to suggest that the Madura Ramnad Chamber of Commerce came to be identified with the Saurashtrian handloom capitalists, while the Tuticorin formation was controlled by sections of the rising Nadar and Bharata merchant groups.

The late 1920s and 1930s marked a turning point with regard to investment of south Indian capital in industry. The depression sharply turned the terms of trade between agriculture and industry in favour of the latter. This brought about a significant shift of capital from agriculture and moneylending to industry. The shrinkage in the volume of foreign trade and the introduction of tariff protection to sugar and cotton textile industries were also among the important factors contributing to a general upswing in industrial activity and internal commerce. A relative buoyancy in industrial investment in Madras from the late 1920s onwards was also due to a set of favourable conditions specific to the region – particularly the phenomenal growth of the textile industry centered around Coimbatore.[34]

The maturing and consolidation of regional capital led to the rise of several new associations. The underlying concern was the need to protect and foster the substantial indigenous and commercial interests linked to the cotton textile industry. Two particularly important associations which emerged during this period and which between them commanded considerable influence were the Indian Chamber of Commerce, Coimbatore (ICC Coimbatore) and the South India Millowners Association (SIMA). Established in 1929, the ICC Coimbatore was conceived by R.K. Shanmukham Chetty as a lobby for the rising commercial and industrial interests in Coimbatore.[35] As an industrialist and an important political personality, Chetty must have realized the importance of this association to provide him access to government patronage as well as an opportunity to establish links with the wider commercial and industrial world. The timing of the establishment of ICC is also quite significant. For, by this time the Federation of Indian Chambers of Commerce (FICC – later FICCI when 'industry' was added to its name) had come into being and the importance of channelizing and projecting the ICC interests through FICC could not have been overlooked. The ICC was in fact admitted as a member of FICC in 1930 and regularly sent delegations to the latter's annual meetings. By virtue of representing the ICC Coimbatore, Shanmukham Chetty was inducted into the executive committee of FICC in 1930 and again in 1932.[36]

Besides traders, a fair number of textile millowners were also associated with ICC. Among those closely involved were P.S.G. Ganga Naidu and C.S. Ratnasabapathy Mudaliar.[37] Initially the organization served as an important forum for articulating the interests of the local millowners.[38] Among the significant achievements of the chamber in its early days was its success in obtaining concessional freight rates for imports of coal from Bengal and for exports of cotton yarn and cloth to Shalimar, Wadibunder and Coconada.[39] These must have contributed to consolidating its hold over the local millowners. Despite his political differences with the Congress, Shanmukham Chetty as a millowner did not fail to notice the long-term gains of the swadeshi and boycott campaigns for the south Indian mills to consolidate their hold over the local market. It is interesting that even after his final rupture with the Congress in January 1930,[40] Chetty continued to play a significant role through the ICC in mobilizing support for the cause of swadeshi, khadi and boycott.[41]

From the mid-1930s till the early 1940s the ICC was fairly active in taking a firm stand on various economic issues, especially those concerning the textile industry. Over a period of time the ICC succeeded in enlarging its membership. A good number of the seventy odd members on its rolls by the late 1930s were fairly influential entrepreneurs associated with the Coimbatore textile industry.[42] The fact that Ratnasabapathy Mudaliar was nominated as vice-president and later as president of FICCI in 1939 also gave the ICC a certain clout and possibly enhanced its stature. With the phenomenal growth of the textile industry in Coimbatore, especially in the early 1930s, initiatives were taken for promoting an association which could cater exclusively to the textile interests. While the available evidence is not very clear, it seems that there was an element of rivalry between the South India Textile Association (SITA) which came into being in 1932 and the ICC both of which claimed to represent broadly similar interests[43], although it is difficult to infer the basis of this conflict.

The South India Millowners Association (SIMA), which also championed the cause of textile industry, was founded in 1933 on the initiative of some leading millowners of Coimbatore, predominantly Indian but a few Europeans as well.[44] Given the composition of the executive committee of the SIMA and the timing of its establishment, it may not be too far-fetched to infer that this was perhaps an attempt to create a cohesive organization comprising various conflicting elements to face the crisis emerging out of the severe competition from the cheaper Japanese textile goods being dumped on to the Indian market.[45] The resultant wage cut, retrenchment and the labour unrest may have provided the impetus to an institutionalization of this broad-based class unity. The phenomenal growth in the textile investment around Coimbatore and the need for rationalizing the production structure in terms of uniformity in working hours and wages could also have provided legitimacy to this move.[46] There was, however, a lot of straddling of members between the three associations namely ICC, SIMA and SITA, particularly between the first two.[47] While SITA continued to survive for a few years more, it was gradually overshadowed by SIMA and, with the changed circumstances, gradually went into oblivion.[48]

A close analysis of the composition of the general membership as well as the executive committee of SIMA, which was the crucial apex decision-making body, belies the general notion, as well as its own exaggerated claim, that it represented a large section, if not the whole industry in south India. Thus, right until 1947 SIMA remained essentially 'Coimbatore-centric'.[49] The majority of the member mills were drawn from in and around Coimbatore. Interestingly, while Binnys and the Cambodia Mills were among the initial and only non-Indian members of SIMA, the Harvey group of mills together with the Chetty mills in Madurai chose to remain out of it. Binnys, a composite mill, concentrated more on cloth manufacture catering to an all-India market, while Harveys manufactured only yarn, and competed with the Coimbatore millowners, often eroding the position of the latter.[50] This may explain the seemingly paradoxical situation.

The minutes of the executive committee meetings of SIMA for the years 1934-40 reveal that effective control was highly concentrated in a handful of the leading textile magnates. These included members of the three principal Naidu families – Lakshmi, PSG and Radhakrishna – the Shanmukham Chetty group, P.S. Sathappa Chettiar and a few others. On the whole SIMA meetings were relatively infrequent and it was most active during periods of crisis, especially during 1937-39, when the industry was gripped by a major crisis as a result of adverse market condition triggered to some extent by the influx of the cheaper Japanese imports. In an effort to overcome the hardship, SIMA recommended curtailment of production and sharp reduction of the working hours. This resulted in an upsurge of labour militancy all over Coimbatore.[51] It is quite revealing that even within the Coimbatore region, on crucial matters relating to production, SIMA's influence over the member mills was not all-pervasive, and only fifteen of the thirty-two odd mills decided to act on SIMA's suggestion of curtailing production by discontinuing the night shift.[52]

The minute books also reveal that even within the executive committee complete consensus on the precise extent of reduction was lacking. In February 1938, when the question of curtailing production came up for deliberation SIMA took the position that individual mills 'shall always have the full liberty to curtail their concerns according to the market conditions and trade demands'.[53] This issue again came up for discussion in early 1939 and continued to receive serious attention until July 1939, when a decision was taken to curtail production to the extent of 50 per cent. Member mills which were working for more than eighteen hours were 'requested at the earliest possible moment to fall in line with the other mills at present working 18 hours'.[54] By early August 1939, possibly as a consequence of the discussions with the minister of industries and labour, SIMA decided to modify its earlier position and reduce output by one-third.[55]

Nevertheless, SIMA and ICC remained effective forums for the millowners to exert influence and pressure on the state to keep labour and wage costs in check. The Congress government in Madras, on its part, despite its election promises of ensuring a fair deal to labour, chose to be pragmatic and was not inclined to alienate the local capitalists. This was most clearly revealed when the government, in deference to the strong reservations of the millowners, decided to bury completely the 'Report of the Court of Enquiry into Labour Unrest in Coimbatore Mills'. While severely indicting the millowners and squarely holding them responsible for the prevailing crisis in industry, the report had recommended reasonable increases in wages for all categories of operatives. The matter was referred for reconsideration to a special committee headed by the Commissioner of Labour D.N. Strathie, which recommended standardization of wages, amounting to very moderate increase barely offsetting the wage cut in force since 1933. Given the general mood of the working class and responding 'to Government's appeal and to secure industrial peace'[56] SIMA urged its member mills to accept the increased rates. The government position was made amply clear by C. Rajagopalachari. He held labour squarely responsible for the crisis in the industry and lamented that 'millowners were in a constant state of fear'. He chided labour not to 'allow itself to be exploited for political purposes by others'. The government, he argued, was determined 'to encourage private enterprise' as a means 'to solve unemployment'.[57]

The process of the cémenting of ties between the substantial sections of Tamil capitalists and the Congress has not been accorded sufficient importance. There is really not much evidence in support of the commonly held view that 'in Madras presidency a large section of the local, capitalist class had become integrated with the power-structure of the Justice Party'.[58] Apart from being at variance with the available evidence, such a view assumes a certain homogeneity for the class in terms of its ideological perceptions, and implicitly rules out the possibility of a more complex and variegated structure. While SIMA did not make any overt political intervention in support of the Congress, most of the leading textile magnates, especially those who exercised enormous control over SIMA, were closely aligned with the Congress. A good number of them were members of the district and town Congress committees and actively campaigned and worked for Congress candidates in the 1937 elections.[59] Election meetings were often held in mill premises.[60] The inability of the Congress to accommodate and support Ratnasabapaty Mudaliar's claim for the Coimbatore urban seat – he was eventually persuaded to withdraw his nomination – did not create any split or rumblings within the ranks of the millowners. This is itself suggestive of maturing of this class and its ability to look beyond the narrow confines of its class interests.

The role of the SICC during the 1930s and early 1940s can be better understood in the context of the fluctuating fortunes of the Nattukottai Chettys, especially some of their leading business houses. Chetty interests overseas received a serious setback with the onset of the depression in the late 1920s. The sharp fall in the prices of primary products and the consequent mounting of bad debts and liquidity crisis disrupted their intricately structured banking system. Though difficult to estimate, the losses incurred by the Chetty firms were believed to be fairly substantial. Several small and a few large Chetty firms were declared insolvent and collapsed.[61] Even the major Chetty houses were in serious trouble as the bulk of their capital was tied up in immovable assets. Nevertheless, the fact that they exercised some control over the Indian Bank in Madras enabled them to utilize the bank's funds in tiding over their difficulties.[62]

The economic crisis in the colonial regions of south - east Asia gave rise to anti-colonial popular nationalist movements, which were generally hostile to the Chettys. For, owning large estates and plantations, they were seen as alien exploiters of the people, and were the target of popular wrath and violence. With a view to maintaining the stability and safeguarding the colonial interests, the governments in the region introduced during the early 1930s measures which had the effect of regulating Chetty banking activities and eventually curtailing their investments. The separation of Burma from India further accentuated the uncertainty of Chetty investments in that region.[63] In the light of these adverse conditions, the question of safeguarding the Chettys' interests became of paramount importance, investing pressure group politics with a new meaning and relevance. The attempts by some leading sections of the Nattukottai Chettys to acquire a firm grip over SICC should be viewed in this context. It is alleged that between 1930 and 1931 Annamalai Chettiar had managed to enrol as many as 150 Chetty businessmen as members of the SICC and all the Chettys together came to constitute 60 per cent of the membership of the SICC.[64] The importance of this control becomes evident in the light of the fact that only the SICC and NNA had representation in the Madras legislative assembly then. Each of these two bodies were allowed to return one member each.

The excessive control over major trade associations, especially the SICC and NNA, by a few leading Chetty houses had the effect of dampening the ongoing process of intra-regional and intra-ethnic corporate unity. This is well illustrated by the case of the Andhra Chamber of Commerce (ACC) which was revived in 1934. This was among the most vocal and forthright of such commercial associations which resented being excluded from the legislative assembly.[65] Alluding to 'the indifference shown towards Andhra commercial, industrial and banking interests by the Southern India Chamber of Commerce',[66] the ACC lamented the fact that 'the Southern India Chamber has latterly become a mere adjunct to the Nattukottai Association, as more than fifty per cent of its members come from the Nattukottai Chetty Community'.[67] Interestingly, opposition to the domination of these commercial bodies by a few families also stemmed from within the Chetty community, especially from its small and middle-level strata, At a Nagarathar conference held in Karaikudi in 1936, these elements expressed their open hostility to the NNA which they characterized as 'an unrepresentative body', and appealed to the government 'to make the reserved seats in the Madras Legislative Council and the Corporation open for contest to the whole Chettiar community'.[68] The conference also urged all Chettys 'to join the Congress and support its candidates in the coming elections'. [69] For the leading Chetty houses the benefit of control over these institutions was not limited to gaining access to levers of power in Madras. It also enabled them to gain entry into FICCI which might help protect their vital overseas interests, experiencing excessive strain at that time. The strategy adopted by the leading Chettys was evidently multi-pronged.

Despite the Chetty domination over SICC, the latter was not reduced to a mere appendage of the NNA, articulating only Chetty interests. It also voiced concern for the economic interests of other indigenous entrepreneurs as is borne out by the proceedings of the SICC annual reports. Throughout the 1930s it took a consistently anti-colonial and nationalist position on almost all the major economic issues. The following resolution passed by the SICC on the question of constitutional guarantees is eloquent testimony to this:

> . . . no scheme of constitutional advance would be satisfactory to the Indian mercantile community if it does not vest in a responsible government full fiscal autonomy including the right to safeguard national interests in every legitimate and recognised manner and the Chamber urges the Indian commercial community to stand uncompromisingly for the power to pursue a national economic policy under the new Constitution'.[70]

The 1930s and early 1940s can, thus, be characterized as a period which witnessed the maturing of industrial and commercial interest groups of varying importance. While each of these bodies was attempting to articulate its demands and interests, they essentially remained disparate, localized and fragmented in character. Even established industrial associations such as SIMA, when invited to accept the membership of SICC as late as 1938, chose not to 'avail itself of the offer' on the plea that 'it would be sufficient if an exchange of correspondence took place on subjects of mutual interest'.[71] That there was as yet no serious attempt by these formations to come together on a trans-regional platform was perhaps partly a reflection of the uneven character of the industrial structure. Paradoxically, a good number of these associations were affiliated to FICCI and strengthened the latter's claim to be a representative all-India forum of industrial and commercial interests.[72] These links with FICCI were, however, quite tenuous and south Indian commercial and industrial interests were at the periphery of the overall FICCI politics. This is revealed in the manner in which the presidentship of FICCI itself was decided. Seeking the advice of Purshotamdas Thakurdas, on the choice of the vice-president in 1930, G.D. Birla expressed his preference for a Muslim. In his view 'Husainbhai Lalbhai will be far better. Madras is an out of the way place; besides I do not think that Jamal Mohammed Saheb would be a great success'.[73] Thakurdas did not share Birla's perception, and argued: 'I fear that Madras will not be satisfied if you give it the go-bye this time. Jamal is the best man and I am afraid there may be great trouble if we give Jamal the go-bye'.[74] But for this warning, Jamal would not have become the federation's vice-president then and president a year later.

III

From the mid-1940s there were clear indications of a basic shift in the position and attitude of the south Indian capitalist class, vis-a-vis capitalists from the other regions. In short, national considerations and objectives seem to have given way to regional and often provincial considerations. There was a latent fear that in the post-war plan for industrial development, Madras would be overlooked. This perceived fear of a possible domination of the south Indian market by the capitalists from other regions provided the basis for the coming together of large sections of regional capital, with SICC providing the leadership.[75] The realignment of capital and the shift in its ideational position must be seen in the light of specific historical and political situation of the 1940s.

While the outbreak of the Second World War and cessation of imports provided an opportunity for south Indian entrepreneurs to amass vast profits both legitimately and through speculative dealings, the 'surplus capital... available for starting new enterprises'[76] could not immediately find an outlet in industry owing to certain constraining factors. These included the government regulatory controls, principally the control of capital issues, the difficulties in securing machinery, and foreign exchange bottleneck for procuring capital goods from non-empire countries. The working of the yarn control order, the imposition of sales tax and excess-profit tax and the embargo on expansion of textile mills were among other reasons which restricted the investment scope of local entrepreneurs, and served to strengthen the regional tendencies.[77] The principle of regionalization of industries introduced by the Government of India provided further impetus to this trend. A close scrutiny of the proceedings of SICC during this period is quite revealing and brings out the shift in its position as compared to the 1930s.

Forwarding its views to the Industrial Planning Committee of the Government of Madras, the Southern India Chamber of Commerce argued that 'a fundamental doubt to be cleared before the public investors can be encouraged to invest in industries and economic enterprises is whether the plan is on an all-India or provincial basis'.[78] The chamber went on to add that if the decision was taken on an all-India basis, Madras would have 'no claim for opening any new textile factory even for weaving, any sugar factories, any cement factories'. But that would be most cruel and unfair for, 'we depend on other provinces for 80 per cent of our cloth, 65 per cent of our cement requirements. . . . We should aim at attaining self-sufficiency in these important commodities'.[79] Justifying the attempts by the provincial government in restricting the flow of north Indian capital into industries in Madras, the chamber argued:

> It may be that citizens of Madras province are being outwitted by nationals of other provinces or other countries in the matter of race for industries and enterprises. In that case the provincial Government's interference so as to restrict issue of shares or transfer of shares to the citizens of other provinces or countries could be well understood.[80]

Again forwarding a memorandum to the popular government in Madras on the eve of the 1946 budget session the Southern India Chamber of Commerce appealed to the ministry to 'do everything possible to improve the trade and industries and help to retain as big a slice of them as possible *for the benefit of the sons of the soil*'[81] (emphasis added). There is some evidence which would suggest that even the South India Millowners Association was tending to take a regional perspective on industrial investment. Thus, in a memorandum submitted to the Madras government it made a strong plea for establishment in the south of a 'manufacturing unit for the production of textile machinery and spare parts'. It went on to add that 'the entire weightage should not be allowed to shift to the North and the interest of the South in matter of industrial undertakings should be adequately protected'.[82]

On the question of securing textile machinery from overseas countries, the textile subcommittee of the government of Madras, represented by two of the leading millowners of Coimbatore, took a categorical position that 'the Government of India should be asked immediately to consult provincial governments before reaching a final decision in regard to allocation of machinery'. Otherwise, the committee warned, 'the case of Madras might go by default being left entirely to the powerful North Indian interests which have a large voice in the committee of selection'.[83]

Almost in the same vein, the first South India Industrial Commercial Conference, held in Madras in 1945 and convened by the Southern India Chamber of Commerce with a view to discussing the prospects of industrialization in Madras, reiterated the regionalization principle. This was in fact one of the important resolutions passed at the conference.[84] This conference was fairly representative and brought together for the first time almost all the leading industrialists of south India on one platform.

The Federation of Indian Chambers of Commerce and Industry was quite disturbed by these developments. It took a very serious view of the way 'certain decisions are being taken by provincial governments', in the name of regionalization of industries. In a communication addressed to the Department of Planning and Development of the Government of India it lamented the tendency to oppose proposals to set up industry in the Madras presidency 'on the ground that the firm sponsoring the establishment of that industry does not belong to that presidency'.[85] 'The present policy of regional development', it added, would 'lead to the creation of monopolies for persons or firms born only in a particular district or province' which would 'have the ultimate effect of arresting even the normal development of industries in various provinces'. Deprecating this attitude it argued that 'private enterprise should be given the full freedom and facilities to establish industries in places most suitable for such development'.[86]

The forging of a broad unity of the regional capitalists tended to conceal temporarily intra-capitalist contradictions. In the late 1940s, however, they surfaced again and resulted in the withdrawal of non-south Indian business communities, principally Marwaris and Gujaratis, from regional associations who went on to form the Hindustan Chamber of Commerce.[87] C.M. Kothari was instrumental in setting up this body. It is claimed that this was the outcome of his being denied the presidentship of SICC.[88] While this may be partially true, it is also possible that this was an expression of his disapproval of the narrow provincial perspective that SICC had come to acquire. Perhaps, at one level, the bogey of regional principle itself was a device to secure vital concessions from the state. It could also be a reflection of the urge to overcome the lag between developed and underdeveloped regions. Above all, it underlines the importance of the politicization of business.

Notes

1. The abrogation of the East India Company's monopoly in 1833 may have provided the stimulus for the European merchants of Madras to come together and 'speak with one voice on subjects concerning them'. See Hilton Brown, *The Parrys of Madras* (Madras 1954), p.66.

2. The only two Indian members, probably *dubashis* of European firms were C. Teerooswamy Naik and G. Sidloo Chetty. See F. Desouza, *The House of Binnys* (Madras 1969), p. 47.

3. In the course of 118 years of the chamber's history extending from 1836 to 1954, sixteen of Parrys' partners or directors occupied the chairmanship of the chamber for a period of thirty-seven years. See Brown *The Parrys*(n.1), p.67. Binnys' influence over the chamber was equally pronounced. For details see Desouza, *The Binnys* (n.2), p.47.

4. FICCI, *Silver Jubilee Souvenir* (Delhi 1951), p.36. The composition of the association even as late as 1947 remained unaltered. The European firms were still dominant. See Padma Balkrishnan (ed.), *The Madras Directory and Who's Who 1947* (Madras 1947), p.3.

5. Desouza, *The Binnys* (n.2), p.118.

6. The Madras and Southern India Millowners Association came into being in 1910. Of the seven founding member mills, all but one were European firms. The association was initially set up with the objective of joining the International Federation of Madras Cotton Spinners and Manufacturers Association. Ibid., pp. 167-8.

7. They accounted for 78 per cent of the spindles in the Madras region. See Raman Mahadevan, 'Conflict and Dependence: Some Aspects of the Evolving Relationship between Indigenous and Foreign Capital in Colonial Madras', Paper presented at the Seminar on Indian industrialisation, 9-12 June 1987, Centre for Development Studies, Trivandrum. p.5.

8. FICCI, *Souvenir* (n.4), p.21.

9. While difficult to quantify, the activities of the provincial industries department and in particular the enlightened initiatives of Chatterton in stimulating indigenous enterprise in textile and tanning may also have had a positive effect in boosting investment. See Padmini Swaminathan, 'State Intervention in Industrial Development. A Case Study of the Madras Presidency', paper presented at the Seminar on South Indian Economy c. 1914-1945, 25-27 April 1988, Centre for Development Studies. Trivandrum.

10. The *Hindu*, 18 April 1910.

11. D. Sadasivan, *The Growth of Public Opinion in the Madras Presidency, 1858-1909* (Madras 1974), p. 106.

12. Ibid.

13. Thus, even after eight years of its existence its financial resources amounted to a paltry eleven thousand rupees. This was 'very insufficient' as admitted apologetically by one of the functionaries of the association 'to start even one small factory'. See The *Hindu*, 25 September 1914.

14. NFIA, *An Interview with the Director of Industries Madras on the Development of Indigenous and Cottage Industries,* hereafter NFIA pamphlet (Madras 1920), p.1.

15. Ibid., p. 9.

16. Sadasivan, *Growth of Public Opinion* (n.11), p. 106.

17. Indian Bank Ltd., *Golden Jubilee Souvenir 1907-1957* (Madras 1957).

18. M.S. Natarajan. 'A Study of the Capital Market of Madras Presidency with Special Reference to its Evolution and Indigenous Institutions.' (D. Phil thesis, University of Madras, 1934), p.60.

19. The *Hindu*, 29 January 1908; also *Swadeshamitran* (Tamil daily) 30 January 1908. Among the Chettys who came to be closely associated with the bank were S.R.M.M.A. Annamalai Chettiar, P.M.A. Muthiah Chettiar, S.R.M.A.R. Ramaswamy Chettiar. The Chettys, it would appear, were not associated with the conception and the promotion of the bank. Thus, the two public circulars issued in 1906 relating to the proposal for a joint-stock bank do not bear the signatures of any of the Chetty bankers. It was only a little later when the idea itself gained sufficient public support and the company itself came into being that some of the prominent Chettys came forward to subscribe a substantial portion of the share capital.

20. The *Hindu*, 2 November 1909.

21. Ibid.

22. SICC, *Report and Correspondence for 1910-1911*. (Madras 1912), see list of members on pp. 192-6.

23. Kochanek seems to overemphasize Chettiar control over SICC during its early years. Stanley Kochanek, *Business and Politics in India* (Berkeley 1974), pp. 151-2.

24. SICC, *Report and Correspondence* (n.22), pp. 151-2.

25. Ibid. See also Kochanek, *Business and Politics* (n.23).

26. Asylum Press, *Almanac and Directory of Madras and Southern India*, (Madras 1920), p. 1785.

27. The *Hindu*, 2 April 1917.

28. C.J. Baker and D.A. Washbrook, *South India* (Delhi 1975), pp. 209-10.

29. The *Hindu*, 7 August 1914.

30. The *Hindu*, 10 October 1917, 17 October 1917, 17 November 1917; G.O. 176, Development Department, 31 January 1924. Tamilnadu Archives (TNA), Madras.

31. D.A. Washbrook, *The Emergence of Provincial Politics : The Madras Presidency 1870-1920*, (Delhi 1977), p. 293; also D. Arnold, *The Congress in Tamilnadu* (Delhi 1977), p.41.

32, The *Hindu*, 28 November 1917,

33. The *Hindu*, 10 September 1917, 21 September 1917, 2 October 1917.

34. Mahadevan, 'Some Aspects of Evolving Relationship', (n.7).

35. ICC Coimbatore, *Silver Jubilee Souvenir 1920-54* (1954), p.20.

36. *FICCI Report of the Proceedings of the Executive Committee 1930-32*. Shanmukham Chetty, however, resigned from the executive committee in October 1932 in protest against FICCI's criticism of the Ottawa agreement and in particular of the bonafide of the non-official delegation. Shanmukham Chetty to Walchand, 29 October 1932, R.K. Shanmukham Chetty papers, hereinafter R.K.S. papers, in the custody of R. Sunderraj of Coimbatore, file no. 3.

37. The *Hindu*, 10 September 1929; also ICC, *Souvenir* (n.35), pp. 27-28.

38. A.G. Guruswami Naidu, Mg. Agents of Radhakrishnan Mills to Secretary FICCI, 10 March 1931, FICCI Papers FICCI office, New Delhi, file no.75, Textile section under the Federation.

39. ICC *Souvenir* (n.35) pp. 21-22.

40. The *Hindu*, 8 January 1930.

41. *Swadeshamitran*, 6 June 1930.

42. Report of ICC Coimbatore 1937-38. See list of members for 1938.

43. R.K. Shanmukham Chety wrote to Palaniswamy on 26 May 1932, 'I hope that during my absence you will keep up the activities of our chamber and take care that it is not swallowed up by the textile Association'. See his letter in R.K.S. Papers, file no. 3.

44. *Nav India* (Tamil daily) Coimbatore, 7 July 1955. Special supplement on the occasion of the inauguration of the new building of SIMA; also *Indian Textile Journal* (ITJ) special souvenir number (Bombay 1954), p. 536.

45. G.O. 869, Development Department, 19 July 1933 (TNA).

46. See Minutes of the Executive Committee of SIMA, hereinafter SIMA minute book, Minute Book 1, resolution 5a, 26 December 1934.

47. Thus R.K. Shanmukham Chetty group, C.S. Ratnasabapathy Mudaliar and P.S.G. Naidu, who were closely associated with ICC, also figure prominently in the executive committee of SIMA. Ratnasabapathy Mudaliar was for about a decade the president of both ICC and SIMA. Similarly, C.V. Venkataramana Ayyanagar, a local businessman, an active Congressman and particularly close to the Stanes group in which he had developed some stakes, was member of both SITA and SIMA.

48. SITA was formally struck off the register of members of FICCI in 1937. See *FICCI Report of the Proceedings of Executive Committee 1937-38.*

49. SIMA Fourteenth Annual Report for 1947-48. See schedule B for list of members. The statement should however be qualified by the fact that SIMA did periodically take a firm stand on larger issues concerning the industry as a whole, especially with reference to protection.

50. Mahadevan, 'Some Aspects of Evolving Relationship' (n.7), pp. 11-12 and note 39.

51. Eamon Murphy, *Unions in Conflict* (Delhi 1981), pp. 194-218.

52. The *Mail*, 26 July 1939.

53. SIMA minute book 1, resolution 2, 17 February 1938.

54. Ibid., 15 July 1939.

55. Ibid., 2 August 1939, 5 August 1939.

56. G.O. 1501 Development Department, 10 June 1939 (TNA). See G. Kuppuswamy Naidu's address to SIMA.

57. The *Hindu*, 29 July 1938.

58. Claude Markovits, *Indian Business and Nationalist Politics, 1931-39* (Bombay 1985), p. 119; also D. Arnold, *Congress in Tamilnadu* (n. 31), p. 158.

59. The *Hindu*, 17 November 1936; 15 February 1937.

60. The *Hindu*, 13 October 1936, 15 February 1937.

61. Raman Mahadevan, 'The Origin and Growth of Entrepreneurship in the Nattukottai Chetty Community of Tamilnadu (Unpublished M. Phil thesis, Jawaharlal Nehru University, 1976), pp. 188-94.

62. C.M. Kothari to Thakurdas (Gujarati) 4 July 1939, Purshotamdas Thakurdas Papers, hereinafter P.T. Papers, file no. 82. Nehru Memorial Museum and Library, New Delhi.

63. Having failed to secure from the colonial authorities the necessary guarantees for the protection of their interests and in view of the enormous financial risks of operating under

the new dispensation, it was strongly rumoured, the Chettys were seriously considering the possibility of withdrawing the capital and investing it in textile mills in India. See *The Hindu*, 9 March 1936; Kothari to Thakurdas (Gujarati), 15 March 1936, PT Papers,file no. 162/I.

64. Kothari to Thakursas (Gujarati), 20 May 1931, PT Papers, file no. 82.

65. *Annual Reports of the Andhra Chamber of Commerce* (ACC) 1935, pp. 10-14. Similar criticism was also voiced by the Madras Swadeshi Merchants Chamber. The *Hindu*, 15 November 1935.

66. *Annual Report ACC* 1935 (n.65), pp. 13-4. That there was an element of exaggeration in this claim is revealed in Govindoss Chathoorbhoojadoss's candid note on some of the unseemly features of commercial organization of the Madras province. He thus, observed: 'The Muslim Chamber of Commerce, Madras and the Andhra Chamber of Commerce Madras were duplication on a minatory scale of the SICC and originated probably on discomfiture of some individual at some election to public body from the SICC... Indirectly most of these organisations can be though not all regarded as existing for individual aggrandisement, advantage and benefits.' See G.O. 2394, Development Department 23 December 1941 (TNA).

67. *Annual Report ACC 1935* (n.65), p. 11.

68. The *Hindu*, 15 November 1936.

69. The *Hindu*, 14 November 1936.

70. *SICC Annual Report*, 1931

71. SIMA Minute Book 2, 22 September 1938. resolution 7.

72. FICCI, Correspondence during the year 1936, vol.II, p. 71.

73. G.D. Birla to Thakurdas, 4 February 1930, P.T. Papers, file no. 42.

74. Thakurdas to G.D. Birla, 8 December 1930, ibid.

75. The evidence, though scattered, clearly suggests that this trend was becoming noticeable from the late 1930s. C.M. Kothari to Thakurdas, 6 July 1936; also Kothari to Thakurdas, 13 October 1938, ibid.; The *Hindu*, 22 April 1936.

76. SICC, the Proceedings of the South India Industrial and Commercial Conference, December 1945, p. 13.

77. The drift of capital to the adjoining princely states assumes relevance in this broad context.

78. SICC, *Annual Report*, January-December 1947, pp. 150-1.

79. Ibid.

80. Ibid.

81. SICC, *Annual Report*, January-December 1946, p. 37.

82. See G.O. 2295, Development Department, 28 April 1949(TNA).

83. G.O. 328, Development Department, 21 January 1946(TNA).

84. See Proceedings of South India Industrial and Commercial Conference (n.76) p. 49.

85. FICCI, *Annual Report*, 1946, vol II, p. 189.

86. Ibid.

87. Kochanek, *Business and Politics* (n.23), pp. 153-4. See also G.O. 5315, Development Department, 15 November 1947, (TNA).

88. Kochanek, *Business and Politics*(n.23), pp. 153-4.

9

Politics and Expatriate Enterprise in India: The Inter-war years

Maria Misra

The decline of the British managing agency houses in India from their dominant position in the import-export and secondary sectors during the inter-war period has been debated extensively. Explanations of this phenomenon can be divided into two broad categories. The first has stressed the inevitability of decline as the unavoidable consequence of the changing international economic structure of the 1920s and 1930s, particularly the diminishing complementarity of the Indian and the British economies. This was a change to which those essentially nineteenth-century entities, the agency houses, were unwilling or unable to adapt. The other explanation has focused instead upon the political context of business activity in the period and has identified the growing impotence of the colonial government as the principal underlying cause of British business weakness. According to this view, the British expatriate business in India, of the managing agency kind, was crucially dependent on government favouritism in financial and commercial matters arising from a cultural, not to say racial, affinity of officials and businessmen. Frustrated by the lack of evidence for this hypothesis in official papers, and not having consulted the papers of the expatriate firms themselves, proponents of this view have often been reduced to asserting that 'everyone' knew this kind of favouritism went on, particularly in the undocumented proceedings of the notoriously exclusive European clubs.[1]

This article proposes to examine the validity of charges of commercial discrimination by the colonial government in the inter-war period and the political rather than commercial response of British businessmen in India to the dual threats of political and economic nationalism in the period. My approach is based largely on the papers of two expatriate firms, Gillanders Arbuthnot, a trading firm which also managed some manufacturing units in Calcutta, and Bird and Company, a larger but essentially similar concern.[2]

I

The connection between British capital in India and the imperial state has come to be seen as almost the paradigmatic case of 'client relationship'. Indeed, one leading authority has gone so far as to say that the major purpose of the state in India was to provide the conditions under which business could prosper, and that the Government of India consistently discriminated in favour of British business interests in a number of ways. The most obvious of these was preferential treatment in the allocation of store-purchasing contracts, but official favouritism went much deeper than that – the rupee exchange rate was held at high level in the 1920s to enable expatriate managing agencies paying dividends to shareholders in Britain, to capitalise their holdings to be repatriated on retirement. Expatriate entrepreneurs had also been given a crucial role in determining the nature of the Indian central bank established in 1934. Despite the mass of Indian opinion in support of the idea that the new Reserve Bank of India should be controlled by the legislature, a combined front of British business groups in India and at home, and the government, steadfastly adhered to the idea of a shareholders' bank, supposedly 'independent of political pressure'.[3]

In transport policy too, pro-British discrimination has been detected in the government policy of granting a continued monopoly on coastal and inland shipping to British shipping companies despite pressure from the Indian shipping interests, particularly Scindia. The owner of Scindia, Walchand Hirachand, referred scathingly to 'the large sums of money which have been paid to the British shipping companies under the mail contracts and the exclusive privileges given to them'.[4] Furthermore, British agency houses still ran many railway lines. Indian interests were unanimous – in the legislative council throughout the First World War, before the Industrial Commission of 1916-18, the Railway Committee of 1920-21, the Fiscal Commission of 1920-22 and subsequently throughout the period of British rule – that the rate structure agreed by British business and government favoured British over indigenous interest.[5] Lord Inchcape – head of the largest corporate entity in India at that time, the Inchcape shipping and agency group – as chairman of the Retrenchment Committee in India, secured for his company a contract for the carriage of coal to Burma for a period of ten years on terms which the government refused to disclose, not giving any opportunity for an Indian company to tender for the contract.[6]

Thirdly, with respect to tariff policy, it has been said that British-owned industries in India fared better than purely Indian interests. Cement and glass, largely Indian, were denied protection; import duties on iron and steel, exclusively Indian, were lowered in 1927. On the other hand, the foreign-dominated match industry was given the protection it requested. On another occasion, the Government of India rejected the recommendation of the Tariff Board for protection to the woolen industry on the ground that two British-controlled units did not support the application.[7] Finally, there is the larger claim that the government cooperated with British business associations such as the Bengal Chamber of Commerce and the Indian Jute Mills Association (IJMA) to maintain the British beachhead on privileges against the rising tide of Indian political and economic nationalism.[8] In other words, by resisting Indian demands for state assistance in developing India's industrial base, the government was protecting the interests of British business. Kidron argues that the government resisted Indian pressure to develop the economy partly in response to lobbying from the British community, which favoured non-intervention, low taxation, and balanced budgets.[9]

These views are popular and widespread, but are not really supported by any papers from the expatriate business houses themselves. When you look at these, you find that the influence enjoyed by expatriate business interests over the colonial government has been exaggerated. It is true that, in the period before the First World War, British businessmen enjoyed privileges as defence stores suppliers, railway contractors, and mail shippers; in the inter-war period, however, this fairly limited kind of favouritism proved of relatively little significance. Faced with a revenue system buckling under the pressure to remit home charges and fund a much enhanced Indian army, the colonial government was increasingly unwilling to give any preference to British business in India which would involve financial sacrifice. Thus, after the First World War British firms in India found themselves unable to secure higher coal prices from the Railway Board or financial support for much-needed railway extensions to the western coast. Meanwhile, as the government imposed unprecedentedly high taxes and export duty on business in general, and on jute exporters in particular, it was simultaneously opening up its paper and timber contracts to competitive tendering from indigenous firms.[10]

This diminution in economic privilege reflected a loss of political influence; faced with the rising tide of nationalism, the colonial government simply could not be seen to give preferential treatment to British business. In the pre-1914 era it had been common practice to consult the various European chambers of commerce on any government bills that might affect their interests; and in this connection the presidents of the main European chambers of commerce and trade associations were often kept abreast of government proposals. In addition to this privileged access to government, British business interests in India retained disproportionate weight in the legislature from 1909. In the subsequent decades, however, there was a marked slackening of the ties between the colonial regime and the non-official British in India, of whom the business community formed a substantial part.

Even as early as 1912, the Government of India showed itself willing to override those interests if they conflicted with the government's greater objective: the stability of the British state in India. With the steady rise of nationalist feeling, securing the state would increasingly entail making concessions to certain indigenous groups. The decisions to move the capital from Calcutta to Delhi in 1912, and to reunify Bengal, while not of immediate relevance to the British business community were, nonetheless, met with dismay and anger. What expatriates found disturbing about these decisions, and about the even more momentous Montagu-Chelmsford reforms, was that they had been made in response to Indian pressure. As *The Englishman*, an organ of non-official British interests, ruefully commented, the government was 'riding roughshod over the British community in an effort to win the applause of a small group of self-interested Indians'.[11]

As a result of economic and political pressures, relations between British business and officialdom markedly deteriorated in the inter-war period. The principal points of conflict were the government's maintenance of excess-profits tax, and its failure to implement the recommendations of the Indian Industrial Commission of 1918, which had advocated, among other things, investment by government in social overhead capital as a catalyst to the further development of industry in India. Investment in better transport facilities was of particular concern to the British-dominated chambers of commerce, and the government's refusal to countenance such expenditure caused much resentment in the period immediately after the First World War. Complaints were made in the European business press about the 'little tin gods in Simla' treating business as a golden goose and perpetrating acts of 'financial chicanery'; while 'the little tin gods' retaliated by denouncing the selfishness of the 'pesky box-wallahs'.[12] Later in the period, officials such as Arthur Clow and George Schuster at the commerce and finance departments were seen by business as closet socialists – Clow because he attempted to implement some of the recommendations of the Royal Commission on Indian Labour of 1929, Schuster because he imposed revenue tariffs which were perceived to be particularly punitive to European importing agencies. In 1935 the European group in the central legislative assembly went so for as to refuse to support the government's budget.[13]

The process of alienation reached its climax at the time of the Cripps Mission in 1942. A lobby from the Bengal Chamber of Commerce managed to secure only a single meeting with Cripps himself, who made it quite clear that the interests of British capital were very low on the government's list of priorities. They had already had, he acidly observed, 'a good innings'.[14] In 1946, it even seemed at one point that the Treasury was willing to sell the expatriate firms 'down the river' over the sterling balances question, when in answer to a question in the legislative assembly, the finance member said that the repatriation of British assets in India was a possible means of paying off some of the sterling debt to India. It is also significant that the British government failed to negotiate a 'most favoured nation' commercial treaty with the nationalist Indian government, and that British business in India after 1947 was greatly disadvantaged by the absence of an agreement on double income tax relief between the two countries.[15]

Clearly, at some point after the First World War, the British authorities in India decided that British private business interests in India were simply not important enough, politically or economically, to be worth serious defence. The British firms themselves first began to suspect that their interests were being downgraded by government in the 1920s over the question of the rupee exchange rate. Indeed, they began to fear that the government was inclining towards discrimination in favour of their Indian rivals: in February 1923 Henry Gladstone of Gillanders noted that the fact that the Bombay exporters favoured the 1s 4d rate would 'no doubt influence the Government to a much greater extent than in the past'.[16]

As we have already seen, the rupee ratio question of the 1920s is usually seen as a clear evidence of official favouritism to British business interests. It is often assumed that while Indian businessmen favoured a low-valued rupee in order to stimulate industrial growth, and currency inflation to ease their credit burden, their British rivals favoured a high-valued rupee to maximize their remittances. The fact that the Government of India decided in favour of the 1s 6d rupee in 1926-27, suggests that the government 'favoured' British interests. In reality, however, the government's reasons for favouring a high rupee had very little to do with the wishes of either business community. The government had persuasive reasons of its own for maintaining a high rupee. First, it reduced the burden of the 'home charges' (payments to London). Secondly, it was thought that social stability would be threatened by inflation induced by higher import prices. Moreover, the position of British business was not straightforward: while it was advantageous for British firms to have a high-valued rupee for remittances, a lower rupee could be preferable during the so-called busy season when their London offices were purchasing large volumes of Indian exports.

Disquiet at the government's handling of the exchange rate began as early as 1920. Following the report of the Babington Smith Committee, which recommended linking the rupee to the gold standard, the Bengal Chamber of Commerce had supported the government's preference for maintaining the exchange rate in the range of the 'gold point'. When, however, the government reversed its position in view of the high cost of maintaining the 'gold point' range during the 1920-21 slump, the chamber accused the government of 'throwing in the sponge'. It was felt that business had been deliberately excluded from the government's confidence, and that the government, instead of intervening on the exchange to support the rupee (as in the past), had left business 'more or less in the dark'.[17] It was clear from the government's action that in future there would be no question of the government tailoring its buying and selling of council bills to suit the needs of business. Thus, the import-export houses in India (along with the exchange banks which financed trade) faced the prospect of unpredictable exchange movements, never knowing whether the government was going to pursue an easy or a tight money policy.

In August 1924 the chamber again took issue with Finance Member Blackett's exchange rate policy, which was now exerting so strong a deflationary pressure that British export houses in India were having difficulty in buying enough rupee to finance their trade. Blackett was unsympathetic to a lobby from the chamber: Albert Gladstone observed that 'you asked him for bread and he gave you a stone'. The commonly held view was that Blackett wished to discourage currency speculation and force prices down – 'in other words flagrant deflation'[18] – a view confirmed in September 1924, when, in reply to renewed pressure from the Bengal Chamber, the finance department stated that it did 'not intend to come to the assistance of trade by increasing supplies of currency'.[19] Although there was a brief flicker of government sympathy for business shortly after this uncompromising statement, the business community remained gloomy. In a speech on September 19, Blackett acknowledged that the 'unusual stringency' was causing difficulties to business and declared that, in the coming busy season, the government 'had every intention of using to the fullest extent necessary their powers for issuing currency against purchases of sterling'.[20] But Albert Gladstone was unimpressed:

> How far the somewhat rapid change in attitude between the letter of the 28th and the statement of 19th . . . may be due to pressure from the India Office, or to local developments, we cannot say. . . . In the absence of an effective ratio between the rupee and gold, [the] Government is the only source whence the supply of currency can be increased [and] . . . would be compelled to come to the assistance of the market in case of need. . . . But it seems . . . that they will only do this sparingly and grudgingly, and not in such abundance as to give cause for exchange to fall.[21]

The evident unpopularity of this policy among the British clearly conflicts with the notion that British business in India always favoured a high-rupee ratio and that the Government of India tended to favour British commercial interests in this respect.

The case of the exchange rate illustrates the way in which an apparent congruence of business and official interests could mask a significant degree of dissension. The question is: how did business respond to this divergence of interests? Was any effort made to retrieve the situation; or did business accept with fatalism the loss of favoured status?

II

One obstacle to a concerted defence of the political position of business was social. This was a factor of which contemporaries were acutely conscious. Many of the seniors in the Calcutta managing agency firms had not been to public school: for example, there was a high concentration of Scotsmen who had been drawn into jute mill management through the Dundee connection. Such men had difficulty establishing rapport with the socially elite officers of the Indian Civil Service(ICS).[22] The number of businessmen who could move easily in government circles was surprisingly small; individuals like the first Lord Inchcape, who sat on a number of government committees, including the post-war Retrenchment Committee, and Sir Edward Benthall, a business representative at the Round Table Conferences and a member of the viceroy's council during the war, were the exceptions, not the rule.

In many ways, this social divide was less significant than the divisions of interest and outlook within the business community itself. To begin with, there were important geographically based conflicts of interest. For example, James Finlay & Sons, a British firm with extensive cotton interests working in close contact with Indian entrepreneurs in Bombay, had a very different political perspective from the more exclusive Calcutta-based firms.[23] Moreover, even within the regional economies, there were conflicts of interest. Typically, the Bombay Chamber of Commerce, which represented both millowners and importers in the cotton textile industry, noted that 'the 1933 duty of 75% on all non-British piece goods hurt the interests of some members of the Chamber who were importers of continental piece goods. . . .' It was, therefore, 'impossible to put forward a unanimous view'.[24]

Nor were the divisions simply between industrial and commercial interests: managing agents with strong industrial presence continued to have interests in trade, for example, in raw materials.[25] There were also conflicts of interest between the older forms of British capital in India, namely the managing agency houses, and the newer forms, the multinational firms. There were even important divisions *within* individual firms, notably the 'generation gap' which separated the more senior partners, usually based in London, from the younger partners and 'assistants' based in Calcutta. The fact that the London partners had the decisive say in any major decision on strategy or investment inevitably led to resentment in India. This had its political aspect as Edward Benthall noted: 'Many of the younger businessmen felt that their seniors were content to buy appeasement [of the nationalists] . . . at any price which would afford peace in their time of service'.[26] In the Bengal Chamber of Commerce debates and correspondence on the constitutional reforms of the 1930s, there was a clear division between the outlook of the younger and the older men. Thus, there were a variety of reasons why the British expatriate firms did not find it easy to present a united political front. Bitter disagreements on strategy regularly arose among the various firms and individuals involved in the chambers of commerce and associations such as IJMA or the Indian Mining Association.

Perhaps the most fundamental handicap to the effective promotion of business interests at the political level, however, was the ambivalent attitude of businessmen towards political activity itself. Although it might be expected that in the colonial context businessmen would naturally regard the state as an ally, in fact most of them by instinct viewed government with suspicion. Mercantile capitalists were not natural corporatists, like some European industrialists of the period. As the case of IJMA illustrates, there was a strong antipathy to the idea of government intervention in economic life, even when it might have been advantageous to business.[27] Particularly among the small to middle-sized private companies, there was great hostility to the use of official connections to extract commercial favours. In 1928 Albert Gladstone was to observe sourly of Lord Inchcape's political philosophy:

> Our attitude generally as regards managers taking up public duties . . . is that we should wish them to participate when circumstances permit, but by no means to lay themselves out for it, as has always been the case with Mackinnons [a firm in the Inchcape group]. Lord Inchcape doubtless finds special advantage accruing to his transport services from the fact of his senior men being in close touch with the Government . . . [but] if our managers serve in the legislative assemblies it is because we regard it as a duty of all leading Britishers to the state, *and not in the expectation of any personal benefits accruing* [emphasis added].[28]

In the same way, the political activity of Sir Edward Benthall also aroused suspicion. There were invariably suspicions that political activity had mercenary motivations – a tendency which clearly impeded effective representation of business interest by delegated representatives, whether in the legislative assemblies or other official bodies.

The establishment of parliamentary institutions in 1919 signalled a major change in the relationship between British commercial groups and the government. British businessmen had, until then, relied on a fairly informal kind of interaction between themselves and government officials. There is evidence that the constitutional reforms were a cause of irritation to the average British businessman as they made far greater demands on his time than he had previously been accustomed to devoting to politics. These reforms, by creating a new layer of provincial government based on corporate representation in the form of several seats for the European chambers of commerce in the Bengal provincial legislature as well as in the central legislature, necessitated the development of a far more coordinated political secretariat than the chambers had ever organized before. It is clear from the annual reports of the Bengal Chamber of Commerce that the requirement to send men to these assemblies was regarded as irksome in the extreme. The correspondence of Gillanders and Duffs is littered with the disgruntled observations of the London partners to the Calcutta partners about the onerous duties of office.[29] Furthermore there seems to have been a persistent belief that real power over economic matters continued to reside in the India Office and not in Delhi even with the coming of fiscal autonomy, with the result that it was not until the 1930s that the organization of political representation in India was taken seriously by business. One businessman commented typically that 'anyone accepting office must resign himself to losing touch with the business. . . . The Legislative Council posts . . . would become the preserve of the retired or the semi-retired'.[30] A frequently aired theme throughout the 1930s was that British businessmen were losing the political initiative to their indigenous competitors, because they (the British) lacked a 'leisured class' to 'do' their politics for them.

In the light of this evidence, it seems fair to conclude that a European representative regarded his tenure in a legislative council as 'an irksome distraction from the important business of making money'.[31] The two seats allotted to the Bengal Chamber of Commerce in the Bengal legislative council had eleven different occupants in the seven years from 1913-1920. The business attitude verged on being blase. Broomfield notes the indifference with which the British business community treated accusations of racial discrimination in respect to the number of seats they were granted in the new legislative councils in 1919: 'They were confident that their security rested on the maintenance of the existing arrangement, with the officials holding real power and according their compatriots a preferential hearing'.[32] But this complacency was superficial. It was viewed as a matter for concern that the decisions to move the capital to Delhi, to reunify Bengal and to introduce some parliamentary representation had been kept secret with the express purpose of preventing the non-official British from exercising influence.[33] *The Statesman* was outraged at this deliberate failure to consult business interests: 'In the interests of commerce it is essential that the English public should know that India is not wholly subject to the caprices of a one-eyed bureaucracy. . . . Public opinion insists on being consulted'.[34]

The establishment of parliamentary institutions, with government responsible to some degree to a representative body in India, inevitably meant that the old methods of confidential access and influence would have to give way to 'sordid political negotiations'. The most alarming prospect for British businessmen was that of power being transferred from British officials to the very Indians who were most antagonistic to the interests of British commerce. In 1917, Lionel Curtis, author of the new Indian constitution, received a beseeching letter from a British businessman: 'If you destroy the present government you must put something in its place which will ensure that our interests are safeguarded as at present, and that we are not placed at the mercy of Bengal Zamindars and lawyers'.[35]

Antagonism to political reforms dated back to the period before 1914, when the Calcutta business community had launched a press campaign in England against any further constitutional reform. Montagu and Chelmsford were accused, with unconscious irony, of riding roughshod over the British community 'to win the applause of small, self-interested group of Indians', and, more importantly, of leaving British commercial interests unprotected.

It is significant, however, that this campaign was a failure. More moderate voices quickly came to the fore. By the last quarter of 1918, the British press in India was printing articles deploring earlier alarmism, and by the 1920s certain elements within the British business community were making a serious effort to adapt to the new parliamentary framework. There is a constant theme running through the reports of and speeches at the annual meetings of the chamber about the need on the part of senior British businessmen to give far more time to political matters. Indeed, there is often a note of reproach in the remarks of the outgoing president at the reluctance of a number of prominent agency houses to sanction the participation of their senior men in the new provincial assembles. The view that 'the businessman in Calcutta should, as far as possible, withhold himself from dabbling in politics [and] should stick to his business, confin[ing] his political activities to questions which immediately affect or threaten commerce' was now losing ground.[36] The 'march of events' after 1918 was so rapid that it was impossible for the businessman to 'stand on one side'. As the Bengal Chamber of Commerce put it :

> It behoves every man to take a hand in the game, so that he may be prepared to resist aggression and defend his rights . . . . The old fashioned idea that some firms have of restraining their senior men from taking any part in public life, must be abandoned if we are not going to run the risk during the next few years of critical change. The business community in Calcutta are [sic] being attacked, and they will be attacked still more in the future, and it requires the very best men that they can produce to put up adequate defences.[37]

Successive presidents of the chamber tried, with varying degrees of success, to galvanize the member firms into political action, sometimes resorting to remarkably strong language such as this :

> It is a wicked and selfish act for any one firm to be willing enough to take advantage of all the Chamber does for it, but unwilling to allow the attention of their senior to be distracted for a moment by any thoughts outside making money for the Home partners. If I had my way such a firm would be ostracised.[38]

Yet, such thunderings could not overcome the persistent aversion of the average businessman to political activity. The efforts of a few individuals were largely nullified by the political apathy of the majority. The official mind was unimpressed by the business community. In 1913 Secretary of State Lord Crewe wrote: 'The [Calcutta] community includes . . . a number of honest and capable people: but I am not less sure that in many respects they are spoilt children, full of their social and historical importance, . . . keen to scent out any 'disloyalty' . . . [and] hidebound in class prejudice'.[39]

The business delegates to the Round Table Conference, Hubert Carr and Edward Benthall, did not enjoy very warm relations with officials of either the Government of India or the India Office. There was strong suspicion among firms like Gillanders and Bird towards the finance members of the viceroy's council, Basil Blackett and later John Grigg. On the question of tariffs, Henry Gladstone observed ruefully that the opposition of the Bengal Chamber was 'a voice in the wilderness, the government being more concerned with pleasing public opinion'.[40] While some of the political and economic changes that had been accelerated by the war in Europe – the integration of labour into the political bargaining system, the erosion of the line between the public and the private, with governments claiming greater regulatory powers over prices, labour, or even the money supply – had filtered into the consciousness of some Indian officials by the 1930s, business remained wedded to a more traditional, liberal view of relations between economy and state. It was in official rather than business circles that new ideas of planned economies and the obsolescence of markets percolated – ideas which were to be crucial in the first phase of Indian independence and to which Indian business proved to be more responsive than its British counterparts.

Relations between the British businessman and officialdom, thus, were far from close in the inter-war period; and attempts by some businessmen to compensate for this by increased political activity enjoyed only limited success. As the controversies such as that over the rupee exchange rate – and others which are not discussed here – illustrate, there were issues on which the British business houses were prepared to mobilize.[41] But they found it difficult to act in concert, and increasingly hard to gain admission to the corridors of power. Divisions within the business community undermined its capacity for collective action, while an ideological aversion to political activity undermined the efforts of the few businessmen who were willing to act. Given the increased politicization of the Indian economy in the turbulent inter-war period, this failure to lobby effectively must be counted as an important factor in the ultimate decline of the managing agency houses.

Yet, a large part of the difficulties experienced by British business reflected the ambiguous position of the Government of India in the inter-war period. Neither a wholly national nor a wholly imperial regime, the Government of India was performing a balancing act, trying to maintain the imperial interests of the British state in India, while at the same time containing Indian nationalism. This involved making concessions to indigenous business groups who, it was hoped, could be lured away from the Congress. The corollary of this was that British business interests were of low political importance to the government. Under these circumstances, there was little to be gained from lobbying officials who increasingly came to regard themselves as fulfilling a transitional role. British official policy, thus, tacitly acknowledged that Indian business counted for more than British.

III

One possible option for the managing agency houses in the face of the decline of their financial strength and of their political influence was to form some kind of political alliance with the rising class of Indian entrepreneurs. As a strategy for survival this had a great deal to recommend it. Joining forces would have solved the problem of capital shortage in the British firms and strengthened the hand of Indian-based business against the influx of multinational capital in the 1930s and 1940s. Moreover, a joint Anglo-Indian lobby would have been a more effective political force in view of the increasingly 'transitional' nature of the Government of India. Why then was such an alliance not formed?

The most obvious answer must be that racial chauvinism disinclined the British businessmen to cooperate too closely with their Indian counterparts. This was certainly a factor. There are innumerable instances of ingrained prejudice, especially among the older men who held the decision-making reins in the inter-war period. There are, however, also examples of Indians joining the boards of managing agency houses in the 1920s and working amicably with their British colleagues.[42] A second obstacle was the antipathy of British business towards the Congress, which was seen as socialist, if not communist, and therefore irreconcilably antagonistic to British business interests. Once again, however, efforts were made to overcome this problem. Some of the more politically imaginative British businessmen of the period believed that it might be possible to detach the Indian capitalist wing from the Congress by forming a cross-racial centre party, or a joint business 'peak' association. This section examines the reasons why these efforts at political rapprochement failed, and considers, in conclusion, the attitude of Indian businessmen to British overtures.[43]

Although economic links between British and Indian business remained half-hearted at best, there were, nevertheless, significant efforts to build political bridges between the two groups. Some more 'progressive' and politically active elements of the expatriate business community considered the possibility of some kind of political alliance with Indians surprisingly early on. With the introduction of a degree of provincial autonomy for Indian ministers in 1919, it was clear to a few British businessmen that they would need to revise their attitudes to Indian politics and politicians, particularly as the new responsibilities devolved on the Indian ministers included the commerce and industry portfolio.

The evolution of a coherent strategy for safeguarding the interests of British business in an increasingly 'Indianized' India went through three distinct stages. In the first, only a 'negative' type of political activity was envisaged. This took the form of discreetly funding an anti-Congress Indian front organization – the Citizens' Protection League(CPL). The second initiative came when, following the failure of the CPL, overtures were made to Tej Bahadur Sapru's Indian Liberal Party. But a parting of ways with this group became inevitable in 1927, when elements in the British business community were implicated in the government's decision to exclude any Indian representation on the Simon Commission. The third and most potentially successful initiative was the foundation of a joint British-Indian capitalist 'centre' party which, although primarily the hobby-horse of Edward Benthall, originated in the efforts of Sir Alexander Murray and Sir Homi Mody to form a joint employers' federation.

The driving force behind all the various initiatives for a political understanding with Indian business was a small group of businessmen, of whom Sir Edward Benthall of Bird and Sir Alexander Murray of Jardine Henderson were the most prominent. They had become aware at the time of the Montagu-Chelmsford reforms of the need to respond in some way to the growth of 'racial' (i.e. nationalist) feeling. In an early assessment of the working of the new provincial assemblies set up by the reforms, Murray, president of the Bengal Chamber at the time, criticized the 'highly controversial and racial character' of much of the Bengal assembly's deliberations: 'The Councils, and especially the Assembly, are beginning to realize their power, and are beginning to look about to see how they can by legislation work off some of their racial jealousies'.[44] Murray entertained, however, hopes of the emergence of a strong Indian moderate party, with whom it would be easy to 'do business', in both senses:

> There is a large number . . . probably a majority of Indians, who have the sense to recognise that India for Indians alone is quite an impossible ideal. They are as a rule, somewhat timid in coming forward and proclaiming their opinions, but the spread of civil disobedience and the threatening of anarchy are driving them to take action, and the new leaders are sound men of common sense, who are willing to join hands with us.[45]

Murray was referring to the little-known Citizens' Protection League, funded by the British business community. The CPL was the first of a number of abortive attempts to get an Indian liberal party off the ground to form a viable alternative channel of nationalist sentiment to the

Congress Party. Murray saw it as a propaganda organization aimed at propagating anti-Congress views: 'This is not a charity gentlemen, it is an insurance premium'.[46] He clearly hoped that suitable propaganda would pave the way for 'finding some common ground on which these racial questions can be settled':

> My last word gentlemen, is to form a solid defence. Hit back, and hit back hard when attacked. Join hands with those Indians of moderate principles who are willing and wishful to work with you, and be sympathetic with their legitimate aspirations as regards the government of their own country. . . . And when this fungus growth of anarchy, hatred and revolution which now dims her lustre has been swept away, India will shine out again and prove that she still is . . . the fairest jewel in the Imperial crown.[47]

Not everyone was as enthusiastic about the Citizens' Protection League as Murray. Henry Gladstone was initially unwilling to contribute to it, observing that such schemes frequently began 'with a flourish, only to be overtaken by apathy, to become just a source of income to their executive officer'. When the respectable shipping firm of Mackinnons agreed to set up an annual subscription of a thousand rupees, Gladstone grudgingly decided upon a modest donation.[48] But on the whole, his pessimistic assessment proved correct. The Citizens' Protection League petered out soon after it was started.

The idea of a political approach to 'moderate' Indian opinion was reviving during the Round Table Conferences, when the British business delegates began seeking ways to bolster the position of Sapru's Indian Liberal Party. Although approaches to the liberals had already been made in the 1920s, they had foundered over the exclusively British composition of the Simon Commission. It was hoped that now this channel could be reopened. The prospective basis for cooperation was that, in return for European support for the liberals in the new assemblies, the liberals would support British business demands for commercial and financial safeguards. But once again the idea came to nothing, as the Round Table Conference ended with a general wave of Indian disillusionment with British intentions.[49]

The failure of these attempts to fortify moderate Indian political forces convinced Edward Benthall of the need for an altogether new and openly Anglo-Indian centre party. This he envisaged as primarily a business party; but possibly receiving additional support from the

Muslim community. Benthall's idea was, however, viewed with suspicion by the European Association in Calcutta, a venerable organization which saw its role as being to rally non-official British groups in India. The association saw Benthall's scheme as a distraction from the main objective of maintaining British unity and putting together a credible 'European Group' to represent non-official opinion in the new provincial and legislative assemblies. It was felt that an Anglo-Indian party was too ambitious an undertaking.[50]

A more realistic scheme was that originally devised by Murray to unite British and Indian business in an economic peak association. The formation of the Employers' Federation of India (EFI) – an Anglo-Indian body representing primarily large industrial rather than mercantile interests – had been set up in 1919. Its origins lay in the controversy surrounding Murray's own selection as the representative of Indian jute interests at the International Labour Conference in Washington. Following government criticism of the mode of his selection, the Indian Jute Mills Association, an exclusively European body, and the Bombay Millowners Association, an Indian body, had agreed to set up a joint Employers' Federation to facilitate a broader representation of business opinion. The momentum behind the scheme had, however, been lost when two of the prime Indian movers died, and an attempt to revive it in 1925 by the Bombay firms came to nothing because the European chambers of commerce refused to affiliate to the EFI. It was not until 1929 that the idea of an Employers' Federation really began to take concrete shape. The Bombay cotton manufacturer Homi Mody envisaged that it would 'take all steps to provide and protect the commercial and industrial development of India; to ensure adequate representation of industrial employers in the new legislatures; to promote schemes for the rationalisation of industries; [and] . . . to promote or oppose legislative and other measures likely to affect members' interests'.[51]

It appears that the proceedings surrounding the introduction of the 1935 Government of India Act had the effect of convincing many British business houses that such cooperation would indeed be a good idea, and in 1933 the Associated Chambers of Commerce (the body representing all the European chambers of commerce in India), became affiliated to the federation. One reason for this change of attitude was undoubtedly Mody's success in winning Benthall's backing for the EFI in 1929. As the president of the Indian Jute Mills Association, the Bengal Chamber of Commerce and the Associated Chambers at various times during the 1930s, Benthall wielded enormous influence in the business community. He now emerged as 'a great believer in the association of Indian capital and management together in business' and pleaded: 'In the altered conditions of business in India it will in future be of the prime importance that the European who goes out to India should not only be prepared to associate with Indian Capital and Management . . . but should be able to mix socially. . . . Social problems have caused economic difficulties'.[52]

Benthall had been most impressed by the support which British business had received from the Bombay millowners during the Congress boycott of British goods, and now latched on to the EFI as a way of resurrecting his idea for a broader kind of political alliance between British and Indian business. For Benthall, the key lay in the new legislatures introduced under the new constitution, which provided for separate representation of Indian and European commerce. Although their interests might diverge on some issues, argued Benthall, 'in many respects the interests of the employers are identical and the cooperation of European and Indian employers is likely to form a community of interests which may be of the utmost value to all'. The principal area of common ground lay in the fact that, under the new constitution, labour was likely to receive substantial representation. In the future, argued Benthall, parties were likely to divide on 'economic' rather than 'racial' lines, with European and Indian business interests combining against 'socialistic' measures.[53] In other words, he envisaged that in the long run the Employers' Federation would evolve into a political force in the legislatures in its own right – a cross-racial capitalist party on the model of his earlier idea for a centre party.

The fundamental premise of Benthall's argument was that the granting of dominion status to India was now inevitable. He was well aware that this would greatly increase the power of Indian business; but his argument was that, for precisely this reason, the sooner an alliance with Indian business was cemented, the better: 'If in the course of time the industrial interests of the Associated Chambers become less predominant owing to the rapid growth of Indian industry, then there would be all the greater need for such interests to be joined with Indian interests for their common protection'.[54]

At the preparatory stages of the Round Table Conference in November 1930, Benthall had raised the idea of closer ties between British and Indian business with the Indian liberal Ramaswamy Mudaliar who also thought that British commerce should not seek separate representation in the assemblies but attempt to establish a joint capitalist party. As Benthall put it in a letter to Sir George Schuster, the Government of India finance member:

> I have often thought we should be in a very much stronger position commercially if we did not represent specifically European commerce but, enlarged our membership, including a large number of Indian firms . . . . Mind you, I do not think that European opinion will favour this yet, but in years to come this is the line of defence which will give us most strength in the future deliberation of Indian legislation over commercial matters.[55]

At the root of Benthall's strategy was the belief that it was in the interests of British business to foster powerful provincial governments at the expense of the political centre. This would have two advantages. First, it would exacerbate the internal divisions within the Congress, as regional leaders would wish to exploit their powers to the full. Secondly, in the event of a transfer of power at the centre to the Congress, there would be limits on the new government's powers. It was even suggested by the European delegation in London that the provincial and the central reforms should be implemented at the same time to allow the development of a new Anglo-Indian party at the national level to counter the influence of the Congress. With Sapru, Mudaliar and B.S. Moonje he discussed the possibility of forming a new party which would concentrate initially on the formation of policy at the federal level, but would later go on to develop a provincial programme. As he put it: 'If it is possible to form a federal party it will be real sound tactics for the European Association to join it as an earnest of our good faith [in the federal scheme]. Then the natural installation of Provincial Autonomy . . . would not be subject to the suspicion that we meant it as a final step'.[56]

In April 1931, Benthalll went so far as to discuss his idea for a new political formation with Sir George Schuster. Benthall envisaged setting up a 'national' party in Bengal, the main policies of which would be: the maintenance of the 1s 6d rupee; the reclamation of the jute tax from central government (a constant bone of contention between the colonial government and the British businessmen in Calcutta, who wanted the proceeds of the jute tax to be used to reduce the Calcutta sales taxes); the repeal of the cotton, sugar and iron duties; the abolition of the salt tax; the imposition of ceilings on the establishment of new jute mills or banks in Bengal; and the initiation of an enquiry into the problem of middle class unemployment. This curious programme – which Benthall summed up gnomically as 'a national policy of relief against Bombay' – was presumably intended to appeal to the peasants and the disaffected middle classes of Bengal, along with the supposedly anti-Bombay Calcuttan indigenous capitalists.[57]

Although Benthall's hopes for a new party of capital were dashed when the Indian moderates decided to throw in their lot with the Congress in July 1932, his approach won recognition from certain Indian businessmen – not only Mody, a known moderate, but also Ghanshyam Das Birla and Purshotamdas Thakurdas, both Congress sympathizers. In 1933, the financier Sir Shanmukham Chetty wrote warmly to Benthall congratulating him on his evidence to the Joint Select Committee on the White Paper:

> The fact that the number of English and Indians who take a reasonable view of things and are anxious to co-operate with one another in the future administration of India is growing by the day [is] a sure sign for the good for India's future. If the Joint Committee of the Houses of Parliament are guided by the arguments of a Churchill rather than those of a Benthall, then I must revise my opinion of those bodies.[58]

In the period of the war before the Quit India campaign, Birla even suggested to Benthall that they, as respective representatives of their business communities, might together resolve the whole question of safeguards, which were seen as a major obstacle to constitutional progress.[59]

Yet ultimately the advocates and supporters of political partnership were in a minority in both communities. The idea of a joint employers federation or a centre party was never going to take off so long as the majority of Indian businessmen gave their support to the Congress. Despite his personal friendship with Benthall, Birla was always lukewarm about the federation idea; and never for a moment contemplated splitting away from the Congress to form a particularist capitalist party with the British. A fatal flaw in the Benthall strategy was his failure to appreciate, behind the socialist rhetoric, the proto-corporatist nature of the Congress relationship with Indian business, which first came to the surface with the adoption of the Birla-inspired Bombay economic plan during the war. Against inducements of this kind there was precious little the British business community could offer their Indian counterparts. Benthall's political strategy of splitting the Congress and frustrating the creation of a strong central government was in direct opposition to the interests of most Indian businessmen who perceived that they had much to gain from a strong nationalist government committed to economic planning.

Notes

1 For the best exposition of the first view see B.R. Tomlinson, 'Colonial Firms in Decline in East India 1914-1947', *Modern Asian Studies*, XV (1981), pp 455-486. For the second view see particularly A.K. Bagchi, *Private Investment India, 1900-1939*, (Cambridge 1972), chapter VI; M. Kidron, *Foreign Private Investment in India* (London, 1965), pp 13-18.

2 I have mainly used in this article the papers of Ogilvy Gillanders, County Clywd Record Office, Chester (henceforth MSS OG). I have consulted the following firms' archives, though they feature in greater detail in my forthcoming Ph.D. thesis: the Thomas Duff papers, Dundee University Library (henceforth MSS TD); James Finlay & Co. papers, Cambridge University Library (henceforth MSS JS); Jardine Skinner papers, Cambridge University Library (henceforth MSS JS); the papers of Andrew Yule & Co., Morgan Grenfall Bank, London (henceforth MSS AY); The Benthall papers, Centre for South Asian Studies, Cambridge (henceforth MSS Benthall).

3 See MSS Benthall, box VI, for correspondence on British business attitudes to an Indian central bank.

4 See the Indian Legislative Assembly Debates on the Haji 'Reservation of Coastal Shipping Bill', 1928.

7 Kidron, *Foreign Private Investment* (n.1), pp. 13-14.

8 Ibid., pp. 11-12.

9 Ibid., pp. 12-26.

10 There are numerous examples of this in the Gillander and Benthall files. For example: On paper see Godfrey to Benthall 25 Nov. 1928. MSS Benthall, box I. On cement see MSS OG, file 2611, 31 July 1924. On coal see *Capital* (Ditcher's column), 24 Jan. 1919.

11 Quoted in J.H. Broomfield, *Elite Conflict in a Plural Society*. (Berkey, 1968), pp. 109.

12. *Capital*, 12 Jan. 1919.

13. C.M. Chapman Mortimer (a member of the European group in the central legislative assembly) to Benthall, 24 July 1935, MSS Benthall, box 15.

14 Thomas Gladstone to Arthur Gladstone, 21 April 1942, MSS OG, file 2632.

15 Speech by Basil Elkins to ASSOCHAM, 1950, MSS OG, File 2636.

16 H.N. Gladstone to Arthur Gladstone, 13 February 1923, MSS OG, file 2610.

17 Arthur Gladstone to H.N. Gladstone, 5 April 1922, MSS OG, file 2610.

18 H.N. Gladstone to Arthur Gladstone, 7 August 1924, MSS OG, file 2611.

19 H.N. Gladstone to Arthur Gladstone, 25 September 1924, MSS OG, file 2611.

20 Ibid.

21 H.N. Gladstone to H.E. Bateson, 22 May 1924, ibid.

22 On the question of social stratification among the Europeans in India see the excellent oral archive at the India Office Library made for the BBC's *Plain Tales from the Raj Series,* broadcast in 1974. Of particular relevance are the following: MSS Eur R 168, Sir J.C. Burns; MSS Eur R 140, E.A. Jenkins; MSS Eur R 3u. Sir Ridgby Foster; MSS Eur R & T 31 Sir Percival Griffiths; MSS Eur T 80, J.T. Banneramn.

23 R.J.F. Sullivan *One Hundred Years of the Bombay Chamber of Commerce* (Bombay, 1936). For example Sullivan notes that on the question of the steel tariff: "to a strongly disapproving motion moved by the Bengal Chamber at the meeting of the Associated Chambers in December 1923, the Bombay Chamber unsuccessfully moved an amendment expressing sympathy with Legitimate Indian aspirations." pp. 161. On the rupee-ratio question of the mid-20s the Bombay Chamber was divided, pp. 219.

24 Ibid. See chapter XVI, pp. 160-171 on the Bombay Chamber's attitude to the cotton tariff issue.

25 The historiography of the agency houses is extensive and usually errs on the side of the purely descriptive. For a comprehensive breakdown of their various areas of operation: R.K. Nigam, *Managing Agents in India* (New Delhi, 1957); B.B. Kling, '*The Origins of the Managing Agency system*' Journal of Asian Studies, XVI (1958), pp. 37-47; P. Lokanathan, *Industrial Organisation in India* (London, 1935), chpts I, VI, VIII & IX; S.K. Basu, *Industrial Finance in India* (Calcutta, 1950), chpts VI; R.S. Rungta, *The Rise of Business Corporations in India 1851-1900* (Cambbidge, 1970), chpt.XII; K.M. Kurian, *The Impact of Foreign Capital on the Indian Economy* (New Delhi, 1966), pp. 263-273; D.R. Gadgil, *The Industrial Evolution of India in Recent Times, 1860-1929,* (Madras, 1929), chpt. XV; S.K. Sen, *The Economic History of Modern India, 1848-1939* (Calcutta, 1981), chpts, III & XII; D.H. Buchanan, *The Development of Capitalist Enterprise in India* (New York, 1934), pp. 165-175.

26 MSS Benthall, Diary, box XII.

27 MSS Benthall, box X, for a discussion of the IJMA.

28 H.N. Gladstone to H. Bateson, 2 February 1921, MSS OG, file 2614.

29 MSS TD, files 86/v/7/i, (23 March 1933) & 86/v/7/iv, (10 April 1938).

30 Minute books of the European Association, Calcutta Branch, 1933, hereinafter EURASSO Minutes. These are in very poor condition and uncatalogued in the office of the British Deputy High Commission, Calcutta).

31 Bengal Chamber of Commerce, *Annual Report, 1921.* Speech by Alexander Murray, pp. viii-ix.

32 Quoted in Broomfield, *Elite Conflict* (n. 11), pp. 106-107.

33 Ibid.

34 *The Statesman*, 2 February 1912.

35 From Lional Curtis's papers relating to the application of the principles of dyarchy to the Government of India, cited in Broomfield (n.11), pp. 107.

36. Bengal Chamber of Commerce, *Annual Report 1922* presidential address, pp. xii.

37 Ibid.

38 Bengal Chamber of Commerce *Annual Report 1924*, presidential report, pp. vii.

39 Lord Hardinge, *My Indian Years, 1910-1916* (London, 1948), pp. 38-50.

40 H.N. Gladstone to A.R. Gladstone, 22 May 1926, MSS OG, file 2611.

41 I am thinking here of the efforts of the European jute mill owners in Calcutta to involve the government in shoring up the Indian Jute Mills Association cartel during its most crisis ridden period in the mid to late 1930s.

42 There were a number of prominent Indian businessmen, who, possibly because of their government connections, sat on the boards of many European firms; e.g., K.P. Goenka, Nalini Sarkar. The only Indian to have a seat on the board of European agency house was Sir Ramjeedas Jatia, followed by his son Onkarmull at Andrew Yule's; this was an unusual firm in its liberal attitude to Indians, one of the original Yule brothers had been a founder of the Indian National Congress.

43 Of the Indian businessmen who were particularly aggressive towards British capital, the most prominent was Walchand Hirchand, who waged a campaign throughout the 1920s and 1930s for the reservation of coastal shipping. In 1937 he initiated a rate war with the British shippers Killick Nixon in the hope of dividing down their share value and taking them over cheaply. Such instances of 'cornering' became more and more common as the inter-war period wore on and reached epidemic proportions in 1946 during the post-war stock exchange boom.

44 'The political Future of Europeans in India' in *The Quarterly Review*, the journal of the European Association, August 1928.

45 Presedential address, Bengal Chamber of Commerce *Annual Report*, 1921.

46 Ibid.

47 Ibid.

48 HN Gladstone to H Bateson, 16 March 1922, MSS OG, file 2609.

49 MSS Benthall, box II on the proceedings of the Round Table Conferences 1932.

50 EURASSO Minutes, 15 April 1932.

51 Correspondence with Sir Homi Mody regarding the Joint Select Committee proceedings on Constitutional Reform, MSS Benthall, box II.

52. Correspondence with Chapman Mortimer, MSS Benthall, box VI.

53 Ibid.

54 Ibid.

55 Ibid.

56 Ibid.

57 Benthall to Sir George Schuster, 18 April 1931, MSS Benthall, box VI.

58 MSS Benthall, box VI.

59 MSS Benthall, box XIV.

10

Big Business and the Peasantry

Kapil Kumar

The struggle for India's freedom from the 1920s onwards was closely interlinked with the perceptions, hopes and aspirations of different social classes or sections. These were related not only to contemporary social reality but also to what place these classes would have in an independent India. It was not merely a question of nationalism *vis-a-vis* the British but also nationalism in relation to class interests – class perception of nationalism.[1]

It was this class perception which governed and determined the attitude of Indian capitalists towards the British, the Congress, Gandhi, the working class and the peasantry. In this attitude, at times, there appeared to be variations or ambiguities due to differing interpretations and projections but in the ultimate analysis, it was the class perception that guided the capitalists' reactions to events, institutions, and personalities. For example G.D. Birla would inform the British that he only financed the Gandhi Seva Sangh, All India Spinners Association or the Harijan Sewak Sangh and had nothing to do with the political activities of the Congress. He took pains to assure the Secretary of State for India Sir Samuel Hoare that he had never taken part or financed the Civil Disobedience movement; he had only been and was a 'severe critic of the financial policy of the Government'.[2] And his closeness to Gandhi was because of his belief that 'men of his [Gandhi's] type are not only friends of India *but also of Great Britain'* (emphasis added).[3] He further stressed that the government 'will find us always ready to work for the economic interest, leaving aside sentiments and politics'.[4] Note the words *sentiments* and *politics.*

Birla was not an exception to this brand of nationalism pursued by capitalists. Lala Shri Ram was worried in 1940 about the troops being posted at the frontiers, which might give an impression to the people that the government did not have adequate force to control the interior. Hence he pleaded with Purshotamdas Thakurdas, another leading capitalist, that 'we could ask the Viceroy . . . that the Government should every now and then *pass some troops with tanks, cars, lorries, guns etc. near or through different towns, so that people may not think that there are no troops left in the country,* or that they are all concentrated either at frontier or at port towns'[5] (emphasis added). The Lala's suggestion obviously was to demoralize people from taking recourse to any kind of agitation or revolt against the government. Almost at the same time Birla wrote to Thakurdas: 'In the name of war industrialization, we should not allow Government to do anything to put up new industries under the control of British interests'.[6]

Similarly, during the Quit India movement a delegation of the Federation of Indian Chambers of Commerce and Industry (FICCI) requested the viceroy to release Gandhi immediately as he alone could check attacks on government property. Members of the delegation felt that if these attacks were not stopped, very soon there would be attacks on private property. And their plea for Gandhi's release was not motivated by nationalism but was due to the 'long-term interests of the British in the country'.[7] Referring to Churchill's assertion that he had not become 'the King's First Minister to preside over the liquidation of the British Empire', Thakurdas said at a meeting of the East India Cotton Association in 1942:

> If it was a warning given to the people of India, I think it necessary to say on behalf of the Indian commercial community that *the various demands put forward by the commercial community did not and could not aim at the liquidation of British Empire*. In fact, that is the *last thing* that any commercial man in the British commonwealth would desire [emphasis added].[8]

The plea for the growth of native industry in a colony was no doubt against the imperialist interests but the prime concern of the Indian capitalists was to safeguard their own interests not only during the national movement but in a free India as well. How were these interests to be guarded? By deriving more and more concessions from the colonial state; by mustering support from nationalist leadership and parties in the name of establishing and encouraging indigenous industry; by increasing the number of their friends and sympathizers within the Congress, and by seeking the umbrella of both nationalists' right wing and the colonial government to crush working-class movements and the left.

A number of works analysing the capitalist development and the political attitude of Indian capitalists have come out in recent years. Their attitude to the peasantry and peasant organizations has, however, received less scholarly attention than it deserves. A balanced understanding demands a proper enquiry into this aspect, and this is what this paper intends to do. It must, however, be admitted at the outset that the theme is too vast to be explored in a short paper and what is being presented here is only a tentative effort.

I

Before going further into the subject, it is necessary to note that many leading capitalists had landed interests. One may cite here the zamindaris of the Tatas and the Birlas.[9] Many big businessmen not only gave donations and contributions to Gandhi and his various *sanghas* and associations; they also indulged in moneylending on a large scale and loaned vast sums to political leaders. C. Rajagopalachari used to get *hundis* of huge amounts from the Birlas[10] but the most telling case is that of Rajendra Prasad. In July 1936, Chiranjilal Bardjatia, manager of the Bachraj Jamnalal firm at Wardha and a founder pillar of the Bharat Jain Mahamandal, on a query from Jamnalal Bajaj regarding Rajendra Prasad's estate and accounts, informed him :

> Birlaji gave Rs 45,000 to Rajendra Babu and in lieu of this on Birlaji's instructions mortgage possession of the estate was taken in your name. He will return the money in 9 years. If it is not returned in 9 years the estate will be ours. Since we have mortgage possession, the interest will keep coming from estate's income every year. If we don't get the money in future, there will be no need to file a suit because the entire estate is in our control due to mortgage possession. We have given Rs 27,000/- and have got the pronote signed in the name of our shop.[11]

In another letter Bardjatia wrote:

> After coming from Chapra I had a talk with Birlaji which was as

> follows: (A) Some land is to be settled. If the settlement takes place 15000 to 20000 rupees can come soon. (B) The sum invested by Babuji [Rajendra Prasad] in Electricity company is being settled with Bihar Bank. If the settlement comes through we get shares on debentures and our invested money won't suffer (would be safe). We have written to Rajendra Prasadji a number of times about settling the estate but he could find no time out of Congress work; hence no sale.[12]

It is to be noted here that Rajendra Prasad was to be the prime architect of the Congress-Zamindar pact in Bihar in opposition to the Kisan Sabha in 1937.[13]

If the capitalists were owning land or indulging in moneylending many political leaders bought shares and debentures in their companies. For example, Indira Gandhi after consulting her father asked Jamnalal Bajaj to buy shares on their behalf: 'I have heard there is great profit in Tatas shares these days', she added.[14] Although our evidence on politicians' corporate investments is scanty at the moment, there is no doubt that this reflects on the mental attitude of the nationalist leadership towards the capitalists and that the interests of both were interlinked to a large extent.

The capitalist reaction to the Bardoli Satyagraha must be viewed in this light. When Thakurdas and Birla acted as intermediaries between the government and Vallabhbhai Patel to bring about a settlement, Thakurdas wrote to Patel: 'I had no doubt that you will always be prepared to settle this question *without humiliation to Government* [empharis added] and at the same time without humiliation to the people whose cause you have espoused'.[15] Thakurdas believed that Patel's leadership and firm stand had 'been successful in so far as it has attracted public notice all over India'.[16] On the other hand Birla strongly argued with Gandhi in favour of a settlement saying '. . . if the only issue be the question of deposit of revenues, I for one would favour the idea of some independent individual making the necessary deposits. This will help the Government save face and will also keep Vallabhbhai free from the tangle'.[17] Birla told Gandhi that the government would 'assume an aggressive posture' and symptoms were wholly favourable for an agreement. Though well aware that the Bardoli struggle was 'likely to be of great help in our work relating to the Simon Commission', Birla urged Gandhi that 'the struggle should be kept apart from the wider issue of political struggle'.[18] The question here is why did Birla want it so? Nothing is spelt out clearly but the inference is clear i.e. the economic interest of the peasantry was to be kept apart from national issues and the peasant movement was not to be allowed to go beyond a point. After the settlement, however, Birla was glad that the Bardoli affairs were 'after all settled and the triumph has been for the people'. He regarded this 'as an eye opener to all the concerned' which would 'put new life into the dwindling forces of nationalism'.[19]

It would be useful for our analysis here to have some idea about Birla's understanding of the peasants' condition. In a letter to W.D. Croft in 1932 he wrote: 'In connection with my business, I had recently to travel in a number of villages and I found that although there was a great economic distress, the agriculturist so far has been able to maintain nearly the same standard of living'.[20] Birla had concluded this on the basis of information received by him that in most cases the zamindars were not getting more than 50 per cent rent, the money-lenders were not receiving interest on loans advanced, and the peasants were selling gold. he felt that the agriculturist was not left with 'much surplus gold' and in case prices did not rise, there would be a total 'refusal to pay rent and interest'.[21] Three months later he averred that 'stabilization of prices at a higher level can undoubtedly reduce the burden of the agriculturist, as he is a debtor and has to pay a fixed revenue for his land'.[22] This he wrote to Gandhi, but the accent in his argument to Lord Lothian was slightly different:

> A rise in price of food stuff alone will help the cultivator only partially, as the cultivator is both a producer as well as a substantial consumer. The cultivator can, therefore, largely gain only if there is a rise in the prices of those articles which are exported, and jute and cotton stand first in the list of such produce.[23]

In these arguments taken together, Birla's concerns are clear. He was worried about the exports of cotton and jute in which he himself traded, and he lamented the loss of rent and interest by zamindars and moneylenders. His reference to the gold stocks of the peasants betrayed his ignorance of the ground realities, and he seems to have overlooked the fact that the rise in prices helped the middlemen and not the cultivator, except in extremely limited cases.

During the period the Congress ministries were in power in most of the provinces, Birla played a crucial role in guiding the Congress right wing and determining its attitude towards working-class and peasant struggles. This was a period when the peasant movement was gaining strength all over the country and the Kisan Sabhas faced a lot of problems with the Congress right wing. I have discussed these issues elsewhere.[24] Here I would attempt to establish the links between the actions of the colonial government, Congress ministers, Congress right wing and Birla in relation to the Kisan Sabha's activities.

In August 1937 the Bihar Kisan Sabha organized a peasants' march to the assembly. The aim was to remind the Congress ministry of the promises made to the peasantry during the election campaigns. The viceroy believed that this was a movement which 'needed careful watching'[25] whereas the governor of Bihar considered it a 'harmless demonstration' – the peasants 'were well-behaved and good humoured . . . rather like a body of tourists on a sight seeing tour'. The viceroy, fearing that in future 'such demonstrations might degenerate into assemblies which might be rather a menace to the public peace',[26] advised the Congress premier of the province to take stern action.

Birla at this time was in England and was being regularly informed about events in India. Feeling that 'indiscipline was getting rampant' he wrote to Mahadev Desai:

> I very much disliked the peasants in Bihar marching to the Assembly house and occupying all the seats of the Assembly and refusing to vacate them in spite of the request of the Prime Minister. And then the Prime Minister addressed them and told them all sorts of sweet things without telling them that they were wrong in occupying the Assembly seats and refusing to vacate them.[27]

Birla feared that 'in course of time indiscipline will grow more and more unless strict measures are taken'. He hoped that the 'Congress authorities are fully alive to the situation and they will take all necessary measures'. The rank and file, according to him, was 'confusing freedom with indiscipline'.[28] He also discussed at great length with the viceroy the growing peasant movement in Bihar and the United Provinces (U.P., now Uttar Pradesh). The viceroy asked him to 'convey it to proper quarters that it would be very bad for the ministers, if the Governor had to use his own responsibility for maintenance of law and order'.[29] Birla assured the viceroy that 'Pant [Govind Ballabh, the Prime Minister of U.P.] was fully conscious of his responsibility'. He told him that 'all big leaders of the Gandhi Sewa Sangh were strenuously working to fight out violence'. The viceroy 'was very happy to hear this'. Nevertheless, Birla made it clear to Mahadev Desai that his own fear was that the Congress ministries in these two provinces had not fully realized the 'seriousness of the growing danger to non-violence'.[30]

Birla was of the view that 'perhaps for the next few months the most important task of the ministers would be to suppress all incitement to violence'. But this was to be done 'partly through prosecution and partly through redressing the grievances of the people'. The root cause of the troubles, according to him, was the 'exaggerated expectations'.[31] Birla believed that the discontent would not subside 'unless the Congress tells the peasants clearly that their position could be improved ultimately through their own hard work alone and not by any stroke of wand'.[32] In his opinion, abolishing the zamindari or nationalization of accumulated wealth would 'hardly add much to the existing income of the masses'.[33] 'Bread is not going to come out of confiscation of Zamindaries', he wrote. 'Our ministers', he further added, 'will have to decide from this very moment as to what they are going to do for ameliorating the condition of the people. If they think that the amelioration depends on the confiscation of the properties, then I think they are deceiving themselves'.[34] And then he presented a frightening scenario:

> The question of discontent just now is linked up with economics and unless steps are taken to make the peasants realise what is possible and what is not, I fear the ferment will grow to such an extent that it will become impossible after a certain stage for the ministers to maintain discipline. And as Bapu has said so many times, inviting the help of the Military will be the death knell of the provincial government.[35]

Thus, what Birla was basically demanding here was a total check on peasants' actions; strict measures by ministers and an end to the talk of confiscation of zamindaris or private property. Here was a case of direct support to zamindars by a private capitalist.

Barely six days after Birla had written the above letter to Mahadev Desai, the Congress leadership put a ban on the Bihar Kisan Sabha on 10 December 1937. This was later ratified by the Congress Working Committee. The speeches of kisan leader were reported by the Central Intelligence Department and their mail intercepted. It was during this period that the Congress under the guidance of Rajendra Prasad, Patel and Maulana Abul Kalam Azad entered into an agreement with the landlords in Bihar, and kisan workers were prosecuted.[36] When all this was going on Mahadev Desai informed Birla that the 'situation has decidedly improved in Bihar'.[37] Similarly, Pant sent a 'very reassuring' letter to Birla saying that 'there was nothing to worry about agrarian trouble and he was keeping his fingers on the pulse'. The viceroy hearing this reassuring news from Birla was 'quite pleased'.[38] But both Birla and Desai were quite upset over Rafi Ahmed Kidwai's declaration at a kisan meeting at Pratapgarh on 20 December that 'the Congress Government would either be forced to adopt coercive measures or get out of office if the peasants did not abide by the laws in force today'.[39] Kidwai was a Congress minister in U.P. but instead of changing the tenancy laws enacted by an alien government, he was asking the peasants to follow them. But the British, Birla and Desai felt that 'a responsible minister cannot run away from his responsibility by offering to resign'.[40] Gandhi agreed with Birla that 'anarchical tendencies are striking roots in the Congress' and assured him that 'I have been exerting my utmost to check this development'.[41] He was not referring to the peasants or workers alone. During this period any kind of mass action, including innocent public welcome of released political prisoners, was condemned by Gandhi, the right wing and Birla.[42]

II

An important development from 1936 onwards was the coming closer of the All-India Trade Union Congress (AITUS) and the All-India Kisan Sabha (AIKS). The latter appealed to peasants to celebrate May Day and cooperate with city workers in their struggles against capitalists. As a prominent kisan leader Sahajanand Saraswati pointed out:

> Till recently it [May Day] had been the international day of only factory workers throughout the world and agrarian workers and peasantry had very little, if at all, realised its significance. Gradually came the turn of the European and American peasants and they began to observe it and thus showed their solidarity with factory comrades. Only last year, the Kisans throughout our country observed the Kisan day on 1 May and thus expressed their solidarity with the workers all over the world.[43]

All affiliates of the AIKS celebrated May Day and by 1938 the slogan *'Kisan mazdur raj kayam ho'* (Let the worker-peasant regime emerge) had gained momentum. The AIKS was attempting to make the peasants aware of their responsibility towards other exploited classes.[44] It also organized the sweepers in Gaya who went on strike for higher wages.

In certain pockets united actions were taken. For example, in December 1937 the Textile Workers Union of Nagpur organized a march to the assembly in association with kisans, demanding that the Congress ministry should outline its labour policy and give immediate relief from wage cuts to textile workers.[45]

When the Congress imposed a ban on the Bihar Kisan Sabha in December 1937, an AITUC session held in January 1938 condemned it in strong language and assured the AIKS of its full support in the fight against landlordism and vested interests. The session also passed resolutions favouring abolition of zamindars and all other intermediaries.[46] The Bihar Kisan Sabha expressed its gratitude to the AITUC for supporting the peasants' cause.[47] In the speeches of virtually all AIKS leaders as well as the peasant leaders operating at local levels, feudalism and capitalism were described as enemies of the poor. For example Baba Ramchandra, in his writings and mobilization work among the peasants in UP, described the zamindars and capitalists as synonyms of peasant exploitation.[48] In November 1938, the Kanpur factory workers expressed solidarity with peasants and denounced the pro-landlord attitude of the Congress ministry in relation to the Tenancy Bill.[49] Sahajanand believed that the entire socio-economic problem revolved around the peasant. This was because a significant proportion of the urban proletariat consisted of those who migrated in search of some relief from suffering confronted in rural areas, and kept alternating between fields and mills.[50] Interestingly, this rural-urban link was described by Birla to Churchill: 'No townsman is a pure townsman in India. Everyone maintains touch with the villages. Twenty-five thousand men that I employ in my mills went to their villages more than once a year. Therefore, on the roll there were more than fifty thousand'.[51]

Gandhi was conscious of the growing unrest among the peasants as he admitted in a letter to Guy Wint in 1939:

> The agrarian unrest is a much greater danger, but if the Congress retains non-violence it is bound to be disciplined. We who believe in non-violence are trying to cope with it, but we may fail. And yet we are not going the way of China. In China peasants can be soldiers at will but not here in India. In India we cannot make soldiers so easily. But I agree that you have spotted the real danger. However, it will cease if the Congress can produce real type of workers for the villages.[52]

The Mahatma 'did not dread' the labour unrest much 'for factory labourers were not more than 20 lakhs' who lived 'only in artificial cities'. Discarding the 'psychological importance' of labour unrest and confident that 'those bent on mischief cannot spread red ruin in the villages' Gandhi advised Wint to 'hook his mind to the villages and not the towns'.[53]

A number of Gandhi Sewa Sangh volunteers were moved into Bihar villages to counter the Kisan Sabha propaganda. Significantly enough, what these volunteers preached was not class adjustment or class collaboration but class submission.[54] And we must take note of the fact that the Sangh was financed by G.D. Birla. The coming together of the working class and the peasants was alarming for the Congress right wing and capitalists who worked hand in hand. For example Ramkrishna Dalmia, an emerging industrialist, had financed the Congress in Bihar during the elections of 1937.[55] The same year Rajendra Prasad advocated the candidature of Dalmia for a by-election to the central assembly as an independent candidate, supported by the Congress. He wrote to Patel:

> As I told you Dalmia would like to have the seat but *on account of his many business connections he does not* like to take the Congress ticket. As you know he has been always helpful and there is a feeling in some of our workers that it is worth-while leaving this seat uncontested. Personally I have confidence that he will support the Congress in most matters [emphasis added].[56]

Prasad also brought to Patel's notice that 'there may be some among Congressmen particularly those connected with Kisan Sabha who may disapprove of this action'.[57] In the earlier election Dalmia had lost to the Congress candidate supported by the Kisan Sabha. Patel turned down Prasad's proposal perhaps because of his fears that support to Dalmia would further aggravate the political challenge to the right wing leadership and its alliance with the capitalists, but this does not detract from the significance of Prasad's suggestion.

The growing unity of the peasants and the working class served them well as several agitations succeeded only because of their mutual support. In this regard the labour strike in a sugar mill at Bihta in Bihar is noteworthy. Promoted by Dalmia in 1932 the mill had been established in response to the protection granted to the sugar industry[58] which encouraged virtually all leading capitalists to invest in this industry. To establish his mill Dalmia sought the help of Rajendra Prasad and Swami Sahajanand Saraswati who, though working for the peasants, was during this phase a staunch Gandhian. The Swami would later regret his association with Dalmia but conceded:

> It was only through this mill that I learnt how shrewdly the rich and selfish capitalists exploit the people. How big leaders and the Mahatma entrapped in their grip, help them in this and are unable to realise it. On the contrary they believe that they are using the capitalists for people's welfare. But in reality it is the capitalist who used them to exploit the poor.[59]

Dalmia faced problems with zamindars of Bihta in buying land for the mill. The vice-chairman of the Danapur local board approached Sahajanand and sought to assure him: 'He should not be worried about donations for his Ashram. Once he helps the *millwalas* in getting land, money would be no problem'.[60] Sahajanand took strong exception to this offer saying:'I piss on such money as it will enslave me to the *millwalas*'.[61] Yet he did help Dalmia in acquiring land because he thought, to quote his own words, 'that since a tax of Rs 6 and 5 annas has been imposed on imported sugar, sugar mills will open in this region. So instead of a foreigner opening it this Dalmia would be much better because he wears a Gandhi cap and calls himself a Congressman. People also consider him so.'[62]

Soon the industrialist's family started visiting the Swami's ashram. Dalmia proposed that his sister's son be allowed to stay in the ashram. The young man's mother and grandmother also supported this request. They wanted to construct a house for their ward in the ashram but Sahajanand refused to go along, saying that he could not break the rules and no servants could be provided in the ashram. The family continued its visits and on various pretexts, like *puja*, birthday, etc., would leave small amounts of money during these visits for sweets to be distributed among the ashramites. Sahajanand put a stop to this also, realizing that Dalmia's generous gestures might tie his hands if he had to stand up against the mill management to espouse the peasant cause in future. To quote his own picturesque language: 'It is said when a thief goes to commit burglary he takes some jaggery for the dogs. When they bark, it is fed to them and this stops their barking. The same is done by capitalists. Knowing that we are going to bark, they offer us jaggery in advance.' [63]

Significantly, Rajendra Prasad was included as a director of the mill and Madan Mohan Malviya was to come for its inauguration. On the occasion of the opening of the mill, a number of promises were made. The workers were promised model houses for themselves and schools for their children; and the peasants were assured high prices for cane. It was stated that an existing rival company in the vicinity, the Beg Sutherland Mills owned by Englishmen, incurred a great deal of avoidable expenditure because of which it paid lower wages to the worker and less price to the grower for his cane. The Dalmia factory would husband its resources carefully; hence the peasants would get high prices for cane, and workers higher wages. And yet the sugar produced here would be cheaper than in the English company.[64] It is quite clear that the management wished to take full advantage of the rising swadeshi sentiments.

But what actually happened in relation to peasants and workers was worse than what was happening in the English mill. The price offered by the Dalmias for cane was three annas per maund as against six annas by the Sutherland Mills. When this was brought to the promoter's notice by Sahajanand, Dalmia's reply was that 'he has to see the principle of demand and supply'. Now the tug of war started. Sahajanand warned the peasants not to give up jaggery-making or else they would become the slaves of the mill. The mill management wanted the peasants to stop producing jaggery to ensure supply of raw material to the mill. Dalmia even accused Sahajanand of opposing the mill out of dudgeon because the latter had asked Dalmia for two thousand rupees, which had been refused. But this did not carry any weight with the peasants and the mill was ultimately forced to abide by its promise and pay seven to eight annas per maund – about one anna more than paid by other mills.[65] Sahajanand informed Nehru of Dalmia's promises and what he was doing now. He believed that Dalmia had trapped Rajendra Prasad into accepting the directorship of the mill. At this time Prasad was imprisoned and Sahajanand believed that Prasad 'realises everything . . . and is ready to resign from the directorship of the Mills . . .; only his confinement is a great obstacle'.[66] But Sahajanand was not aware of the actual relationship between Prasad and Dalmia to which we have referred earlier.

The cane growers were not fully satisfied with the value they received for their produce and the workers' discontent in the meantime was also mounting. The result was that the Dalmia mill witnessed as many as three strikes within a brief period of two years between 1936 and 1938. The first strike was in 1936, the issue being sugarcane prices. For months the peasants stopped the supply of sugercane to the factory. The mill procured it from different places at 12 to 14 annas per maund but was not prepared to offer the same price to local cultivators. The peasants picketed the bullock-carts that carried cane to the mill and many were arrested. Though the mill suffered heavy losses the strike failed.[67] Yet the success lay elsewhere. The peasants had learnt their first lesson in strike against a capitalist and were better prepared next time.

In January 1937 the millworkers went on strike for higher wages. In support of workers the peasants stopped supplying sugercane to the mill. This forced the mill to accept the workers' demands within forty-eight hours of the commencement of the strike. Towards the end of 1938, the workers again went on strike on the ground of non-implementation of the agreement. But only 250 workers could hold on due to threats and repression by the management. Again the peasants came to their rescue and refused to supply cane. About 250 of them were jailed within a brief span of two days. This time the management approached Sahajanand with a lump sum donation of ten thousand rupees and two hundred per month for the ashram. The emissary who came with this offer had to flee the ashram for his life and ultimately the mill had to concede the demands.[68]

The peasant-worker joint action perturbed the capitalists and alarmed the sugar syndicate. Besides Dalmia, Birla, Shri Ram and Jamnalal Bajaj owned sugar factories in UP and Bihar.[69] The Congress depended on the sugar lobby for funds. As Pant wrote to Bajaj: 'There are many sugar factories in Gorakhpur. In case you can take pains to go there, I firmly believe, you will be able to get a good amount of money. . . . It will create inconvenience to you but . . . it is for you to save us from financial difficulties.'[70] This perhaps explains why even Jawaharlal Nehru chose to silence Shibhanlal Saxena in Gorakhpur. Saxena was mobilizing the sugarcane growers and other peasants in the 1930s. The sugar lobby complained against him to the viceroy and Gandhi. Jawaharlal wrote to the viceroy: 'I must confess he [Saxena] is crude of speech and occasionally his tongue runs away with him when he discusses the plight of the peasantry. *We have warned him privately several times* and our advice has had effect on him'.[71] (emphasis added).

These instances demonstrate that by the late 1930s the kisan sabhas and the pro-peasant leadership were not only advocating the peasants' cause but also opposing both the zamindars and capitalists. This stance is reflected not only in their position on economic demands but the way these demands were related to the political struggle against the

British. All this added to the coming closer of the right wing Congress-men and the capitalists. The capitalists left no stone unturned to guide and strengthen the right wing in checking not only the working class but the awakening among the peasants also. Birla's condemnation of peasant marches and stress on discipline is one amongst the many cases that can be cited in this context. The friendly relationship of the capitalists with the British on the one hand and their growing influence in the Congress on the other remained a constant factor in the freedom struggle. A unique feature of the Indian transition towards capitalism has been not the conflict between capitalism and feudalism, but their mutual cooperation and accommodation. Devising methods to crush the peasant struggle was a part of this mutual understanding duly supported by the Congress right wing.

Notes

1. See Kapil Kumar (ed) *Congress and Classes*, (New Delhi, 1988), Introduction.

2. G.D. Birla to Samuel Hoare, 14 March 1932, G.D. Birla: *Bapu A Unique Association*, (Bombay, 1977) v.1, p.181.

3. Ibid. In the same letter Birla also wrote that "Gandhiji is the greatest force on the side of peace and order. He alone is responsible for keeping the left wing in India under check".

4. Ibid.

5. Shri Ram to Purshotamdas, 6 June 1940, Purshotamdas Thakurdas Papers, hereinafter PT Papers, file no. 239/I Nehru; Memorial Museum and Library, New Delhi.

6. G.D. Birla to Purshotamdas, 25 June 1940, ibid.

7. Ibid., file no. 239/V.

8. Ibid.

9. Birla had purchased a big estate in Chhotanagpur for Rs.8 Lakhs. G.D. Birla to Mirabehn, 7 July 1939, Birla, *Bapu* (n.2), vol. 3, p. 343.

10. There are references to this in C. Rajagopalachari Papers available in Nehru Memorial Museum and Library, New Delhi.

11. Jamnalal Bajaj, *Patravyavahar*, (New Delhi 1969), vol. VII, pp.131-32.

12. Ibid., p.132.

13. See Kapil Kumar, "Congress Peasant Relationship in the late 1930's" in D.N. Panigrahi (ed.), *Aspects of Economy, Society and Politics in Modern India* (New Delhi 1984), p. 242.

14. Indira Gandhi to Jamnalal Bajaj, 30 October 1941, Jamnalal Bajaj, *Patravyavahar*, (New Delhi 1958), vol. I, p.13.

15. Thakurdas to Patel, 14 June 1928, PT Papers, file no. 74/II.

16. Ibid.

17. Birla to Gandhi, 25 July 1928, Birla, *Bapu*(n.2), vol. 1, p. 103.

18. Ibid.

19. Birla to Thakurdas, 7 August 1928, PT Papers, file no. 74/I.

20. Birla to Croft, 30 April 1932, Birla, Bapu (n.2), v. 1, pp. 181-2.

21. Ibid.

22. Birla to Gandhi, 22 July 1932, ibid., p.201.

23. Birla to Lothian, 4 August 1932, ibid., p.213.

24. See Kumar (ed.), *Congress and Classes* (n.1), pp.238-251.

25. Linlithgow to Hallet, 25 August 1937, Linlithgow Papers (LP), s.no. 113, Nehru Memorial Museum and Library, New Delhi.

26. Hallet to Linlithgow, 3 September 1937, ibid.

27. Birla to Desai, 4 September 1937, Birla *Bapu* (n.2), vol. 3, pp. 76-7.

28. Ibid.

29. Birla to Desai, 4 December 1937, ibid., pp. 105-6.

30. Ibid.

31. For details of these expectations, see Kumar (ed.), *Congress and Classes* (n.1), pp.235-36.

32. Birla to Desai, 4 December 1937, Birla, *Bapu* (n.2), vol. 3, p. 106.

33. Ibid.

34. Ibid.

35. Ibid.

36. See Kumar (ed), *Congress and Classes* (n.1), pp. 242-43.

37. Desai to Birla, 22 December 1937 Birla, *Bapu* (n.2), vol. 3, p.127.

38. Birla to Desai, 21 December 1937, ibid., p.124.

39. *Modern Review,* LXII (1938), p. 119.

40. Birla, *Bapu*(n.2), v.3, pp.132, 141.

41. Gandhi to Birla, 26 August 1938, ibid., p.187.

42. See Kumar (ed.), *Congress and Classes* (n.2), p.249.

43. *All India Kisan Bulletin* (AIKB), 16 April 1937.

44. Ibid., 22 April 1938

45. Ibid., 10 December 1937

46. Ibid., 14 January 1938

47. Ibid., 4 February 1938.

48. During the late 1930s, Baba Ram Chandra was very critical of capitalist domination. Baba Ramchandra Papers, subject files no. 3, Nehru Memorial Museum and Library, New Delhi. For his work amongst peasants, see. Kapil Kumar, *Peasants in Revolt,* (New Delhi 1984).

49. *AIKB,* 11 November 1938.

50. *Congress Socialist,* 26 December 1936.

51. Birla to Churchill, August 1935, Birla, *Bapu* (n.2), vol. 2, p. 141.

52. Ibid., vol.3 p. 224.

53. Ibid.

54. See Kapil Kumar, "Ideology, Congress and Peasants In 1930s: Class Adjustment or Submission?" *Social Scientist,* XIV-89 (August-September 1986), pp. 40-55.

55. There are many letters exchanged between Dalmia, Bajaj and Rajendra Prasad in this regard.

56. Rajendra Prasad to Patel. 5 May 1937, Rajendra Prasad Papers, Nehru Memorial Museum and Library, New Delhi.

57. Ibid.

58. See Sanjay Baru, "State and Industrialization : The Political Economy of Sugar Policy, 1932-1947", in Panigrahi (ed.), *Economy and Society* (n.13), p.105.

59. Sahajanand Saraswati, *Mera Jiwan Sangarsh* (Patna 1952), p. 455.

60. Ibid.

61. Ibid.

62. Ibid.

63. Ibid., p. 456.

64. Ibid.

65. Ibid.

66. Shajanand to J. Nehru, 2 November 1933, J. Nehru Papers, vol. 91, Nehru Memorial Museum and Library, New Delhi.

67. Sahajanand Saraswati, *Mera Jiwan* (n.59), p.459.

68. Ibid. Such struggles continued in future also against retrenchment of workers.

69. Sanjay Baru, "State and Industrialization" (n.58), p.108.

70. Bajaj, *Patravyavhar* (n.14), p.42.

71. J. Nehru to Viceroy, 6 October 1939, J. Nehru Papers, vol. 42.

11

Businessmen and the Partition of India*

Claude Markovits

The vast and still growing literature on the partition of India does not place much emphasis on its economic aspects, and the role of businessmen remains one of the most obscure points in the story. It is not claimed here that the attitudes of the Indian capitalists were a central factor in the most dramatic event in the modern history of the subcontinent. The underlying causes of partition are to be sought in long-term trends and policies which, after a certain point in time, were beyond the control of any of the actors involved. Therefore, even if Indian big business had, on grounds of economic rationality, unanimously opposed the partition, it would not have been able to prevent it. The interesting point, however, is precisely that, on the whole, Indian big business did not oppose the partition, but, at least from 1942 onwards, seems to have been increasingly favourable to it. This is true not only of Muslim businessmen, but also of their non-Muslim colleagues. On the first point, an apparent rationale is furnished by W.C. Smith's thesis of the contrast between a relatively advanced Hindu bourgeoisie and a retarded Muslim capitalist class. But the second point is more puzzling.

The great weakness of all existing rationalizations including Smith's is that they do not sufficiently disaggregate the data, that they tend to treat both the Muslim and non-Muslim capitalists as more or less homogeneous entities, while in fact there were major internal differences within these two categories. The emphasis of this paper will, therefore, be on presenting a picture as disaggregated as is possible on the basis of the limited empirical evidence available to the author. But, before embarking upon that kind of study, it is necessary to make a few preliminary remarks of a general nature on the kind of framework most appropriate for analysing the relationship between Indian business and communal politics. This has been done in the first section of this paper. The second section will deal with developments in communal politics in the period prior to 1942, while the third section will consider the attitudes of businessmen in the years immediately preceding partition. The final section sums up the conclusions derived from this analysis.

I

While communalism in India has been generally defined as a middle-class movement and a middle-class ideology, little attention has been paid to the role played in its emergence by merchants and capitalists. Actually there seems to be a sort of consensus that communalism as a distinct and somewhat articulate ideology evolved in the late nineteenth century among non-capitalist middle-class elements, such as government servants, professionals and sections of intelligentsia and spread during the twentieth century both to the lower classes and to the emerging capitalist bourgeoisie. Forms of community consciousness were, however, undoubtedly present among various strata even before the advent of colonialism[1] and they are germane to the later elaboration of a communalist ideology. Various movements of religious reform throughout the nineteenth century were manifestations of that community consciousness but could not be described as full-fledged statements of a communalist view of society.

What is of relevance to our topic is that merchant communities often seem to have been closely connected to some of these movements. Unfortunately, little is known of the attitude of Muslim business people to the various movements of 'Islamicization' which, throughout the nineteenth century, sought to 'purify' Indian Islam and to bring about some homogenization of beliefs and practices among a very diverse and heterogeneous religious community.[2] It is interesting to note, however, that the first specifically 'Muslim' association in India, the Anjuman-i-Islam, was created in the 1870s in the major commercial city of Bombay, and that two of the richest and most prominent local Muslim businessmen were closely associated with its birth.[3] More is known about the contribution of some Hindu merchant communities to the growth of various shades of Hindu 'revivalist' movements, particularly in northern India. Recent studies[4] have pointed to the important role played by trading communities in the Cow Protection Agitation of the 1890s in the United Provinces and Bihar. Hindu commercial men appear to have been actively involved in financing the various cow protection societies and to have had often a prominent part in their organization. Pre-existing links between some north Indian merchants and the Arya Samaj, (the Hindu revivalist sect) which played an important role in the genesis of the movement, facilitated their involvement. Similarly the movement for the propagation of Hindi, with its strong anti-Muslim overtones, got support from Hindu businessmen in many localities of northern India.[5]

The interpretation of these facts, however, remains a problem. 'Religious' community consciousness was only one of the variegated forms of community consciousness which developed in India during that period. Other groupings, which tended to emphasize divisions within the religious communities rather than their unity, also became important foci of loyalty for many Indians, Hindu and Muslim alike. One has only to think of the tremendous surge in caste-based organizations in India under the stimulus of the population censuses. Merchants were not the last ones to organize on that basis. Therefore, 'Hindu' or 'Muslim' was only one of the categories which a trader or a businessman could use to define his social identity. The advantages to be derived from its use would be primarily of a symbolic nature, such as a rise in the self-esteem of men who did not occupy a very exalted position in the accepted social hierarchy. But it did not obliterate other forms of consciousness.

To take one example, in undivided India, a businessman who was a Muslim by religion had many categories to choose from in order to define his social identity: he could identify himself primarily as a member of a small community, sect or quasi-caste (i.e. in Gujarat as a Bohra, a Khoja, or a Memon, to mention three groups to which most of the prominent Muslim businessmen of western India belonged, with further subdivisions into Daudi and Sulaimani Bohra, Ismaili and Itna'ashari Khoja, Kutchi and Halai Memon); or he could emphasize the regional connection and see himself as a Gujarati, a Bengali or a Tamilian; he could also stress a feeling of corporate identity (merchant vs non-merchant) which was highly developed in the towns and cities of Gujarat and northern India.[6] With the rise of Indian nationalism, there was also a growing tendency among Indian businessmen to stress the indigenous-expatriate divide, especially since they were subjected to various disabilities in comparison with European and particularly British businessmen.[7] Lastly, of course, a Muslim businessman could identify himself primarily as a Muslim, either because of a deep religious faith (not a very common occurrence though, according to a keen observer of Indian Muslim society[8]) or of desire to differentiate himself from his Indian non-Muslim colleagues. Needless to say, these identities were mutually overlapping, and whether the emphasis was put on one or another did not depend only on individual strategic choices. There is no reason, however, to assume *a priori* that, because a businessman was Muslim by religion, he saw himself first and foremost as a 'Muslim businessman'.

Therefore, as far as political alignments are concerned, one could not automatically infer that Muslim businessmen would support Muslim communal movements and organizations after the 1909 reforms established separate electorates and the Muslim League started putting forward its claim to represent a specific 'Muslim' interest in politics. Nor could it be inferred that non-Muslim, and particularly Hindu businessmen, would necessarily adopt a 'nationalist' outlook.

II

To this day, the most influential statement regarding the relationship between the economic role of Muslims in India and the growth of Muslim communal politics remains the one put forward in 1943 by W.C. Smith in his *Modern Islam in India.* A radical critique of capitalism, Smith saw in the specific kind of capitalism which evolved in India under colonial conditions a fertile ground for the development of communalism.[9] Specifically concerned with Muslim communalism, he defined it in its most recent phase as 'the nationalist ideology adopted by the emergent and precarious Muslim middle class in its struggle against domination within India by the much more developed Hindu middle class'.[10] Although he was ideologically opposed to communalism, Smith tended to rationalize Muslim communalism as the response of an emergent but still weak Muslim bourgeoisie to the attempt by an already entrenched Hindu bourgeoisie to thwart its growth. He did not, however, muster any empirical evidence to prove his point regarding the 'retardation' of the Muslim capitalist class. His views have recently been challenged by Bipan Chandra who stresses that, at least prior to the 1940s,'Hindu bourgeoisie' and 'Muslim bourgeoisie' were not meaningful categories.[11] His refutation of Smith's thesis also is not, however, based on a detailed empirical study of the role of Muslim and non-Muslim capitalists in the Indian economy.

In a recently published study I have presented some data on the position of Muslim businessmen in the Indian economy, drawn mainly from the 1921 census and various primary and secondary sources.[12] Treating, for convenience sake, 'Muslims' as one category, I have concluded that, during the first half of the twentieth century, Muslim businessmen still occupied fairly important positions in the commercial life of India in spite of wide regional variations. I have stressed the contrast between the situation in the regions which at a later stage formed Pakistan, in particular Bengal and the Punjab, where Muslims, although a majority in the population, did not occupy dominant positions in trade and finance, and in other regions where a numerically small Muslim population often played an important role in the commercial life. On an all-India basis their main area of weakness, albeit a crucial one no doubt, was finance. It appears also that Muslim representation in the ranks of large-scale industrialists, although not insignificant in the 1920s, tended to decrease in the 1930s.[13]

It seems that the 1930s represented a watershed in the perception that many Muslim businessmen had of their role in the economic life of India. Before that date, they do not seem to have nursed a particular sense of grievance, as shown by the fact that they did not create separate commercial associations but participated, often actively, with their Hindu, Jain and Parsi colleagues, in major Indian commercial bodies.[14] Nor were partnerships between Muslim and non-Muslim businessmen a totally unknown feature in principal commercial and industrial cities of India. It is true that there are not many instances of that kind of partnership, at least outside Bombay. But it should be remembered that in India business partnerships were generally family or kinship-based, which in any case restricted possibilities of cross-communal associations. Marwaris for instance chose only Marwaris as business partners, but did not exclude Muslims more than Parsis or members of other Hindu communities. This kind of exclusiveness operated also within the Muslim community: thus in western India Khojas rarely formed business partnerships with Memons. A common religion was no strong bond in the business world of India, which was fragmented along the lines of caste and kin.

From the 1930s onwards, however,attempts were made by some Muslim businessmen to forge business linkages with coreligionists belonging to other groups and regions. These attempts were not very successful before the 1940s when, at the prompting of Jinnah and the Muslim League, there developed a movement specifically aimed at creating the so-called 'Muslim enterprises'.[15] Although it achieved some results, this movement does not seem to have been received with great enthusiasm by at least a section of the Muslim business elite.

More successful and of more far-reaching importance was the movement which developed from 1932 onwards to create separate Muslim associations. Starting with the foundation in 1932 of the Muslim Chamber of Commerce in Calcutta, it gathered momentum throughout the 1930s and 1940s and at the time of partition the number of such bodies had grown enormously.[16] The reasons for this mushrooming of Muslim commercial associations are, however, far from clear. The Muslim Chamber of Commerce in Calcutta was created to take advantage of the political reforms in Bengal: under the new regime one seat in the provincial legislature was reserved for a Muslim commercial association. Since none existed, a few prominent Muslim businessmen of Calcutta, such as M.A.H. Ispahani and Adamji Haji Dawood,[17] moved in to fill the vacuum. But it is not easy to discover what their real motivations were. They did not raise, as could have been expected, the bogie of 'Marwari domination' of business in Calcutta; on the contrary, they tended to overestimate the strength of Muslim business interest there.[18] And it is interesting to note that, prior to 1942, the Muslim Chamber of Commerce did not raise any specific 'Muslim' issues; actually its resolutions largely paralleled those passed during the same period by the Indian Chamber of Commerce.[19] It also seems that some members of the new Muslim Chamber continued with their membership of the Indian Chamber.

The creation of the Muslim Chamber, thus need not be seen as a clear sign of an increasing polarization in the Calcutta business world along 'communal' lines. The more plausible interpretation is in terms of factional conflict: big Muslim businessmen such as Ispahani and Adamji, like some of their Hindu colleagues, increasingly resented the heavy-handed leadership exercised by the Birla brothers, G.D. Birla in particular, over the Indian Chamber and their autocratic methods. By creating a separate chamber, they could escape their domination; 'Muslim' came in handy as a label, since it could also bring in political advantages, but the term hardly had any 'communal' meaning. Once that kind of movement was launched, however, it acquired a dynamics of its own, which was beyond the control of its promoters, and the creation of separate Muslim commercial bodies did contribute to dividing the business world along communal lines. The process culminated with the creation in 1945 of a Federation of Muslim Chambers of Commerce and Industry which was conceived by Jinnah as a counterpart of the Federation of Indian Chambers of Commerce and Industry (FICCI) which had increasingly tended to align itself with the Indian National Congress.[20]

Post-partition accounts of that period, coming in particular from Pakistan, have tended to stress the existence of a growing gap between Muslim and Hindu businessmen.[21] It is true that most of the spectacularly successful businessmen of the 1930s and 1940s happened to be Hindus.[22] As I have shown elsewhere,[23] however, there is no hard evidence that, as opportunities in the trading sector diminished under the impact of the world depression, Muslim businessmen were systematically barred from entry into industry by entrenched Hindu interests. The absence of large Muslim banks has often been cited as a major handicap for would-be Muslim industrialists. But banks did not play a major role in financing industries in India; most capital for industry was raised through credit networks which remained largely 'informal' and were generally controlled by some specialized communities like the Marwaris. It cannot be demonstrated convincingly that the controllers of credit in India, who were mostly Hindus, discriminated against Muslim businessmen because they were Muslims. Such an assertion, to be plausible, would have to be based on a statistical study of all cases of refusal of credit for industrial projects, a study which is of course impossible.

In history facts are, however, often less important than perceptions, even though distorted. Although its empirical foundations were, to say the least, flimsy, the idea seems to have gained ground in some Muslim business circles that Hindus were doing their utmost to prevent Muslim businessmen from succeeding and, as the years went by, this kind of crude rationalization became accepted as an undisputed truth. It led to increasing demands for 'positive discrimination' in favour of Muslim business interests which were difficult to accommodate within a unitary political framework. In this way, Muslim separatism, the demand for a political separation of the Muslim-majority areas from the rest of India, acquired an economic dimension.

This was, however, a late development. Prior to the 1940s, the idiom of communal politics in India was steeped in the preoccupations of the landed elite and of the non-capitalist middle classes. Problems of unequal educational entitlements with their purported consequences at the level of competition for scarce jobs in the government and service sector and of delicate landholder-tenant relationships figured much more prominently in discussions of the 'communal question' than views on the structure of industrial credit. The existence of links between businessmen and 'communal' politicians did not mean that communal 'lobbies' articulated business interests in a coherent fashion. In that respect, there were significant regional differences. The Punjab and Bengal were two specific cases, and they deserve a separate treatment.

In the Punjab, the 1919 reforms had resulted in the coming to power in the province of a coalition of 'rural' interests in which Muslim landholders occupied a dominant position. The urban interests, mainly Hindu traders and moneylenders, had been pushed aside and they resented the orientation of provincial politics and the 'rural bias' of the provincial government. Although Hindu and Sikh landholders were very much part of the Unionist Party power structure, the urban-rural divide was given a clear communal twist by the political representatives of the urban commercial classes. The cities and towns of the Punjab were Arya Samaj strongholds and politicians like Lala Lajpat Rai, who had close links with the sect, became the spokesmen of the urban Hindu interests in the province. In the Punjab the dominant Hindu business interests, thus, became clearly identified with a communal outlook in politics.

Sir Gokul Chand Narang, head of one of the largest business groups in the Punjab (with large interests in the sugar industry) was also one of the most outspoken representatives of Hindu communalist views. As far as the much smaller Muslim business class of the Punjab is concerned, it seems to have solidly supported the Unionist ministry which in its turn bestowed favours on it. Although no detailed study of this is available, an indication of the trend is the rapid and spectacular rise of the Muslim firm of Wazir Ali, headed by Sir Syed Maratib Ali,[24] which became the largest contractor of military canteens in the Punjab, a hugely profitable activity in a province which sheltered so many garrisons. Since Punjabi regionalism was the main platform of Muslim politicians in the province,[25] local Muslim businessmen did not show much interest in all-India Muslim politics and, even after 1937, did not support the Muslim League. In the richest agricultural province of India, however, the landholding interest always remained paramount, and urban businessmen played only a marginal role.

Things were different in Bengal, the other Muslim-majority province, because of the weight of Calcutta and of its business interests. In this old stronghold of Indian nationalism, the death of C.R. Das in 1925 opened an era of gradual decline for the Congress and of growing assertion of communal forces in politics.[26] While British firms still occupied a dominant position in the business world of Calcutta till the 1940s, an increasingly important role was played by Indian businessmen, particularly Hindu Marwaris, and also non-Bengali Muslims of various origins.[27] Although provincial politics was dominated by the *bhadralok* of Calcutta and the rising Muslim *jotedars* of eastern Bengal, the various factions contending for control of the province had to seek some business support to fill their coffers. No study of the involvement of businessmen in Bengal politics is available, but one can focus rapidly on three businessmen who played an important role at various moments.

G.D. Birla emerged in the mid-1920s as the most influential leader of the Calcutta Marwaris, displacing the more conservative and pro-British Rai Badridas Goenka. Although Birla was a staunch nationalist and a follower of Gandhi in all-India politics, he maintained close links with the conservative Hindu leader Pandit M.M. Malaviya, whose friends in Bengal opposed a compromise between Hindus and Muslims in the province.[28] In 1934 Birla sided with Malaviya in opposing the Communal Award, which gave Muslims a majority of seats in the provincial legislature, and criticized Gandhi's stand.[29] His outlook on Bengal affairs, therefore, was close to that of the Hindu communalists and of the Hindu Mahasabha, although he had at an early stage severed his links with the latter organization. It seems that many Calcutta Marwaris feared that a Muslim-dominated provincial government might take measures detrimental to their interests. Nevertheless, when the Fazl-ul-Huq ministry, the first Muslim-dominated ministry in Bengal, was formed after the 1937 provincial elections, the finance portfolio was given to N.R. Sarker, a Bengali Hindu businessman-politician (with large interests in insurance), who had close links with the Marwari business community, particularly G.D. Birla. In spite of its radical stand, the Huq ministry did nothing to upset the powerful Marwari business interests of the province. But the Marwaris remained suspicious of Muslim intentions.

As far as Muslim businessmen are concerned, their main representative in Bengal politics was the Cambridge-educated M.A.M. Ispahani, scion of an illustrious family of Persian origin. He represented the Young Party on which Jinnah increasingly relied to intervene in the faction-ridden world of Bengal Muslim politics. In the 1940s Ispahani emerged as the main financier of the Muslim League and a major figure in all-India Muslim politics. In spite of a growing communal polarization of politics, there was more room in Bengal than in the Punjab for an accommodation between Hindu and Muslim business interests. The existence of an active urban Muslim commercial class based in Calcutta made a difference: the growing west Bengal-east Bengal divide did not totally coincide with the communal alignment. Nevertheless, in so far as the Marwari businessmen were gaining in strength (largely at the expense of British interests)[30] and self-assurance, there was a possibility that they would increasingly resent the prospect of Muslim political domination of the province.

In the two large Muslim-majority provinces, Hindu and Muslim businessmen developed divergent appreciations of the problem of centre-province relations. Given their close links with the provincial governments, Muslim businessmen favoured greater provincial autonomy, especially in financial and economic matters, while their Hindu colleagues put their hopes in a strong central government, because Muslims would necessarily wield less influence with it than Hindus.

In the other provinces, where Muslims were not in a majority, but where Muslim businessmen often played an important role in commercial life (particularly in the Bombay and Madras presidencies), communal considerations were not central to the politics of business, be it Hindu, Parsi or Muslim. In the United Provinces, which was the birthplace of Muslim separatism, businessmen do not figure prominently in accounts of the growth of the movement,[31] which drew support mainly from landlords, urban professionals and government servants. In the Bombay presidency, a Hindu-Muslim divide in the commercial world was revealed for the first time during the civil disobedience movement when the pro-government stand of most Muslim traders formed a clear contrast to the pro-Gandhian enthusiasm of the majority of the Hindu commercial class.[32] It does not seem, however, to have created a permanent rift within the commercial community along the Hindu-Muslim divide: the business world of western India was too complex and interdependent, with the Parsis in particular still playing an important role.

A new conflict arose in 1936 around the question of the separation of Sind from the Bombay presidency. The local Hindu business community opposed the move, which was bound to result in the creation of one more Muslim-dominated province, and some Bombay businessmen supported their stand.[33] In spite of this, communal politics did not deeply penetrate western India, and Muslim traders continued to be active in the Indian Merchants Chamber in Bombay.

The 1937 provincial elections revealed that the Muslim League, reorganized by Jinnah from 1934 onwards, had more support among the commercially oriented Muslim communities of the Bombay and

Madras presidencies than in the predominantly rural and agrarian communities of the other provinces.[34] But the League, in spite of its claim to represent a specific 'Muslim' interest in all-India politics was still operating within the broad ideological framework of Indian nationalism and did not advocate separatism. It, therefore, appears that the Muslim business communities of western and southern India, which were the most active and the richest in the subcontinent, still conceived their future within a unitary India and were not averse to a strong centre, since, because of the sheer law of numbers, they had little hope of playing a decisive role in provincial politics.

The transformation of the Muslim League during the 1937-47 period from an organization seeking guarantees for Muslim interests within a unitary structure of government into a spokesman for the separation of Muslim-majority areas was a complex and gradual process. Actually it has been argued in a recently published book that Jinnah's aim remained till the very end a united India with a strong centre in which Muslims would have parity of representation with Hindus and that he eventually settled for a separate Muslim state as only the second-best option.[35] According to this view, he used the separatist demand formulated in very ambiguous terms in the famous Pakistan resolution of 1940 as a bargaining counter to obtain concessions from the British and the Congress. But, whatever were Jinnah's ultimate intentions, the demand for Pakistan gathered a momentum of its own, and, from 1942 onwards, its shadow loomed large over India's political landscape. Businessmen, Muslim and non-Muslim, increasingly had to take it into account and to define their position with regard to it.

III

Prior to 1942 the British had always thought of the political future of India in unitary terms and therefore the possibility of a partition of the country had never been seriously entertained by anyone. The first intimation that partition might be a practical possibility came with the Cripps mission offer of the 'provincial option' to resolve the Indian deadlock. A. Jalal has shown that it aimed mainly at driving a wedge between Jinnah and the Muslim leaders of Bengal and the Punjab, who were more interested in getting increased freedom of action for their own provinces than in obtaining concessions for Muslim interests in a united India.[36] Jinnah was saved from an open breach with those leaders by the opposition that the provincial option met from both Linlithgow and the Congress leadership. Of all the Congress leaders, only the astute

Rajagopalachari understood that Cripps' proposal offered a way to break the 'communal' deadlock by dividing the Muslim camp, but his advice was ignored.[37]

It is nevertheless interesting to note that one of the Congress's main business supporters, G.D. Birla, tended to echo Rajaji's views in a letter written to Gandhi's secretary in July 1942. Birla wrote:

> You know my views about Pakistan. I am in favour of separation and I do not think it is impracticable, or against the interest of Hindus or of India. As long as we will quarrel, there is no salvation of India. Besides, we should not forget that the Muslims – every one of them – now want it. Even the Congress Muslims are no longer exception. How could then we resist?[38]

Birla gave an interpretation of the Pakistan movement in purely 'communal' terms and did not mention its regional dimension. It shows that, contrary to what has been asserted by some,[39] he clearly thought of the problem in communal terms. This led him to overlook the deep divisions within the Muslim camp that Rajaji was precisely keen on exploiting. But he clearly understood that Muslim demands had become a fact of the political life of India and that they could not be brushed aside.

That is precisely what his fellow businessman Lala Shri Ram, the big Delhi industrialist who also thought in communal terms, failed to grasp. In a private letter written in September 1942, in the aftermath of the Quit India movement, he took the line that 'we [the Hindus? the Congress?] should not pay any price for Independence to the Muslims, either in the way of Pakistan or increase in percentage of seats in the Centre or residual power in the Provinces'.[40] Shri Ram was advocating a line of total rejection of all the demands put forward by Muslim politicians. It was certainly closer to the dominant stand of the Congress than Birla's conciliatory approach. The president of the Bombay Millowners Association publicly defended the same strong unitary line.[41] It seems, therefore, that there was a clear division of opinion in the ranks of non-Muslim big business regarding the question of partition, which was reflected in the inability of the FICCI, the mouthpiece of the dominant business interests, to define a clear position in the matter.

There is nothing surprising in this, given the complexity of the issues involved. From a strictly economic point of view, partitioning India did not seem to make much sense. Thus Sir Ardeshir Dalal, a member of Tata board and one of the most influential figures in Bombay big business, argued the economic case against partition in a pamphlet released in February 1943 entitled 'An Alternative to Pakistan'. Stressing that Pakistan would be a poor country, he added:

> With innumerable problems . . . to be handled and a burden of debt difficult to repay, it will cut itself off from the great economic and industrial future which a self-governing India may look forward to. There will be a great urge to impose heavy custom duties on goods from 'Hindustan' to fill its depleted coffers and that in itself will not only hinder industrial progress but might be a fertile source of trouble between the two states.[42]

In conclusion, Sir Ardeshir urged Hindus to make sacrifices to placate Muslims so as to keep the country united. He proposed a plan for a federation in which the constituent units would have important powers. Dalal's views partly reflected the specific interests of the Tata group, the most 'national' of all the Indian business groups since the market for its products was the entire country. But with the growing integration of the Indian market brought about by customs protection and wartime restrictions of imports, most big business groups had an interest in the preservation of the subcontinent as one market.

For instance, the Ahmedabad millowners sold a lot of cloth to Bengal and separation of that area could be harmful to the prosperity of their mills. There was a lot of 'Hindu' capital invested in factories in the Muslim-majority provinces. Birla controlled two large jute mills in Calcutta and one cotton mill in the Punjab; Shri Ram had a cotton mill in Lyallpur in western Punjab and one sewing-machine factory in Calcutta; the Associated Cement Companies (controlled by Hindu, Parsi and British businessmen) had several plants in the Pubjab and Sind; the Narang group and Lahore Electric were two major Hindu-controlled operations in western Punjab. For 'Hindu' big business, however, the losses would be minimized if Calcutta, with its large trade and many industries, remained in 'Hindustan', but this required a partition of Bengal between the Hindu west and Muslim east which hurt Bengali feelings and may not be easy to bring about. Muslim businessmen in the areas which would not go to Pakistan might also face great difficulties, unless they were ready to migrate to the Muslim-majority areas, a move that was not so easy to contemplate. Their colleagues in the Punjab and Sind were the only ones who could really expect immediate gains from a political separation of their provinces. For Muslim businessmen in Bengal, who were mostly Calcutta-based, a lot depended whether Calcutta would or would not go to a Muslim-dominated Bengal.

In spite of these economic problems, there seems to have been increasing support to partition from most businessmen especially from 1945 onwards. The essential reason, more than the intrinsic merits of the case, was the absence of an attractive alternative. For Jinnah's cherished dream of a unitary state with parity between Hindus and Muslims was rapidly fading in the face of determined Congress opposition. The only way to avoid partition seemed now to be the acceptance of a loose federal regime with a weak central government having limited powers and limited finances, most powers and revenue going to the provinces. That is what Maulana Azad advocated in 1945[43] and Jinnah seems to have rallied to the idea in 1946 when he realized that he would never get parity at the centre.[44] Big business, especially the dominant non-Muslim interests which were behind the 1944 Bombay Plan, found such a prospect distasteful. They wanted a strong centre, and their blueprint for the economic development of independent India assumed the existence of a unitary India, in which a central plan could be implemented without hindrance from powerful provincial governments.[45]

A practical step in that direction had been the Industrial Policy Statement of April 1945, the last significant economic measure taken by the colonial government, which transferred responsibility for most large-scale industries from the provinces to the centre,[46] reversing the trend inaugurated by the Montagu-Chelmsford reforms of 1919. For big business, there was no question of going back on this and of allowing provincial interests to interfere in the definition of economic policy. It is significant that a resolution passed at the FICCI session of March 1947 explicitly criticized the Cabinet Mission plan of 1946 for the vagueness of its formulations regarding the powers of the central government.[47] At the same session a resolution on 'the powers and policy of the government of the Indian Union' was adopted recommending that the central government be given all powers in matters of monetary policy, custom duties, protection, defence and communications.[48]

To achieve a unitary India with a strong centre, big business was ready to pay a price in the separation of the Muslim-majority provinces, provided the non-Muslim areas of Bengal and the Punjab were incorporated into the Indian Union. This solution, a separate Muslim country, also suited Muslim businessmen in Sind and Punjab, since it promised to free them from the stranglehold of Bombay non-Muslim big business.

The prospect was less attractive to Muslim businessmen in Calcutta since it meant they would have to migrate from the city where they had been operating for long. But they had no other choice than to accept it, since the alternative prospect of a united independent Bengal was, as we shall see, even more distasteful to them. As for Muslim businessmen in the rest of India, many of them, although not all, seem to have reconciled themselves to a migration which seemed to offer new economic opportunities.[49] Therefore, partition eventually emerged as the solution most responsive to the needs and aspirations of a very large section of big business, Muslim as well as non-Muslim, because it combined the attractions of a strong unitary structure which appealed to non-Muslims and of the separation of Muslim-majority areas which satisfied the Muslims.

The most delicate question was, nevertheless, the partition of Bengal, because Bengalis were sentimentally opposed to it, and this popular opposition found an echo among some politicians. The Muslim League leader H.S. Suhrawardy, thus, sought to reach an agreement with a section of the Bengal Congress led by Sarat Bose on a programme of unity and independence for Bengal.[50] His attempt was, however, sabotaged both by a section of the provincial Muslim League and by the all-India Congress leadership,[51] although Jinnah on his part appeared ready to condone it. It seems that big business, both Muslim and Hindu, had a hand in the failure of Suhrawardy's attempt. Ispahani and Adamji, the two biggest Muslim businessmen of Bengal, had always sided with Suhrawardy's rivals in the complicated factional struggles which had rattled the Bengal Muslim League during the early 1940s, culminating in their dismissal from the ministry in 1943.[52] They did everything in their power to sabotage his efforts at conciliation. As for Hindu big business, it supported the campaign launched at the end of 1946 by the Hindu Mahasabha for the partition of the province.[53] Sarat Bose complained that in Bengal it was mainly the middle classes which were for partition,[54] and he must certainly have included businessmen among them. Businessmen seem to have feared that the only common platform which could unite Suhrawardy and Sarat Bose was radical populism, and Ispahani and Adamji preferred to leave Calcutta rather than live in a populist Bengal, even if Suhrawardy claimed that he was acting within an Islamic tradition.

As Calcutta was eventually awarded to India,[55] the last obstacle to partition in the eyes of Hindu big business was removed. Nothing could be done to save the big Hindu interests in the western Punjab and in

April 1947 a huge flight of capital and personnel occurred from that area, which Jinnah's reassuring declarations could do nothing to stem.[56] With Calcutta in Indian hands and the Punjab and Sind stripped of most of Hindu capital, Birla was in a position to argue that the overall cost of partition to non-Muslim business was slight. He could emphasize the fact that almost all the industrial assets of India were in the Indian Union[57] and that the trade balance between the two countries would be clearly favourable to India.[58] One worrying aspect was that the Calcutta jute mills would be cut off from their supplying areas of raw material in eastern Bengal. The situation could, however, be improved if jute cultivation developed in western Bengal and adjoining areas. For Muslim businessmen, the massive flight of Hindu traders and money-lenders from the western Punjab, Sind and eastern Bengal created a void which Muslim immigrant traders from Bombay, Calcutta and other areas could step into, notwithstanding that the economic prospects of Pakistan were uncertain.

A development not foreseen by businessmen on either side of the new border was that partition would bring into being two mutually hostile country and that the resulting escalation in the defence budgets of the two countries would tend to slow down their rate of economic growth. For it was considered likely at the time that there would be some form of common defence agreement between the two countries to face a potential threat from the north-west.[59]

How far did the attitudes and policies of businessmen influence the decisions of the major actors, i.e. the British government, the Muslim League leadership and the Congress High Command? Regarding the former's role, a close examination of the attitudes of British business and of the way it may have influenced government policies would be necessary, and it falls outside the scope of this study. Suffice it to mention here that British business in Calcutta clearly showed its preference for the inclusion of the city in the Indian Union,[60] a fact which may have influenced the policy of the British government in that matter.

As far as the two major Indian political organizations are concerned, there were some similarities in the way they interacted with big businessmen. In particular, a parallel has often been drawn between the role of Birla *vis-a-vis* the Congress and that of Ispahani in relation to the League. The League at the all-India level was, however, more dependent for its functioning on the contributions of a few wealthy business supporters than the Congress, which drew support from a wider range of interests in society. But, since the League derived most of its strength, especially in 1946-47, from regional sentiments, the nature of its central organization did not influence its policies to such an extent.

In the Punjab and Bengal, the two key Muslim-majority provinces which formed the backbone of Pakistan, the League's eventual political success was due to the rallying to it of the dominant Muslim rural interests. Its urban supporters, who were few in any case given the overwhelmingly rural character of the Muslim population in the two provinces, never played a major role. Even in Bengal the rising *jotedars* of eastern Bengal eventually mattered more than a few business magnates of Calcutta. The rural bosses of the western Punjab and eastern Bengal were motivated mainly by their hostility to urban interests which happened to be largely Hindu but they did not particularly relish the prospect of a massive migration of displaced Muslim businessmen from the Indian Union. They were regionalists more than 'communalists'. Muslim businessmen had more influence on regional 'Muslim' politics in the Bombay and Madras presidencies but were increasingly peripheral to the concerns of the Muslim League. Although the business supporters of the League at the all-India level may, as is suggested by A. Jalal,[61] have played some role in Jinnah's retreat from his cherished dream of power-sharing with the Congress at the centre, their part was not crucial;Jinnah would in any case have been forced to lower his sights.

What, then, of the possible influence of non-Muslim big business over the final acceptance by the Congress of a partition the idea of which the nationalist party had obstinately resisted between 1942 and 1946? Given the fact that the most influential business supporter of the Congress, G.D. Birla, had been converted to the inevitability of Pakistan as early as 1942, it is tempting to speculate whether Birla's pressure did not have something to do with the change in the attitude of the Congress High Command in 1947, particularly since the main architect of the shift in Congress policy was Vallabhbhai Patel,[62] the crucial link between the Congress High Command and big business since the late 1930s.[63] Patel, however, had a mind of his own. He was in favour of a strong centre, since he could hope to control it. Actually, in the absence of convincing evidence of big business pressure on Patel regarding the question of partition, let us be content with signalling the existence of a clear coincidence of views between the strong man of the Congress and his friends from big business.

Also striking is the simultaneousness of the adoption by the FICCI of its resolution on the powers of the Union at its session of March 1947 and of the passing by the Constituent Assembly on 28 April of the first report of the Union Powers Committee. The latter, by putting forward a very extensive conception of the powers of the central government of the future Indian state, 'slammed the door shut on Jinnah and the League once and for all'.[64] Leaving aside the question whether they were or were not 'communal' in their outlook, big non-Muslim businessmen had very precise reasons for not relishing the prospect of a co - sharing of power between the League and the Congress at the centre. They feared the capacity of the League to exploit the internal contradictions of the Congress by proposing anti-business measures, as Liaqat Ali Khan had done in March 1947 at the time of the budget of the interim government.[65] Knowing how tenuous was the hold of the right-wing leaders over the Congress organization, they were mortally afraid of the emergence of a 'populist' combination of Muslim and non-Muslim politicians which would have taken measures against big business interests. In this, there was also a clear coincidence of interests between non-Muslim big business and the Congress right-wing leadership.

IV

Although many businessmen came to accept the partition of India as the most satisfactory solution to the political deadlock, it is not suggested here that capitalists as a class were a major influence in the developments which led to it. Big business influence was probably crucial in so far as the fate of Calcutta was concerned, but in the Punjab urban capitalists were not the deciding factor.

Feelings of 'communal' solidarity, cutting across differences of caste and class, certainly existed among some businessmen, but they do not really provide a rationale for the behaviour of the business class. To argue, for instance, that Muslim business magnates in Bombay suddenly felt that they had more in common with the poorest peasants of East Bengal than with their Hindu or Parsi fellow businessmen of Bombay does not appear very sound. Attitudes towards Pakistan and partition were determined more by considerations of personal advantage than by religious sentiments. This is not meant to imply that, from the economic point of view, partition was a perfectly rational solution. Actually in strictly economic terms, it could be shown to be a zero-sum game, the gains of some being offset by the losses of others.

Those who gained most were undoubtedly some Muslim businessmen in the Punjab, Sind and East Bengal, as well as some business immigrants from Bombay, Madras and Calcutta who settled in Pakistan. They were able to take advantage of the void created by the massive departure of Hindu traders and moneylenders from the areas which went to Pakistan. They also benefited by the pro-business policy adopted by the authorities of the new country which were keen to foster industrialization in an almost exclusively agricultural country. But not all Muslim businessmen benefited by the establishment of Pakistan. The Muslim business communities remaining in the Indian Union faced a difficult situation as the more dynamic elements which were generally in a position of leadership left for Pakistan. And many Muslim businessmen who settled in Pakistan had lost almost everything they owned and had to start again from scratch. For non-Muslim businessmen who fled Pakistan and settled in India, there were the same problems, with the added difficulty that they entered a more competitive world, for in India the departure of Muslim traders had never created a void comparable to the one that existed in Pakistan.

The separation of rich agricultural areas deprived several Indian industries of a more or less captive market. Actually, Indo-Pakistani trade was very rapidly reduced to almost nothing, a development which had not been anticipated by Birla in 1947. Particularly hard hit was the Indian cotton textile industry which, after having lost a lucrative market in the Punjab and Sind, was faced with increased competition from the new Pakistani mills on the foreign markets to which it had turned to offset the loss of a part of its domestic market. The jute mills of Calcutta, having faced for a few years the problem of supply of raw material, also had to contend in the export market with the competition of the new mills of East Bengal which could exploit a large pool of cheaper labour.

In economic terms, partition can ultimately be analysed as a response to the problem of the uneven pace of capitalist development in colonial India.[66] The formation of a new state allowed some of the least industrialized areas of India to create a minimal industrial infrastructure which had been denied to them by the workings of colonial capitalism. Those regions were under - industrialized not because they had a mainly Muslim population; other regions of the subcontinent with mainly Hindu populations (like Orissa or large tracts of central India) were no better off from that point of view. But, not having a Muslim population, they could not separate themselves and escape the domination of Bombay or Calcutta-based big business.

All the same, the inter - regional contradictions which were a powerful (although obviously not the only) factor in the partition of India did not disappear with partition. In the new independent state of Pakistan, capitalism developed in an even more unbalanced way than in colonial India; the Punjab and Karachi got most of the benefits while the peripheral regions, and in particular East Bengal remained sadly neglected. The independence of Bengladesh was only the logical outcome of this whole process. On the other hand, in the Indian Union, the unitary structure which was created after 1947 has probably become one of the major obstacles to the economic development of the country and is increasingly criticized by regional capitalists. All this tends to show that the 1947 partition could not be, contrary to what some big businessmen expected, a durable solution to the problem of growing regional economic imbalance which the colonial regime bequeathed to its successors.

Notes

*The author wishes to thank the Foreign Affairs Ministry of the Government of France for financial support to participate in the IIMA Seminar where an earlier version of this paper was presented.

1. See C.A. Bayly, 'The Pre-History of "Communalism"? Religious Conflict in India, 1700-1860', *Modern Asian Studies* IXX (1985), pp. 177-203.

2. On the various movements such as that of Sayid Ahmad of Bareilly and the *fara'izi*, see P. Hardy, *The Muslims of British India* (Cambridge 1972), pp. 50-60. For a detailed account of developments in Bengal, see R. Ahmed, *The Bengal Mulsims, 1871-1906: A Quest for Identity* (Delhi 1981), pp. 39-105.

3. The Tyabji brothers, leaders of the *Sulaimani Bohra* community and Muhammad Ali Roghay, a Konkani Muslim belonging to a leading shipowning family. C. Dobbin, *Urban Leadership in Western India: Politics and Communities in Bombay City, 1840-1885* (Oxford 1972), p. 231.

4. As for instance, G. Pandey, 'Rallying Round the Cow: Sectarian Strife in the Bhojpuri Region, c. 1888-1917', in R. Guha (ed.), *Subaltern Studies II, Writings on South Asian History and Society* (Delhi 1983), pp. 60-129.

5. See C.A. Bayly, 'Patrons and Politics in Northern India', *Modern Asian Studies* VII (1973), pp. 349-88.

6. On the corporate world of the north Indian merchants, see C.A. Bayly, *Rulers, Townsmen and Bazars. North Indian Society in the Age of British Expansion, 1770-1870* (Cambridge, 1983).

7. See A.K. Bagchi, 'European and Indian Entrepreneurship in India, 1900-1930', in E. Leach and S.N. Mukherjee (eds.), *Elites in South Asia* (Cambridge 1970), pp. 223-56.

8. W.C. Smith, *Modern Islam in India* (Lahore 1946, 2nd, reprint 1963), pp. 203-4: 'It is difficult to discover what, if anything, they mean when they say "Islam", except the Muslim community and loyalty to it. . . . Usually they do not govern their lives by their religion in any other sense . . . .'

9. He wrote: 'Capitalist society is favourable to the growth of communalism. Indian capitalist society is especially favourable to the growth of Muslim communalism'. Ibid., p. 199.

10. Ibid., p. 200.

11. B. Chandra, *Communalism in Modern India* (Delhi 1984), p. 75.

12. C. Markovits, 'Les hommes d'affaires musulmans dans la premiere moitie du XXe siecle', *Purusartha*, IX (1986), pp. 111-26.

13. The 1930s witnessed in particular the collapse of the largest Muslim-controlled (although not exclusively Muslim-owned) industrial group in India, the Bombay-based Currimbhoy group with its large interest in cotton textiles.

14. An analysis of the names of the members of the major chambers of commerce in the principal cities of India shows a fair proportion of Muslim names. There were also Muslims in the committees of the various chambers and at times several chambers had a Muslim president.

15. On this movement, see H. Papanek, 'Pakistan's Big Businessmen: Muslim Separatism, Entrepreneurship and Partial Modernization', *Economic Development and Cultural Change* XXI (1972), pp. 1-32.

16. The *Muslim Yearbook of India and Who's Who* compiled by S.M.Jamal (Bombay 1949) listed eighty-eight Muslim commercial associations.

17. On Ispahani, see K. Macpherson, *The Muslim Microcosm: Calcutta 1918 to 1935* (Wiesbaden 1974), pp. 120-51.

18. In a 'Note by the Muslim Chamber of Commerce on the Memorandum containing the proposals of the Government of Bengal on the Delimitation of Constituencies for the Federal Legislation under the Reformed Constitution', it was claimed that Muslim traders controlled a large share of the import-export trade of Calcutta. See Muslim Chamber of Commerce, Calcutta. *Annual Report of the Committee for the year 1935* (Calcutta 1936), Appendix A, pp. 134-40. The hollowness of these claims was exposed in an article by N.K. Basu in the *Amrita Bazar Patrika* of 12 September 1935.

19. As shown by a systematic comparison of the resolutions passed by the two chambers between 1932 and 1942.

20. On the prolonged battle waged by Jinnah to convince the major Muslim business magnates to join the federation and the resistances he encountered, see M.A.H. Ispahani, *Qaid-e-Azam Jinnah as I knew him* (Karachi 1976), pp. 119-25.

21. In particular M.A.H. Ispahani, 'Factors Leading to the Partition of British India', in C.H. Philips and M.D. Wainwright (eds.), *The Partition of India: Policies and Perspectives, 1935-1947* (London 1970), pp. 331-59.

22. See C. Markovits, *Indian Business and Nationalist Politics 1931-39: The Indigenous Capitalist Class and the Rise of the Congress Party* (Cambridge 1985), pp. 64-7, for some case studies.

23. Markovits, 'Les hommes d'affaires mussulmans . . . ' (n.12), *passim.*

24. See the entry in the *Muslim Yearbook of India and Who's Who* (n.16), Sir Syed, born in 1884, managing proprietor of the firm of M/S Syed Ali & M. Wazir Ali, secretary of the All-India Canteen Contractors Association from 1922 to 1926, became a director of the Reserve Bank of India in 1935.

25. On Muslim politics in the Punjab, see D. Page, *Prelude to Partition: The Indian Muslims and the Imperial System of Control 1920-1932* (Delhi 1982), in particular pp. 46.72.

26. See J. Gallagher, 'Congress in Decline: Bengal 1930 to 1939', *Modern Asian Studies* VII (1973), pp. 269-325.

27. On Muslim businessmen in Calcutta, see K. Macpherson (n.17), p. 22.

28. According to Page (n.25), p. 130, G.D. Birla and Malaviya were behind the agitation

of the *Karmi Sangha* to have C.R. Das's Bengal Pact rescinded.

29. See Birla to Gandhi, 14 April 1934, in which the business magnate asked the Mahatma to allow the members of the Swaraj Party 'to fight the Communal Award in their own way'. G.D. Birla, *In the Shadow of the Mahatma* (London 1955), p. 127.

30. Although there remains a question mark as to the extent of Marwari control of the jute industry.

31. See F.C.R. Robinson, *Separatism among Indian Muslims: The Politics of the United Provinces Muslims, 1860-1923* (Cambridge 1974).

32. The point is made in R. Kumar, 'From Swaraj to Purna Swaraj: Nationalist Politics in the City of Bombay, 1920-1932', in D.A. Low (ed.), *Congress and the Raj: Facets of the Indian Struggle, 1917-1947* (Delhi 1977), p. 97.

33. See Purshotamdas Thakurdas Papers, file no. 72, 'Separation of Sind', Nehru Memorial Museum and Library, New Delhi.

34. In Bombay, the League won twenty of the thirty-nine Muslim seats, and only one out of eighty-six in the Punjab. See A. Jalal, *The Sole Spokesman: Jinnah, the Muslim League and the Demand for Pakistan* (Cambridge 1985), p. 32.

35. Ibid., pp. 59, 175.

36. Ibid., p. 75: 'By offering a provincial not a communal option, Cripps hoped to provide a powerful incentive for those very constituents on whom Jinnah's strategy depended to unhitch their wagons from the League's train'.

37. On 2 May 1942 the All-India Congress Committee rejected Rajagopalachari's resolution allowing separation of the Muslim provinces. Ibid., p. 83.

38. G.D. Birla to Mahadev Desai, 14 July 1942, in G.D. Birla: *Bapu, a Unique Association* (Bombay 1977), vol. 1, pp. 315-17.

39. Thus, Bipan Chandra writes in *Communalism in Modern India* (n. 11), p. 71: 'The Indian capitalist class was not Hindu in any sense other than that its majority followed the Hindu religion. At no stage did any section of the Indian bourgeoisie think of itself or act objectively or subjectively as a Hindu (or Parsi) bourgeoisie or in communal terms'.

40. Lala Shri Ram to Sir Purshotamdas Thakurdas, 29 September 1942, Purshotamdas Thakurdas Papers, file no. 239.

41. In his presidential address at the annual session of the Bombay Millowners' Association, V.N. Chandavarkar declared that 'any scheme that was likely to result in the disintegration and disunity of the country was not likely to be welcomed'. Quoted in the *Times of India*, 25 March 1942.

42. A.R. Dalal, *An Alternative to Pakistan* (Bombay 1943), p. 45.

43. Mentioned in Jalal *The Sole Spokesman* (n.34), p. 135.

44. Ibid., p. 211.

45. See P. Thakurdas et al., *Memorandum Outlining a Plan of Economic Development for India* (Bombay 1945).

46. The text of the statement is found in India Office Records, Economic and Overseas Department Collection, L/E/8/3618.

47. FICCI, *Proceedings of the 20th Annual Session of the Federation of Indian Chambers of Commerce and Industry* (Delhi 1947), p. 138.

48. Ibid.

49. In April 1946, Chaudhary Khaliquzzaman mentioned to the Cabinet delegation that Muslim industrialists from Bombay might wish to transfer their business to the Punjab. See 'Note on meeting of the Cabinet Delegation with Mohammad Ismail, I.I. Chundrigar, Chaudry Khaliquzzamman and Maulana Syed Abdur Rauf', 8 April 1946, reproduced in P.S.N. Mansergh (ed.), *India: The Transfer of Power, 1942-1947* (London 1970-1983), vol. VII, pp. 166-9.

50. jalal, *The Sole Spokesman* (n.34), pp. 265-6.

51. A resolution passed by the Congress Working Committee on 8 March 1947 endorsed the demand for a partition of the Punjab, opening the way for the partition of Bengal. Reproduced in Mansergh (ed.), *Transfer of Power* (n.49), vol. IX, pp. 900-1.

52. The victory of Suhrawardy's faction over Nazimuddin's at the meeting of the Bengal Provincial League Committee in November 1943 led to Ispahani and Adamji's exit from the provincial cabinet. Jalal, *The Sole Spokesman* (n.34), p. 103.

53. S. Sarkar, *Modern India, 1885-1947* (Delhi 1983), p. 436.

54. Sarat Bose to Patel, 27 May 1947, reproduced in D. Das (ed.), *Sardar Patel's Correspondence, 1945-50* (Ahmedabad 1971-74), vol. IV, pp. 45-6.

55. In spite of the governor's efforts to have declared it as a free city. Jalal, *The Sole Spokesmen* (n.34), p. 266.

56. Capital flight from the Punjab was estimated to be as high as Rs.250 crore, and a Hindu banker declared: 'We are leaving Pakistan an economic desert'. See *Times of India*, 6 May 1947.

57. In a pamphlet brought out by G.D. Birla in 1947 under the title: 'Basic Facts Relating to Pakistan and Hindustan', it was underlined that Pakistan would get only 9 out of 389 cotton mills, none of the 108 jute mills, 10 of the 166 sugar mills, none of the 18 iron and steel mills, only 3 cement plants and none of the 16 paper mills. Quoted in *Times of India*, 7 June 1947.

58. Exports from India to Pakistan were estimated to amount to Rs. 850 million (mainly cloth, coal, steel and manufactured items) while exports from Pakistan to India amounted only to Rs.700 million (mainly cereals and raw jute, and some raw cotton). Ibid.

59. See M. Zinkin's note on Pakistan in Mansergh (ed.), *Transfer of Power* (n.49), vol. VI, pp. 801-5.

60. See Cabinet Delegation to India, Paper C.D.I. (1)[1], ibid., vol. VI, p. 953.

61. According to her, the business supporters of the League strongly reacted to Nehru's press statement of 10 July 1946 in which he defended a strong centre capable of deploying 'central authority to restrict the freedom of action of Muslim-majority provinces in their provincial domains'. To them 'this meant the supremacy of the Tatas, the Birlas and the Dalmias in the competitive wilds of an independent India'. Jalal, *The Sole Spokesman* (n.34), p. 210. It was clear that Jinnah and Nehru's ideas about the centre were not compatible, and therefore some form of Pakistan was inevitable.

62. It was Patel who, on 25 April 1947 conveyed to Mountbatten that, if the League was not ready to accept the Cabinet Mission's proposals, the Congress would demand partition. Mountbatten's interview with Patel, eighth miscellaneous meeting, 25 April 1947 in Mansergh (ed.), *Transfer of Power* (n.49), vol. IX, pp. 424-6.

63. See Markovits, *Indian Business and Nationalist Politics* (n.22), p. 181, on Patel's role as a 'privileged broker' of big business interests.

64. The wide definitions given to the three headings of 'Defence', 'Foreign Affairs' and

'Communications' allowed the central government to exercise its control over most economic activities and forbid the provincial governments to impose restrictions on the doings of any citizen of the Union. Muslim-majority provinces would therefore not have been permitted to discriminate against non-Muslim businessmen. See Jalal, *The Sole Spokesman* (n.34), pp. 261-2.

65. Liaqat Ali Khan, who was finance minister of the Congress-League interim government, introduced in the budget project proposals for taxation of high profits and a capital tax. He had initially the support of Nehru and Azad, but big business reaction was so strong that the Congress then stepped in to water down his proposals. The Congress-Hindu big business equation was thus planted in the minds of many, as Liaqat had probably anticipated. On this episode, see M.A.K. Azad, *India Wins Freedom* (Delhi 1959), pp. 205-6 and C.M. Ali, *The Emergence of Pakistan* (New york 1967), p. 105.

66. For an analysis of the problem, see A.K. Bagchi, 'Reflections on Patterns of Regional Growth in India during the Period of British Rule', *Bengal Past and Present,* XCV (I)-180 (Jan.-June 1976), pp. 247-89.

12

Indian Business and Economic Planning (1930-56)

Raghabendra Chattopadhyay

Indian capitalists were probably unique in the third world in demanding a planned economy. The leaders of the Indian bourgeoisie had made their demands known through the publication of the so-called Bombay Plan in 1944. This fact is well known but it neglects the historiography of Indian planning. In their effort to establish an independent nationalist nature of the plan programmes initiated by the post-colonial state in India, the historiographers, irrespective of their ideological positions, gloss over the formative period of the idea of planning which belonged to the colonial past. There appears to be an active forgetfulness regarding the close link and resemblance between the First Five-Year Plan and the preceding British plans, and of the strong influence that the Indian business community exerted in giving form to the idea of planning. The Bombay Plan is mentioned only *en passant* and as no more than a part of the 'pre-history' of a process supposed to have commenced only after the transfer of power,[1] and no notice is taken of the early British efforts in the 1930s.[2]

The fact of the matter, however, is that the Indian business community did play a crucial role in developing the concept of planning, particularly during the two decades before independence. In the early post-colonial years, too, during the formative stage of the plan strategies, the leaders of this community left their mark upon it. A historical analysis of the evolution of the idea of planning in India brings this out clearly.

I

The success of the first plan in Soviet Russia during 1928-33, in sharp contrast to the prevailing crisis of the Great Depression in the capitalist world, made the entire world plan-conscious. That success encouraged many non-socialist nations to attempt to solve their economic problems through planned state intervention. In the USSR the idea of planning served as a political concept to mobilize the entire people to transform society. Having nationalized all the major branches of the economy, it was incumbent upon the state to direct and control, and thus plan all economic activities. But planning within that system was more than just an alternative to a market-based economy. It was a central aspect of the socialist ideology of the dictatorship of the proletariat. Rapid industrialization of society was a part of that ideology, and not its central goal. But the aspect of Soviet planning which attracted the non-socialist nations was not its function as a means to achieve a comprehensive social transformation, but its mechanics, that is, planning as an economic method divorced from politics and intended merely to bolster capitalism through state intervention. In India, the communists were not the first to advocate planning. From Visvesvaraiya, the first Indian planner, to Nehru, its principal architect, all the 'pioneers' dealt with planning as a merely economic exercise. It was for them, an effective method to industrialize the Indian economy.

Modernization through industrialization had remained the central point around which the dominant strand of Indian economic thought developed since the days of Telang, Ranade, and their followers. Ideologically, this strand represented the characteristic demand of the Indian capitalists as they grew in number and strength since the second half of the last century. The eagerness shown by almost all the nationalists in the 1930s, excepting Gandhi and a few of his close followers, to adopt planning as the only way to reconstruct and develop the economy, can be best understood if we study the history of this idea as an aspect of Indian nationalism. The immediate impetus might have come from the success of Soviet planning; but the genesis of the idea lay in the *etatisme* which was integral to 'economic nationalism' as it evolved through Telang, Ranade, Naoroji, Dutt and their followers. A study of the development of this strand throws light not only on the ideological basis of planning within Indian nationalist thought, but also the resistance it encountered, even at its incipient stage, from Gandhism. The development of what may be called Indian economic thought cannot be comprehensively discussed here, but we may sketch here a brief outline of the central problem that concerned the Indian socio-economic thinkers since the middle of the nineteenth century up to 1930, when the idea of planning was first mooted officially by the British in India.

The second half of the nineteenth century witnessed some major political and economic changes in India. After 1857 the British Crown took over the administration of the Indian colony from the East India Company and India became the direct responsibility of the British Parliament. The avowed economic dictum of the period in Britain was that of *laissez-faire.*[3] In the name of that policy Indian indigenous manufacturing – particularly the handloom industry – continued to be destroyed through the fiscal policies adopted by the Government of India. But the cotton mill industry in India began developing during the same period despite the efforts by the Lancashire textile industry to retain its hold over the Indian market. The number of cotton mills increased from just one in 1954 to twelve in 1861 and within another eighteen years, in 1879, India had fifty-four cotton mills working with 1,550,000 spindles.[4] In effect the rise of the Indian cotton mills did not encroach upon the interests of Manchester in India. Restricted mainly to the Bombay area, the mills were catering to the residual demand within the country and were exporting Indian cotton cloth to countries of Asia and Africa.[5] The other region of India which witnessed industrial growth was Bengal where jute, a major industry, was overwhelmingly dominated by European, more narrowly, British businessmen.

This period also marked the rise of nationalist thinking in India, Poona in the Bombay presidency, and Calcutta in the eastern region taking the lead. The urban middle-class elite and some of the forerunners of the indigenous factory systems in these cities began to voice their anxiety over the adverse effect of the *laissez-faire* policy on the Indian economy. The swadeshi movement can be traced back to 1849, when Gopalrao Deshmukh of Poona advocated, in the columns of *Prabhakar*, the use of Indian products in place of imported ones.[6] In Bengal, Nabogopal Mitra organized the 'Hindu Mela' (or National Gathering as they called it in English) in 1867 which regularly met once a year for nearly fourteen years.[7] One of the major functions of the *mela* was the promotion of the use of indigenous manufactures by organizing exhibitions of the products of Indian arts and crafts.

Sumit Sarkar has identified four different political trends within the swadeshi movement as it developed through the second half of the nineteenth century: moderate; the trend towards self-development without inviting political clash – 'constructive Swadeshi'; political extremism using extended boycott or passive resistance in addition to self-help efforts; and terrorism.[8] In terms of economic thinking there were various shades of differences between these strands. But in the main, these may be said to have constituted two major tendencies. The first, expounded at great length by the 'moderates', looked forward to an industrialized modern India, while the second, espoused by Sarkar's other three categories in varying degrees, fell back upon the traditional handicrafts and artisan mode of production as the source of prosperity. The latter emphasized the glorious past of the Indian village community. The revivalism inherent in this tendency found expression in the rejuvenated interest in the Hindu religion. Dayananda in northern India, Vivekananda and Bankim Chandra in Bengal and Tilak and his followers in western India became the new proponents of Hindu society as such. Rabindranath Tagore also wrote for a time in a Hindu nationalist vein, upholding the ideal of rural society in ancient India. In economic terms, the emphasis in this thinking was on self-reliance and boycott of all foreign commodities (with the implied rejection of the western mode of life). It opposed British rule because the latter intervened and disrupted the stability of traditional Indian society through the destruction of its indigenous manufactures.[9] Indeed, it denied the state any role at all in the economic activities of society. In a sense Gandhi's *Hind Swaraj* published much later, was a logical culmination of this variety of socio-economic thought worked out to its fullest logical extent.[10] For convenience, we shall use the term 'swadeshi' only for this strand of thought.

It was, however, the moderate school which actually dominated the thinking of the early 'nationalists'. People like Telang, Naoroji, Ranade, M.V. Joshi and R.C. Dutt belonged to this school. Protectionism was the key word to them for the remedy of the economic distress of the country. To both the 'moderate' and the 'swadeshi' schools, the reasons for the abysmal poverty in India were to be found in the policies adopted by the British government which resulted in an economic 'drain' of the country. Agriculture was ruined by the new system of land revenue introduced under the Raj.[11] The indigenous industries were destroyed. Extravagant expenditure by the government on civilian and military personnel brought from England bled the country white financially. All this added up to an 'un-British rule'.[12] The remedy, according to the moderates, lay in the industrialization of the country. The view of this school was cogently summarized by Justice Ranade in his inaugural speech to the first Industrial Conference in Poona in 1890.[13] He pointed out the phenomenal poverty of the existing soviety and its growing dependence 'upon the single and precarious resources of agriculture'. He particularly emphasized the disproportion that existed between the increasing production of raw agricultural produce and the backwardness in the production and distribution of 'manufactured produce'. He observed that 'no hand-made industry [could] hope to thrive in competition with industry moved by cheap natural agents. The free use of natural agents . . . [made] large investments of capital a necessity, and this handicapped all individual efforts beyond rivalry'. Therefore 'the organization for industry and capital on joint-stock principle for collective and large undertakings' was vitally necessary. Thus lack of large-scale industrialization was recognized as the major cause of Indian poverty. This was an important distinction from other trends in the swadeshi movement which considered the development of indigenous traditional handicrafts through individual and community efforts as the panacea for the prevalent economic ills.

Once large-scale industrialization was accepted as the means to develop the Indian economy, the role of the state became vital in such a programme. The country with its 'scanty capital resources' could not hope to develop its industries in the face of stiff foreign competition, particularly when the state itself was encouraging foreign (British) interests in the name of its *laissez-faire* policy. Protest against the latter and demand for protection was a distinguishing feature of this strand of economic thinking.

One of the earliest pleas for protectionism was made by K.T. Telang in 1877 in his long essay on 'Free Trade and Protection from an Indian Point of View'. Free trade may have benefited England, but for India, he argued, it had been the cause of industrial decline. Protectionism alone could save the country under the prevailing circumstances. It would help in mobilizing idle resources.[14] G.V. Joshi went further and clearly advocated state participation in industrial development:

> First of all, we must have the Government thoroughly with us, heart and soul. Without its help in our economic weakness and unpreparedness, we could hope to accomplish but little in the direction of national progress, in the face of such fierce competition as we are exposed to – Government must recognise the true wants of the nation and cordially identify itself with the cause of national industries.[15]

Ranade elaborated on this argument when he pointed out that in European countries there was a decided reaction against the *laissez-*

faire policy. Even in England, he observed, 'the recent factory legislation, the qualified reorganisation of the law of trade unionism, the Poor Law System, and the Irish Land Settlement are all instances which indicate the same change of mind'.[16] He went on to make a case for positive state intervention in economic activities, emulating England and other developed countries where 'the State [was] . . . more and more recognised as the national organ for taking care of national needs in all matters in which individual and corporate efforts [were] not likely to be so effective and economical as national effort. This [was] the correct view to take of the true functions of the State'. [17]

The early criticism of the British *laissez-faire* policy in India, thus, gradually developed into an idea of positive state participation in the economic activities of the nation. R.C. Dutt actually tried to put this idea into practice when he became the revenue minister of the princely state of Baroda in 1904. He attempted to organize state help to private enterprise to make Baroda, 'a model state in India . . . in the prosperity of the agricultural people, the briskness of trade and enterprise, the starting of new mills and industries'.[18]

The role of the state to these thinkers was not confined merely to protecting the nascent Indian industries from foreign competition but often included the responsibility of bringing about agricultural and social reforms.[19] It was from this understanding of the role of the state that Gokhale observed in 1903: 'What the situation really demands is that a large and comprehensive scheme for the moral and material well-being of the people should be chalked out with particular care and pre-sight and then it should be firmly and steadily adhered to and the progress made examined from year to year'.[20] Although the idea of planning had not yet emerged in Indian economic thought, Gokhale's demand was almost a harbinger of what was later to take the form of a conscious effort in that direction.

The plea for state participation continued unabated throughout the period up to the First World War. The colonial authority, however, continued to adhere to the doctrine of *laissez-faire* up to 1916. Lord Curzon, who claimed to be a staunch champion of industrial effort, admonished the proponents of state intervention for imagining 'that by any stroke of an enchanter's wand, the present Government, or any Government of India, can effect a revolution in the economic, social or industrial conditions of this vast continent'.[21] The official view at the time considered the government 'ill qualified' to promote industrial development by direct action and wanted all such matters to be left to private enterprise.[22] Against this sort of argument the Indian elite cited the examples of the railways, cinchona, tea and coffee plantations and coal mining, where the Government of India either subsidized and underwrote private investment or even directly participated for a long time. It amounted to saying that the government was not really averse to the principle of state aid, but refused it in the case of indigenous efforts.

But the *laissez-faire* policy broke down with the Government of India's entry into the First World War. Orders had to be placed with the Indian firms to meet the war needs. For the Indian industrialist, a welcome change in the attitude of the government was discernible in regard to excise duty on cotton, when Viceroy Lord Hardinge said before the legislative assembly in 1916:

> I need hardly say that the Govt. of India have no desire to create controversies here, in England or elsewhere at the present time by the discussion of the question affecting Indian interests; but they are glad to have had that the import duty on cotton fabrics should be raised and the excise duty should for the present, remain at its actual figure and an assurance given that it will be abolished as soon as financial conditions will permit.[23]

The plea put forward by the moderate Indian nationalists for so many years now started showing some result, and they rendered whole-hearted support to the British war effort.

Industrial development in India during the war was hindered by several factors, the most important being the short supply of plant and machinery for expanding capacity. There was no machine-making industry in India, not even for nails and screws.[24] But all through the war, Indian industries were automatically protected from foreign competition. Britain's war needs also helped. Many new industries were started to meet urgent civil and military requirements, manufacture of glass, hardware, cutlery and cement being the more important.[25] The pre-war industries were also encouraged to expand their capacity. Tata Iron and Steel Company, for example, registered a steep rise in its production under the stimulus of increased demand, high prices and quasi-monopoly. The output of rolled steel rose from 48,872 tons in 1913-14 to 1,230,800 tons in 1917-18.[26] The cotton mills too experienced an unparalleled prosperity. Though very few new mills could be set up owing to the difficulties in importing plant and machinery, the existing ones worked at maximum capacity, earning large profits.[27] The Government of India also assisted Indian industrialists in forming the Indian Munition Board in February 1917 and placed orders for government stores and railways with Indian firms.[28]

With the end of the war, Indian industries were again subjected to severe foreign competition and the demand for protection mounted. A new generation of economists now took up the cause. V.C. Kale, Benoy Sarkar, P.N. Bose, K.T. Shah, C.N. Vakil, R.K. Mukerjee, D.R. Gadgil and others who had succeeded the early nationalist thinkers, were almost all staunch supporters of state protection and encouragement to industrialization. But now the arguments and visions were much more complex than before. New ideas were being incorporated in the national movement. M.K. Gandhi with his revivalist ideology was emerging as the undisputed leader of the Indian National Congress. The swadeshi movement of the early decades had lost its vigour but its ideas became an effective weapon in his hands. Communism and socialism also began to make an impact on socio-economic thinking, especially in the wake of the success of the Bolshevik revolution in Russia.

The conflicting ideas of the time can be discerned in the writings of contemporary economists. People like P.P. Pillai were re-reading their economic history: 'India was never a great manufacturing country in any adequate sense of the term. The only industry she had developed on any extensive scale was hand-spinning and weaving'.[29] He went on:

> It is indisputable that tariff policy has contributed its own share to checking the development of this textile industry; but this share has generally been overestimated. . . . The reason that tariff policy has loomed so large in the eyes of Indian writers is that it was persisted in by the Government in flagrant defiance of popular wishes, and that its supporters have invariably employed language of a most provocative character. [30]

Another interesting writer of the early 1920s was K.T. Shah, a professor of Economics in the University of Bombay, whose writings may be considered as prototypes of the new economic thinking. In his *Trade, Tariffs and Transport in India,* published in Bombay in 1923, Shah was concerned not only with the protection of Indian industries but also with the idea of distributive justice. His support for protection to private enterprise was also a qualified one:

> The real danger . . . of an active State aid for the building up of industry lies in [the problem that] . . . should industry develop by such means under the aegis of private enterprise, a much more serious problem in distributive justice would have been created, of which doctrinaire free trader usually takes no cognizance. . . . The concentration of riches, in ever increasing proportion, in a steadily diminishing number of hands, brought about demonstrably by such active assistance granted by the community collectively, intensifies the class cleavage that is universally regretted as the most undesirable feature of modern industry. The only solution that I can think of for avoiding the otherwise certain disaster would be frankly to accept the socialist principle of collective enterprise, at least in new industries where no vested interests are concerned.[31]

But knowing full well that socialism was a far-cry in the then Indian situation, he prescribed the alternative that 'the authority responsible for the supervision and guidance of the economic system' should treat the problem 'as a comprehensive whole instead of breaking it up into parts'.[32]

Such a comprehensive outlook could be the starting point of planning. After Gokhale prescribed it as early as 1903, others took it up, the most prominent among them being M. Visvesvaraiya. By training an engineer, he was neither a politician nor an economist. As the *dewan* of the princely state of Mysore he earned fame, spurring his state to modernize its administration and economy. He also served the British administration in India in different capacities and travelled round the world to 'gain experiences' from the workings of the economies of Japan, the USA, Cananda and other European countries.[33] With a clear idea of the nation's needs, he published *Reconstructing Indian Economy* in 1920, in which he pinpointed the causes of Indian underdevelopment and discussed how the new Government of India Act(1919) could be made to work for the country's development.[34] Ranade, Naoroji and Dutt too had come to similar conclusions earlier. The problems of Indian poverty were, according to him, (a) low standard of living caused by the protracted negligence of the rulers; (b) low level of education – general and technical; (c) dependence on agriculture which was primitive and overburdened; (d) lack of industrialization and destruction of indigenous industries due to British tariff and fiscal policies, etc. But the potential was immense. Although literacy was even less than 7 per cent, the absolute number of literates in India far exceeded that in the United

Kingdom. India also had abundant natural resources. What was lacking was the effort on the part of the governmental authority to harness the natural and human resources, he asserted.

To prove his point Visvesvaraiya gave the examples of developed countries like the United States, Great Britain, Canada and Japan. All of them according to him developed only under the protective umbrella of state aid and policies. He added:

> The first lesson to be drawn from this survey by the Government and the people of India, is that industries and trade do not grow of themselves, but have to be willed, planned and systematically developed. In India the Government has shown some enterprise in developing railways and irrigation; but the expansion of trade and industry has been a matter of British domination and has left the people of the country disinterested, with no share in the control of policy or its operation.[35]

In this respect, too, Visvesvaraiya was but echoing the demands made earlier by Ranade, Naoroji, Joshi, Dutt and other moderates.

The 'statism' of early Indian economic thinking has been noticed by many scholars. One of them, P.K. Gopalakrishnan has attributed to these nineteenth century thinkers the notion of actually planning 'mixed economy' within the framework of parliamentary democracy: 'What they probably had in mind was a state armed with more effective legal powers and with the more monopolistic economic units – owned by the state and directed to the public interest'.[36] This may be stretching the point too far. For there was no basis either in the material or the intellectual conditions of nineteenth-century India to foster any indigenous idea of planning or of mixed economy. The perception of abject poverty and economic backwardness and exposure to the western capitalist world had led the thinkers of that epoch to the conviction that the path to development lay in industrializing the economy. But in so far as this tendency within nationalist thought stood apart from the traditional swadeshi ideology with its opposition to any kind of state interference, in so far as it argued for a positive intervention – it was not merely a plea for 'protection' from foreign trade but actual participation by the state – it may be said to have anticipated some of the fundamental presuppositions which were to characterize the discussion on planning during the two decades prior to independence. The planners of pre-independence India were, thus, in a direct line of descent from moderates like Ranade and Naoroji. It was not total state control that they envisaged. Rather, the idea was to seek aid for the indigenous bourgeoisie to stand on their own, and the state was to participate in those sectors where private enterprise was absent. As Visvesvaraiya recommended:

> The provincial government may make a start by pioneering some of the larger industries like shipbuilding, machinery, engines, motor transport, chemicals, paper, etc. and also some of the many key industries needed, with the object of making them a success and subsequently transferring them to the people. There are few technical secrets that are not readily available or that cannot be secured by the expenditure of money.[37]

It was not the aspiration of an individual but of a whole class which was thus represented – the aspiration indeed of the Indian capitalist class.

Beginning with K.T. Telang's demand for protection in 1877 the Indian bourgeoisie and its ideologues took more than forty years to spell out their economic aims and goals clearly. Politically the demand for self-rule or independence had been mooted much earlier by the proponents of traditional swadeshi. But that particular kind of nationalism did not speak fully for the Indian bourgeoisie whose leading organization, the Indian National Congress, paid only lip-service to the swadeshi movement associated with the 'extremists', and often even denounced it. When Gandhi championed swadeshi, it was of a different variety, politically speaking, from the earlier movement. Even so, the Mahatma's swadeshi idea did not strike a deep root within the Congress.

The Gandhian vision of 'Hind Swaraj' attempted to evolve an alternative not only to British rule in India, but also to the social structure based on the concept of western capitalism. This was the first attempt, however utopian, to transform the entire society by decentralizing political power and situating it at the basic level of social organization – the village community. But this vision did not agree with the 'modernizing' ideas of the ideologues of Indian bourgeoisie. As a consequence, although Gandhi was the universally acknowledged leader of the national movement in his mass-mobilizing role, and latter-day plannners and politicians tried to uphold the Indian five-year plans of the 1950s as efforts towards Gandhian socialism,[38] his blueprint for a sovereign India was never really accepted by the dominant leadership in his own party. This was so, because the latter had chosen economic modernization rather than social transformation as their principal objective. With them, as with Visvesvaraiya, Nehru and most other Indian planners, modernization came to be synonymous with industrialization and planning with 'industrialism'. In fact, this hiatus was one of the principal reasons for Gandhi's resignation from the Indian National Congress.[39]

II

We have seen in the preceding section how Indian economic thinking – which had begun with a criticism of the British *laissez-faire* policy in India – developed into a full-blooded protectionist and state-interventionist industrializing ideology by the turn of the century. This statist demand provided Indian economic thinking with a fertile soil where the idea of planning could germinate and grow rapidly from the seeds brought from abroad.

By the 1930s the entire world had become plan-conscious. The impact of the Great Depression and the parallel success shown in the very early years of the first five-year plan in Russia forced the 'free world' to give up finally the moribund theory of *laissez-faire*. Roosevelt's New Deal policies drove the final nail in its coffin. Lord Keynes performed the last rites later when he published his *General Theory*.

The idea of planning struck firm roots in India by the mid-1930s. By 1934 at least two Indians had published their buleprints for planning in India. M. Visvesvaraiya's *Planned Economy for India* and S.C. Mitter's *A Recovery Plan for Bengal* were both published in the same year, the first from Bangalore and the second from Calcutta. The idea had already gained wide currency and a substantial degree of acceptance within the colonial bureaucracy. When Sir George Schuster, the then finance member in the viceroy's council, and his advisors in the bureaucracy tried to set up a plan machinery in 1930, they drew inspiration from the Economic Advisory Council in Great Britain set up to advise the government there in its efforts to come out of the crisis of the Great Depression. In India, planning was designed by the colonial regime as an economic solution for the political crisis created by the growing tide of the nationalist movement during the late 1920s.[40] It was in this connection that the Indian capitalist class first entered the area of planning and its leadership showed its political acumen.

The Indian business community, including the industrialists, were never a homogeneous lot. Yet, when G.D. Birla, the doyen of Indian capitalism, together with Purshotamdas Thakurdas, formed in 1927 the Federation of Indian Chambers of Commerce and Industry (FICCI) as a petulant gesture of defiance against the Associated Chambers of Commerce (ASSOCHAM) which represented the European, primarily British, business interest in India, it signified the beginning of the emergence of the Indian capitalists as a class by itself. FICCI soon became the apex body of Indian business organizations and represented the majority of the Indian business community. Throughout the period of the nationalist movement, the FICCI had consciously and ably led the class it represented. The leadership of Birla and Thakurdas was most evident in their handling of the question of planning in India.

When Schuster first attempted to form the Economic Advisory Council in India, he and his colleagues in the viceroy's council wanted to incorporate 'unofficial advisers' to give this body a neutral colour and to prove to the Indian masses that the colonial regime was earnest in developing the economy in a planned manner. Schuster invited some unofficial representatives including Birla and Thakurdas to a meeting with him and his colleagues to discuss the formation of the council. Both Birla and Thakurdas declined to accept the idea of such a council where Indians would be included merely to rubberstamp, and thus sanctify, the British effort.[41]

The leaders of Indian capitalism did not abhor the idea of planning as such. That the class took keen interest in the idea of planning and that its leadership had understood the import of the concept was soon evident. In 1934, while Schuster was busy making his final, futile attempt to introduce planning in India, FICCI was deliberating on the issue with all earnestness. In its annual meeting that year, there were at least two speeches dwelling at length upon the necessity of planning in this country. Two of its very prominent members, G.D. Birla and N.R. Sarkar (president in 1934) actually sketched their own plans. Birla, in a long speech delivered at the annual general meeting of the FICCI in 1934 – twenty-two printed pages – surveyed the economic condition of India and outlined a plan for the development of the country.[42] Sarkar used his entire presidential speech on the same occasion – fifty-three pages long – to explicate the idea of planning and its possible content.[43]

By 1934, thus, the idea of planning had already attracted the attention of the business community and its opinion was voiced through its leaders. Such an early and positive response from this class should not surprise us in the light of our discussion in the last section. The ground had been already prepared for it during the past seventy years. We have seen that when Indian industrial capitalism was still nascent, the demand for state intervention was already gaining support from that section of

Indian social thinkers who had envisaged an industrial future for the subcontinent. In western Europe, Britain in particular, industrial capitalism during its developing stage had desired, and succeeded in realizing, minimal state intervention over economic activities. In India the situation was entirely different.

In European countries the capital accumulated through mercantile expansion was seeking avenues for productive investment, requiring expansion of market and availability of productive inputs. Hence the demand for minimal control and a liberal non-interfering state. In India on the other hand indigenous capitalism had to develop under the aegis of colonialism. The traditional technological and production bases were, by and large, destroyed by the imperialist rule. The indigenous industrial capitalist class was dependent on imported technology and had to struggle for survival in the face of an overwhelming monopolistic control of its potential market by alien business interests backed by an alien state. For more than a century before the birth of an indigenous industrial base, Indian economy was being denuded of all its surplus by the foreign power. Overall capital formation, thus, was poor. Appropriate technology was hard to come by and the foreigners' monopoly of the market left only the periphery for the indigenous capital to exploit, severely restricting the scope for Indian industrial capitalism. The demand for protection, thus, was natural to Indian economic thinking. This had a dual content: on the one hand it was a critique of the 'un-British rule' seeking to correct the prejudice of the existing state against its Indian subjects – including the business community – and on the other hand it signified the recognition of an aspiring capitalism which desired to unfold itself. The path taken by the colonial Indian bourgeoisie, therefore, had to be different from the one followed by their forerunners in Europe. Not surprisingly, Birla and Sarkar could speak aloud so confidently on the necessity of planning.

Birla's and Sarkar's speeches and the works of Visvesvaraiya and Mitter have some interesting features. The starting point of their discussions, like those of their predecessors in the nineteenth century, was the question of poverty. The solution lay in industrializing the economy which would raise the standard of living. Visvesvaraiya could foresee that 'left to private enterprise, industries [would] not make satisfactory progress. Government should take the lead as every progressive government [was] doing [then].[44] This was, in a sense, the ground on which the idea of planning itself evolved in India – from the understanding that the Indian private enterprise, developed under the colonial aegis was unable to carry forward on its own the task of industrialization. Birla appeared to add to Visvesvaraiya's argument by pointing out that an improvement in the standard of living meant an increase in the purchasing power of the people. Planning was the most desirable goal from that angle as well: 'If there is no wherewithal to buy, then increased production [would] be simply decorating the warehouse of the producers'.[45] So, 'we should not forget that the success of a plan which contemplates increased production depends directly on a parallel increase in the purchasing power of the masses'.[46] Economic development required not only planned progress in the production system, but also some distribution of income to raise the purchasing power of the masses without which capitalism could not expand. It was only through planned effort that the question of production and distribution could be resolved in the interest of a proper capitalist development.

Sarkar expanded this view further: 'In any scheme of planned economy for India, our foremost attention should be directed towards agriculture – the biggest industry of the country. Whatever degree of inter-dependence with other parts of the world may be permissible and economically justifiable in other matters, India should aim to complete self-sufficiency in food'.[47] It was on this understanding that Birla could assert:

> . . . in the industrial sphere there may not be any need of direct [and immediate] encouragement. Protection, tariffs and the increasing purchasing power of the masses [would] take care of the job; but in the case of agricultural produce [which in 1934 was yet to recover from the impact of the Depression and the droughts of the preceding years] some big concentrated effort [would] have to be made to improve the situation and nothing short of subsidy [would] be sufficient to induce the producer to produce more.[48]

Mitter was equally in favour of planned industrial development as a panacea for the problem of Indian poverty, but to him equilibrium between agriculture and industries was more important.[49]

Although all these pioneers expressed their anxiety about the state of Indian agriculture, none of them was ready to prescribe any drastic change in agrarian relations. They would all stress the need to increase productivity and ensure equitable distribution of income but without spelling out the structural impediments in the system, because of their fear of communism. They advocated a planned economy but not a 'communistic' one. And any proposal for a drastic structural change might lead to such 'danger'. Visvesvaraiya was of the view that 'the Indian plan should avoid communistic tendencies, its basic policy should be to encourage collective effort without intervening with individual initiative'.[50] The Russian experience was valuable for planning but, according to him 'the doctrines of communism should be discouraged as unsuited to India'.[51] Mitter observed that 'a plan to be successful should proceed along the lines not only of least resistance but also of maximum social satisfaction. Government control [was] necessary but not necessarily aggressive . . . India does not aspire after socialism'.[52] Birla praised the New Deal of President Roosevelt because 'there is no surer method of inviting Bolshevism, Communism or anarchism than to create an unhealthy disparity between the higher and the lower strata of society'.[53] Hence his emphasis on the distribution of wealth through planning to raise the purchasing power of the people. Sarkar declared that 'the extreme type of State Socialism and economic regimentation that have been enforced in Russia [were] hardly acceptable or applicable to India. The basic principles of the Russian experiment [were] contradictory to the tradition, outlook and philosophy of the Indian people'. He was, however, careful to argue that 'while we reject the communistic basis of economic planning as adopted by Russia, we would be exceedingly unwise to offer opposition to planning itself'.[54]

We need not go any deeper into the content of the speeches and the writings of these early proponents of Indian planning. Suffice it to mention here that all of them had not only tried to establish the necessity of planned economic development in India, they had also discussed in detail the methods to adopt in planning and what physical objectives to set and how to raise the necessary revenue for such planning by the state. They desired an overall planned industrial growth together with increasing agricultural productivity, without endangering the existing socio-economic structure lest the idea of socialism or communism took roots in India.

The keen interest shown by the leaders of the Indian business community and others like Visvesvaraiya and Mitter was in direct response to Schuster's attempt during 1930-34. This phase ended with his departure for England in 1934. Soon after, the Government of India Act of 1935 was passed and elections were held in 1937 which returned the Indian National Congress in most of the provinces. The Congress formed ministries in the United Provinces, Bihar, Orissa, Central Provinces, Bombay and Madras initially and about a year later in North West

Frontier Provinces and Assam. With ministries came power and responsibility, and the party soon adopted a resolution (in Wardha in August 1937) recommending to the Congress ministries 'the appointment of a Committee of Experts to consider urgent and vital problems the solution of which is necessary to any scheme of national reconstruction and social planning'.[55] This was the first time that the concept of planning was mentioned in an official document of the Congress. The resolution was, however, rather vague as it stood and for almost a year merely remained on paper. Thereafter, the party empowered Subhas Chandra Bose, the Congress president, to take necessary steps. Bose called for a conference of the ministers of industries in October 1938 where he announced the formation of National Planning Committee (NPC). The committee was given the task of formulating a comprehensive scheme of national planning to solve 'the problem of poverty and unemployment, of National Defence and of the economic regeneration in general through a programme of industrialization'. Moreover, 'this scheme should provide for the development of heavy key industries, medium scale industries and cottage industries, keeping in view our national requirements, the resources of the country, as also the peculiar circumstances prevailing in the country'.[56] The journey that had begun with the 'rise of economic nationalism' in the second half of the last century was now drawing to a close. Telang, Ranade, Naoroji and Dutt had all begun with the problem of poverty, and prescribed industrialization as the remedy. The conference of 1938 echoed the ideas voiced by these early thinkers.

It is noteworthy that socialism was nowhere mentioned in 1938. It was only later that the party, and Jawaharlal Nehru in particular, began to stress that 'planning' was a step towards socialism in India. When the formation of the National Planning Committee was announced, persons like G.D. Birla, Lala Shri Ram, Lala Shankarlal and M. Visvesvaraiya were present as special invitees to the conference.[57] Later, Bose nominated the following members of the committee: Jawaharlal Nehru (chairman), K.T. Shah (general secretary), Sir M. Visvesvaraiya, Dr. Meghnad Saha, A.K. Saha, Dr. Nazir Ahmed, Dr. V.S. Dubey, Dr. J.C. Ghosh, Sir Purshotamdas Thakurdas, A.D. Shroff and Ambalal Sarabhai. Subsequently, J.C. Kumarappa, N.M. Joshi, Prof. Radha Kamal Mukherjee and Walchand Hirachand were co-opted.[58] Thus the committee consisted of politicians, professionals including scientists and economists and leaders of the Indian business community. Thakurdas, Shroff, Sarabhai and Hirachand were all leading merchants and industrialists belonging to FICCI. Apart from Nehru, only K.T. Shah and

Meghnad Saha were known for their socialist leanings. It is interesting to note that although the Indian business community was so closely associated with the efforts for planning from the beginning, Nehru, perhaps to paint the planning activity with a socialist colour, later wrote in the *Discovery of India:* 'Big business was definitely apprehensive and critical [of the National Planning Committee], and probably joined up because it felt that it could look after its interests better from inside than outside'.[59]

The Big business did indeed look after its interests thoroughly 'from inside'. The NPC, during its short span of life, faced only a few major differences of opinion among its members. One of these related to the place of cottage and large-scale industries in the total scheme of things. J.C. Kumarappa, a staunch Gandhian, actually questioned the authority of the committee to discuss large-scale industrialization. His opposition in this respect stemmed from the Congress view on swadeshi and large industries. This reopened the whole question of industrialization on which both Bose and Nehru had deliberated at length during the inaugural session of the NPC. Nehru now reiterated his earlier view that there was no necessary conflict between small and large industries. Moreover, 'now that the Congress [was], to some extent, indemnifying itself with the sate it [could] not ignore the question of establishing and encouraging large-scale industries'.[60] Nehru's stand was naturally supported by the representatives of the business community and Kumarappa was defeated.

Once the issue of large-scale industrialization was clinched, there arose the question of the role of the state in the plan for industrialization. There was unanimity in the committee that the defence industries must be owned and controlled by the state. Public utilities too should be owned by some organs of the state, such as the central government, provincial governments or local board. On the question of 'key' industries, however, the business group differed with the majority opinion that these should also be state-owned. The business representatives could concede only state control over the 'key' industries but not state ownership.[61] (The definitions of defence and key industries and public utilities were given in the Red Book published by K.T. Shah on behalf of the committee[62]). A.D. Shroff voiced his differences quite sharply and put his note of dissent to the interim report of the public finance sub-committee set up by the NPC.[63] Shroff's dissent was accepted by the NPC and the sub-committee report, which had assumed that all the 'key' industries would be nationalized rather than 'controlled' by the state, was amended accordingly.[64] (We should note here that each of the twenty-eight sub-committees of NPC had a number of business representatives as members.)

The two debates mentioned above had far reaching implications for, and in a sense shaped the structure of, the planning process in independent India. At the very early stage of the deliberations the highest authority in the Congress – the future ruling party which Nehru had represented in the NPC – had decided that future planning would be geared towards large-scale industrialization, though leaving enough space for private capital to grow and prosper even in the field of 'key' industries. The concept of the 'mixed economy' developed through these debates. The nineteenth-century 'economic nationalists', the early ideologues of Indian capital, had created the ground for the future emergence of the idea of planning in India. The Indian business community ably championed the cause of planning in the early 1930s and now at the fag end of that decade the leaders of the community moulded this idea of planning and give it content which would suit them most.

The NPC had a very short life and virtually died with the advent of the Second World War. But while it lasted, big business exerted its influence on the outcome of its activities. When the provincial Congress governments resigned and the leaders including Nehru were put behind bars, K.T. Shah tried to publish the documents already prepared by the NPC and its twenty-eight sub-committees. Nehru sent his consent from jail. But Shah was known for his radical inclinations and the business representatives were worried that he would publish only the views in favour of state ownership of all 'key' industries. Thus, Thakurdas and Shroff, two important leaders of this community, took steps to scuttle Shah's efforts and ultimately invoked Gandhi's authority to overrule Nehru's consent.[65] It was only in 1948 that Shah was ultimately able to publish these documents. But by then the situation had undergone a sea-change.[66]

III

The next phase of the evolution of planning in India started with the onset of the Second World War. The Indian bourgeoisie again played a very important role in this effort. The war provided them with ample opportunities not only to consolidate their economic position but also establish themselves as the most organized pressure group to influence and even formulate plan strategies that the Indian state would adopt.

The colonial state renewed its own efforts at planning soon after the war started. The experiences of the First World War and the subsequent Great Depression had made the entire world plan-conscious. During the Second World War, all the big powers engaged in the struggle for supremacy set up their own plans for a new world economic order. During the early 1940s, Germany, Japan, Britain and the United States were all busy formulating post-war plans not only for their respective economies but for the entire world.[67] By mid-1941, an Inter-departmental Post-War Reconstruction Committee was formed by the Government of India to 'prepare developmental plans for India'.[68] By March 1943 this committee was replaced by a Reconstruction Committee of the [viceroy's] Council (RCC). The new committee set up a number of policy committees comprising representatives of the provincial governments and princely states, and prominent 'non-officials'.[69]

We may recall here that back in 1930 Schuster had made a similar attempt to rope in the 'unofficial advisers' but failed due to non-cooperation from the leaders of the FICCI. Since the birth of industrial capitalism in India, indigenous industrial and commercial interests had been clamouring for assistance from the state in their efforts to develop as a class. In 1930 when the government had first indicated its eagerness to help by offering accommodation on the still-born Economic Advisory Council, the hostile political atmosphere and the impending nationalist movements had created difficulties. In 1943 the situation was different. The Quit India movement had been brutally crushed. The Congress was in complete disarray with all its leaders behind bars. On the other hand, the war had boosted the economy through war demands. International competition in the Indian market had almost ceased. Even the pressure of British export interests on the Government of India had eased to some extent. At the same time a huge sterling balance was piling up with the Indian treasury in the form of trade surplus from the supply of war materials to the allied army.[70] The colonial state, faced with the crisis generated by the war, was more eager now to seek help from 'non-officials' and non-officials had much more to gain by collaborating. The participation of the indigenous big business in the viceroy's policy committees, therefore, was quite in keeping with the logic of these developments. And nearly all the representatives of Indian business houses joined these committees with enthusiasm. They could once again exert influence 'from inside'.

The result was that all the policy committees and the apex body itself – the Post-War Reconstruction Committee – had a large number of established Indian businessmen as members. Members of the committee included G.D. Birla, A.D. Shroff, G.L. Mehta, P. Thakurdas, Muthiah Chettiar, N.R. Sarkar and M.A. Ispahani. Many representatives of Indian business served simultaneously on the National Planning Committee or its numerous sub-committees and the Reconstruction Committee or its various policy committees. Thus, neither the nationalists nor the colonial state could do without the leaders of Indian business. It is noteworthy that most of the professional experts serving on the NPC such as K.T. Shah, and Meghnad Saha were excluded from the Reconstruction Committee.

Soon after the reorganization of the Reconstruction Committee, the government set up a new department exclusively for planning and development. The suggestion to create this department came from G.D. Birla.[71] Lord Wavell, the then viceroy, also accepted Birla's nomination of Ardeshir Dalal as the new member of the viceroy's council in charge of that department – against the wishes of the Secretary of State Lord Amery. Dalal, a retired ICS officer, was then a director in a Tata company.[72] He was also one of the authors of the so-called Bombay Plan produced by the leaders of Indian capitalism, not from any academic interest but to pre-empt directly and thus influence the state effort in formulating strategies of planning in India. Big business in India had collaborated with the colonial state in many spheres during the 1940s, but it did so from a position of strength which it had gained because of the crisis of the state. The appearance of the Bombay Plan was one of the manifestations of this strength.

The document resulted from an initiative the leaders of Indian big business took when Stafford Cripps and Bevin were busy trying to convince Churchill in Britain and Linlithgow in India of the necessity of initiating a planned economic development 'to enlist the sympathy of the workers and peasants by immediate action on their behalf'[73] and thus 'wean' them away from the nationalist movement. Birla and Thakurdas enlisted the support of J.R.D. Tata and organized a secret meeting of some leading businessmen in the Bombay office of Tata Sons Limited. The Tatas showed great enthusiasm to set up an informal committee and lent all infrastructural support to it. John Matthai, who was then in the employment of Tata Sons Limited, prepared background papers for this meeting and, later when the committee started functioning, all its clerical and research tasks were performed by the statistical department of Tata Sons. The Tatas bore half the expenses of investigation for the committee while the other members of the committee (Purshotamdas Thakurdas, Shri Ram, G.D. Birla, Kasturbhai Lalbhai, A.D. Shroff and Ardeshir Dalal) financed the rest.[74] (Dalal was not present in the first meeting.)[75]

The interest of Indian big business in formulating a plan document had two aspects. Apart from the long-term perspective that the doyens of Indian capitalism such as Birla and Thakurdas had, the immediate impetus came from the worries the Indian business community had developed in the early years of the war regarding the ever-increasing sterling balances and the possible use of it by the British in India. They feared that British industrialists both in India and in Britain would try, with the connivance of the Government of India and the India Office, to place pre-emptive orders for capital goods with firms in Britain for delivery after the war and, thus, block the use by Indian firms of the reconstruction fund created by the Government of India to utilize a part of the sterling balances.[76]

The fear was not entirely without basis. Indeed, British firms like Imperial Chemical Industries (ICI) were already moving in that direction.[77] The Federation of British Industries had advised all the British chambers of commerce in India that the latter should make plans for starting and acquiring industrial units with rupee capital so that in the post-war period they would be in a position to compete with Indian firms.[78] The Government of India's decision in 1942 to increase the import of consumer goods from the United Kingdom and to control the inflow of capital equipment only added to the anxieties of the Indian business community regarding the intentions of the colonial state.[79]

In turn, Indian business began organizing itself to put up a joint front against these imperialist designs. The authors of the Bombay Plan were not an isolated group. Other indigenous business interests were also moving in that direction.[80] S.C. Majumdar, who headed the Hindustan Cooperative Insurance Society Ltd. of Bombay, had corresponded with Thakurdas suggesting to him that he should form a Post-War Association of India and give leadership to the community together with Birla, Dalal and others to formulate a post-war economic plan programme for India.[81]

Apart from the immediate exigency, the authors of the Bombay Plan bore in mind the post-war situation. They had already anticipated the possibility of India gaining independence in the near future. In the first meeting of the committee formed by these planners, held on 11 December 1942, they formulated a general attitude on the question of economic planning on the basis of the political assumptions that if a national government came into existence after the war, it would (a) 'embrace the whole of India', (b) be on a 'federal basis with residual powers vested in the local governments', and (c) be 'completely free in respect of economic matters'.[82]

The maturity developed by the leaders of Indian capitalism was evident in the proceedings of this meeting. The committee decided that 'its aim should not be to vindicate capitalism as an institution but impartially to analyse capitalism', with a view to determining what modifications were necessary 'to enable it [capitalism] to render the best possible service to the country'. The planners were unanimous in their opinion that the role of the state was vital in this regard. Enquiries were to be initiated on the subject of state control with a study of the 'defects of capitalism, particularly in respect of planning distribution'. The system of wartime control, according to the committee, could be a proper subject to determine the merits and demerits of state control. In general, it was agreed that the state should lay down a general plan for the development of industries, and its control should carry with it an obligation to assist industries where such assistance was needed. Its control was to be exercised through a machinery composed of representatives of employers, labour and the state, and care should be taken to maintain freedom and initiative and avoid over-centralization. Licensing of industries was considered to be a suitable means of enforcing state control in respect of regional distribution of industries and also of social and economic conditions within each industry.

In selecting subjects for investigation, the committee decided, among other things, that 'problems relating to agriculture should be examined not merely in relation to their bearing on industrial development but on its own merits as the most vital economic activity of the country', and that consideration should be given (clearly under the influence of Keynesian economics) to the question of providing public works on a long-term basis and the building of houses in industrial areas and in villages as a means of remedying cyclical fluctuations. At the same time it was felt that 'Public Works as a means of providing employment should, as far as possible, relate to directly productive works'.[83]

The committee worked very efficiently because of the help rendered by the statistical department of Tata Sons Ltd. The initial note on planning prepared by Matthai in June 1943 was considered by the committee in its meeting held in August. By December of that year, an outline, drafted by Matthai[84] with the help of, amongst others, P.S. Lokanathan – a noted economist of the time – was ready.[85] It envisaged an increase of 55 per cent in industrial production as against 60 per cent in agriculture. But both Thakurdas and Birla criticized this on the ground that this would expose the committee 'to the charge of industrial bias' and suggested, instead, a 100 per cent increase in agriculture production over fifteen years of planning. Accordingly, the outline was revised incorporating these suggestions.[86]

The plan called *A Brief Memorandum Outlining a Plan of Development of India,* was presented at a press conference held at Tata's Bombay House on 19 January 1944.[87] Initially, the idea was to publish it by the end of January after arranging some good publicity. But the committee decided to bring forward the date to take advantage of the meeting of the general policy committee of the Reconstruction Committee, which was scheduled to be held on 17-18 January.[88] Since A.D. Shroff, P. Thakurdas and G.D. Birla were members of this committee, they wanted to use this occasion to make an impact on the Government of India with the production of their own plan. Although this resulted in insufficient publicity, the authors were successful in drawing the attention of the policy-makers of the state to their efforts.[89]

The Bombay Plan caused quite a stir in official circles.[90] Arrangements were made to analyse different aspects of this document by various departments of the Government of India.[91] All the departments expressed their agreement with the general objective of the plan, but most were concerned with the financial aspects.[92] Theodore Gregory, the economic advisor to the viceroy, in his note pointed out the difficulty in carrying out such an elaborate plan for economic development under the prevalent constitution based on provincial autonomy. He was of the opinion that 'planning on a national scale [had] hitherto been attempted in a thoroughgoing way only in Russia, Germany and (to smaller degree) in Italy', and that all these countries were under totalitarian forms of government.[93] This observation did not, however, stop the government from going ahead with its consideration of the plan. The research department of the Reserve Bank of India was given the task of analysing the financial aspects.[94]

The Government of India at that time was 'working on a statement of broad policy to be followed as regards post-war development.[95] This was necessitated by the pressure created by Ernest Bevin and Stafford Cripps in the war cabinet, and Churchill's support for them on the question of 'social and economic policy' in India. As a result the government decided to consult the authors of the Bombay Plan for clarification of the points raised by different government officials. J.P. Srivastava, the member for food in the viceroy's council and deputy president of the Reconstruction Committee was entrusted with the task.[96] He wrote to Thakurdas that in view of the proposed statement of policy by the government, on which his committee was working at the time, it would be 'most useful to have the Bombay Plan explained' to the government by the authors.[97] He suggested a meeting between the authors and government officials at his place. In the meeting held in April 1944, the government was represented, apart from Srivastava, by the finance and the supply members of the viceroy's council and the secretaries of RCC, and of the departments of industries, finance, education, health and land and commerce. The economic adviser to the viceroy and a few other government officials also attended. Amongst the authors Thakurdas, Tata, Dalal, Shri Ram, Shroff and Matthai were present.[98]

The first point, raised by Srivastava, was 'whether the Plan contemplated the continuance of provincial autonomy [under the 1935 Act] or a revision of the Constitution in regard to the respective functions of the Centre and Province'.[99] This was obviously an effort to sidetrack the issue of national government as the prerequisite to planning. The authors of the Bombay Plan reiterated their stand on the necessity of a national government and observed that such a government would have to be invested with 'adequate power of control and direction as regards economic matters both in the Provinces and in the States'. We may recall here that the major opposition of the Congress and other political parties in India against the 1935 Act was related to the power that it devolved to the princely states in the proposed federal system.[100] The authors of the Bombay Plan, in a sense, echoed the Congress views in their demand for a strong central authority in economic mattes. The government side conceded this point in principle.[101] It was agreed by both sides, however, that the existing 'government must initiate planning on the basis of the [prevalent] Constitution and with regard to its constitutional relations with Provinces and States'.[102]

The authors stressed that the existing government should immediately 'declare their intentions and policy regarding post-war development over the whole field and in particular, the industrialisation of the country', initiate action for and modify the conditions and restrictions which stood in the way of 'developing key industries, arrange imports of machinery and plant, etc., and the priorities required'. This, they thought, would be in conformity with the policy of a future national government which should be instituted without delay. They also emphasized the importance of 'giving preference to Indian nationals in the matter of prospecting and mining licences and avoiding the intervention of foreign vested interests'. All these demands of the leaders of the Indian bourgeoisie were obviously directed to pre-empting the efforts that British and other foreign economic interests would make in using India's sterling balances during the post-war period. By publishing the Bombay Plan they were trying to force the government to commit itself regarding the direction of its post-war policies. The importance that was attached to this document by various groups of people – Indian and otherwise – is evident by the fact that within three months of its publication, the Bombay plan had two editions and two reprints.[103]

The meeting of April 1944 also revealed the attitude of the Indian bourgeoisie regarding the role of the state in the economy. The authors of the Bombay Plan stressed that they contemplated three kinds of government intervention in industry, namely government control, government ownership and government management: 'The relation between the National Government and Industry should be in the direction of a large measure of Government control, considerable Government ownership in view of the large expenditure of Government finances that would be involved, and a minimum of Government management.'[104] The authors did not want state ownership or government management in those cases where 'private capital was forthcoming for an enterprise'. They were of the opinion that apart from the armament industry only public utilities and 'some units of basic industries might be Government-owned.'[105]

In this view they were following the same argument they had put forward in the NPC on the issue of government control of 'key' industries. It may be recalled that the NPC initially favoured the nationalization of all 'key' industries. Shroff, Thakurdas and Walchand Hirachand succeeded, however, in whittling down the resolutions regarding this matter.[106] The leaders of the Indian bourgeoisie knew very clearly what they wanted from the state. In their scheme of things the state was to minimize regional disparity in distribution of industries, promote or subsidize non-remunerative enterprises and build up public utilities and basic industries which, though essential for industrial growth, were characteristically non-remunerative. Private enterprise was to be given a free hand to choose its own fields of operation. Hence not only the entire consumer goods industry, but even some of the basic industries in which private enterprise might find it profitable to invest, was to be kept free from state intervention. It is interesting to observe that people like Nehru and his followers, who hoped to promote 'socialism' through economic planning, agreed to these typically capitalistic proposals as early as 1938-39.[107]

In their attempt to protect the interest of private enterprise the authors of the Bombay Plan convinced the officials in the meeting that 'it would not be possible or desirable to set out in advance the industries or enterprises which should be owned by the Government'.[108] It was also agreed by both the sides that the question of policy regarding state controls should be decided through the reconstruction policy committees in association with the non-official experts, so that Indian capitalists could exercise some control on Indian experts by influencing their selection.

A decision on economic planning could not leave out agricultural issues from its purview. In the NPC discussions, the question of agriculture had figured only as an afterthought when Sarabhai had pointed out its omission from the programme.[109] By contrast the Bombay Plan did discuss the problems of Indian agriculture and suggested increasing size of average landholding and readjustment of the areas under cultivation of different crops. The change in agriculture, the authors thought, could be achieved through cooperative farming which should be introduced, even if it meant 'some measure of compulsion'.[110] The vagueness of this prescription came in for some criticism by the government side. Characteristically, the objections related to only the technical aspects of the problem. They pointed out that to increase agricultural production by 130 per cent over fifteen years would require 'advanced agricultural research and technique'. The authors agreed that 'the question required further examination' and the 'problems of cooperative farming and consolidation of holdings would need further study and consideration'.[111]

The inability of the leaders of industry to conceptualize or prescribe any concrete structural change of the land system is evident here. They discussed size of landholding, rural indebtedness, and low agricultural productivity but could not come to a firm decision even with regard to cooperative farming that they had prescribed as a solution. This failure followed from the evolutionary approach to economic development adopted not only by the Indian bourgeoisie but by almost the entire nationalist leadership including Nehru. Whenever they talked of 'planning', they thought only of industrializing the economy. As a result, the question of agriculture was dealt with in a perfunctory manner – sometimes as an afterthought, sometimes only as a matter of technology. (As far as the Congress was concerned, even the most daring measure on its part – the U.P. Tenancy Act of 1938 – was not aimed at any basic change in the land system). The inability of the bourgeoisie to prescribe any radical change in the land system led them to suggest cooperative farming as a solution to the problems of agriculture. But since it was obvious to them that the prevalent land system was itself the largest hurdle in introducing cooperative farming, they vaguely suggested 'some measure of compulsion' without spelling out the 'measure'.

Another crucial debate in the meeting, however, revolved around finance. The government negotiators were of the opinion that the plan involved heavy taxation and depended too much on 'a heavy overdraft on the future'. Moreover, since the budget for the plan was estimated on the pre-war (1931-39) price level, the actual finance, they argued, would be much more than the estimated figure of ten thousand crore rupees. They suggested that 'in view of this the social schemes of educational and public health development should be held back until the national income had been stepped up by the expansion of industry and other remunerative schemes'. The authors agreed that the plan involved heavy taxation, but hoped that it would not be difficult for a national government enjoying popular support to raise the necessary finance. They also acknowledged that the taxation involved distribution problems and promised to clarify their views on this issue in a separate publication. By the end of the year they brought out a second document called *Memorandum Outlining a Plan of Economic Development for India*, Part II.[112] But by then there had been a number of publications on planning from different quarters of the Indian society – including plan documents of the Government of India.

We have now enough evidence to understand the extent to which the Bombay planners had made their impact on the Government of India. A detailed study of the functioning of the Reconstruction Committee of the Council and its policy committees would indicate the level of involvement of the Indian business representatives in formulating strategies and policies of the Government of India during the 1940s.[113]

The impact of the Bombay Plan on the government formulation of plan strategies was particularly evident in the Industrial Policy of the Government of India published in 1945.[114] The government itself recognized within the official circles that the policy was formulated generally in line with that of the Bombay Plan.[115] The policy was based on the constitution of 1935 under which industry was a provincial subject. The Government of India in its policy statement declared its intention to bring important industries, 'in which a common policy was desirable' under central control. These included twenty basic industries, such as iron and steel, machines, plants and tools, electricals, chemicals, transport, cement etc. and some consumer goods industries like textiles, sugar, automobiles, etc. In brief, almost the entire large-scale industry was to be brought under central control. The statement also accepted the suggestions mooted in the Bombay Plan on the role of the state in industrial enterprise. The ordnance factories, public utilities and railways were already largely state-owned. The government envisaged direct state investment in other 'basic industries of national importance' in which adequate private capital was not forthcoming. Listed among these were aircraft, automobiles and tractors, chemicals and dyes, iron and steel, prime movers, transport vehicles, electrical machinery, machine tools, electro-chemical and non-ferrous metals. It contemplated to nationalize certain industries in which the 'tax element' predominated the profit element. All other industries were to be left to private enterprise under varying degrees of state control. Some industries such as shipbuilding and manufacture of locomotives and boilers would be run by the state as well as by private capitalists. In some other areas the government favoured public corporations or private agencies.

Overall industrial development would be controlled, according to the policy statement, by introducing the system of industrial licence except for small industrial enterprises. Any new industry beyond a certain capital value would require licence from the government to operate. This would enable the government to distribute industries all over the country and check over-concentration in certain locations. Further state control for a planned development was to be achieved through capital issues by the government to 'secure balanced investment in Industry, Agriculture and Social Services'. The policy also declared the government's intention to introduce legislation for better working conditions and a fair wage to workers. Excess profit made through monopoly was to be eliminated.

The government acknowledged its responsibility for developing infrastructural prerequisities for industrial progress. It envisaged augmentation of transport and irrigation facilities and development of electrical power and universal resources. It also promised to assist industries by providing loan facilities, guaranteeing a minimum dividend on capital in special cases to meet revenue losses for a fixed number of years, enhancing research facilities in universities and procuring capital goods from abroad.[116]

This brief review of the statement of Industrial Policy of 1945 would enable us to discern that not only was the policy in line with the strategy set out in the Bombay Plan, but it remained the basis on which virtually all subsequent industrial policies of post-independence India were formulated. The policy statement by Jawaharlal Nehru's government in 1956, just before the Second Five-Year Plan was launched, has unambiguous similarities with this statement of 1945. In other words, the Bombay Plan had defined and set the limits of the domain of the state in the socio-economic field of the country, particularly as far as the industrial development was concerned – and industrialism was seen as the remedy by the Indian state for all its economic ills.

Although the business leaders collaborated with the state in the 1940s and they were greatly involved in formulating plan strategies by the state during the period, it does not mean that the collaboration was total. The class was fighting for its space. To the extent it could benefit from the association with the crises-ridden state of the period, it collaborated. But it was also firm in fighting for its own interest whenever the government's economic policies clashed with its own perception. Ardeshir Dalal who was the representative of this class in the viceroy's council, continued to launch battles on behalf of his peers. On issues like commercial safeguard clauses of the act of 1935 and use of sterling and dollar balances, the business community was at loggerheads with the government. These matters pointed to inherent contradictions between the interest of indigenous capitalist class and that of the imperialist regime in India.

The commercial safeguard clauses were incorporated in the constitution of 1935 to protect the British business houses operating in India. The general effect of these provisions was that any law which purported to give special facilities to Indian nationals as against British subjects domiciled in the UK would be infructuous. The sections provided full protection to British colonial interest in exploiting the Indian market.[117] The commercial safeguards became crucial in 1944-45 when the Government of India tried to define the industrial policy for India. Dalal, soon after he became member of the planning and development department, took up the issue with Wavell. Dalal demanded that the new industrial development should be financed and controlled by Indians as far as possible. The government acquiesced in principle – after a long-drawn battle with the business representatives – but as the law stood, it could not discriminate against any British company.[118] Dalal wanted to discuss the problems with British officials and industrialists to find a solution. The viceroy's council agreed with Dalal's proposal and later sent him to Britain with a white paper on the issue. The British government headed by Churchill, however, paid no need to Dalal's pleas and he returned to India empty-handed. This, together with the British stand on the use of sterling balances in favour of India led to Dalal's resignation from the council in January 1946.[119]

The events around the sterling balances also revealed the contradiction inherent in the relations between the imperial government and the Indian business interests. Not only had India accumulated a large sterling balance reserve, it also had a very favourable balance of trade with the United States during the war. Indian industrialists had pinned their hopes on the possibility of using these surpluses to import capital goods necessary for industrial development. But these hopes clashed with the interests of the metropolitan country. For, the government of the United Kingdom was far from eager to part with these balances for the development of a colonial economy. As far as India's dollar earnings were concerned, the Government of India was forced to contribute it to the Empire Dollar Pool[120] created by the British government for the purchase of essential war materials. As a result, although India had a net earning of three hundred million dollars during the period from September 1939 to March 1945,[121] it received back only forty million dollars out of the pool. The sterling balance to the credit of India amounted to about 1,515 million pounds by the end of March 1945. It was not only that Britain had utilized India's dollar earning during the war, it also made every effort to repudiate India's sterling balances. Churchill and his supporters used all kinds of arguments to disown this debt to India.[122]

Any programme of post-war industrialization depended entirely on the availability of the sterling balance and dollar earnings to India. After the war, when it became obvious that Britain was not ready to repay the debts to India in the near future,[123] the Government of India had to give up its early enthusiasm over the question of industrial development. It opted for 'short-term' plans to develop irrigation and power and other non-industrial activities. The abandonment of the ideas of industrialization naturally made the Indian industrialists unhappy. FICCI renewed its tirade against the government's policies, Dalal resigned and the wartime *entente* between the Indian business and the government was over. The former had, however, by that time left its indelible mark upon the plan programmes of the Indian state.

IV

After the war, the government's attitude towards the Indian capitalists hardened and they found their dreams of industrial planning shattered. There was an acute shortage of capital goods but the imperial power refused to allow India to import necessary machinery from abroad. The argument put forward was that capital was more necessary to revitalize British and other European economies devastated by the war.[124] The 'short-term' plans that the Government of India adopted during 1945-46, contained hardly any industrial programme. Irrigation had hydro power projects were given priority. When the central and provincial plans were estimated in 1945, expenditure under industries amounted to only Rs. 360 million out of a total estimated expenditure of Rs. 13,450 million. Of these 360 million rupees, 100 million represented expenditure on Sindri Fertilizers and five million were for the expansion of Hindustan Aircraft at Bangalore – both central schemes. The rest was made up of provincial expenditure which was confined to provision of technical training and the development of cottage and small-scale industries. The estimate of provincial expenditure for industry was actually less than 3 per cent of the total expenditure on all provincial plans.[125]

It would be inaccurate to conclude from the above that the government had decided to leave the issue of industrial development in the hands of private capitalists. It had, in fact, full control over expansion of private investment in India through measures introduced during the war : licensing for new industries or for the expansion of old ones, import-export restrictions, regulations for capital issue, and similar other decisions. Birla, in early 1946, bitterly criticized the government for not taking any positive action for industrial development and cited evidence to show that it was deliberately trying to thwart all initiatives for industrialization through these controls.[126] G.L. Mehta joined Birla in this criticism. Citing debates in the legislative assembly, he showed that between January 1945 and June 1946 the government had released more than thirty-nine crore rupees in dollar resources for industrial imports, but out of these only 7.29 crore rupees were made available for import of capital goods, while more than thirty-two crores were earmarked for consumer goods. (British business houses enjoyed the benefit).[127]

The *entente* thus ended. The new attitude of the state was a bitter experience for the Indian capitalists. They also appeared to have learnt their lesson. Thus, when Attlee's government declared the British intention to leave India by 1948 and Wavell installed an Interim Government at the centre comprising a coalition of the Congress and the Muslim League, the Indian bourgeoisie was much more cautious in its approach towards this new government.

The Interim Government was first formed by the Congress alone in September 1946; the Muslim League joined it only in November of that year. Jawaharlal Nehru's very first act as its head was to institute an advisory planning board to go into the question of planning and to suggest to the government ways and means to form a planning commission in the near future. This board did not include any business representative in it. This is not, however, surprising. The collaboration between the Indian capitalists and the British government during the war had irked many a Congress leader including Nehru. There was also popular discontent against the way Indian business had taken to profiteering during and after the war. The Congress had also mobilized this discontent to its favour during the election campaign. Nehru is on record promising, during his election campaign in Calcutta, to hang the black-marketeers on the nearest lamp-posts. Given this kind of volatile atmosphere, the Congress could neither invite business representatives to join in its governmental programmes, nor could the capitalists show any interest. This does not, however, mean that the Indian bourgeoisie surrendered before the emerging state. On the contrary, it now organized itself even more strongly to confront the infant state.

This was most evident in the events that occurred around the budget proposal by Liaqat Ali Khan, the finance minister of the coalition Interim Government.[128] When Liaqat introduced high tax rates on big business to curtail the latter's monopoly power, the entire Indian business world was mobilized by its leaders to stand up against the budget. The stock-markets were closed down for days; the established press went all out to condemn the budget; important leaders of the Congress, like Vallabhbhai Patel and Rajegopalachari branded the budget as 'communal' and even Jawaharlal Nehru was forced to backtrack from his early support to it. In short, the budget was spiked due to the immense pressure that the Indian business community mounted against it within and outside the Congress and the government. Nehru had to lose many a friend on this issue. The entire left block within the Congress had supported this budget; it felt cheated by Nehru's volte-face in favour of big business. In fact, when the Congress Socialists broke away from the party to form the Socialist Party of India, the most significant accusation they made against the Congress, and Nehru in particular, was the latter's support to big business.[129] The apparent over-reaction of the Indian bourgeoisie against Liaqat's budget may be regarded as only a pre-emptive move by the former against the attempt of the emerging state to establish control over it. The budget itself was inconsequential. Matthai had in fact pointed out during the debate that followed over the issue that the proposed tax burden was less than that of the previous year.[130]

From 1946 onwards the business community could no more work

'from inside'. As a result, the methods that the class would adopt to influence the state would be through exerting pressure and lobbying. It is significant that both Birla and Tata had gone to Delhi to convince the Congress high command of the necessity to kill Liaqat's budget. The tactics appeared to have worked. Not only was the budget watered down, the new state's attitude to the community also became quite submissive. At a time when the new government faced difficulties on all fronts, non-cooperation from the business community added to its woes. Production in the existing industries went down and the capitalists went for an 'investment strike' to force the government to come out with a definite promise not to nationalize any existing industry.

As in the case of Liaqat's budget, the events around the nationaliization controversy indicate that it was a proxy fight. The idea of nationalizing large industries was mooted by the left within the Congress in 1946 during the election campaigns. The advisory planning board had, however, tried to allay the fear of large-scale nationalization in the near future by stating clearly that the industries to be nationalized would include, apart from defence industries, coal, mineral oils, iron and steel, motor and air and river transport and 'any industry where private capital was reluctant to invest'.[131] As if this were not enough, Nehru's government immediately after assuming power gave even more categorical assurance against nationalization, as we shall see later.

The socio-political aftermath of the partition delayed Nehru's and the bourgeoisie's dream of a planned economy. The National Planning Commission could not be constituted before 1950. The intervening period, 1947-49, witnessed the pattern of economic policies to be pursued in future by the state in India. These policies followed very closely the trends set at the time of the Interim Government when the Congress, as we have noticed, openly sided with the Indian bourgeoisie against the economic and fiscal policies proposed by the Muslim League leader in the cabinet. Unable to build up a capital-goods base, the Indian bourgeoisie wanted the state to intervene in the sphere of 'basic' or 'key' industries, leaving the rest of the market free for private enterprise. As the Congress leadership was not in a position to gear the state activity to fulfil the task of industrializing the economy, it more than compensated the capitalist class by opening up the consumer goods market in an unrestricted manner.

This is clear from the fact that one of the first acts of the Congress government after independence was to withdraw all controls over the consumer goods market. Many of the wartime controls had been retained by the British government to facilitate stabilization of the economy. Cotton, jute, major cereals, oil and oilseeds, and sugar were the main items the prices of which were fixed by the government. The distribution of essential commodities like cloth and food were also controlled by the state. Soon after independence, in August 1947, the new government appointed a foodgrains policy committee under the chairmanship of P. Thakurdas, superseding the commodity prices board set up by Liaqat Ali Khan a few months earlier.[132] In December 1947 sugar was decontrolled, followed by foodgrains in January 1948 and textiles a few months later. The government also granted liberal increases in the controlled prices of iron and steel in January 1948 itself.[133]

On the question of nationalization Nehru was categorical. 'Far too much attention is often paid to acquiring existing industries than to the building of new industries by the State or under state control', he said in his speech at the tripartite industrial conference in Delhi in December 1947. 'It seems to me a far better approach to the problem for the State to concentrate more and more on new industries of the latest type and to control them in a large measure instead of merely trying to get hold of something which exists'.[134] Again in 1949, he explained to the FICCI that the government's declaration that it 'would not touch' the basic and key industries for ten years, 'did not mean that [it] would necessarily touch them after the ten-year period'.[135] Sardar Patel also assured the capitalists that there would be no nationalization in the foreseeable future. 'Take it from me', he said, 'if anyone talks of nationalization, it is only for the sake of leadership'.[136]

Thus, the bogey of nationalization raised by big business could not have been from a genuine fear. Big industrialists like J.R.D. Tata were confident that the government would not go for any programme of nationalization of the existing industries. They were also aware that if they were to expand their production capacity, they would benefit from the unlikely eventuality of nationalization, simply because the increased market value of the assets of the company would increase the compensation owing to them.[137] All the same, big business wanted to ensure that the state would not 'touch' them. It was, in fact, aiming at establishing a new equation with the new state.

The labours of big business bore immediate fruit. In 1948 the independent Government of India published its first Industrial Policy Resolution.[138] If we compare this with the Industrial Policy Statement of 1945, an interesting difference emerges. The 1945 document had identified certain basic industries – including aircraft, automobiles and tractors, chemicals and dyes, iron and steel, prime movers, transport vehicles, electrical machinery, machine tools, electro-chemicals and non-ferrous metals – which might be nationalized in the absence of sufficient private investment in the field. It had also comtemplated nationalizing defence, railways and public utilities industries. The resolution of 1948, on the other hand, chose only six industries – coal, iron and steel, aircraft, shipbuilding, mineral oils and telephone, telegraph etc. – apart from defence, railways and public utilities, where the new undertakings might be the exclusive responsibility of the state. The resolution also declared that the government had 'decided to let existing undertakings in these fields develop for a period of ten years' during which period they would be allowed 'all facilities for efficient working and reasonable expansion'. At the end of this period, the matter would be 'reviewed and a decision taken, in the light of circumstances obtaining at the time'. If it was decided that the state should acquire any unit, the fundamental rights guaranteed by the constitution would be observed and compensation would be awarded on a 'fair and equitable basis'.[139]

It is not only that the resolution of 1948 was more liberal towards private enterprise than envisaged by the plan programmes of the mid-1940s. Even the advisory planning board set up by the Nehru government itself in 1946 had recommended stricter controls over the private sector.[140] The scrupulous avoidance of the word 'nationalization' in the entire body of the 1948 resolution also seems significant. Actually, the word became almost a taboo in official circles and the leaders of the Congress went out of their way to assure businessmen that nationalization was not on the cards. We have already referred to Patel's and Nehru's assurances. Further evidence would be superfluous.

The First Five-Year Plan launched in 1951 had nothing much either to enthuse or antagonize the business community. The plan appeared, however, to have succeeded in its objective of stabilizing the economy, raising the hopes of the Nehruvian 'socialists' to venture on industrialization more vigorously during the next five years. The Second Plan launched with the bold claim of ushering in a socialist pattern of society, was preceded by a new Industrial Policy Resolution (1956). This plan has been criticized by many a scholar from different angles of vision and the striking similarities between its objectives and those of the Bombay Plan have caught the attention of at least one leftist commentator.[141] We may also add that the Industrial Policy Resolution of 1956 almost replicated the first industrial policy formulated by the alien Government of India in 1945.

The 1956 resolution classified industries in three categories. The first, shown in schedule A, consisted of industries for the future development of which the state would accept exclusive 'responsibility'. Railways and air transport, arms and ammunition and atomic energy were to be developed as central monopolies. This did not, however, foreclose the expansion of the existing privately owned units or 'the possibility of the State securing the cooperation of private enterprise in the establishment of new units' when the 'national interests' would so require. In cases where the cooperation of the private enterprise would be sought, state control would be exercised 'either through majority participation in the capital or otherwise'. Under schedule B were listed those industries where both the state and private enterprise would operate side by side, the former establishing new undertakings 'with a view to accelerating their future development'. All the remaining industries would fall under the third category, the development of which was to be 'undertaken ordinarily through the initiative and enterprise of the private sector, though it [would] be open to the State to start any industry in this category'. The resolution declared, however, that 'it [would] be the policy of the State to facilitate and encourage the development of these industries [under the third category] in the private sector, in accordance with the programmes formulated in successive Five-Year Plans'. Thus we find that if the document of 1956 differed from that of 1945 at all, it did so to ensure the position of private enterprise more securely.

We have been concerned in this paper with the attitude of the Indian business community towards planning. The endeavour has been also to produce a discourse on the march of capital in India. We have, however, confined ourselves to analysing only one aspect of the purposes of this march – to define the role of the state to facilitate the development of indigenous capital. A more complete study would require the analysis of agrarian policies, among other things, as well.

It is often said that a bourgeois revolution calls for drastic agrarian reforms and that the failure of the Indian bourgeoisie to lead the nation towards such a reform indicates its weakness. Unless there is an implicit assumption of a missionary role for the class, this claim appears to be untenable. Capitalism necessitated changing the feudal structure of society to facilitate its development. It called for commoditization of the life of society. In India, the British had broken the feudal bondage over labour mobility, if there was any, through their policies and rules long before Indian industrial capital was born. Again, almost the entire production system was brought under the aegis of commodity production through the forced commercialization of agriculture long before the beginnings of modern industry.

The growth of Indian capital was hindered not so much because of the semi-feudal land relations but because of the alien rule which would not allow the capital market and the product market to develop. The late industrializers, therefore, required a strong state working on their behalf. Viewed in this manner, agrarian reform was not on the agenda. There was, however, a link between agriculture and industry. Birla's warning regarding the 'purchasing power' of the masses was pointer to the fact that capital was aware of the shortcomings of a backward agriculture. But this had to be weighed against the possible danger of unleashing the forces which might destroy capital altogether – the fear of 'Bolshevism'. Thus the march of capital could only be in the way of a 'passive revolution'. Technology would solve the problem of agricultural productivity.

The strength of Indian capitalism lay in its ability to identify its own needs very early in its development and in formulating a broad overall perspective to influence the course that the country would adopt. The idea of planning was central to this vision of the future. To the extent the plans in India would fulfil the demands of the class, the capitalists lent their support to it. Whenever the state made any effort to transgress the limits the class set for it, the bourgeoisie took necessary steps to check this transgression or redefine the limits. The tussle goes on.

Notes

1. A.H. Hanson, *The Process of Planning: A Study of India's Five Year Plans, 1950-64* (Oxford 1966),pp. 27-49.

2. R. Chattopadhyay, 'An Early British Government Initiative in the Genesis of Indian Planning', *Economic and Political Weekly*, XXII-5, (31 January 1987), pp. PE 19-PE 29.

3. For a detailed exposition of the *laissez-faire* policy of the Government of India, see S. Bhattacharya, 'Laissez-faire in India', *The Indian Economic and Social History Review*, II (1965), pp. 1-22.

4. Y.P. Verma, *Growth of Protection in India* (Delhi 1974),p.36.

5. Amiya Kumar Bagchi, *Private Investment in India, 1900-1939* (Cambridge 1972), pp.229-31.

6. Bipan Chandra, *The Rise and Growth of Economic Nationalism in India* (New Delhi 1966), p.123.

7. Jogesh Chandra Bagal, *Hindu Melar Itibritta* (Calcutta 1968), p. 3.

8. Sumit Sarkar, *The Swadeshi Movement in Bengal, 1903-1908* (New Delhi), p.33.

9. Ibid., ch.3.

10. For a critique of Gandhi's *Hind Swaraj*, see Partha Chatterjee, 'Gandhi and the Critique of Civil Society', in Ranajit Guha (ed.), *Subaltern Studies* (New Delhi 1984), vol.III, p. 153-195.

11. R.C. Dutt, *Economic History of India in the Victorian Age* (London 1903).

12. Dadabhai Naoroji, *Poverty and Un-British Rule in India* (London 1901).

13. M.G. Ranade, *Essays on Indian Economics* (Bombay 1899), pp. 180-94.

14. Quoted in Chandra, *Economic Nationalism*(n.6),p. 725.

15. G.V. Joshi, *Writings and Speeches* (Poona 1912), p.743.

16. Ranade, *Essays* (n.13), p. 31.

17. Ibid., p.32.

18. J.N. Gupta, *Life and Work of R.C. Dutt* (London 1911), p. 402.

19. See, for example, Ranade's speeches on 'Emancipation of Serfs in Russia' and 'Prussian Land Legislation and the Bengal Tenancy Bill' in his *Essays* (n.13).

20. Quoted in Chandra, *Economic Nationalism* (n.6), p. 120.

21. Quoted in ibid., p. 114.

22. Govt. of India, *Report of the Indian Industrial Commission* 1916-1918 (Delhi 1918), p. 2.

23. Verma, *Growth of Protection* (n.4), p. 32.

24. A.G. Clow, *The State and Industry* (Calcutta 1928), p.8.

25. Verma, *Growth of Protection* (n.4), p.32.

26. H.L. Day, *The Indian Tariff Problems in Relation to Industry and Taxation* (London 1921), p.160.

27. Vera Anstay, *The Economic Development of India* (London 1957), p. 262.

28. Verma, *Growth of Protection*(n.4), p.33.

29. P.P. Pillai, *Economic Conditions in India* (London 1925), p.40.

30. Ibid.

31. K.T. Shah, *Trade, Tariffs and Transport in India* (London 1923), p.257.

32. Ibid., p.263.

33. M. Visvesvaraiya, *Memoirs of My Working Life*, (New Delhi 1960).

34. M. Visvesvaraiya, *Reconstructing Indian Economy* (London 1920).

35. Ibid., pp. 133-4.

36. P.K. Gopalakrishnan, *Development of Economic Ideas in India, 1880-1950* (New Delhi 1959), p.183.

37. Ibid., p.154.

38. See e.g. S.N. Agarwal, *Socialism in Indian Planning* (Bombay 1964), ch. II.

39. Gandhi to Vallabhbhai Patel, 19 August 1934 and 'before September 5' 1934 in Government of India, *Collected Works of Mahatma Gandhi* (New Delhi 1974), vol. LVIII, p. 330. See also his statement to the Press dated 17 September 1934 in ibid., vol. LIX, pp. 3-4.

40. See R. Chattopadhyay, 'An Early British Initiative' (n.2), for a detailed discussion on the first British effort.

41. Ibid., p. PE 22.

42. G.D. Birla, *Indian Prosperity: A Plea for Planning* (published as a booklet by FICCI, 1934).

43. FICCI, Presidential Address of Mr. N.R. Sarkar at the Annual General Meeting 1934, Walchand Hirachand Papers, file no.6(a) in Nehru Memorial Museum and Library, New Delhi.

44. M. Visvesvaraiya, *Planned Economy for India* (Bangalore 1934), p. 282.

45. Birla, *Indian Prosperity* (n.42), p. 12.

46. Ibid., p.19.

47. Sarkar's *Presidential Address* (n.43), p.18.

48. Birla, *Indian Prosperity* (n.42), p.16.

49. S.C. Mitter, *A Recovery Plan for Bengal* (Calcutta 1934), p. 12.

50. Visvesvaraiya, *Planned Economy* (n.44), p. 7.

51. Ibid., p.50.

52. Mitter, *A Recovery Plan* (n.49), p.9.

53. Birla, *Indian Prosperity* (n.42), p.20.

54. Sarkar's Presidential Address (n.43), p.16.

55. A.M. Zaidi and S.G. Zaidi (eds.), *The Encyclopaedia of Indian National Congress*, hereafter ENC (Delhi 1981), vol. XI, p. 291.

56. Quoted in *National Planning Committee: A Booklet* (hereafter NPCB), published by K.T. Shah, hon. gen. secretary of the National Planning Committee, from Bombay (n.d), p.9. This booklet was later known as the Red Book in NPC parlance.

57. Jawaharlal Nehru Papers, hereafter JNP, vol. II, file no. 135/I (documents relating to the National Planning Committee), in Nehru Memorial Museum and Library, New Delhi.

58. NPCB, p.12.

59. Jawaharlal Nehru, *The Discovery of India* (London 1951), p. 373.

60. 'Minutes of the Proceedings of the NPC', dated 18 December 1938 in JNP, vol. II, file no. 135/I.

61. 'Chairman's Memorandum to all the Members of the NPC' dated 12 February 1940 in ibid., 135/III.

62. We have already referred to this Red Book (n.56). Page 102 of this Red Book contained a tentative list of defence industries, key industries and the public utilities which are reproduced below.

Defence Industries

1. Fire arms (land, air and marine) and their parts
2. Munitions, cartidges, explosives, shells, torpedoes, etc.
3. Tanks and armoured cars and other forms of mechanical equipment especially designed for military purposes
4. Warships of all types including submarines
5. Military aircraft of all kinds
6. Gases for warfare and gas-masks.

Key Industries

1. Power - Hydro and thermal (generator)
2. Fuel, coal and fuel wood, mineral oil, power alcohol, natural gases

3. Metals, ferrous and important non-ferrous including mining of ore for them
4. Industries for the making of machine tools
5. Industries for the making of machinery and machinery parts
6. Heavy engineering industries for the building of ships, locomotives, wagons, automobiles, aircraft and the like (vital)
7. Instruments and apparatus - commercial, industrial and scientific (standards)
8. Chemicals, heavy chemicals, fine chemicals including dyes (some vital), fertilizers and refractories.

Public Utilities

1. Distribution of electricity, gas and other forms of energy
2. Public transport and communication services
3. Water supply
4. Sanitation.

Banking and Insurance were reserved for consideration later.

63. 'Minutes of Dissent by Mr. A.D. Shroff, etc.' dated 13 March 1940 in Purshotamdas Thakurdas Papers (PTP), file no.223, Nehru Memorial Museum and Library, New Delhi.

64. 'Minutes of the Proceedings of the NPC' dated 24 June 1940 in JNP, vol. II, file no. 135/III.

65. K.T. Shah to P. Thakurdas, 30 April 1941 in PTP, file no. 220/II.

66. The NPC series was published by Vora & Co. from Bombay in 1948.

67. League of Nations, *The Transition from War to Peace Economics: Report of the Delegation on Economic Depression,* (Geneva 1943), pt I, passim.

68. 'Press Note' by Government of India, Commerce Department, 24 June 1941, on 'Post-War Reconstruction' in PTP, file no. 260.

69. Secretary to the Government of India to the Secretary, FICCI, 27 March 1943 in ibid.

70. Amiya K. Bagchi, 'Private Investment and Partial Planning in India' (unpublished Ph.D. thesis, Cambridge, 1963), ch. IV. See also Bipan Chandra, 'Colonialism and Modernization' in his *Nationalism and Colonialism in Modern India* (Delhi 1979), 1-37.

71. Note by Wavell on interview with G.D. Birla, 6 March 1944, in N. Mansergh (ed.), *India: The Transfer of Power, 1942-1947,* hereafter TOP (London, 1973), vol. IV, doc. 411.

72. Wavell to Amery, 14 March 1944, in ibid., doc. 430.

73. Ibid., vol. II, doc. 678.

74. 'Proceedings of the first Meeting of the Committee' held on 11 December 1942, in PTP, file no. 291.

75. Tata to Thakurdas, 30 November 1942 in ibid.

76. S.C. Majumdar to Thakurdas, 10 March 1943 in ibid.

77. Amery to Linlithgow, 2 March 1943, TOP, vol. III, doc. 556.

78. See news report 'Indian Industry and Central Government, Breach of Faith Alleged', *Times of India (Bombay)*, 22 December 1942.

79. Govt. of India, Ministry of Commerce, *Handbook on Import of Trade Control*, (Delhi 1950); also Bagchi, 'Private Investment and Partial Planning in India' (n.70).

80. S.C. Majumdar to Thakurdas, 3 March 1943 in PTP, file no. 291.

81. Ibid. Majumdar appears to have been in touch with Thakurdas also before the constitution of the committee regarding post-war reconstruction and planning in India. See 'A Note on Post-War Reconstruction and Post-War Planning as it Affects India' by S.C. Majumdar, 28 October 1942 in PTP, file no. 260.

82. 'Proceedings of the Meeting of the Committee on Post-War Economic Development', 11 December 1942, in PTP, file no. 291.

83. Ibid.

84. J. Matthai to Thakurdas, 8 December 1943, ibid.

85. 'Notes by Dr. P.S. Lokanathan', 17 December 1943, ibid.

86. See Thakurdas to Matthai, 13 December 1943 and G.D. Birla to Matthai, 3 January 1944, ibid.

87. N. Salivati of the *Hindu,* to Thakurdas, 20 January 1944, ibid.

88. Ibid.

89. F. James to Tata, 27 January 1944, ibid.

90. Wavell to Amery, 25 January 1944, TOP, vol. IV, doc.344.

91. Note by the Secretary, Finance, on Bombay Plan, 4 February 1944 in Government of India, Finance, Planning Branch I, file no. 13(2)-P/44 of 1945, National Archives of India, New Delhi.

92. Ibid., passim.

93. T.E. Gregory's note, 21 March 1944 in ibid.

94. Confidential Circular to 'All Directors of the Central Board of the Reserve Bank of India' from the Secretary, R.B.I. ref.no. Sy.26(a), 27 January 1944 in ibid.

95. Wavell to Amery, 12 January 1944, TOP, vol. IV, doc. 324.

96. 'Secret Brief for the use of Honourable Members at the meeting with the representatives of the Bombay Plan', 14 April 1944, Government of India, Finance (n.91).

97. Srivastava to Thakurdas, 30 March 1944 in PTP, file no. 260.

98. 'Brief Record of an informal conference with the authors of 'A Plan of Economic Development for India', 20 April 1944, ibid.

99. Ibid., p.2.

100. R.J. Moore, *Crisis of Indian Unity, 1917-1940* (Oxford 1974), ch. 7.

101. 'Brief Record' (n.98), p.3.

102. Ibid.

103. See Thakurdas et al., *A Brief Memorandum, . . .* (Bombay 1944).

104. 'Brief Record' (n.98), pp. 4-5.

105. Ibid., p.4.

106. See note 64 above.

107. 'Brief Record' (n.98),p.5.

108. Ibid.

109. 'Minutes of the NPC' (n.60).

110. Thakurdas et al., *Brief Memorandum* (n.103), pp.30-1.

111. 'Brief Record' (n.98), p.6.

112. The two booklets were combinedly published as 'A Penguin Special' in 1945 under the title : *Memorandum Outlining a Plan of Economic Development for India.*

113. Interested readers may see R. Chattopadhyay 'The Idea of Planning in India 1930-1951' (Ph.D. Thesis, Australian National university, Canbera, 1985), ch. V.

114. The Statement of the Industrial Policy is reproduced in Planning and Development Department, file no. 8(5)-P/45, appendix III, National Archives of India, New Delhi.

115. Dalal's speech in ibid., file no. 8(1)-P/45, para 11.

116. Ibid., para 8.

117. Government of India Act 1935 (Delhi 1935).

118. Wavell to Amery, 2 January 1945, in TOP, vol. V, doc.178.

119. Wavell to Pethick-Lawrence, 9 December 1945, ibid., vol. VI, doc. 276.

120. Reserve Bank of India, *History of the Reserve Bank of India* (Bombay 1970), p.369.

121. Ibid., p.373.

122. Ibid., pp.375-6.

123. TOP vol.V., doc. 469.

124. Ibid.

125. 'Summary of the Five-Year Plans (Industries) in Government of India, Finance, Planning Branch I, file no. 12(12)- PI/46, National Archices of India, New Delhi.

126. See G.D. Birla, *A Critique of Government Planning* (Speech delivered at the nineteenth Annual Session of the FICCI); *FICCI Annual Report* (Delhi 1946).

127. G.L. Mehta's Speech in ibid.

128. R. Chattopadhyay, 'Liaqat Ali Khan's Budget of 1947-48: The Tryst with Destiny' in *Social Scientist*, XVI-6, 7 (June-July 1988), pp. 77-89 for a detailed study on this issue.

129. *Nasik Report* - the booklet giving a comprehensive report of the Socialist party's sixth conference at Nasik held in March 1948 (published by the party from Bombay 1948).

130. Chattopadhyay, 'Liaquat Ali Khan's Budget' (n.128), p.88.

131. Government of India, *Report of the Advisory Planning Board* (Delhi 1946), p. 15.

132. N.V. Sovani, *Planning of Post-War Economic Development in India* (Poona 1951), p. 60.

133. D.R. Gadgil's foreword in N.V. Sovani, *Post War Inflation in India* (Poona 1949), p. vii.

134. See Nehru's Speech, 'Production the First Essential' in Government of India, *Independence and After* (Delhi 1949), pp. 153-4.

135. M. Kidron, *Foreign Investment in India* (London 1965), p.85.

136. Ibid., p.97.

137. Amiya K. Bagchi, *'Private Investment and Partial Planning in* India' (n.70), p. 106.

138. For details of this resolution, see Government of India, *Report of the Fiscal Commission, 1949-50,* vol.I, appendix III, pp. 409-15.

139. Ibid., p.410.

140. *Report of the Advisory Planning Board* (n.132), p. 15.

141. See E.M.S. Namboodiripad, *Economics and Politics of India's Socialistic Pattern* (Delhi, 1966), pp. 113-21.

Bibliography

Abraham, Meera, *Two Medieval Merchant Guilds of South India* (Delhi, 1988).

Adhya, G.L., *Early Indian Economics: Studies in the Economic Life of Northern and Western India, c.1200 B.C.- 300 A.D.* (Bombay, 1966).

Aggarwal, S.N., *Socialism in Indian Planning* (Bombay, 1964).

Ahmed, R., *The Bengal Muslims, 1871-1906: A Quest for Identity* (Delhi, 1981).

Alam, Muzaffar, *The Crisis of Empire in Mughal North India: Awadh and the Punjab, 1707-48* (Delhi, 1986).

Ali, Athar M., *The Mughal Nobility Under Aurangzeb* (Bombay,1970).

Ali, C.M., *The Emergence of Pakistan* (New York, 1967).

Ali, Yusuf, *Ahwal-i-Mahabat Jang*, translated by Jadunath Sarkar in *Bengal Nawabs* (Calcutta, 1952).

Ambirajan, S., and R. Rajagopalan, "Science: Teacher, Servant or Master?", *Bulletin of the Madras Institute of Development Studies*, XVI (1986).

Amin, B.D., *The Rise and Growth of the Alembic Chemical Works* (Baroda, 1939).

Anstey, Vera, *The Economic Development of India* (London, 1957).

Appadorai, A., *Economic Conditions in Southern India, 1100-1500 A.D.* (Madras, 1936).

Arasaratnam, S., "The Coromandel-South East Asia Trade, 1650-1740", *Journal of Asian History*, XVIII (1984).

* Only books and articles cited in this volume are listed here. Primary documentary sources have been by and large left out.

——," India and Indian Ocean: The Seventeenth Century", in *India and the Indian Ocean, 1500-1800*, edited by Ashin Das Gupta and M.N.Pearson (Calcutta, 1987).

Arnold, D., *The Congress in Tamilnadu*, (Delhi, 1977).

Audholia, B.S. and D.Tripathi (eds.), Gleanings from Gandhian Thought (Jabalpur, 1959).

Azad, M.A.K., *India Wins Freedom* (Delhi, 1959).

Baddeley, T.V., "Industrial Disputes and Their Settlement", *Indian Textile Journal: Jubilee Souvenir, 1890-1940* (Bombay, 1940).

Bagal, Jogesh Chandra, *Hindu Melar Itibritta* (Calcutta, 1968).

Bagchi, Amiya K., Private Investment and Partial Planning in India (Unpublished Ph.D. thesis, University of Cambridge, Cambridge, 1963).

——,"European and Indian Entrepreneurship in India, 1900-1930", in *Elites in South Asia*, edited by S.N.Mukherjee and E. Leach (Cambridge, 1970).

——, *Private Investment in India, 1900-1939* (Cambridge, 1972).

——, "Reflections on Patterns of Regional Growth in India during the Period of British Rule", *Bengal Past and Present*, XCV (1976).

——, *The Evolution of the State Bank of India: The Roots, 1806-1876* (Bombay, 1987).

Bajaj, Ramkrishna (ed.), *Patra Vyavahar*, Correspondence of Jamnalal Bajaj in Hindi (Delhi, 1958).

Baker, C.J., and D.A.Washbrook, *South India* (Delhi, 1975).

Balakrishnan, Padma (ed.), *Madras Directory and Who is Who* (Madras, 1947).

Banaji, Jairus, "The Comintern and Indian Nationalism", in *National and Left Movements in India*, edited by K.N.Panikkar (New Delhi, 1980).

Banarsidas, *Ardhkathanaka (Half a Tale)* edited by Mukund Lath (Jaipur, 1981).

Bandhopadhyaya, Kumkum, "Indigenous trade, Finance and Politics-A Study of Patna and its Hinterland, 1757 to 1813", (Unpublished Ph.D. thesis, Calcutta University, 1987).

Basu, S.K., *Industrial Finance in India* (Calcutta, 1950).

Bayly, C.A., "Patrons and Politics in Northern India", *Modern Asian Studies*, VII (1973).

——, *Rulers, Townsmen and Bazaars: North Indian Society in the Age of British Expansion, 1770-1870* (Cambridge, 1983).

——," The Pre-History of Communalism: Religious Conflict in India,

1700-1860", *Modern Asian Studies*, XIX (1985).

Besant, Annie, *How India Wrought for Freedom* (New Delhi, 1975).

Bhagat, Niranjan et al. (eds.), *Tribute to Ethics: Remembering Kasturbhai Lalbhai* (Ahmedabad, 1983).

Bhargava, B.K., *Indigenous Banking in Ancient and Medieval India* (Bombay, 1934).

Bhatia, B.M., *Famines in India (1860-1965)* (Delhi, 1967).

Bhattacharya, S., "Cotton Mills and Spinning Wheels : Swadeshi and the India Capitalist Class, 1920-22", in *National and Left Movements in India*, edited by K.N.Panikkar (New Delhi, 1980).

——, "Laissez-Faire in India", *The Indian Economic and Social History Review.*, II (1965).

Birla, G.D., *Path to Prosperity* (Allahabad, 1950).

——, *In the Shadow of the Mahatma* (Bombay, 1953).

——, *Bapu: A Unique Association* (Bombay, 1977).

——, *Words to Remember* (Bombay, 1983)

Bombay Dying and Manufacturing Co., *Diamond Jubilee, 1879-1939* (Bombay, 1940).

——, *The First Hundred Years, 1879-1979* (Bombay, 1979).

Bombay Millowners' Association, *Centenary Souvenir, 1875-1975* (Bombay, 1979).

Broomfield, J.H., *Elite Conflict in a Plural Society* (Berkeley, 1968).

Broughton, Thomas Dyer, *Letters from a Mahratta Camp during the year 1809* (Calcutta, 1977, reprint).

Brwon, Hilton, *Parrys of Madras* (Madras, 1954).

Buchanan, D.H., *The Development of Capitalist Enterprise in India* (New York, 1934).

Cashman, Richard I., *The Myth of Lokamanya Tilak and Mass Politics in Maharashtra* (Berkeley, 1975).

Charkrabarty, Dipesh, "The Colonial Context of the Bengal Renaissance : A Note on Early Railway Thinking in Bengal", *Indian Economic and Social History Review*, XVI (1974).

Chandra, Bipan, *The Rise and Growth of Economic Nationalism in India* (New Delhi, 1966)

——, *Nationalism and Colonialism in Modern India* (Delhi, 1979).

——, (ed.), *The Indian Left: Critical Appraisals* (New Delhi, 1983).

——, et al., *India's Struggle for Independence, 1857-1947* (New Delhi, 1988)

Chandra, Moti, *Kashi Ka Itihas* (Banaras, 1985).

Chatterjee, Partha, "Gandhi and the Critique of Civil Society" in *Subaltern*

Studies, edited by Ranajit Guha, Vol.III (New Delhi, 1984).
——, *National Thought and the Colonial World : A Derivative Discourse* (Delhi, 1987).
Chattopadhyay, R., "An Early British Initiative in the Genesis of Planning", *Economic and Political Weekly* (Review of Political Economy), XXII-5 (31 January 1987).
——, "Liaquat Ali Khan's Budget of 1947-48 : The Tryst with Destiny", *Social Scientist,* XVI (1988).
——, "The Idea of Planning in India, 1930-1951" (unpublished Ph.D. thesis, Australian National University, Canberra, 1985).
Chaudhari, K.N., *Trade and Civilization in the Indian Ocean: An Economic History from the Rise of Islam to 1750* (Cambridge, 1985).
Chaudhuri, S., "Sirajuddaulah, the English Company and the Plassey Conspiracy", *Indian Historical Review,,* XIII (1986-1987)
——, "Merchants, Companies and Rulers: Bengal in the 18th Century", *Journal of the Economic and Social History of the Orient,* XXXI (1988).
Checkland, Sydney, *The Rise of Industrial Society in England, 1815-1885* (London, 1964).
Clow, A.G., *The State and Industry* (Calcutta, 1928).
Cohn, B.S., "The Initial British Impact on India: A Case Study of the Benares Region", *Journal of Asian Studies,* XIX (1960).
Cooke, C.N., *Rise, Progress and Present Condition of Banking in India* (Calcutta, 1863).
Dalal, A.R., *An Alternative to Pakistan* (Bombay, 1943).
Dalmia, Ramkrishna, *A Short Sketch of the Beginning of My Life and a Guide to Bliss* (New Delhi, 1962).
Das Gupta, A., "The Merchants of Surat, c.1700-1750" in *Elites in South Asia,* edited by S.N. Mukherjee and E. Leach (Cambridge, 1970).
——, *Indian Merchants and the Decline of Surat, 1700-1740,* (Weisbaden, 1979).
——, "Indian Merchants and the Western Indian Ocean: The Early Seventeenth Century" in *Modern Asian Studies,* XIX (1985).
——, and M.N. Pearson (eds.) *India and the Indian Ocean, 1500-1800* (Delhi, 1987).
Davids, T.W. Rhys, *Buddhist India* (London, 1911).
Day, H.L., *The Indian Tariff Problems in Relation to Industry and Taxation* (London, 1921).
Democratic Research Service, *Indian Communist Party Documents, 1930-1956* (Bombay, 1957).

Desai, N.N., *Directory of Ahmedabad Mill Industry, 1929-1956* (Ahmedabad, 1957).

Desouza, F., *The House of Binny* (Madras, 1969).

Dewey, Clive and A.G. Hopkins (eds.), *The Imperial Impact: Studies in the Economic History of Africa and India* (London, 1978).

Dobbin, Christine, *Urban Leadership in Western India: Politics and Communities in Bombay City, 1840-1895* (Oxford, 1972).

Duff, James Grant, *A History of the Mahrattas* (Calcutta, 1912), 3 Vols..

Dutt, R.C., *Economic History of India in the Victorian Age* (London, 1903).

——, *Speeches and Papers on Indian Questions, 1892-1900* (Calcutta, 1904).

Edwardes, S.M., *The Bombay City Police: A Historical Sketch* (London, 1923).

Elwin, Verrier, *The Story of Tata Steel* (Privately printed, 1958).

Fazl, Abul, *Ain-i-Akbari*, trans. H. Blochman (Delhi, 1965, reprint).

Fischer, Louis, *The Life of Mahatma Gandhi* (Bombay, 1983).

Forum of Free Enterprise, *The Bombay Plan and Other Essays* (Bombay, 1968).

Foster, Sir William (ed.), *English Factories in India, 1618-1621* (Oxford, 1906-1927).

Gadgil, D.R., *The Industrial Evolution of India in Recent Times, 1860-1939* (Bombay, 1971).

Gallagher, J., "Congress in Decline: Bengal 1930 to 1939", *Modern Asian Studies*, VII (1973).

Ghosh, Suniti Kumar, *The Indian Big Bourgeoisie* (Calcutta, 1985).

Gopalkrishnan, P.K., *Development of Economic Ideas in India, 1880-1950* (New Delhi, 1959).

Gordon, A.D.D., *Business and Politics: Rising Nationalism and Modernising Economy in Bombay, 1915-1933* (New Delhi, 1978).

Goswami, Omkar, "Then Came the Marwaris: Some Aspects of the Changes in the Pattern of Industrial Control in Eastern India", *Indian Economic and Social History Review*, XXII (1985)

Govt. of Bombay, *Gazetteer of the Bombay Presidency*, vol. II: *Surat and Broach* (Bombay, 1877).

Govt. of India, *Report of the Indian Industrial Commission* (Calcutta, 1918).

——, *History of the Indian Tarriff, 1924-1939* (New Delhi, 1940).

Govt. of U.P., *Freedom Struggle in Uttar Pradesh* (Lucknow, 1957-1960).

Guha, Amlendu, "Comprador Role of Parsi Seths, 1750-1850", *Economic and Political Weekly*, V-58 (28 November 1970).

Gupta, J.N., *Life and Work of R.C. Dutt* (London, 1911).

Gupta, Prem Sagar, *A Short History of the All India Trade Union Congress, 1920-47* (Bombay, 1980).

Habib, Irfan, "Banking in Mughal India", *Contributions to Indian Economic History* edited by T. Raychaudhuri (Calcutta, 1960)

Hanson, A.H., *The Process of Planning: A Study of India's Five Year Plans, 1950-64* (Oxford, 1966).

Hardiman, David, *Peasant Nationalists of Gujarat: Kheda District, 1917-1939* (Delhi, 1981).

Hardinge, Lord, *My Indian Years* (London, 1910).

Hardy, P., *The Muslims of British India* (Cambridge, 1972).

Harris, F.R., *Jamsetji Nusserwanji Tata - A Chronicle of His Life* (Glasgow, 1958).

Harrison, G., *Birds and Company, 1860-1960* (London, 1962).

Hasan, Mushirul (ed.), *Muslims and the Congress: Selected Correspondence of Dr. M.A. Ansari, 1912-1935* (New Delhi, 1979).

I.C.C. Coimbatore, *Silver Jubilee Souvenir, 1920-54* (Madras, 1954).

Indian Bank Ltd., *Golden Jubilee Souvenir, 1907-1957* (Madras, 1958).

Indian Merchants' Chamber, *Platinum Jubilee Commemoration Volume* (Bombay, 1982).

Indian National Congress, *Resolutions on Economic Policy and Allied Matters* (New Delhi, 1969).

Indian National Congress, *Congress Presidential Addresses* (Madras, n.d.).

Indian Textile Journal, *Jubilee Souvenir, 1890-1940* (Bombay, 1940).

Ispahani, M.A.H., "Factors Leading to the Partition of British India", *The Partition of India, Policies and Perspectives, 1935-1947*, edited by C.H. Philips and M.D. Wainwright (London, 1970).

——, *Qaid-e-Azam Jinnah as I Knew Him* (Karachi, 1976).

Jackson, S., *The Sassoons* (London, 1968).

Jalal, A., *The Sole Spokesman: Jinnah, the Muslim League and the Demand for Pakistan* (Cambridge, 1985).

Jalbhoy, R.H., *The Portrait Gallery of Western India* (Bombay, 1886).

Jamal, S.M. (ed.), *Muslim Yearbook of India and Who's Who* (Bombay, 1949).

Jamnadas, Chhagunlal, *The Life of Late Sheth Damodher Thackersey Mooljee, J.P.* (Bombay, 1895).

Jeejeebhoy, J.R.B., *Bribery and Corruption in Bombay* (Bombay, 1952).

Jenkins, Sir Owen, *Memoirs of a Merchant Prince* (London, 1988).

Jog, N.G., *Narottam Morarjee: Architect of Modern Indian Shipping* (Bombay, 1977).

Jones, Stephanie, *One Hundred Years of Overseas Trading: The Origins and Development of the Inchcape Group* (London, 1988).

Josh, Bhagwan, "Nationalism, Third International and Indian Communists", in *The Indian Left: Critical Appraisals* edited by Bipan Chandra (New Delhi, 1983).

——, "Understanding Indian Communists: A Survey of Approaches to the Study of the Communist Movement in India, 1920-47", in *Situating Indian History,* edited by S. Bhattacharya and Romila Thapar (New Delhi, 1986).

——, "The Left and the Indian National Movement, 1934-41" (Ph.D. thesis, Jawaharlal Nehru University, New Delhi, 1987).

——, "The Colonial State and Its Enemies", Presented at the Indo-German Seminar, Centre for Historical Studies, Jawaharlal Nehru University, New Delhi, 10-12 March, 1988.

Joshi, Arun, *Lala Shri Ram* (New Delhi, 1975).

Joshi, G.V., *Writings and Speeches* (Poona, 1912).

Joshi, Shashi, "Nehru and the Emergence of the Left Bloc, 1927-29", in *The Indian Left: Critical Appraisals,* edited by Bipan Chandra (New Delhi, 1983).

——, "The Left and the Indian National Movement, 1920-34," (Ph. D. thesis, Jawaharlal Nehru University, New Delhi, 1984).

Kaji, H.L., *The Life and Speeches of Sir Vithaldas Thackersey* (Bombay, 1934).

Kalekar, Kaka (ed.), *To a Gandhian Capitalist: Correspondence between Mahatma Gandhi and Jamnalal Bajaj* (Wardha, 1951).

Kannangara, A.P., "Indian Millowners and Indian Nationalism Before 1914", *Past and Present,* No. 40 (July 1968).

Karaka, D.F., *History of the Parsis* (London, 1884).

Karnik, V.B., *Strikes in India* (Bombay, 1967).

Khan, Abdul Majid, *The Transition in Bengal, 1756-1775* (Cambridge, 1969).

Khan, Gholam Hossein, *The Seir Mutagherin,* translated by Nota Manus (Delhi, 1986, Reprint).

——, *The Riyaz-us-Salatin,* translated by Abdus Salam (Calcutta, 1902).

Khanolkar, G.D., *Walchand Hirchand: Man, His Times and Achievements* (Bombay, 1969).

Kidron, M., *Foreign Investment in India* (London, 1965).

Kirloskar, S.L., *Cactus and Roses* (Pune, 1982).

Kirloskar, S.V., *Yantrikanchi Yatra* (in Marathi, Kirloskarwadi, 1958).

Kling, B.B., "The Origins of the Managing Agency System", *Journal of Asian Studies*, XXVI (1958).

Kochanek, Stanley, *Business and Politics in India* (Berkeley, 1974).

Kothari, M.L., *Industrial Combinations* (Allahabad, 1967).

Kulkarni, V.B., *History of the Indian Cotton Textile Industry* (Bombay, 1979).

Kumar, Kapil, "Congress-Peasant Relationship in the late 1930s" in *Aspects of Economy, Society and Politics in Modern India*, edited by D.N. Panigrahi (New Delhi, 1984).

——, *Peasants in Revolt* (New Delhi, 1984).

——, "Ideology, Congress and Peasants in 1930s: Class Adjustment or Submission?", *Social Scientist*, XIV (1986).

——, (ed.), *Congress and Classes* (New Delhi, 1988).

Kumar, Ravinder, "From Swaraj to Purna Swaraj: Nationalist Politics in the City of Bombay, 1920-1932", in *Congress and the Raj: Facets of the Indian Struggle, 1917-1947*, edited by D.A. Low

——, *Western India in the Nineteenth Century* (London, 1968).

Kurian, K.M., *The Impact of Foreign Capital on the Indian Economy* (New Delhi, 1966).

Lakhanpal, P.L., *History of the Congress Socialist Party* (Lahore, 1946).

Leonard, Karen, "The Great Firm Theory of the Decline of the Mughal Empire", *Comparative Studies in Society and History*, XXI (1979).

——, "The Hyderabad Political System and its Participants", *The Journal of Asian Studies*, vol. XXX (1971).

Little, J.H., *The House of Jagatseth* (Calcutta, 1967, reprint).

Lokanathan, P., *Industrial Organisation in India* (London, 1935).

Low, D.A., "The Forgotten Bania; Merchant Communities and the Indian National Congress", in *The Indian National Congress: Centenary Highlights* ed. by D. A. Low (Delhi, 1988).

MacPherson, K., *The Muslim Microcosm: Calcutta 1918 to 1935* (Weisbaden, 1974).

Mahadevan, Raman, "The Origin and Growth of Entrepreneurship in the Nattukottai Chetty Community of Tamilnadu" (unpublished M.Phil. thesis, Jawaharlal Nehru University, 1976).

——, "Conflict and Dependence: Some Aspects of the Evolving Relationship Between Indigenous and Foreign Capital in Colonial Madras", paper presented at the Seminar on Indian Industrialisation, 1987, Centre for Development Studies, Trivandrum, June 9-12, 1987.

Manucci, N., *Mogul India or Storia do Mogor*, translated by Sir William Irvine (London, 1907). 4 Vols.

Markovits, Claude, "Indian Business and the Congress Provincial Governments, 1937-39", *Modern Asian Studies,* XV (1981).

——, *Indian Business and Nationalist Politics, 1931-39: The Indigenous Capitalist Class and the Rise of the Congress Party* (Cambridge, 1985).

——, "Les Hommes d'affaires Musulman dans ia Premiere Moitie du XXe Siecle", *Purusartha,* IX (1986).

Marshall, P.J., *East Indian Fortunes: The British in Bengal in the Eighteenth Century* (Oxford, 1976).

Martin, B., *New India, 1885* (Bombay, 1970).

Masani, M.R., *The Communist Party of India* (London, 1954).

Mehrotra, S.R., *Towards India' s Freedom and Partition* (Delhi, 1979).

Mehta, M.J., "Some Aspects of Surat as a Trading Centre", *The Indian Historical Review,* I (1974).

Mehta, S.D., *Cotton Mills of India, 1854-1954* (Bombay, 1954).

Mehta, Shirin, "Social Background of Swadeshi Movement in Gujarat, 1875-1903", *Vidya, IVX* (1981).

Mende, Tibor, *Conversations with Mr. Nehru* (London, 1957).

Mishra,, K.P., *Banaras in Transition, 1738-1795: A Socio-Economic Study* (New Delhi, 1975).

Mitter, S.C., *A Recovery Plan for Bengal* (Calcutta, 1934).

Mody, J.R.P., *Jamsetjee Jeejeebhoy: The First Indian Knight and Baronet, 1783-1859* (Bombay, 1959).

Moore, R.J., *Crisis of Indian Unity, 1917-1940* (Oxford, 1974).

Moosvi, Shireen, *The Economy of the Mughal Empire, c.1595* (Delhi, 1987).

Moraes, Frank, *Purshotamdas Thakurdas* (Bombay, 1967).

Moreland, W.H., *From Akbar to Aurangzeb: A Study in Indian Economic History* (London, 1923).

——, *India at the Death of Akbar,* (Delhi, 1962, reprint).

Mukherjee, Aditya, "The Indian Capitalist Class : Aspects of its Economic, Political and Ideological Development in the Colonial Period, 1927-47" in *Situating Indian History* edited by S. Bhattacharya and Romila Thapar (New Delhi, 1986).

Mukherjee, Hiren, *Gandhi: A Study* (New Delhi, 1979).

Mukhopadhyay, Rajivlochan, *Maharaja Krishnachandra Rayasya Charitram,* (Calcutta, 1805).

Murphy, Eamon, *Unions in Conflict* (New Delhi, 1981).

Naik J.V., "An Early Appraisal of the British Colonial Policy", *Journal of the University of Bombay*, XLIV and XLV, new series, (1975 and 1976).

Namboodiripad, E.M.S., *The Mahatma and the Ism* (New Delhi, 1958).

Nambudiripad, K.N.S., *A Short History of Indian Currency* (Poona, 1955).

Namjoshi, M.V., *Chambers of Commerce in India* (Bombay, 1967).

Nanda, B.R., *Gokhale, the Indian Moderates and the British Raj* (Delhi, 1977).

——, *Gandhi and His Critics* (Delhi, 1987).

——, *In Gandhi's Footsteps: The Life and Times of Jamnalal Bajaj* (Delhi, 1990).

Naoroji, Dadabhai, *Essays, Speeches and Writings*, edited by C.L. Parekh (Bombay, 1887).

——, *Poverty and UnBritish Rule in India* (London, 1901).

Narayan, J.P., *Why Socialism?* (Varanasi, 1936).

Narayan, Shriman, *Window on Gandhi and Nehru* (Bombay, 1971).

Natarajan, M.S., "A Study of the Capital Market of Madras Presidency with Special Reference to Its Evolution and Indigenous Institutions" (Ph.D. thesis, University of Madras, 1934).

Nehru, Jawaharlal, *Autobiography* (London, 1936).

——, *Discovery of India* (Calcutta, 1946).

——, *Independence and After* (Delhi, 1949).

——, *Mahatma Gandhi* (New Delhi, 1966).

Nigam, R.K., *Managing Agency in India* (New Delhi, 1957).

Niyogi, Pushpa, *Contribution to the Economic History of Northern India from the Tenth to the Twelfth Century A.D.* (Calcutta, 1962).

Orme, Robert, *A History of the Military Transactions of the British Nation in Indostan* (London, 1768).

Overstreet, Gene, D. and M. Windmiller, *Communism in India* (Berkeley, 1960).

Page, D., *Prelude to Partition: The Indian Muslims and the Imperial System of Control, 1920-1932* (Delhi, 1982).

Pandey, G., "Rallying Round the Cow : Sectarian Strife in the Bhojpuri Region, c. 1888-1917", *Subaltern Studies II*, edited by R. Guha (Delhi, 1983).

Papanek, H., "Pakistan's Big Business: Muslim Separatism, Entrepreneurship and Partial Modernization", *Economic Development and Cultural Change*, XXI (1972).

Parekh, Bhikhu, *Colonialism, Tradition and Reform* (Delhi, 1989).

Pillai, P.P., *Economic Conditions in India* (London, 1925).

Pillai, Vednayagam, *Pratapa Mudaliar Charitram* (Madras, 1957).

Piramal, G., "A History of the Morarjee Gokuldas Spinning and Weaving Mills, 1871-1934" (M.A. dissertation, Bombay University, 1981).

——, "Industrial Entrepreneurship in Historical Perspective: A Case Study of the Thackersey Group (1873-1939)" (Ph. D. thesis, Bombay University, 1988).

Pradhan, G.P., and A.K. Bhagwat, *Lokmanya Tilak* (Bombay, 1958).

Prakash, Om, *The Dutch East India Company and the Economy of Bengal, 1630-1720* (Delhi, 1988).

Price, Major David, *Memoirs of the Emperor Jahangir*, written by himself and translated from a Persian manuscript (Calcutta, 1904).

Ramaswamy, Vijaya, *Textiles and Weavers in Medieval South India* (Delhi, 1985).

Ranade, M.G., *Essays on Indian Economics: A Collection of Essays and Speeches* (Madras, 1906).

Ray, Rajat K., *Industrialization in India* (Delhi, 1979).

Ray, Ratna and Rajat K., "European Monopoly Corporations and Indian Entrepreneurship, 1913-1922 : Early Politics of Coal in Eastern India", *Economic and Political Weekly*, IX-20 (25 May 1974).

Ray, Sibnarayan (ed.), *Selected Works of M.N. Roy* (Delhi, 1987).

Raychaudhuri, Tapan, "The Mughal Empire" in *The Cambridge Economic History of India*, vol. I, c. 1200-c. 1750, edited by T. Raychaudhuri and Irfan Habib (Cambridge, 1982).

——, *Europe Reconsidered: Perceptions of the West in Nineteenth Century Bengal* (Delhi, 1988).

Reeves, P.D., *Sleeman in Oudh* (Cambridge, 1971).

Reserve Bank of India, *History of the Reserve Bank of India* (Bombay, 1970).

Richards, J.F., "Mughal State Finance and the Pre-Modern World Economy", *Comparative Studies in Society and History*, XXIII (1981).

Robinson, F.C., *Separatism Among Indian Muslims: The Politics of the United Provinces Muslims, 1860-1923* (Cambridge, 1974).

Rungta, R.S., *The Rise of Business Corporations in India, 1850-1900* (Cambridge, 1971).

Rutnagar, S.M., *The Bombay Industries: The Cotton Mills* (Bombay, 1927).

Sadasivan, D., *The Growth of Public Opinion in the Madras Presidency, 1858-1909* (Madras, 1974).

Saklatvala, Sir S., "The Indian Cotton Textile Industry", *Indian Textile Journal,* Jubilee Souvenir, 1890-1940 (Bombay, 1940)

Saletore, R.N., *Early Indian Economic History* (Bombay, 1973).

Sarkar, J.N., *Fall of the Mughal Empire* (Bombay, 1954).

Sarkar, S., *Modern India, 1885-1947* (Delhi, 1983).

——, *The Swadeshi Movement in Bengal, 1903-1908* (New Delhi, 1977).

——, "The Logic of Gandhian Nationalism: The Civil Disobedience and the Gandhi-Irwin Pact (1930-31)", *Indian Historical Review,* III (1976).

Sarkar, Susobhan, *On the Bengal Renaissance* (Calcutta, 1985).

Scrafto, Luke, *Reflections on the Government of Indostan* (Calcutta, 1975, reprint).

Sen, S.K., *The House of Tatas* (Calcutta, 1975).

——, *The Economic History of Modern India, 1848-1939* (Calcutta, 1981).

Sen, S.P., *Dictionary of National Biography* (Calcutta, 1973).

Shah, K.T., *Trade, Tariffs and Transport in India* (London, 1923).

Singh, Khushwant, and Arun Joshi, *Shri Ram: A Biography* (Bombay, 1968).

Singh, M.P., "Mulla Muhammed Ali: The Merchant Prince of Surat", Indian History Congress, *Proceedings* 38th Session (Bhubaneswar, 1977).

Sinha, N.K., "Indian Business Enterprise: Its Failure in Calcutta (1800-1848)", *Bengal Past and Present,* Diamond Jubilee Number (July-December 1967).

Sitaramayya, B. Pattabhi, *History of the Indian National Congress* (Bombay, 1946).

Smith, W.C., *Modern Islam in India* (Lahore, 1946, reprint, 1963).

Sovani, N.V., *Planning of Post-War Economic Development in India* (Poona, 1951).

Subrahmanyam, N., *Sangam Polity* (Bombay, 1966).

Subramanian, L., "Bombay and the West Coast in the 1740s", *Indian Economic and Social History Review,* XXVIII (1981).

——, "The West Coast of India : The Eighteenth Century", (unpublished Ph. D. dissertation, Viswa Bharati University, Shantiniketan, 1984).

——, "The Castle Revolution of 1759 and the Banias of Surat: Changing British-Indian Relationships in Western India", in *State and Business in India : A Historical Perspective,* edited by. D. Tripathi (New Delhi, 1987).

——, "Banias and the British : The Role of Indigenous Credit in the

Process of Imperial Expansion in Western India in the Second Half of the 18th Century", *Modern Asian Studies,* XXI (1987).

Sullivan, R.J.F., *One Hundred Years of the Bombay Chamber of Commerce* (Bombay, 1936).

Swaminathan, Padmini, "State Intervention in Industrial Development: A case Study of Madras Presidency", paper presented at a seminar on South Indian Economy held at Centre for Development Studies, Trivandrum, 25-27 April 1988.

Tandon, Prakash, *Punjabi Saga* (Calcutta, 1988).

Tavernier, Jean Baptiste, *Travels in India,* translated by V.Ball, edited by W. Crooke (London, 1925).

Tendulkar, D.G., *Mahatma 1* (Delhi, 1951).

Thakurdas, P., et al., *A Brief Memorandum Outlining a Plan of Economic Development for India* (Bombay, 1944).

Tikekar, A., *The Cloister's Pale* (Bombay, 1984).

——, "The Ferment : Political Activities Before 1885", in *100 Glorious Years: Indian National Congress, 1885-1985* ed. by R. Zakaria (Bombay, 1985).

Timberg, Thomas, *The Marwaris: From Traders to Industrialists* (New Delhi, 1978).

Tomlinson, B.R., *The Indian National Congress and the Raj, 1929-1942* (London, 1976).

Tripathi, Dwijendra, "Silver Question: India and America", *Journal of Indian History,* XLIV (1966).

——, *Dynamics of a Tradition: Kasturbhai Lalbhai and His Entrepreneurship* (New Delhi, 1981).

——, "Occupational Mobility and Industrial Entrepreneurship in India: A Historical Analysis", *Developing Economics,* IXX (1981).

——, (ed.), *Business Communities of India: A Historical Perspective* (New Delhi, 1984).

——, (ed.), *State and Business in India: A Historical Perspective* (New Delhi, 1987).

——, and Priti Misra, *Towards a New Frontier: History of the Bank of Baroda, 1908-1983* (New Delhi, 1985).

Tyabji, Husain B., *Badruddin Tyabji: A Biography* (Bombay, 1952).

Unwin, George, *Industrial Organisation in the Sixteenth and Seventeenth Centuries* (London, 1963).

Venkatasubbiah, H., *Enterprise and Economic Change: 50 Years of FICCI* (New Delhi, 1977).

Verma, V.P., *Growth of Protection in India* (Delhi, 1974).

Visvesvaraya, M., *Reconstructing Indian Economy* (London, 1920).

——, *Planned Economy for India* (Bangalore, 1934).

——, *Memoirs of My Working Life* (Delhi, 1960).

Wacha, D.E., *Premchand Roychand: His Early Life and Career* (Bombay, 1913).

——, *The Life and Work of J.N. Tata* (Madras, 1915).

——, *Shells from the Sands of Bombay: Being My Recollections and Reminiscenes, 1860-1875* (Bombay, 1920).

Warmington, E.H., *The Commerce between the Roman Empire and India* (Cambridge, 1928).

Washbrook, D.A., *The Emergence of Provincial Politics: The Madras Presidency, 1870-1920* (Delhi, 1977).

Wilson, Charles, *England's Apprenticeship, 1603-1763* (London, 1965).

Wink, Andre, *Land and Sovereignty in India: Agrarian Society and Politics under the Eighteenth Century Maratha Swarajya* (Cambridge, 1986).

Zaidi, A.M. and S.G. Zaidi (eds.), *The Encyclopaedia of Indian National Congress* (Delhi, 1981).

Index